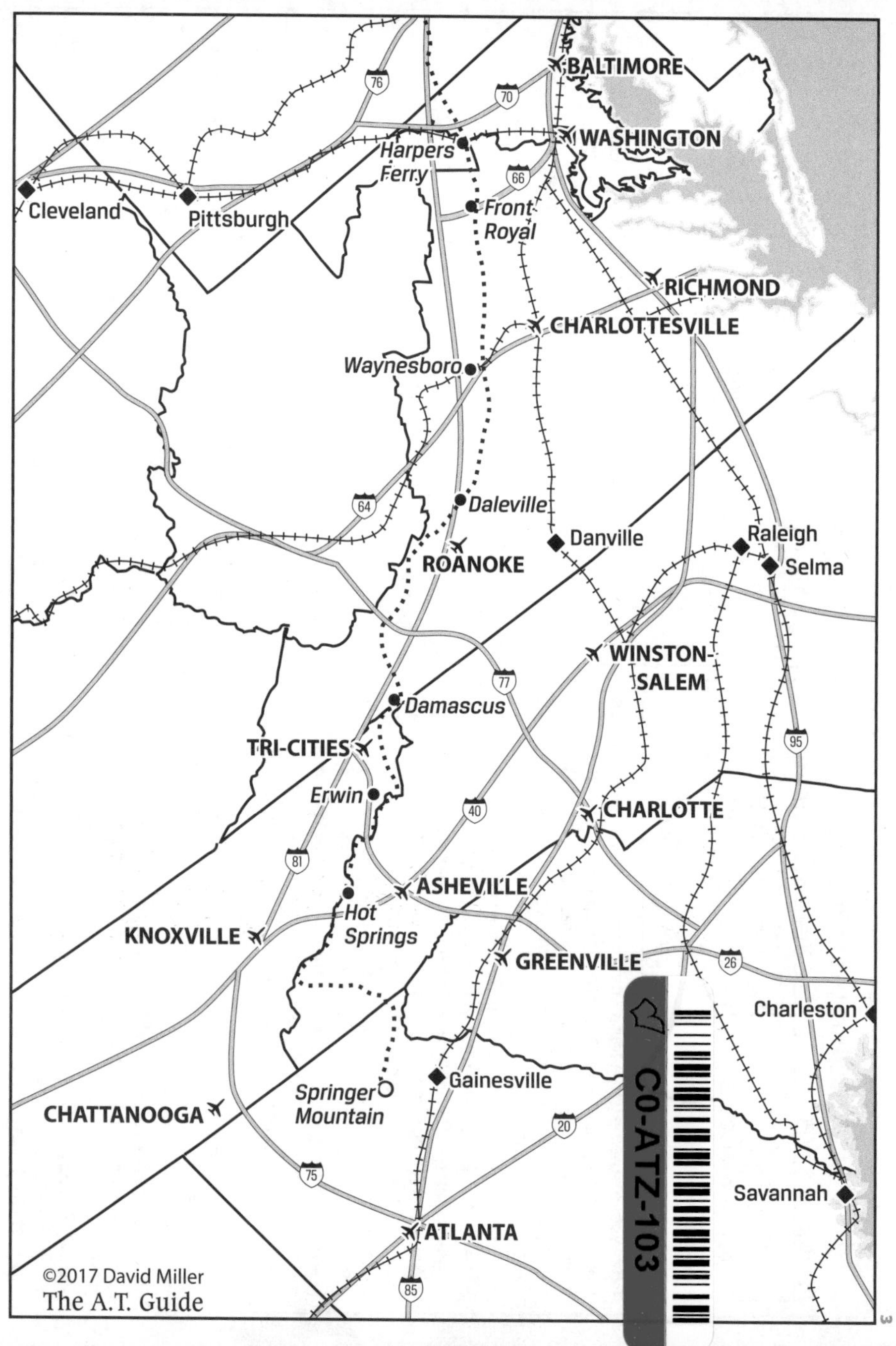
BALTIMORE
WASHINGTON
Harpers Ferry
Front Royal
Cleveland
Pittsburgh
RICHMOND
CHARLOTTESVILLE
Waynesboro
Daleville
Danville
Raleigh
Selma
ROANOKE
WINSTON-SALEM
Damascus
TRI-CITIES
Erwin
CHARLOTTE
ASHEVILLE
Hot Springs
KNOXVILLE
GREENVILLE
Charleston
Gainesville
Springer Mountain
CHATTANOOGA
Savannah
ATLANTA
76
70
66
64
77
95
40
81
26
20
75
85
©2017 David Miller
The A.T. Guide

Maildrop Guidelines

Packages sent to PO:	Packages sent to businesses
John Doe C/O General Delivery Trail Town, VA 12345 Please hold for AT hiker ETA May 16, 2017	John Doe C/O Hiker Hostel 2176 Appalachian Way Trail Town, VA 12345 Please hold for AT hiker ETA May 16, 2017

- ►Use your real name (not a trail name), include an ETA & return address.
- ►Only send "General Delivery" mail to a Post office.
- ►FedEx and UPS packages cannot be addressed to PO boxes.
- ►USPS will forward unopened general delivery mail for free if it was shipped by Priority Mail.
- ►Be prepared to show an ID when you retrieve your mail.
- ►The "C/O" name is essential when mailing to a business's PO Box; without it, they may not be able to retrieve your mail.
- ►When sending mail somewhere other than a PO, it's best to call first.
- ►Hostels & outfitters go out of business. Consider adding your phone number or email so they have a way to contact you about your mail.
- ►Send maildrops to a lodging facility only if you plan to stay there. If your plans change, offer to pay for the service of holding your mail.
- ►Many outfitters hold maildrops. Although none have rules about what you send, it's bad form to buy from an on-line retailer and have it shipped to a store where you could have bought it.

Maildrop services: these businesses offer small quantities of typical resupply items, packaged and mailed to you on the AT:
Son Driven Outfitters 276-781-6994 ⟨www.SonDriven.com⟩ Gear, food & toiletries. Free shipping any CONUS address on orders over $39.99, no sales tax.
Zero Day Resupply ⟨www.ZeroDayResupply.com⟩ Maildrop resupply for thru-hikers. No sales tax, no handling fee, next day shipping. Eat what you want, where you want, when you want it.

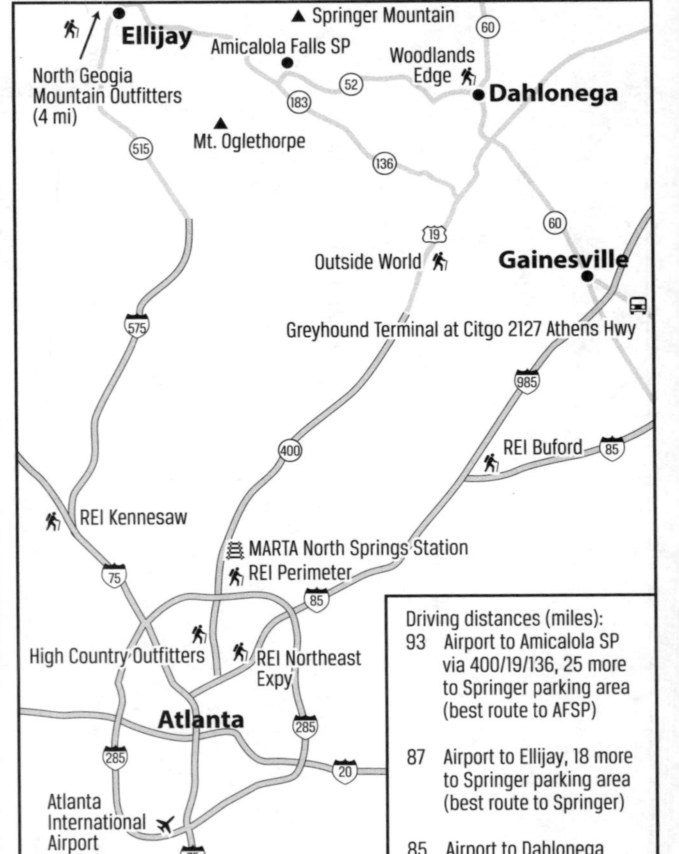

About the Book - The A.T. Guide is an on-trail reference, so its size is constrained. Infomation that can be researched before the hike is not included. Descriptions are terse. Tips and items of interest are scattered throughout where space is avail.

Book Organization - A spread is the pair of pages seen when the book is laid open. *The A.T. Guide* contains a spread of trail data followed by a spread of services available to hikers within that section. Occasionally there are back-to-back spreads of the same type.

Data Spreads have landmarks, mileages and elevations. Every spread covers approximately 39.8 miles of trail (19.9 miles per page). An elevation profile is "watermarked" on the data. Lines of text that describe landmarks are spaced so that they intersect the profile map at the approximate location of each landmark. Small triangular pointers below the profile line identify shelter locations. The vertical exaggeration of the profile maps is 7.6:1.

Services Spreads provide resupply information for towns that the trail passes through or near. Businesses are selectively included, and maps may only show a portion of town closest to the trail. Places of business that appear to be adjacent may be separated by one or more unspecified buildings or roads. When a map is provided, post office information will be on the map. Information presented in the map is not repeated in the text unless more elaboration is needed. The width of the mapped area is at the bottom or top of the map.

Prices are listed as given in fall of 2016. **No one is obliged to maintain these prices.** Lodging prices are dynamic, but most facilities listed will do their best for hikers. Let them know if you are thru-hiking; there may be a "thru-hiker rate."

✖On what page is the dinosaur?

Miles from Katahdin | *Miles from Springer* | *Elevation profile & elevation in feet.*

1966.9 222.2 **Tri-Corner Knob Shelter** . . . . . ☽ 💧 ∠ (12) 5897
20.1◄12.6◄5.2◄►7.7►14.8►25.3 Cables.

The next 3 shelters to the north are 7.7, 14.8 and 25.3 miles from this shelter. (5.2, 12.6, and 20.1 to the south).

There is a privy, water source, and shelter (capacity 12) at this location.

Directions

North/South: At many points along the trail, a northbound hiker will be heading some direction other than compass north, but this book will always refer to "north" as the direction on the AT that ultimately leads to Katahdin. When reference is made to the true bearing, the word "compass" will precede the direction (e.g.: "compass south"). If the trail joins a section of road, enters a park, or enters a town, the "south" end is where a northbound hiker first arrives, and the "north" end is where he/she leaves.

East/West: "East" is to the right of the trail for a northbound hiker and "west" is to their left, regardless of the compass reading. Most east-west directions are abbreviated along with a distance in miles. For example, three-tenths of a mile east is written "0.3E."

Left/Right: If a road leads to a town that is to the west, then a northbound hiker would go to their left, and the southbound hiker to their right. Once on the road both hikers are headed in the same direction, so any additional directions are given using the words "left" and "right." "Left" and "right" are also used to describe features near a shelter, ***from the perspective of a person outside of the shelter looking in***.

2017 is expected to be a popular year for hiking the AT. Most thru-hikers travel north, starting in Georgia in March or April. Other plans lessen impact on the trail and may better suit hikers seeking a more secluded experience or a longer window of mild weather. Learn more about alternative hikes and the benefits here: http://appalachiantrail.org/home/explore-the-trail/thru-hiking/alternative

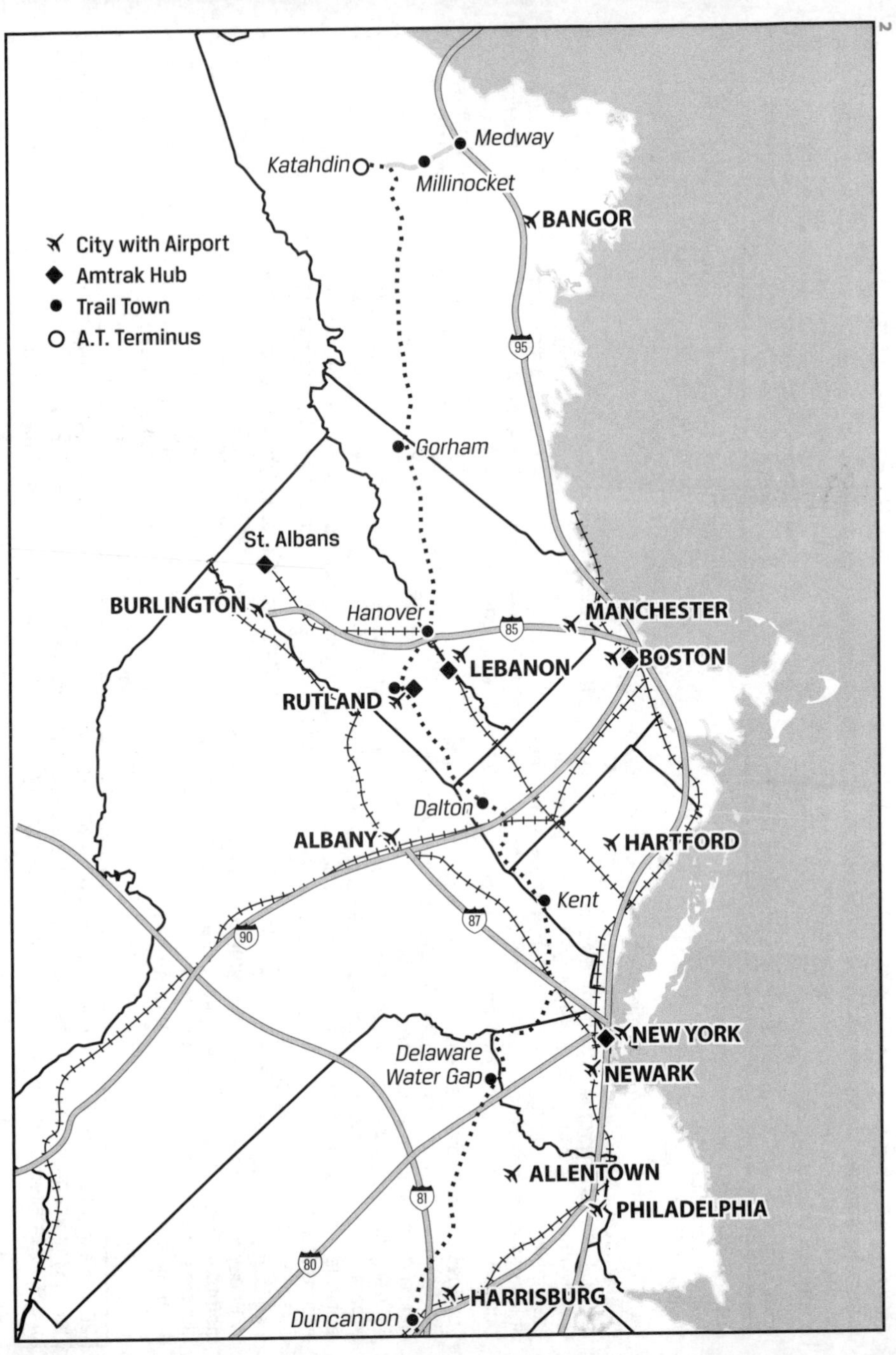

City with Airport
Amtrak Hub
Trail Town
A.T. Terminus
Medway
Katahdin
Millinocket
BANGOR
95
Gorham
St. Albans
BURLINGTON
Hanover
85
MANCHESTER
LEBANON
BOSTON
RUTLAND
Dalton
ALBANY
HARTFORD
Kent
87
90
NEW YORK
Delaware
Water Gap
NEWARK
ALLENTOWN
81
PHILADELPHIA
80
HARRISBURG
Duncannon

Getting to Springer Mountain

The southern terminus of the AT on Springer Mountain is accessible only by foot. The 8.8-mi. Approach Trail originating at the Visitor Center in Amicalola Falls SP is one means of getting there. Or you can drive to Springer Parking area on USFS 42, a dirt road passable by most vehicles unless there is bad-weather washout. From the parking area, hike south 1 mi. on the AT to Springer Mtn. Your hike would begin by retracing your steps. (See Start of Trail map pg. 10)

The closest major city is Atlanta, GA, 82 mi. south. If you fly or take AMTRAK into Atlanta, take the MARTA rail system to the North Springs Station; shuttlers pickup from there. There is also Greyhound bus service to Gainesville, GA, 38 mi. from the park.

Survivor Dave's Trail Shuttle 678.469.0978 (No texts please) Shuttle service to/from Atlanta Airport & North Springs MARTA Station to Amicalola Falls SP, Springer Mountain, & all trailheads up to Fontana Dam. Will stop at outfitter and/or supermarket for supplies (time permitting). Stove fuels available on-board. Well behaved dogs welcome. Will respond promptly to phone messages.

Ron Brown Cell: 706.669.0919, Home: 706.636.2825 hikershuttles@outlook.com. Flat rate shuttles to/from the AT or trail towns up to Fontana, incl. Amicalola Falls SP, Atlanta airport, & Gainesville, GA. Dogs welcome; extra stops OK. Fuel on request.

Hiker Hostel Package deal incl. shuttle, see pg. 11.

Sam Duke 706.994.6633 In Blairsville; range Atlanta-Fontana.

Henry Carter 678.525.3497 Ranging from Atlanta-all of GA.

Appalachian Adventure Company 706.265.9454, 865.456.7677 Shuttles, slackpacking, guided hikes, tours for Ga, NC, TN. Will p/u or d/o ATL, AVL, or TYS airports, bus or Amtrak. Fees vary based on length, accessibility and # of passengers. Max 10 hikers w/gear. Pet friendly.

Subman Shuttles 706.889.7044 2003 & 2016 thru-hiker provides shuttles from Atlanta to start of trail.

Outfitters Near the Southern Terminus

Mountain Crossings 706.745.6095 (see pg. 11)

North Georgia Mountain Outfitters 706.698.4453 Full service outfitter. Tu-Sa 10-6. ⟨www.HikeNorthGeorgia.com⟩

Woodlands Edge 706.864.5358 Open 10-5, 363 days a year (closed Easter and Christmas Day). Full service outfitter, fuel/oz, ask about shuttles. 36 North Park Street Dahlonega, GA 30533

Outside World 706.265.4500 471 Quill Dr, Dawsonville, GA 30534

Half Moon Outfitters 404.249.7921 1034 N. Highland Ave. NE, Atlanta, GA 30306

High Country Outfitters 404.814.0999 3906 Roswell Rd. #B, Atlanta, GA 30342

REI Four Atlanta area stores:

- 1800 Northeast Expy NE, Atlanta, GA 30329, 404.633.6508
- 1165 Perimeter Ctr W Ste 200, Atlanta, GA 30338, 770.901.9200
- 740 Barrett Pkwy, Ste 450, Kennesaw, GA 30144, 770.425.4480
- 1600 Mall of Georgia Blvd, Buford, GA 30519, 770.831.0676

Stay Up to Date on all Updates, Advisories & Trail Information

A.T. Guide Updates .... theATGuide.com/Updates.html
ATC Trail Camping & Fire Updates (pg. 61) .... appalachiantrail.org/camping
ATC Trail Trailwide Updates (pg. 61).......... appalachiantrail.org/home/explore-the-trail/trail-updates
ATC Trail Trailwide Updates (pg. 61).......... appalachiantrail.org/home/explore-the-trail/trail-updates
Baxter State Park (pg. 224) .... baxterstateparkauthority.com
Report a Change or Suggestion to The A.T. Guide.......... email: atgupdates@theatguide.com
Shenandoah National Park (SNP) (pg.88) .... nps.gov/shen

Amicalola Falls State Park

⟨www.www.amicalolafallslodge.com⟩ 706.265.8888 Hikers may use lot across from the visitor center for long-term parking ($50 for 2 weeks or more, even for the duration of a thru-hike) if space is available. You must register if you plan to leave your car overnight. There is $5 fee to park anywhere in the park. Dogs are allowed, but must be leashed.

The Lodge at Amicalola Falls
Rooms in the lodge and cottages throughout the park. Rates are seasonal; reservations strongly recommended. Many campsites are also available; most hold 2 tents and up to 6 persons. Pets allowed in campsites and in designated cottages. WiFi in Lodge common area only. Mail: Arriving hiker "your name", 418 Amicalola Falls Lodge Rd, Dawsonville, GA 30534.

The Len Foote Hike Inn (5 mi.)
800.581.8032 ⟨www.hike-inn.com⟩
Currently $117S $170D (higher on Saturdays & holidays). Includes hearty family-style dinner & breakfast. 20 rooms with bunkbeds & common bath areas. Reservations recommended and can be made on-line. Check in at Amicalola Falls Visitor Center by 2pm; arrive early enough for 5pm orientation and 6pm dinner. This is an eco-friendly facility accessible only by foot. There are hot showers and electricity, but no outlets in the rooms. No Pets. Please do not use cell phones, beepers or radios. Open year round.

Appalachian Trail Kick-Off (ATKO)
March 3-5. Enjoy demonstrations and workshops by hikers and retailers covering gear and trip preparation.

Max Epperson Shelter (free, for use by thru-hikers only)

Visitor Center Carries guidebooks, maps and a small selection of cold drinks and snacks. There is a hiker register inside and a pack scale outside.

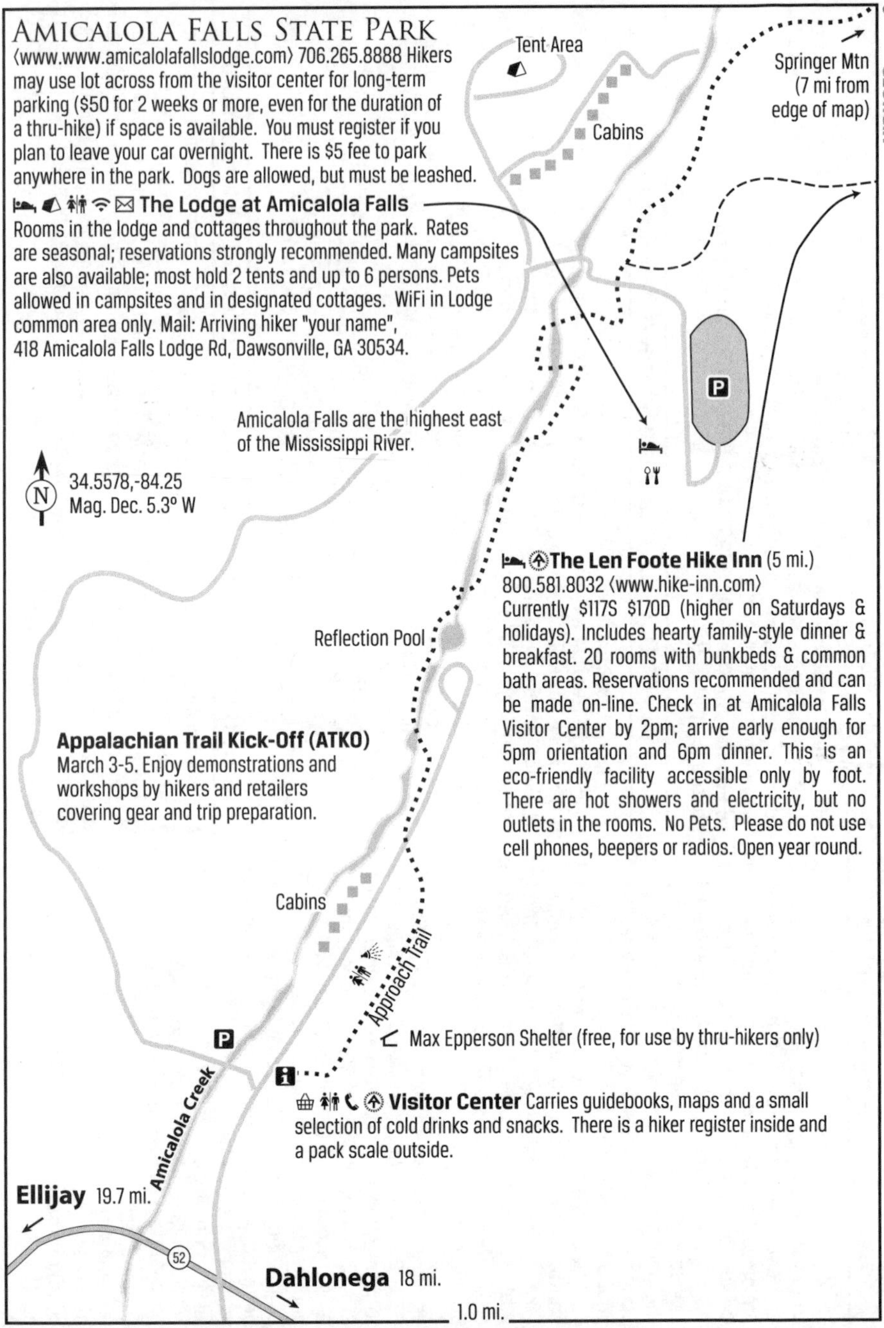

SoBo	NoBo	The Approach Trail		Elev
8.8	0.0	**Amicalola Falls State Park,** archway behind Visitor Center		1800
8.7	0.1	**Max Epperson Shelter,** for thru-hiker use only	(12)	1858
8.4	0.4	Reflection Pond at base of falls		2003
8.1	0.7	Staircase - 604 steps to the top of the Falls		2216
7.7	1.1	Parking, side trail to Lodge	P	2639
7.6	1.2	Lodge Road (lodge to east)		2642
7.5	1.3	Trail to **Len Foote Hike Inn** (5.0E) blazed lime-green.	**(pg. 6)**	2656
7.3	1.5	USFS Road 46, steps on north side		2584
5.6	3.2	High Shoals Road.		2841
4.0	4.8	Frosty Mountain. Spring (0.2E) is unreliable.		3384
3.7	5.1	Frosty Mountain Road, USFS Road 46		3178
3.4	5.4	Trail to **Len Foote Hike Inn** (1.0E) blazed lime-green	**(pg. 6)**	3353
3.1	5.7	Woody Knob.		3406
2.8	6.0	Nimblewill Gap, USFS Road 28		3100
2.6	6.2	Spring (left of trail), unreliable		3419
1.5	7.3	**Black Gap Shelter** (0.1W) Spring is on opposite side of the Approach Trail (0.1E).	(6) (7)	3300
0.0	8.8	Springer Mountain		3782

2000 3000 4000

2189.8	0.0	Springer Mountain southern terminus, register on back of rock with plaque. . 📷	3782
2189.6	0.2	**Springer Mountain Shelter** (0.2E) Tent pads . . . . ☽💧⛺(18) ∠(12) 0.0◄0.0◄0.0◄►2.6►7.9►15.6 150 yards north, Benton MacKaye Trail to east.	3720
2188.8	1.0	Big Stamp Gap, USFS 42 . . . . 34.6376,-84.1954 🅿	3350
2187.8	2.0	Benton MacKaye Trail.	3268
2187.1	2.7	Footbridge, stream . . . . 💧	2918
2187.0	2.8	**Stover Creek Shelter** (0.1E) (2006). . . . . ☽💧⛺(3) ∠(14) 0.0◄0.0◄2.6◄►5.3►13.0►25.1	2916
2186.9	2.9	Footbridge, stream . . . . 💧	2873
2186.4	3.4	Stream. . . . . 💧	2693
2185.6	4.2	Benton MacKaye / Duncan Ridge Trail to east	2586
2185.5	4.3	Three Forks, USFS 58, footbridge . . . . 💧	2530
2184.6	5.2	Benton MacKaye / Duncan Ridge Trail to west . . . . 💧 Trail to Long Creek Falls	2800
2183.6	6.2	Dirt road, 0.2W to Hickory Flats Cemetery, pavilion . . . . ☽	3081
2182.4	7.4	Hawk Mountain campsite (0.2W) 30 designated tent pads . . . . . . ☽💧⛺(30)	3220
2181.7	8.1	**Hawk Mountain Shelter** (0.2W) (1993) tenting restricted for 2017. . ☽💧∠(12) 0.0◄7.9◄5.3◄►7.7►19.8►20.9 Water south on AT and 0.1 mile behind shelter.	3194
2181.2	8.6	Hightower Gap, junction USFS 42 & 69 . . . . 34.6635,-84.1297 🅿	2854
2179.3	10.5	Horse Gap	2681
2178.3	11.5	Sassafras Mountain	3347
2177.5	12.3	Cooper Gap, USFS 15, 42 & 80 . . . . 34.653,-84.0846 🅿	2929
2177.0	12.8	Justus Mountain	3219
2176.3	13.5	Dirt road	2752
2175.4	14.4	Justus Creek. Use designated campsites north of creek, to west . . . . 💧⛺(6)	2589
2174.9	14.9	Stream. . . . . 💧	2636
2174.3	15.5	Blackwell Creek . . . . 💧⛺	2656
2174.0	15.8	**Gooch Mountain Shelter** (0.1W) (2001) Water behind shelter ☽💧⛺(6) ∠(14) 15.6◄13.0◄7.7◄►12.1►13.2►22.3 Designated tentsites, cables.	2789
2173.0	16.8	Spring to the east . . . . 💧	2831
2172.7	17.1	Gooch Gap, USFS 42 (gravel) . . . . 34.6521,-84.0323 🅿💧 **Suches, GA** (2.7W - see Woody Gap entry) water north of rd 0.1E on marked trail	2824
2171.7	18.1	Roadbed.	2939
2171.5	18.3	Liss Gap	3052
2170.9	18.9	Ramrock Mountain . . . . 📷	3222

SoBo	NoBo	Feature	Elev
2169.6	20.2	Seasonal springs	3208
2169.2	20.6	Woody Gap, GA 60 . . . 34.6777,-84.0000 P (pg. 11) **Suches, GA** (2.0W); Hostel (6.0E); spring north of road 0.2W.	3198
2168.3	21.5	Preaching Rock, view to east. Woody Lake in Suches in view to west.	3593
2168.0	21.8	Big Cedar Mountain, rock ledges and views.	3737
2167.8	22.0	Spring to west	3659
2166.9	22.9	Spring to west	3325
2166.0	23.8	Dockery Lake Trail	3050
2165.6	24.2	Lance Creek, camp in designated sites north of footbridge . . . (6)	2865
2164.9	24.9	Henry Gap (unmarked) is 70 yards west on side trail, woods road to GA 180. P	3083

> A hard-shell bear-resistant canister is required for hikers overnighting between Jarrard Gap and Neel Gap from Mar 1 - Jun 1. No fires (year-round) from Slaughter Creek Trail to Neel Gap.

SoBo	NoBo	Feature	Elev
2163.4	26.4	Jarrard Gap, dirt road . . . (0.3W) (pg. 11)	3250
2163.2	26.6	Gaddis Mountain	3402
2162.0	27.8	Turkey Stamp	3742
2161.9	27.9	**Woods Hole Shelter** (0.4W) 25.1◄19.8◄12.1◄►1.1►10.2►15.0 . . . (7) Bird Gap, Freeman Trail east bypasses Blood Mtn & rejoins AT at Flatrock Gap	3662
2161.6	28.2	Slaughter Creek Trail, spring on AT, campsite 0.1 North on AT . . . (8)	3800
2161.2	28.6	Duncan Ridge Trail, Coosa Trail to west	4168
2160.8	29.0	**Blood Mountain Shelter** (1934) 20.9◄13.2◄1.1◄►9.1►13.9►21.2 . . . (8) Privy 50 yards south. No fires. Stream (0.8S). Many views from AT North of shelter	4457
2159.5	30.3	Flatrock Gap, Freeman Trail east bypasses Blood Mtn; west. . . . P (0.2W) to Byron Reece parking area. Balance Rock 150 yards north.	3487
2158.4	31.4	Neel Gap, US 19 . . . 34.7411,-83.9206 P (pg. 11)	3125
2157.3	32.5	Bull Gap, spring 0.1W	3685
2156.7	33.1	Levelland Mountain, view	3870
2155.5	34.3	Swaim Gap, spring to west.	3536
2154.8	35.0	Wolf Laurel Top, views to east	3780

> ✽ **Mayapple – White flower ball dangling under an umbrella of broad leaves. Plant is about a foot tall.**

SoBo	NoBo	Feature	Elev
2153.4	36.4	Cowrock Mountain	3842
2152.4	37.4	Tesnatee Gap, GA 348, Russell Hwy . . . 34.7262,-83.8476 P (pg. 11)	3138
2151.9	37.9	Wildcat Mountain.	3637
2151.7	38.1	**Whitley Gap Shelter** (1.2E) Spring 0.3 mi. behind shelter. . . . (3) (7) 22.3◄10.2◄9.1◄►4.8►12.1►20.2 Campsite 0.1E with view just beyond.	3625
2151.5	38.3	Hogpen Gap, GA 348, Water S of rd, E of AT . . . 34.7259,-83.8399 P (pg. 11)	3444
2150.6	39.2	White Oak Stamp	3470

Temperatures decrease about 3.5° Farenheit for every 1000' gain in elevation. The decrease is even greated in clear weather. If you see a forecast of 50° for Dahlonega (1450'), expect temperatures below 40° on Blood Mountain (4461').

Check weather conditions anywhere on the AT: **www.atweather.org**

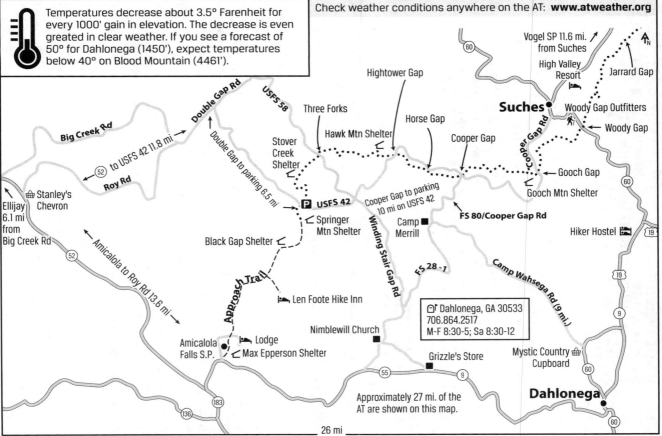

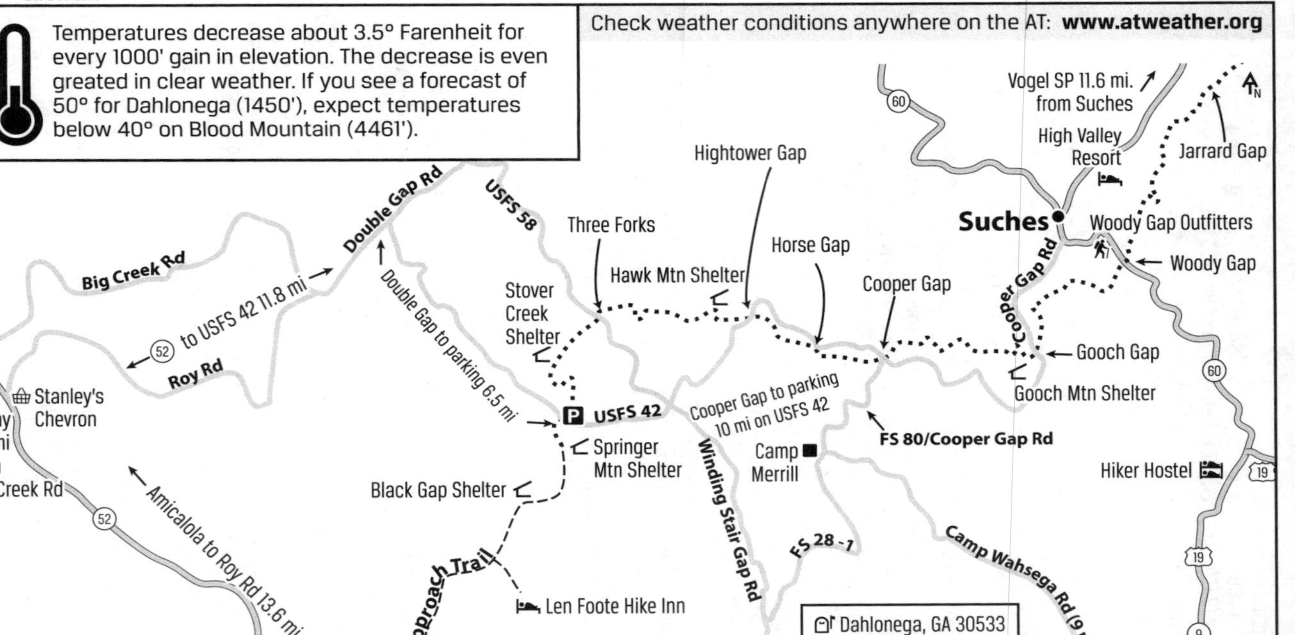

20.6 Woody Gap, GA Hwy 60

Hiker Hostel (6.0E) 770.312.7342 hikerhostel@yahoo.com Open yr-round. $19PP Bunks, $45 Private room for 2, $55-$65 Private Cabin for 2. Stay incl. b'fast, bed linens, towel & shower. Computer w/internet & wireless. Laundry $3. SPECIAL(Feb 24-Apr 20): $85 P/U from Atlanta North Springs MARTA Station or Gainesville, overnight stay bunk, b'fast, shuttle to Amicalola or Springer, 8oz of white gas/alcohol. Canister fuel & limited gear avail. for purchase. Feb 24-Apr 27 5p FREE daily pickup at Woody Gap. Shuttles from Atlanta & Gainesville & to all trailheads in GA by reservation for hostel guests. Mail: (USPS) PO Box 802 or (FedEx/UPS) 7693 Hwy 19N, Dahlonega, GA 30533 ‹www.hikerhostel.com›

Woody Gap Outfitters (0.5W) 678.262.8406 CLOSED FOR 2017 will open late season/early 2018. Full service discount outfitter specializing in thru-hiker needs. Pack shakedowns by triplecrowner Bob "Sir-Packs-Alot" Gabrielsen, resupply, pizza & snacks. Open daily 10-4, Feb 15 - Jun 1. Easy downhill road walk. ‹woodygapoutfitters.com›

Suches, GA 30572 (2W) (pronounced "such-is")

M–F 12:15-4:15, 706.747.2611

High Valley Resort (0.7W) of PO, 404.720.0087 Open Apr-Oct. Camping $15PP, bunkhouse $55PP, both have access to bathhouse, showers and lodge with satellite TV. Cabins $125/night Su-Wed; $165 Th-Sat, some sleep 4, some sleep up to 8 persons. ‹www.highvalleyresort.com›

Wildcat Lodge and Campground 706.973.0321. (7W) $15 bunkroom, $12 camping. Lodge room sleeps 8 $100D, $25EAP. Camp store has Coleman & canisters. Diner serves B/L.

Wes Wisson 706.747.2671, 706.781.4333 Shuttles covering trailheads in north Georgia.

26.4 Jarrard Gap

Lake Winfield Scott Recreation Area (1.0W) 706.747.3816 tent sites $18/up to 5 persons, showers & bathrooms, leash dogs. (Due to the drought in 2016, sometimes at times there may be no water, bathrooms, or showers. Sites $9 when no water.)

31.4 Neel Gap, US 19

Mountain Crossings 706.745.6095 Full-service outfitter, full resupply, gear shakedown, alcohol/oz, bunkroom $18PP incl. shower w/towel. No Pets. Shower without stay $5. Laundry $5. Ask about shuttles. Outgoing shipping avail. Maildrops (USPS/UPS/FedEx) held for 2 weeks, $1 fee at pickup, 12471 Gainesville Hwy, Blairsville, GA 30512. ‹www.mountaincrossings.com›

✖What shoe is over the hostel door?

Blood Mountain Cabins (0.3E) 706.745.9454, 800.284.6866 Thru-hiker rate $72. Cabin w/kitchen, sat. TV, holds 4 adults + 2 children under age of 13. Laundry free w/stay. Wifi at lodge. No pets. Pizza & wings in store. ‹www.bloodmountain.com›

Vogel State Park (3W) 706.745.2628 Primitive tent sites $25, cabins for 2-10 persons $100-$200. $2 shower for tenters & visitors. Long term parking $5. ‹www.gastateparks.org›

(3.5W) **Goose Creek Cabins** 706.781.8593, 706.745.5111 Cabins & shuttles avail. Call for details.

Blairsville, GA 30514 (14W) All major services.

Misty Mtn Inn 706.745.4786 Misty Mtn Inn B&B rooms $125 ($110 w/o b'fast), cabins for 2-10 $105-$125. Free P/U & return from Neel, Tesnatee or Hogpen Gap. Slackpacking w/multi-night stay. info@mistymtninn.com ‹www.mistymtninn.com›

Jim's Smokin' BBQ Th-Sa 11-8.

Blairsville Hikes and Bikes 706.745.8141 M-Sa 10-5:30. Hiking essentials incl. poles, fuel & hiker food.

Sam Duke 706.994.6633 Shuttle range Atlanta-Fontana.

Dahlonega, GA 30597 (17E) All major services.

37.4 Tesnatee Gap,

38.3 Hogpen Gap, ***Blairsville, GA 30514*** (14W) listings above.

2149.5	40.3	Poor Mountain		3620

> **!** Get the most out of your guidebook: pay attention to lines that end with a page number. The page that is referenced will list the services avail. at or near the trailhead.

2147.8	42.0	Sheep Rock Top		3558
2146.9	42.9	**Low Gap Shelter** 15.1◄13.9◄4.8◄►7.3►15.4►22.8 Water 30 yards in front of shelter. Cables. Privy on steep hill beyond shelter.	☽ 💧 ⛺ (4) ∠ (7)	3024
2146.5	43.3	Stream.	💧	3183
2145.5	44.3	Poplar Stamp Gap, spring 0.1E, gap and side trail unmarked.	💧 ⛺	3345
2144.8	45.0	Spring to west	💧	3550
2143.5	46.3	Stream with cascade, several streams in area	💧	3464
2143.0	46.8	Cold Springs Gap		3495
2141.9	47.9	Chattahoochee Gap, Jacks Gap Trail to west, spring 0.5E	💧	3584
2141.2	48.6	Red Clay Gap	(pg. 14)	3485
2140.6	49.2	Site of former Rocky Knob Shelter	💧	3630
2140.3	49.5	Spring west of trail down slope	💧	3606
2139.6	50.2	**Blue Mountain Shelter** 21.2◄12.1◄7.3◄►8.1►15.5►23.6 Bear cables. Spring on AT (0.1S), camping west of AT, south of shelter.	☽ 💧 ⛺ (4) ∠ (7)	3880
2138.7	51.1	Blue Mountain		4025
2137.2	52.6	Unicoi Gap, GA 75, **Helen, GA** (9.0E) **Hiawassee, GA** (12.0W)	34.8017,-83.7428 🅿 (pg. 14)	2949
2136.5	53.3	Stream.	💧	3502
2136.3	53.5	Rocky Mountain Trail to west	💧	3715
2135.8	54.0	Rocky Mountain, views from AT 0.1 north of summit	📷 ⛺	4017
2134.5	55.3	Indian Grave Gap, USFS 283 Andrews Cove Trail to east.	34.7927,-83.7143 🅿	3113
2133.8	56.0	Tray Mountain Rd (gravel), USFS 79, piped stream east on road	💧	3480
2133.5	56.3	Cheese factory site, water (0.1W) on blue-blazed trail	💧 ⛺	3579
2132.8	57.0	Tray Gap, Tray Mountain Rd, USFS 79	34.7993,-83.691 🅿	3847
2132.0	57.8	Tray Mountain	📷	4430
2131.5	58.3	**Tray Mountain Shelter** (0.2W) 20.2◄15.4◄8.1◄►7.4►15.5►22.8 Spring 0.1 mile behind shelter. Cables.	☽ 💧 ⛺ (3) ∠ (7)	4193
2130.3	59.5	Wolfpen Gap		3550

2129.8	60.0	Steeltrap Gap, water 0.5E	💧	3448
2129.2	60.6	Young Lick Knob		3748
2127.9	61.9	Swag of the Blue Ridge		3451
2126.8	63.0	Sassafras Gap, water 0.2E on steep blue-blazed trail	💧 ⛺	3500
2125.9	63.9	Addis Gap,. Campsite 0.5E down old fire road, stream to right of campsite.	💧 ⛺	3304
2124.9	64.9	Kelly Knob, trail skirts summit		4126
2124.1	65.7	**Deep Gap Shelter** (0.3E) 22.8◄15.5◄7.4◄►8.1►15.4►20.3 Water 0.1 before shelter.	☽ 💧 ⛺ (4) ⊏ (12)	3554
2123.0	66.8	"Vista" blue-blaze leads 0.1E to campsite.	⛺	3886
2122.7	67.1	Powell Mountain		3850

.ıll No phone signal at Dicks Creek Gap. If you need ride, call from Shelter or Powell Mtn.

2121.5	68.3	Moreland Gap, water to east	💧	3015
2120.5	69.3	Dicks Creek Gap, US 76 34.9121,-83.6188 Water, picnic tables at the gap, **Hiawassee, GA** (11.0W)	Ѫ **P** ◊ **(pg. 14)**	2675
2119.5	70.3	Campsite, 200 yards to water	💧 ⛺	3177
2118.7	71.1	Cowart Gap	💧	2900
2117.3	72.5	Buzzard Knob		3679
2117.2	72.6	Bull Gap		3541
2116.5	73.3	Spring	💧	3317
2116.0	73.8	**Plumorchard Gap Shelter** (0.2E) Privy 0.2 mi down steep tr. 23.6◄15.5◄8.1◄►7.3►12.2►19.8 Creek on trail to shelter & spring (0.1W) of AT.	☽ 💧 ⛺ (6) ⊏ (14)	3144
2115.3	74.5	As Knob		3460
2114.8	75.0	Blue Ridge Gap, dirt road (no longer passable by car)		3090
2113.8	76.0	Spring to west, campsite	💧 ⛺	3403
2113.1	76.7	Rich Cove Gap		3532
2112.9	76.9	Rocky Knob		3574
2111.6	78.2	**GA-NC** border		3821
2111.5	78.3	Bly Gap, signed spring a 30 ft east of A.T. located between GA-NC border & Bly Gap. Old and twisted tree often photographed. Signed camping area on blue blazed trail 100yds north of Bly Gap.	💧 ⛺	3840
2110.2	79.6	Couthouse Bald, summit 0.1W		4708

SoBo NoBo 2000 3000 4000

48.6 Red Clay Gap

Enota Mountain Retreat 706.896.9966, No sign & trail not blazed; be certain of location if you walk. Marked on some maps by its previous name "Camp Pioneer." Trail is downhill to Joel's Creek & follows creek into camp. Driving from Unicoi Gap: 2.4W on Hwy 17, then left 2.4 mi. on Hwy 180. Tentsites & cabins - check rates online, bunkhouse ($35PP), laundry. Store w/snacks & small gear items. Beautiful waterfall, trout pond, work for stay possible on organic farm. Mail (guests/free, non-guest/$15): 1000 Highway 180 Hiawassee, GA 30546

52.6 Unicoi Gap, GA 75

Enota Mountain Retreat (4.8W, see listing above)

Helen, GA 30545 (9E) Lodging tax 15%

M-F 9-12:30 & 1:30-4, Sa 9-12, 706.878.2422

Tourist town with many hotels, restaurants, gift shops, ice cream shops, river rafting and tubing rentals. Visitor Center on Bruckenstrasse (near the PO) has information about places to stay and a free phone for making reservations.

Best Western Motel 706.878.2111 Hiker rate Mar 15-Apr 30; $55S + $5EAP up to 4. Incl. b'fast buffet.

Helendorf River Inn 800.445.2271 Prices 1 or 2 persons Su-Th; Nov-Mar $44, Apr-May $54, Jun-Aug $84, +tax, $10EAP. Weekend rates higher. Pets $20. Incl. cont B. Visa/MC/ Disc accepted.

Super 8 Motel 706.878.2191, ask for hiker room $55+tax for 1 or 2 persons, pet fee $25.

Econo Lodge 706.878.8000 Weekdays $60, weekends higher, incl. cont. b'fast. Pets under 20 pounds with $20 fee.

Country Inn and Suites 706.878.9000 Call for rates, hiker discount, incl. full hot b'fast, indoor pool & hot tub

Betty's Country Store 706.878.2943 Open 7 days 7a-9p.

laundromat

Hiawassee, GA 30545 (12E) *(see Dicks Creek Gap)*

69.3 Dicks Creek Gap, US 76

Top of Georgia Hostel & Hiking Center (0.5W) 706.982.3252 Open yr-round 7a-7p. Downhill blue-blazed road walk (NoBo left / SoBo right). Full service discount outfitter. Delivery of gear where you need it when you need it. Full resupply. Bunk & shower $25, full hostel kitchen. Free shuttles yr-round to Hiawassee, Dicks Creek Gap & Unicoi Gap for all overnight guests. Slackpacking options & shuttles ranging from Springer to NOC for a fee. Hearty, hot b'fast $6. Pizza & snacks avail. Laundry $5/ load. Computer, free WiFi. Free (Appalachian Trail School) nightly seminar "11 Keys for a Successful Thru-Hike". Pack shakedowns by proprietor, Triple Crowner & guide Bob "Sir-Packs-Alot" Gabrielsen. Separate suite for hikers w/pets. No drugs/alcohol. Mail ($1 fee) held for 30 days; ID required: 7675 US Hwy 76 E, Hiawassee GA 30546. ⟨www.topofgeorgiahostel.com⟩

Henson Cove B&B (5W) 800.714.5542, relax@henson-cove-place.com. Cabin for 1-6 persons, full kitchen, 3BR, 1.5BA: $100 for 3, $135 for 4-5, $150 for 6. B'fast $8PP. Standard B&B rooms $100D, b'fast incl. All stays w/free ride to/from AT from Dick's Creek Gap or Unicoi Gap, or into town for provisions. Free laundry & internet. Slack packing. CC OK, well behaved pets OK. Shuttles, parking for section hikers. Mail: 1137 Car Miles Rd, Hiawassee, GA 30546.

Affordable Taxi 706.970.0794 based in Hiawassee w/ service to/from Dicks Creek Gap & Unicoi Gap; longer shuttles can be arranged.

Hiawassee, GA 30546 (11W)

Hiker Fool Bash Mar 31-Apr 1, info at Budget Inn. Food, fun & games ⟨hikerfoolbash.com⟩

Budget Inn 706.896.4121, $39.99S, $5EAP, pets $10, coin laundry. Guests: free ride to/from Dick's Creek Gap or Unicoi Gap (9a & 11a) Mar-Apr. Non-guest shuttles for a fee. **Mountain Crossings** outfitters on-site. CC ok. Comp. guest maildrop transfer to Franklin Budget or Sapphire Inn. Mail: 193 S Main St, Hiawassee, GA 30546 ⟨www.hiawasseebudgetinn.com⟩

Holiday Inn Express 706.896.8884 $79/up, all major CC. Full b'fast included, laundry, indoor pool, hot tub, no pets. Mail: 300 Big Sky Dr, Hiawassee, GA 30546.

Mull's Inn 706.896.4195 $50/up, no pets, shuttles by arrangement. Guest Mail: 213 N Main St, Hiawassee, GA 30546

Lake Chatugue Lodge 706.896.5253 $89/up incl. c. b'fast. **Chophouse Restahiurant** on site.

Mountain Roots Outfitters 706.896.1873 M-Sa 11-5 Canister fuel, freeze-dried meals, small gear items.

Ingles 706.896.8312, 7-10, 7 days. Pharmacy 9-9, **Starbucks**, deli, bakery, salad bar.

■ **Goin' Postal** 706.896.1844 FedEx and UPS shipping 10-5 M-F.

85.1 Deep Gap, USFS 71
(3.7W) **Standing Indian Campground (**See Rock Gap)

105.8 Rock Gap
(1.5W) **Standing Indian Campground** 828.369.0442, 828.524.6441 Campsites $16, open Apr 1 - Nov 30. Camp store (closes Oct 31) has small selection of foods.

Macon County Transit See entry pg. 18.

Due to the devastating wildfires of late 2016, Services & trail conditions thru GA, NC & TN are uncertain for 2017. Trail conditions & all amenities such as maildrops, hostels etc. should be verified in advance.

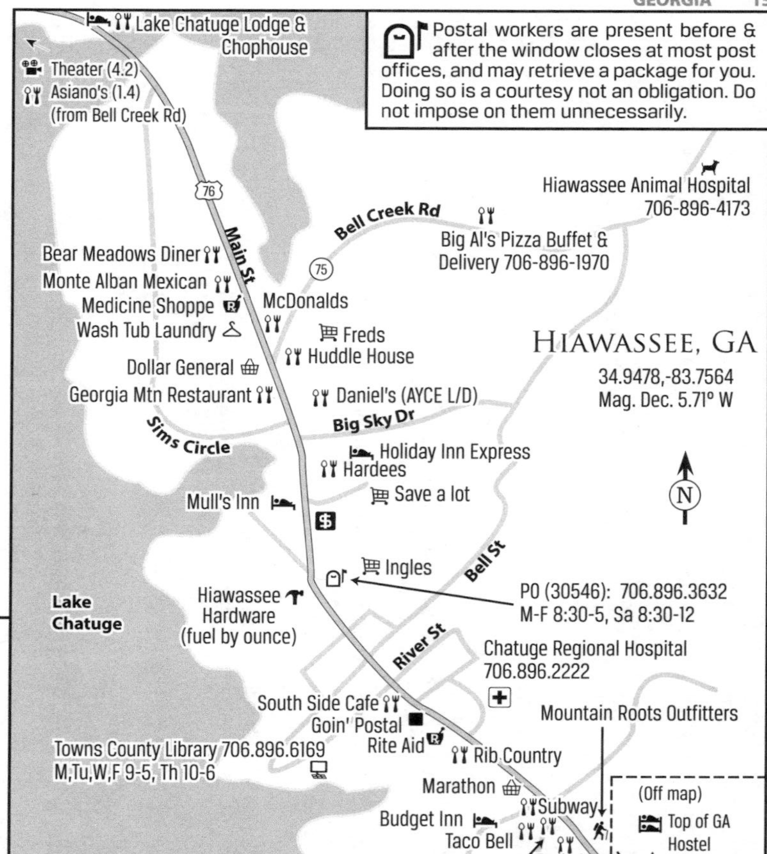

SOBO	NOBO	Location	Services	Elev.
2109.6	80.2	Sassafras Gap		4300
2109.3	80.5	Piped Spring	water	4513
2108.7	81.1	**Muskrat Creek Shelter** 22.8◄15.4◄7.3◄►4.9►12.5►21.2	(6)	4562
2107.9	81.9	Whiteoak Stamp, old roadbed, Chunky Gal Trail to west, blue blazed water trail A.T. east, blue blazed camp trail A.T. west signed with register box.	water, camping	4620
2106.8	83.0	Wateroak Gap		4490
2106.5	83.3	Spring	water	4568
2105.3	84.5	Spring	water	4548
2104.7	85.1	Deep Gap, USFS 71, Kimsey Creek Trail. 35.0396,-83.5525 Signed campsite with register box on KC Trail & blue blazed water trail	P, water, camping (pg. 15)	4341
2104.3	85.5	Spring to west	water	4516
2103.8	86.0	**Standing Indian Shelter,** creek 70 yards downhill 20.3◄12.2◄4.9◄►7.6►16.3►19.7	(8)	4742
2103.5	86.3	Spring	water	4815
2102.3	87.5	Standing Indian Mountain, summit (0.1E). Campsites on side trail to summit. Lower Ridge Trail to west.	view	5435
2100.4	89.4	Spring.	water	4944
2099.4	90.4	Beech Gap Tenting area with water.	water, camping	4460
2098.3	91.5	Stream.	water	4404
2097.7	92.1	Coleman Gap		4221
2096.7	93.1	Timber Ridge Trail to west		4639
2096.2	93.6	**Carter Gap Shelter**. 19.8◄12.5◄7.6◄►8.7►12.1►20.1 Spring south of shelter, 100 yards downhill.		4528
2095.6	94.2	Stream.	water (unreliable)	4738
2095.1	94.7	Spring	water	4921

⚠ PATH (Protecting the Appalachian Trail Hiking Expeience):
The NHC is working to increase camping capacity at shelters & established campsites between Bly Gap & Wesser, NC in order to decrease the number of single tent sites located within sight of the trail. There are signed locations (No Camping/Revegetation Area) with recommended alternative camping locations. Please use the register boxes at campsites to help gather visitor use info.

SOBO	NOBO	Location	Services	Elev.
2092.5	97.3	Betty Creek Gap, Several tent sites west on blue blazed Betty Creek Trail. Campsite with register box	water, camping	4300
2091.7	98.1	Mooney Gap, USFS 83, Ball Creek Rd, stream 0.1 north.		4498
2090.3	99.5	USFS 67, To bypass Albert Mt, take road 0.2W to parking area, then take side trail 0.2 from parking area back to AT north of summit		4843

2090.0 99.8 Albert Mountain, fire tower 5250
2089.8 100.0 Albert Mountain bypass, west 0.2 to parking on USFS 67 . . . . . P 5052
2089.4 100.4 Site of former Big Spring Shelter. Land reclamation underway, no camping 4978

> **White blazes on the north side of trees are identical to the blazes on the south side. Make sure you are headed in the right direction, especially when sleepily leaving shelters in the morning.**

2087.5 102.3 **Long Branch Shelter** (0.1W)(2012) seven tent pads . . . . . (16) 4479
21.2◄16.3◄8.7◄►3.4►11.4►18.2
2086.7 103.1 Glassmine Gap, Long Branch Trail 2.0W to USFS 67 4185

> **A "kick-over" double blaze indicates that you should watch for a turn in the direction of the upper blaze (a right turn in this image).**

2084.1 105.7 **Rock Gap Shelter** (1965), four tent pads. . . . . . (8) 3772
19.7◄12.1◄3.4◄►8.0►14.8►19.6
2084.0 105.8 Rock Gap, 0.7E to Wasalik Poplar and water. . . . . 35.094,-83.5226 P **(pg. 15)** 3732
2083.4 106.4 Wallace Gap, W. Old Murphy Rd, stream to north 3738

2080.3 109.5 Winding Stair Gap, US 64. . . . . 35.1196,-83.548 P **(pg. 18)** 3690
piped spring east of steps, **Franklin, NC** (10.0E)
2080.1 109.7 Forest Service road, waterfall 3727
2080.0 109.8 Stream, No camping here, camp at Moore Creek campsite 3812
2079.7 110.1 Logging road 4026
2079.5 110.3 Moore Creek Campsite to west, signed & blazed 4011
Water & level area for 8 tents with register box.
2079.2 110.6 Swinging Lick Gap 4100
2078.3 111.5 Panther Gap 4480

2076.1 113.7 **Siler Bald Shelter** (0.5E steep), south end of shelter loop trail . . (8) 4769
20.1◄11.4◄8.0◄►6.8►11.6►17.4
2075.7 114.1 Siler Bald, summit (0.2W), shelter (0.3E), north end of shelter loop trail 5001
2074.9 114.9 Piped spring 4481
2074.6 115.2 Footbridge, stream 4374
2074.5 115.3 Wayah Crest Picnic Area (0.1W) . . . . . 35.154,-83.5807 P 4258
2074.4 115.4 Wayah Gap, Wayah Rd . . . . . **(pg. 18)** 4180
2074.0 115.8 AT skirts USFS 69 4352
2073.6 116.2 USFS 69, meadow 4480
2073.2 116.6 Wilson Lick Trail, 0.2W to historic site 4630
2072.7 117.1 USFS 69, piped spring to east 4993
2072.3 117.5 Bartram Trail to west 5236
2072.1 117.7 0.1E to Wine Spring Rd, meadow, campsites 0.1E, water on west side of AT . . 5290

2070.6 119.2 USFS 69 5188
2070.4 119.4 Paved footpath to latrines and parking . . . . . 35.179,-83.5622 P 5298

109.5 Winding Stair Gap, US 64 ***Franklin, NC*** (10E)

Haven's Budget Inn and Baltimore Jack's Place Hostel (10E) 828.524.4403 $39.99S, $5EAP, $50 pet deposit. Bunkroom $20. Owner Ron Haven makes trips at 9 & 11a Mar-Apr to D/O & P/U at Rock, Wallace & Winding Stair Gaps. Motel guests may call for free P/U Mar-Apr & get 4p shuttle around town. Internet & coin laundry on-site. Print Smokies permit for free. Shower w/o stay $5. Mail: 433 East Palmer St, Franklin, NC 28734.

Gooder Grove AT & Adventure Hostel 828.332.0228 Bunks $25, pvt room $43, tent/hammock $13PP. Deduct your $3 Macon Transit fare from prices. Shuttles, slackpacking, sectionhiker parking. Laundry-$6, shower-$5. Lounge w/movie library, activities on-site, coupons for local discounts. Pets OK. Mail: 130 Hayes Circle, Franklin, NC 28734.

Sapphire Inn 828.524.4406 $49.95 S/D/King, $59.95 2 Queen (up to 4PP), pet fee $15. Mail: 761 East Main St, Bus 441, Franklin, NC 28734. sapphireinnfranklin@gmail.com

Microtel Inn & Suites 828.349.9000 Prices vary, cont. b'fast, $25 per pet. Mail: 81 Allman Dr, Franklin, NC 28734

Comfort Inn 828.369.9200 10% thru-hiker discount, hot b'fast, laundry on-site. Call in advance if you need pet-friendly room. Mail: 313 Cunningham Rd. Franklin, NC 28734

Outdoor 76 828.349.7676 Open M–Sa 10-7. Specialty hiking store w/lightweight gear, food, fuel & draft beer in center of town. Footwear experts w/trained staff to deal w/injuries & various foot issues. 10% off for thru-hikers. Shipping services, free internet, in town shuttles. No charge for Mail: 35 E Main St, Franklin, NC 28734. ⟨www.outdoor76.com⟩ **Rock House Lodge** taproom/restaurant inside Outdoor 76, M-Sa 10-9. 18 beers on tap, wine & food, Darts, indoor shuffleboard, community instruments for hikers, Big screen TV & occasional live music. Weekly specials.

1st Baptist Church Free B'fast daily from Mar 12 - Apr 9.

Lazy Hiker Brewing Co. Food Truck, computer/printer, pet friendly. Please sign taproom wall, ask about summit card. Spring/Summer M-Th 12-9, F/Sa 12-11, Su 12-6.

Three Eagles Outfitters 828.524.9061 Two locations in Franklin: 78 Siler Rd, & 7 Derby St. Call # for both locations. Full-svc outfitter. 22 yrs experience on the AT. Footwear specialists, canister & fuel/oz. UL gear, rainwear, clothing & footwear. 10% AT thru-hiker discount. Shuttle list avail. Will hold/ship pkgs. Siler Rd has **coffee & espresso bar** & free beer for shoppers.

Macon County Transit 828.349.2222 Shuttles M-F from Feb 27-May 26, (other dates call). Stops: Winding Stair Gap 9:30, 12:30, & 3:30; Rock Gap 9:45, 12:45, 3:45. $3PP per ride. Multiple pick-up locations in town at 9, 12 & 3. Call day ahead to arrange pickup.

Beverly Carini 850.572.7352 Amicalola - Davenport Gap. Not avail. Su 9-noon.

Jim Granato 828.342.1573 Atlanta - Davenport Gap. Spks Italian/German/Spanish

Chuck Allen 828.371.6460 Springer to Fontana, call after 1p.

City Taxi 828.369.5042 Rides up to 6pm, later by appt.

Roadrunner Driving Services 706.201.7719 where2@mac.com Long distance shuttles covering Atlanta to Damascus.

Larry's Taxi Service 828.421.4987, shuttles anywhere.

Zen Shuttles 828.332.0228 GA-VA

Lenzo Animal Hospital 828.369.2635 M-F 8:30-5:00, Sa 8:30-noon. Emergency clinic 828.665.4399.

Visitor Center (Chamber of Commerce) 828.524.3161 M–F 9–5 yr-round, Sa 10-4 (May-Oct). List of hiker services & shuttles. facc@franklinnc.com ⟨www.visitfranklin.com⟩

115.4 Wayah Gap, Wayah Rd.
124.1 Burningtown Gap, NC 1397
128.9 Tellico Gap, Otter Creek Rd.

Nantahala Mtn Lodge 828.321.2340, after 7:30p 828.321.9949. Run by 2010 thru-hiker "Wiggy." Mar 1-Jun 1. ALL rates incl. b'fast. Bunks $35PP (bedding provided), prvt room w/2 twins $70, prvt room w/king & bathroom $80. P/U & return from/to Wayah Gap (115.4) & Telico Gap (128.9) $5PP/trip, Burningtown Gap (124.1) FREE. 3-Course evening meal $12.50. Laundry $5. Short term resupply; packaged meals, candy, etc. Slackpacking options Rock Gap to Fontana w/reservations. Parking for section hikers. No pets. Mail for guests only: 63 Britannia Dr, Aquone, NC 28781

Enterprise Rent-A-Car 800.736.8227 Car rental w/free pickup/return can be as economical as shuttles. ATC has arranged for hiker discount, use code W15509. Locations include Franklin, NC, Abingdon, VA, Pearisburg, VA, Roanoke, VA, Waynesboro, VA, Front Royal, VA, Charles Town, WV, Carlisle, PA, East Stroudsburg, PA, Warwick, NY, Pittsfield, MA, Bennington, VT, Rutland, VT, West Lebanon, NH, Gorham, NH.

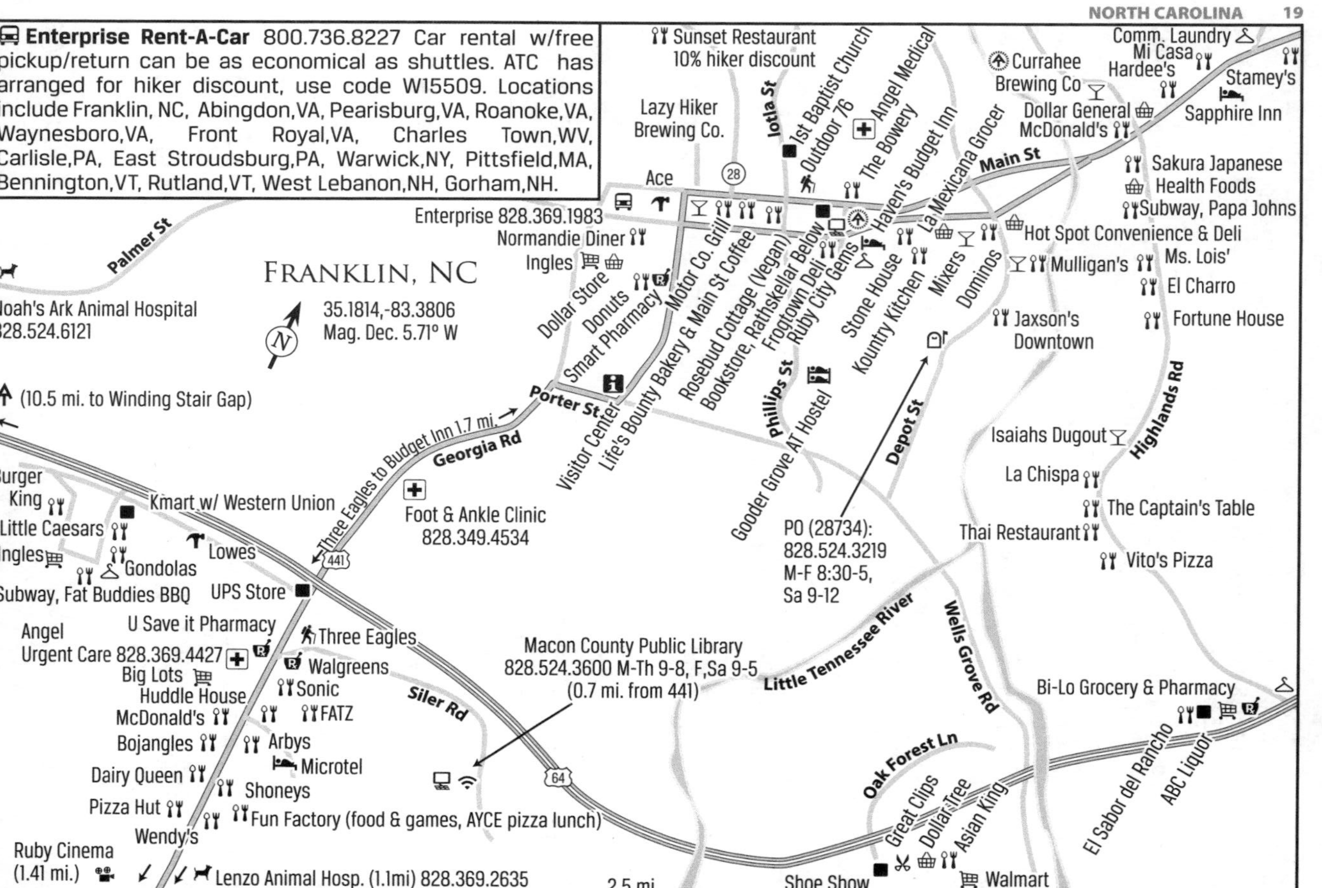

2070.2 119.6 Wayah Bald, stone tower and paved footpath 5342

2069.6 120.2 ⚠NoBos: AT to left, Bartram Trail to east, campsite, spring to west of trail . . 4887

2069.3 120.5 **Wayah Bald Shelter,** east to shelter, west 0.2 to water. . . . . . . (8) 4712
18.2◄14.8◄6.8◄►4.8►10.6►15.5 10 tent sites.

2068.0 121.8 Licklog Gap, signed tent sites with register box along . . . . (0.5W) 4440
blue blaze water trail just out of site of the A.T.

2066.6 123.2 Intersection with old roadbed and side trails, AT turns to east 4515

2066.0 123.8 Stream. 4323

2065.7 124.1 Burningtown Gap, NC 1397 . . . . 35.2223,-83.5622 P (pg. 18) 4236

2065.3 124.5 Spring 4511

2064.5 125.3 **Cold Spring Shelter** (Built by CCC in 1930's) . . . . (6) 4926
19.6◄11.6◄4.8◄►5.8►10.7►18.4 Trail to 10 tentsites on ridge 100 yds N on AT.

2063.8 126.0 Copper Ridge Bald, views 5080

2062.6 127.2 Side trail 0.1E to Rocky Bald, views 5030

2062.4 127.4 Big Branch Campsite, signed 4978
four tent sites with register box, spring

2060.9 128.9 Tellico Gap, NC 1365 Otter Creek Rd . . . . 35.268,-83.5726 P (pg. 18) 3850

2059.5 130.3 Wesser Bald, east 40 yards to observation tower, panoramic views 4627

2058.8 131.0 Spring-fed stone cistern on blue-blazed trail (0.1E) 4208

2058.7 131.1 **Wesser Bald Shelter** (0.1W) . . . . (8) 4092
17.4◄10.6◄5.8◄►4.9►12.6►21.7 Spring 0.1S on AT (at switchback).
Cables. Just north of shelter trail, Wesser Creek Trail to east.

2056.9 132.9 The Jumpoff, views 3940

2055.3 134.5 Weak spring. 3008

2053.8 136.0 **A. Rufus Morgan Shelter** . . . . (6) 2184
15.5◄10.7◄4.9◄►7.7►16.8►22.9 Shelter in view to east, stream west of AT.

2053.3 136.5 Multiple streams and footbridges 1997

2052.8 137.0 US 19 & 74, **Nantahala Outdoor Center** . . . . . . 35.3312,-83.5922 P (pg. 24) 1732

2052.7 137.1 Side trail to bunkhouse 1771

2051.3 138.5 Wright Gap, dirt road 2403

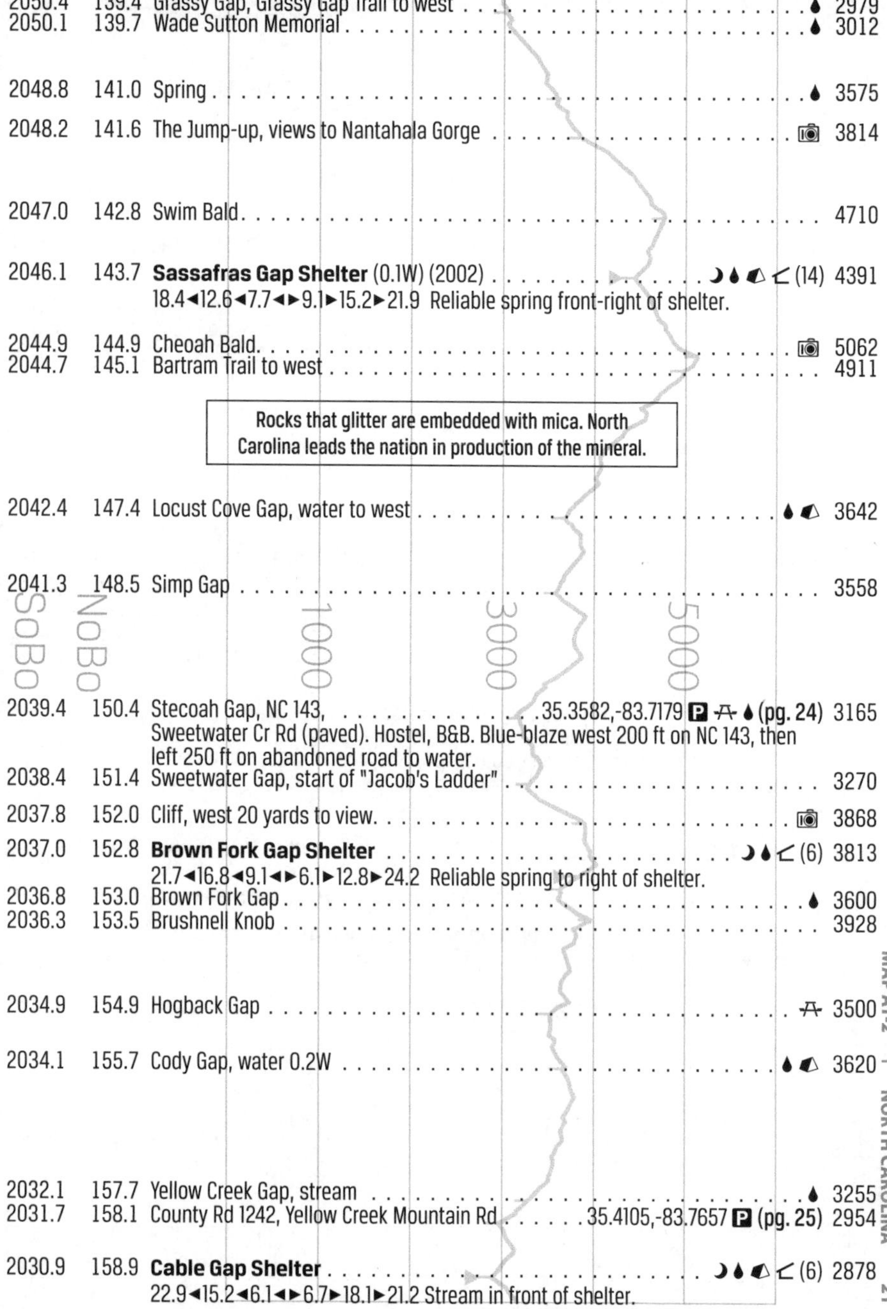

2050.4 139.4 Grassy Gap, Grassy Gap Trail to west 2979
2050.1 139.7 Wade Sutton Memorial 3012

2048.8 141.0 Spring 3575

2048.2 141.6 The Jump-up, views to Nantahala Gorge 3814

2047.0 142.8 Swim Bald 4710

2046.1 143.7 **Sassafras Gap Shelter** (0.1W) (2002) . . . . . (14) 4391
18.4◄12.6◄7.7◄►9.1►15.2►21.9 Reliable spring front-right of shelter.

2044.9 144.9 Cheoah Bald. 5062
2044.7 145.1 Bartram Trail to west 4911

Rocks that glitter are embedded with mica. North Carolina leads the nation in production of the mineral.

2042.4 147.4 Locust Cove Gap, water to west 3642

2041.3 148.5 Simp Gap 3558

2039.4 150.4 Stecoah Gap, NC 143, ... 35.3582,-83.7179 P **(pg. 24)** 3165
Sweetwater Cr Rd (paved). Hostel, B&B. Blue-blaze west 200 ft on NC 143, then left 250 ft on abandoned road to water.
2038.4 151.4 Sweetwater Gap, start of "Jacob's Ladder" 3270

2037.8 152.0 Cliff, west 20 yards to view. 3868

2037.0 152.8 **Brown Fork Gap Shelter** . . . . . (6) 3813
21.7◄16.8◄9.1◄►6.1►12.8►24.2 Reliable spring to right of shelter.
2036.8 153.0 Brown Fork Gap 3600
2036.3 153.5 Brushnell Knob 3928

2034.9 154.9 Hogback Gap 3500

2034.1 155.7 Cody Gap, water 0.2W 3620

2032.1 157.7 Yellow Creek Gap, stream 3255
2031.7 158.1 County Rd 1242, Yellow Creek Mountain Rd . . . . . 35.4105,-83.7657 P **(pg. 25)** 2954

2030.9 158.9 **Cable Gap Shelter** . . . . . (6) 2878
22.9◄15.2◄6.1◄►6.7►18.1►21.2 Stream in front of shelter.

2029.5	160.3	Black Gum Gap		3403
2028.1	161.7	Walker Gap		3450
2027.8	162.0	Footbridge, stream		3266
2026.1	163.7	Spring		2287
2025.4	164.4	NC 28 (paved). **Fontana 28 AT Crossing, Fontana Dam, NC** (2.0W)	35.4414,-83.7968 P (pg. 25)	1756
2024.2	165.6	**Fontana Dam Shelter** "Fontana Hilton" (0.1E) 21.9◄12.8◄6.7◄►11.4►14.5►17.3	(20)	1853
2023.8	166.0	**Dam Visitor Center**	35.452,-83.8013 P i (pg. 25)	1700
2022.7	167.1	Great Smoky Mountains National Park southern boundary NoBo reenter woods, SoBo join road. Benton MacKaye Trail northbound diverges from the AT and follows road to east. The BMT reconnects with the AT at Davenport Gap in approximately 100 miles (BMT miles).	(pg. 28)	1862
2020.7	169.1	Boulder jumble, throne-shaped rock		3314
2020.4	169.4	Stream.		3487
2019.3	170.5	Shuckstack, fire tower 0.1E.		3889
2018.9	170.9	Sassafras Gap		3667
2018.0	171.8	Birch Spring Gap Campsite west 100 yards down slope, tent pads, cables, spring unreliable.		3736
2016.1	173.7	Side trail 3.1W to Gregory Bald		4443
2015.9	173.9	Doe Knob, NoBo follow NC/TN border; SoBo enter NC.		4520
2015.6	174.2	Mud Gap		4325
2014.5	175.3	Ekaneetlee Gap		3842
2012.8	177.0	**Mollies Ridge Shelter,** spring. 24.2◄18.1◄11.4◄►3.1►5.9►12.0	(12)	4586
2012.1	177.7	Devils Tater Patch.		4775
2011.1	178.7	Little Abrams Gap		4120
2010.7	179.1	Big Abrams Gap		4115

2009.7 180.1 **Russell Field Shelter,** spring 0.1W (14) 4348
21.2◄14.5◄3.1◄►2.8►8.9►14.6

2008.3 181.5 Stream. 4747

✽ Sarvis Tree – Also called "serviceberry." Blooms with plentiful petite white-petaled flowers.

2006.9 182.9 **Spence Field Shelter** (0.2E) on Eagle Creek Trail (12) 4916
17.3◄5.9◄2.8◄►6.1►11.8►13.5 100 yards north, Bote Mountain Trail to west.
2006.5 183.3 Jenkins Ridge trail to east 4948

2005.7 184.1 Rocky Top, views 5440

2005.1 184.7 Thunderhead Mountain 5527

2004.4 185.4 Water to west 4964

2002.5 187.3 Starkey Gap 4552

2001.8 188.0 Sugar Tree Gap 4435

2000.8 189.0 **Derrick Knob Shelter** (12) 4882
12.0◄8.9◄6.1◄►5.7►7.4►13.5 Reliable spring near shelter. Cables.
2000.5 189.3 Sams Gap, water 100 yards west, on left side of Greenbrier Ridge Trail 4758

1998.5 191.3 Cold Spring Knob 5203
1998.3 191.5 Miry Ridge Trail to west. 4944
1998.1 191.7 Buckeye Gap 4817

1995.1 194.7 **Silers Bald Shelter,** spring 75 yds right of shelter (12) 5453
14.6◄11.8◄5.7◄►1.7►7.8►15.1
1994.9 194.9 Silers Bald, survey mark on boulder, AT turns to east 5607
1994.7 195.1 Welch Ridge Trail to east 5444

1993.4 196.4 **Double Spring Gap Shelter** 13.5◄7.4◄1.7◄►6.1►13.4►20.7 (12) 5510
Best water 15 yards from crest on NC side. Water is also 35 yards down TN side.
1992.8 197.0 Goshen Prong Trail to west. 5778

1991.0 198.8 Mt Buckley 6590
1990.9 198.9 Trail 0.5E to Clingman's parking area ⚠ NoBo: AT is left fork of this intersection 6518

137.0 US 19 & 74

Nantahala Outdoor Center 888.905.7238 Complex w/lodging, food, gear & whitewater rafting. Non-guest coinop showers Apr-Oct. In-season office hrs 8-5. Reservations recommended, even for hostel. Walk-ins w/out reservation, check-in at General Store or **River's End Restaurant**. CC ok. Campus WiFi. ⟨www.noc.com⟩

Events at NOC: ***Southern Ruck*** Jan 13-16. **NOC Trail Festival** Apr 8-9 Movies, soda & popcorn Fr., thruhiker dinner Sa. Live music, lightweight backpacking, cooking, & ATC clinics, fun & giveaways, gear reps for support & repairs. Extended restaurant & store hrs.

Motel rooms $69.99/up. Prices higher mid-summer, weekends & holidays. Basic rooms do not have TV or phone. Rooms w/more amenities can be economical for groups; ask about prices.

Base Camp Bunkhouse $39.99/2 persons, $79.99/4, $109.99/6, $139.99/8 incl. shower, common area & kitchen.

River's End Restaurant (B/L/D); **Big Wesser BBQ/ Pourover Pub** Live music, opens mid-April.

NOC Outfitters Full line of gear, trail food, fuel/oz. Gear shakedowns. Open daily, extended hours in summer. Can print Smokies permits. Ask about shuttles. Thru-hikers 10% off 1 full price item. Mail: dated & marked "Hold for AT Hiker", 13077 Hwy 19W, Bryson City, NC 28713.

Wesser General Store Open Mar-Oct.

Nantahala General Store & Lodge (0.9E) 828.488.4559 Camping Cabins (up to 4) with mini-kitchen $69.95, offseason (Nov-May) $49.95. 3-bedroom cabins (up to 8) $129. Free pickup/return for guests.

Nantahala Cabins 828.488.1622 (2.5E) 8 Cabins, 4-8 People. Call for thru hiker rate. Hot tubs, kitchen/bath, Wifi, some w/laundry. Shuttles avail., prices vary. ⟨www.nantahalacabins.com⟩

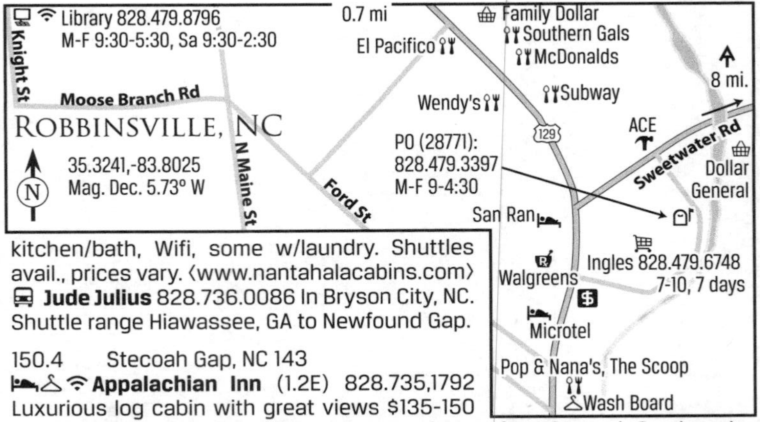

Jude Julius 828.736.0086 In Bryson City, NC. Shuttle range Hiawassee, GA to Newfound Gap.

150.4 Stecoah Gap, NC 143

Appalachian Inn (1.2E) 828.735,1792 Luxurious log cabin with great views $135-150 double, 1.2E from Stecoah Gap. Incl. pickup/return from Stecoah Gap,laundry & full country b'fast. Additional charge for lunch/ dinner. Some rooms have jacuzzi tubs. Cash/check/cc. info@appalachianinn.com.

(3.0E) **Cabin in the Woods** Donna 828.735.1930 or Phil 828.735.3368 Hiker lodging $20PP incl. ride to/from Stecoah Gap, shower, bathroom. Private cabins avail. but are often booked (reserve early). $15 resupplytrip to Robbinsville. For-fee shuttles ranging from Amicalola to Hot Springs or to Knoxville/Asheville bus stations & airports. Family style b'fast $5, dinner $8, laundry $3/load. Cash or check only, no CC. No Maildrops.

The Owl's Perch 828.479.9791 (18.4W) Open Mar-Dec. Hiker rate $70S, $100D incl. P/U &return from Stecoah Gap w/quick stop at Ingles. Simple b'fast. Our "bunkhouse" is a separate structure w/Queen bed, full bath, linens, kitchenette, grill & b'fast. Fee for dinner if requested. W/D avail. No pets. CC or cash. ⟨www.grahamcountytravel.com/the-owls-perch/⟩

Buffalo Creek B&B (19.0W) 828.479.3892 Hiker rate (no drive-ins) $65S, $55D, $45PP for 3+. Incl. Stecoah Gap P/U & return, Robbinsville resupply stop, laundry, b'fast, hot tub, free home brew. Open Apr-Oct, call for avail. other months. Print Smokies permit here. Guest only mail: 4989 W. Buffalo Rd, Robbinsville, NC 28771.

Robbinsville, NC (8W from Stecoah Gap)
San Ran Motel 828.479.3256 Call for rates. Fridge & m'wave. No smoking/pets.
Microtel 828.479.6772 Call for rates. Pet fee $50.

158.1 Yellow Creek Mountain Rd.
(1.8W) **Creekside Paradise on the A.T.** 828.346.1076 Cynthia/Jeff, postandwilson@gmail.com. Room: $60PP, $45PP if 2+per room. Camping $10. Stay incl. P/U & return from Yellow Creek Gap, resupply trip to Robbinsville, laundry, hot tub, & free slackpack. B'fast incl. w/room rental, $10 for campers. Dinner $15PP. P/U & return from Stecoah Gap/Fontana $5, NOC $15. Pets welcome. Mail: 259 Upper Cove Rd, Robbinsville, NC, 28771.
Revonda Williams (1.0W) 828-735-1300 Mobile home rental for up to 5 $75/night Apr 1 - Oct 31.

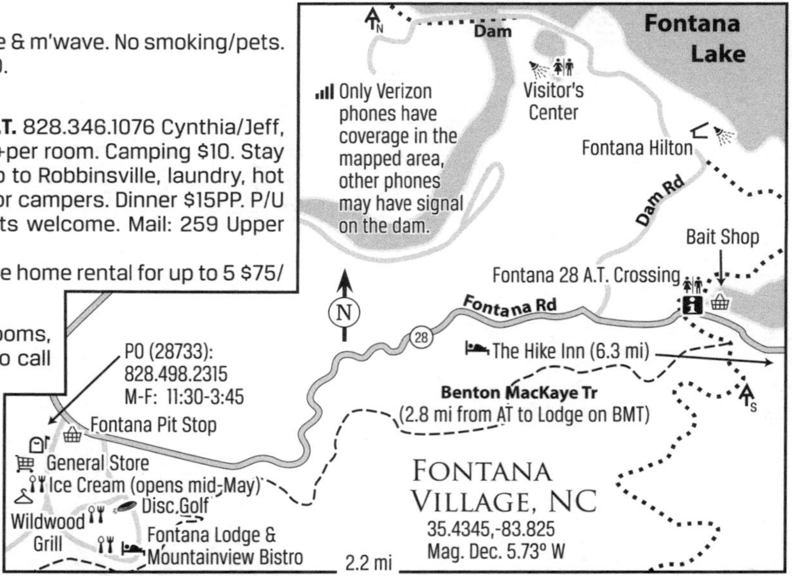

164.4 NC 28 **Fontana 28 AT Crossing** Bathrooms, vending machines, GSMNP maps ($1), house phone to call for shuttle. Snacks & canned meats avail. from bait store on dock 0.1E.
Fontana Shuttle 828.498.2211 Shuttle $3PP ea way between AT Crossing (Marina) or Visitor Center & Fontana Village. 8:30-6 daily Feb 15- May 15. Call for avail. of rides outside these dates.

Fontana Village, NC (2W from NC 28) For all facilities contact: 800.849.2258 or 828.498.2211
Fontana Lodge 800.849.2258, 828.498.2211 Thru-hiker rate (ask) $79 (up to 4), no pets. Price higher on high-demand nights. Cabins $79/BR, pets welcome. Computer & printer in lobby can be used for Smokies permit. Mail ($5 non-guest fee): Fontana Village Resort, ATTN: [Hiker Name], 300 Woods Rd, Fontana Dam, NC 28733.
General Store Grocery store, frz-dried food, Coleman/alcohol/oz, canister fuel during thru-hiker season, small selection of gear. Open Mar 10-Thksgvg.
Fontana Pit Stop Hot dogs, microwave fare, soda & coffee. Stocks hiker food & fuel when General Store closed. Open daily 9-5, later in summer.
Mountainview Bistro, Wildwood Grill Bistro open yr-round B/L/D, Grill Apr-Oct
Laundromat 7 days, yr-round. Detergent at General Store if front desk closed.
Steve Claxton 828.736.7501, 828.479.9608 Licensed shuttle range Springer-Hot Springs & 3 area airports. Slackpacking. 2016 Thru hiker.

166.0 **Fontana Dam Visitor Center**
828.498.2234 Soda machine outside, ice cream sold inside when open (9a-6p daily May-Oct), free showers.
(6.3E) **The Hike Inn** 828.479.3677 A hiker-only service run by Jeff & Nancy Hoch since 1993. BY RESERVATION ONLY. We ask that all long distance hikers call us pre-hike so that we can better accommodate you. Open yr-round for accommodations & transportation. Please call, e-mail (hikeinn@graham.main.nc.us), or visit ⟨www.thehikeinn.com⟩ for more info, reservations & directions.

1990.7	199.1	Clingmans Tower Path, paved path between tower and parking area		6643
1990.5	199.3	Clingmans Dome, tower to east	(pg. 28)	6667
1989.9	199.9	Mt Love		6446
1988.7	201.1	Collins Gap		5750
1987.7	202.1	Mt Collins		6187
1987.3	202.5	Sugarland Mtn Trail, **Mt Collins Shelter** (0.5W) 13.5◄7.8◄6.1◄►7.3►14.6►19.4 Cables. Small spring 0.1 beyond shelter.	(12)	5962
1987.0	202.8	Fork Mountain Trail east ot Clingmans Dome Rd		5882
1986.2	203.6	Spring		5628
1984.6	205.2	Road Prong Trail, AT skirts Clingmans Dome Rd.	35.6094,-83.4467 P	5273
1984.3	205.5	Mingus Ridge, two wild hog containment bridges		5437
1983.0	206.8	Newfound Gap, US 441 Large parking area, restrooms. No potable water. ✖The "Hands That Built" display shows a photograph of a shirtless man using what tool? **Gatlinburg, TN** (15.0W)	35.6112,-83.4257 P (pg. 28)	5045
1981.3	208.5	Sweat Heifer Creek Trail to east		5821
1980.3	209.5	0.2W to Mt Kephart, 0.6W to Jumpoff (views), Blvd Trail 5.5W to Mt LeConte		6036
1980.0	209.8	**Icewater Spring Shelter** to east 15.1◄13.4◄7.3◄►7.3►12.1►19.8 Spring 75 yards north on AT.	(12)	5935
1979.1	210.7	South end of Charlies Bunion Loop Trail (0.1W)		5522
1979.0	210.8	North end of Charlies Bunion Loop Trail		5475
1978.8	211.0	Unmarked side trail 0.1W to original Charlies Bunion.		5420
1978.6	211.2	Dry Sluice Gap Trail to east		5398
1978.0	211.8	The Sawteeth		5400
1977.7	212.1	Porters Gap		5364
1975.0	214.8	View		5746
1974.0	215.8	Bradleys View		5476
1972.7	217.1	**Pecks Corner Shelter** (0.5E) on Hughes Ridge Trail 20.7◄14.6◄7.3◄►4.8►12.5►19.6 Spring just south of shelter side trail.	(12)	5556
1971.9	217.9	Eagle Rocks, view.		5834
1971.1	218.7	Copper Gap		5514

NoBo	SoBo	Location		Elev
1970.5	219.3	Mt Sequoyah, AT skirts summit		5945
1968.6	221.2	East ridge of Mt Chapman		6216
1967.9	221.9	**Tri-Corner Knob Shelter** 19.4◄12.1◄4.8◄►7.7►14.8►25.3	(12)	5897
1967.8	222.0	Balsam Trail to east.		5962
1966.5	223.3	Guyot Spring, trail skirts Mt Guyot		6302
1966.0	223.8	Spring		6225
1965.0	224.8	Deer Creek Gap		6054
1964.3	225.5	Yellow Creek Gap		5902
1964.2	225.6	Plane wreckage		5876
1964.1	225.7	Snake Den Ridge Trail, 5.3W to Cosby Campground		5791
1961.8	228.0	Camel Gap, Camel Gap Trail to east		4674
1960.2	229.6	**Cosby Knob Shelter,** 100 yards east 19.8◄12.5◄7.7◄►7.1►17.6►25.9	(12)	4766
1959.4	230.4	Low Gap, 2.5W to Cosby Campground		4242
1957.3	232.5	Mt Cammerer Trail, 0.6W to summit, lookout tower		4950
1957.0	232.8	Spring		4691
1955.1	234.7	Lower Mt Cammerer Trail, Cosby Campground (7.8W)		3468
1954.1	235.7	Chestnut Branch Trail, 2.1E to parking at Big Creek Ranger Station and north end of BMT.	35.7593,-83.1069 P (2.0E)	2876
1953.9	235.9	Spring		2823
1953.1	236.7	**Davenport Gap Shelter,** spring to left of shelter 19.6◄14.8◄7.1◄►10.5►18.8►23.6	(12)	2591
1952.2	237.6	TN 32, NC 284, Davenport Gap, cross road where pavement ends Great Smoky Mountains National Park northern boundary	**(pg. 29)**	1975
1951.1	238.7	Stateline Branch, multiple crossings		1698

Great Smoky Mountains NP ⟨www.nps.gov/grsm⟩
Backcountry Info: 865.436.1297
Reservations: 865.436.1231

A permit is required and there is a backcountry fee -$4PP/night up to $20PP for up to 7 nights/8 days. An on-line system allows you to pay & print a permit up to 30 days in advance. Hikers who meet the definition of an Appalachian Trail thru-hiker (those who begin & end their hike at least 50 miles outside the park and only travel on the A.T. in the park) are eligible for a $20 thru-hiker permit (valid for 38 days from the date issued for an up to 8 day hike through the Park) ⟨www.smokiespermits.nps.gov⟩

Shelters - The only near-trail campsite is Birch Spring, otherwise hikers must stay in shelters. Reservations required for section hikers. If the shelter is full, thru-hikers must give up bunk space and tent in the vicinity of the shelter. Hikers must use bear cables to secure food.

Bear activity has been reported at various shelters in the park. Hikers must use the food storage cables provided at all backcountry campsites in the park. Occasionally shelters are closed when bear activity becomes especially problematic. Check website for closures.

No pets - Dogs are not permitted in the park. Below are kenneling options, vaccination records often required:

Loving Care Kennels 865.453.2028, 3779 Tinker Hollow Rd, Pigeon Forge, TN 37863. Pickup your dog at Fontana Dam & return him/her to Davenport Gap. $350 for one dog, $500 for two. Will deliver maildrops upon pickup/return. Call at least 2 days in advance (preferably from NOC if NoBo). ⟨www.LovingCareKennels.com⟩

Barks and Recreation 865.325.8245 Does not offer rides, but you can drop-off & P/U from 2159 East Pkwy Gatlinburg, TN. M-Sa 7a-8p, Su 10-6 ⟨www.barksandrecgatlinburg.com⟩

Standing Bear Farm (see pg. 34)

199.3 **Clingmans Dome** 35.5572,-83.4939 Highest point on the AT. Parking lot, trash cans & restrooms 0.5E on a paved walkway. There are no sinks in restrooms. Gift shop near parking area sells water 10a-6p Apr 1-Nov 30 but often sells out. It's 7 mi from the parking area to Newfound Gap on Clingmans Dome Rd; Rd is closed to cars Dec 1 - Apr 1.

206.8 Newfound Gap, US 441 (AT&T weak) ***Gatlinburg, TN*** (15W)

Grand Prix Motel 865.436.4561 $39.99, $5 EAP, coin laundry, computer. Mail: 235 Ski Mtn Rd, Gatlinburg, TN 37738. ⟨www.grandprixmotel.com⟩

Microtel Gatlinburg 865.436.0107 $44.95/up, cont B, pets $10. Maildrop with reservation: 211 Historic Nature Trail, Gatlinburg, TN 37738.

Motel 6 865.436.7813 Reasonable rates. Pool, pets under 25 lbs free, 26-50 lbs $10, 50+lbs $20. Trolley stops at the front door. All major CC. Mail: 309 Ownby St, Gatlinburg, TN 37738.

Days Inn 865.436.5811

Best Western 865.436.5121

Qualla Motel & Cabins (15E) 828.497.5161 Hiker rates, free laundry, WiFi, across street from grocery/pharmacy. Pets ok. ⟨www.cherokeecabins.com⟩

NOC Great Outpost 865.277.8209 Open 7 days 10-9, (Jan-May 10-6). Full line of gear, white gas/denatured/oz. Free showers & pack storage. Mail: 1138 Parkway, Gatlinburg, TN 37738.

The Day Hiker 865.430.0970 Year-round 7 days. Basic hiking supplies w/shoes & fuel (no food). Hours vary by season.

Highlands Shuttle Service (Ron McGaha) 423.625.0739 or 865.322.2752, shuttles from Standing Indian (NC) to Damascus, VA. Also P/U & drop-off at Knoxville & Asheville airports & bus stations.

A Walk in the Woods 865.436.8283 Guides Vesna & Erik Plakanis resupply & shuttling (hikers & dogs). Shuttle range Springer to Damascus (company based in Gatlinburg). Special thru-hiker rates ⟨www.aWalkintheWoods.com⟩

Cherokee Cab 828.269.8621 Short & long distance shuttles 24/7 covering all trailheads in the Smokies & nearby cities. Call for rates.

Cherokee Transit 866.388.6071 ⟨www.cherokeetransit.com⟩

■ **Roger Bailey, LMT** 865.250.0676, 865.250.0676 Special thru-hiker rate $70/hr massage.

Cherokee, NC (21E) Large town, many services.
Microtel Inn & Suites 828.497.7800 $65, higher on wkends, incl. b'fast, free local/long distance phone. Coin laundry, pool. Adjacent supermarket, fast-food, shoe store. Mail: (Fed Ex/UPS only) 674 Casino Tr, Cherokee, NC 28719.

237.6 Davenport Gap *(See map pg. 34)*, **Great Smoky Mountain NP**
(2.3E) **Big Creek Campground** 865.436.1297, 865.436.1231 $14/ site, no showers or electricity. Open early Apr - late Oct. Rates/dates may change, call. Chestnut Branch Trail (2.0mi) connects campground to AT 0.1S of Davenport Gap Shelter. From ranger station on CBT, compass north 0.3 mi to Country Store, compass south 0.6 mi to campsites.
Big Creek Country Store (1.0S) 828.476.4492 Hiker friendly resupply. Adding showers & laundry by 2017 season.

239.5 I-40
Highlands Shuttle Service (see entry pg 28)

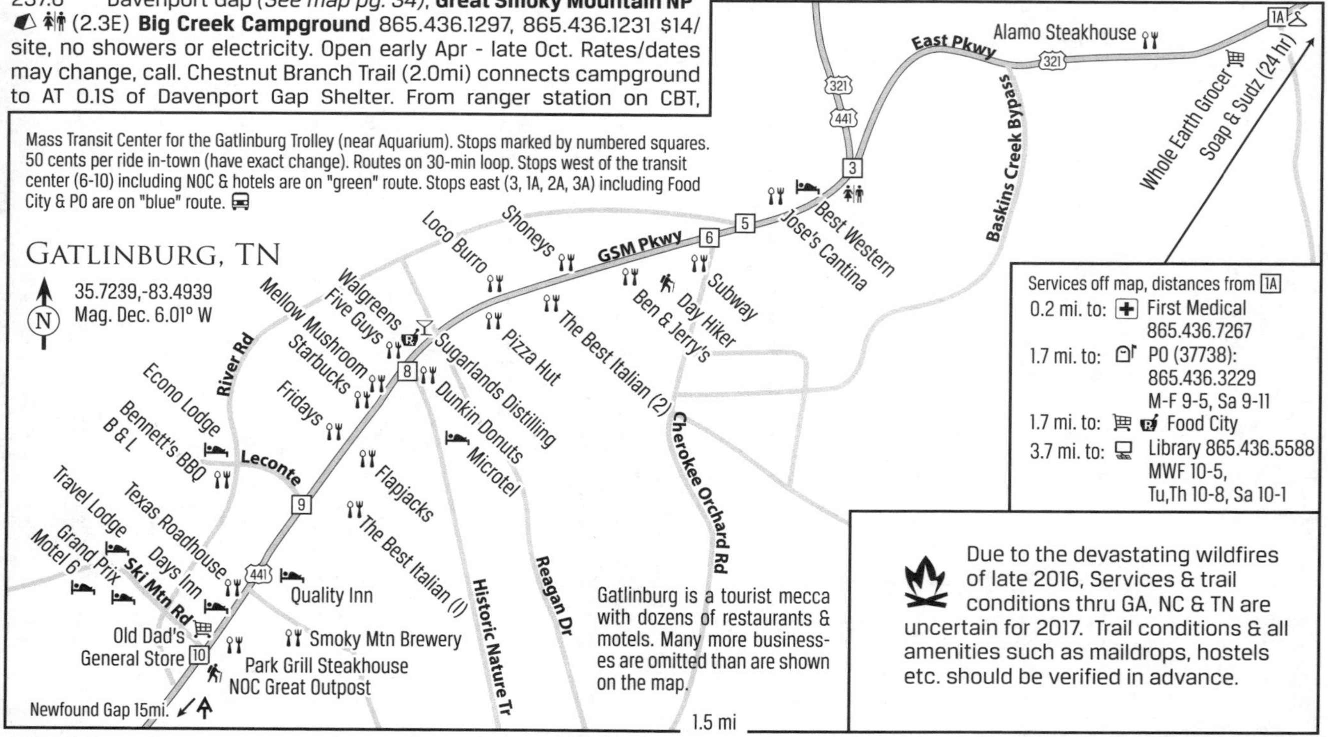

Mass Transit Center for the Gatlinburg Trolley (near Aquarium). Stops marked by numbered squares. 50 cents per ride in-town (have exact change). Routes on 30-min loop. Stops west of the transit center (6-10) including NOC & hotels are on "green" route. Stops east (3, 1A, 2A, 3A) including Food City & PO are on "blue" route.

GATLINBURG, TN

35.7239,-83.4939
Mag. Dec. 6.01° W

Services off map, distances from 1A
0.2 mi. to: First Medical 865.436.7267
1.7 mi. to: PO (37738): 865.436.3229 M-F 9-5, Sa 9-11
1.7 mi. to: Food City
3.7 mi. to: Library 865.436.5588 MWF 10-5, Tu,Th 10-8, Sa 10-1

Gatlinburg is a tourist mecca with dozens of restaurants & motels. Many more businesses are omitted than are shown on the map.

Due to the devastating wildfires of late 2016, Services & trail conditions thru GA, NC & TN are uncertain for 2017. Trail conditions & all amenities such as maildrops, hostels etc. should be verified in advance.

Alamo Steakhouse
East Pkwy
Whole Earth Grocer
Soap & Sudz (24 hr)
Baskins Creek Bypass
Best Western
Jose's Cantina
GSM Pkwy
Subway
Day Hiker
Ben & Jerry's
Shoneys
Loco Burro
The Best Italian (2)
Pizza Hut
Sugarlands Distilling
Dunkin Donuts
Microtel
Walgreens
Five Guys
Mellow Mushroom
Starbucks
Fridays
Flapjacks
The Best Italian (1)
Cherokee Orchard Rd
Reagan Dr
Historic Nature Tr
River Rd
Leconte
Econo Lodge
Bennett's BBQ
B & L
Texas Roadhouse
Days Inn
Travel Lodge
Grand Prix
Motel 6
Ski Mtn Rd
Quality Inn
Smoky Mtn Brewery
Park Grill Steakhouse
NOC Great Outpost
Old Dad's General Store
Newfound Gap 15mi.
1.5 mi

1950.6	239.2	Pigeon River Bridge		1373
1950.3	239.5	I-40 underpass	(pg. 29)	1439
1950.1	239.7	Stream		1569
1949.5	240.3	Green Corner Rd (gravel) hostel to west	(pg. 34)	1788
1947.4	242.4	Painter Branch, cross branch to campsites. Blue-blazed trail east across Painter Creek to campsite and spring.		2844
1947.1	242.7	Stream		3099
1946.5	243.3	Spanish Oak Gap, trail joins old roadbed		3470
1945.1	244.7	Snowbird Mountain, grassy bald, side trail 50 yards to FAA tower on summit.		4263
1944.3	245.5	Wildcat Spring uphill from trail		4065
1943.6	246.2	Turkey Gap		3648
1942.8	247.0	Spring		3034
1942.6	247.2	Deep Gap, **Groundhog Creek Shelter** (0.2E) 25.3◄17.6◄10.5◄►8.3►13.1►23.0 Stone shelter, reliable spring to left. Cables.	(6)	2911
1940.8	249.0	Spring downhill, east 30 yards		3563
1940.3	249.5	Rube Rock Trail to Hawks Roost		3853
1939.7	250.1	Brown Gap, USFS 148A		3500

"Max Patch" is a homophone that replaced the original name "Mack's Patch". The summit was cleared for cattle and is maintained as a bald.

1937.2	252.6	Cherry Creek Trail, water 0.3E		4341
1936.9	252.9	SR 1182, Max Patch Rd, stream to north	35.7963,-82.9627 P	4259
1936.6	253.2	Dirt road, west to parking, east to Buckeye Ridge	P	4397
1936.2	253.6	Max Patch Summit (no fires) ⚠ NoBos turn right at north end of bald		4629
1935.7	254.1	Stream		4384
1935.2	254.6	Roadbed, Buckeye Ridge Trail to east		4215
1934.6	255.2	Stream		4121
1934.4	255.4	Water to east (signed)		4026
1934.3	255.5	**Roaring Fork Shelter,** water 0.1S or 0.4N, 7 tent pads, cables 25.9◄18.8◄8.3◄►4.8►14.7►28.9	(10)	4019
1933.9	255.9	Footbridge, stream		3936
1933.2	256.6	Footbridge		3742
1932.8	257.0	Stream (many in area)		3639
1932.1	257.7	Two streams about 0.1 mile apart		3455
1931.3	258.5	Footbridge		3558
1931.0	258.8	Footbridge, stream		3496

SoBo	NoBo	Location	Elevation
1930.8	259.0	Lemon Gap, NC 1182, TN 107	3550
1930.1	259.7	Stream. 💧	3951
1929.6	260.2	Walnut Mountain, grassy clearing	4293
1929.5	260.3	**Walnut Mountain Shelter** 23.6◄13.1◄4.8◄►9.9►24.1►32.7 (6) Walnut Mt tr. to west. Cables. Water 0.1 behind, campsite in field beyond water.	4245
1928.8	261.0	Kale Gap, campsite 125 yards north on AT.	3700
1928.1	261.7	Catpen Gap, 0.1 east to campsite atop small knoll	4130
1927.7	262.1	Streams 💧	4262
1927.4	262.4	Unnamed gap	4452
1927.1	262.7	Bluff Mountain	4686
1926.4	263.4	Spring 50 yards west. 💧	4195
1925.8	264.0	Old roadbed, spring. 💧	3921
1925.5	264.3	Big Rock Spring located in ravine 💧	3730
1924.9	264.9	Dirt road	3407
1924.3	265.5	Brook with cascades 💧	2978
1923.9	265.9	Old Rd	2710
1923.0	266.8	Garenflo Gap, Shut-In Trail to west 35.8534,-82.8759 P	2500
1922.3	267.5	Taylor Hollow Gap, two footbridges, one over a stream 💧	2639
1919.6	270.2	**Deer Park Mountain Shelter** (0.2E) water at gap west of AT. (5) 23.0◄14.7◄9.9◄►14.2►22.8►30.1 Cables. Gragg Gap 0.1 north on AT.	2319
1918.8	271.0	Deer Park Mountain.	2571
1916.4	273.4	NC 209 + US 25/70, **Hot Springs, NC** 35.8895,-82.8323 P **(pg. 34)**	1326
1916.0	273.8	French Broad River, US 25/70 bridge ⚠ NoBo turn east through gap in guardrail immediately after crossing river.	1339
1915.1	274.7	Lovers Leap Rock, several rock outcroppings, Silver Mine Trail to west 📷 💧	1686
1913.1	276.7	Pump Gap, trail crossing	2130
1912.7	277.1	Springs 💧	2299
1912.2	277.6	North intersection with Pump Gap Loop Trail	2410
1911.6	278.2	Pond with boxed spring, campsite. 💧	2467
1911.3	278.5	⚠ NoBo: AT 0.3W on dirt road. Cross Mill Ridge to gravel road. (double-blazed oak tree). Go 0.1W on gravel road and reenter woods to east.	2604

SoBo NoBo 1000 3000 5000

SoBo	NoBo	Feature	Elev
1910.8	279.0	Stream.	2429
1910.5	279.3	Tanyard Gap, US 25/70 overpass . . . 35.91,-82.791 P	2270
1909.1	280.7	Piped spring	3039
1908.6	281.2	Roundtop Ridge Trail west 3.5 miles to Hot Springs (former path of AT)	3237
1908.1	281.7	Side trail 0.1W to campsite, Rich Mountain Lookout Tower, piped spring north on AT.	3532
1907.6	282.2	Spring	3202
1907.2	282.6	Hurricane Gap, northmost of two gravel road crossings	2968
1906.9	282.9	Grave stone	2983
1905.4	284.4	**Spring Mountain Shelter** 28.9◄24.1◄14.2◄►8.6►15.9►22.6 . . . (5) Water 75 yards down blue-blazed trail on east side of AT. Cables.	3538
1903.6	286.2	Deep Gap, Little Paint Creek Trail, west 200 yards to spring	2892
1902.2	287.6	Spring in ravine 30 yards west	2757
1901.6	288.2	NC 208, TN 70, Allen Gap, Paint Creek 0.2W	2223
1900.6	289.2	AT skirts gravel road	2338
1900.1	289.7	Log Cabin Drive, hostel to west. . . . (pg. 35) Private home in view to east, please do not trespass.	2371
1896.8	293.0	**Little Laurel Shelter** 32.7◄22.8◄8.6◄►7.3►14.0►22.8 . . . (5) Boxed spring 100 yards down blue-blazed trail behind shelter. Campsites west side of AT, south of shelter. Cables.	3656
1895.0	294.8	Pounding Mill Trail to east. 0.2W to Camp Creek Bald Lookout Tower. Tower is beyond first cluster of buildings and catwalk is locked (no view)	4750
1894.2	295.6	Jones Meadow, spring 100 yards south	4450
1893.2	296.6	Trail west to Jones Meadow, 30 yards east to Whiterock Cliff..	4465
1893.0	296.8	0.1W to view from Blackstack Cliffs	4496
1892.8	297.0	Bearwallow Gap, Jerry Miller Trail to east, Firescald bypass to west reconnects with AT 1.5 miles north. AT between bypass points is rocky and strenuous.	4432
1892.1	297.7	Big Firescald Knob	4544
1891.2	298.6	Firescald bypass to west, reconnects with AT 1.5 miles south.	4182

1890.5	299.3	Round Knob Trail to west		4284
1889.7	300.1	Fork Ridge Trail to east		4274
1889.5	300.3	Chestnut Log Gap, **Jerry Cabin Shelter** 30.1◄15.9◄7.3◄►6.7►15.5►25.6 Water opposite shelter. Cables.	(6)	4148
1888.7	301.1	Bald Ridge		4543
1888.3	301.5	Sarvis Cove Trail to west		4569
1887.9	301.9	Howard C. Bassett Memorial, old roadbed before and after		4687
1887.6	302.2	Big Butt Mountain, summit to west, short bypass trail.		4812
1887.2	302.6	Blue-blazed trail to west		4674
1885.8	304.0	Shelton Gravesite to east		4451

AT northbound from Flint Gap to Rice Gap is compass south.

1884.3	305.5	Cross stream		3941
1883.5	306.3	Flint Gap		3449
1882.8	307.0	**Flint Mountain Shelter,** water on AT 50 yards north of shelter. Bear cables. 22.6◄14.0◄6.7◄►8.8►18.9►29.5	(8)	3557
1882.7	307.1	Spring		3564
1881.8	308.0	Spring		3374
1881.4	308.4	AT + roadbed south end		3280
1881.3	308.5	Spring		3272
1880.7	309.1	AT + roadbed north end		3309
1880.3	309.5	Devil Fork Gap, NC 212	36.0105,-82.6086 P	3104
1879.8	310.0	Rector Laurel Rd, spring north on AT.	36.0065,-82.607 P (pg. 35)	2938
1879.4	310.4	Stream		3205
1879.1	310.7	Cascade		3399
1878.9	310.9	Stream		3565
1878.3	311.5	Sugarloaf Gap		4036
1876.9	312.9	Lick Rock		4541
1876.2	313.6	Big Flat, campsite to east		4267
1875.2	314.6	Rice Gap, dirt road		3800
1874.0	315.8	**Hogback Ridge Shelter** (0.1E) 22.8◄15.5◄8.8◄►10.1►20.7►31.2 Spring 0.2 mile beyond shelter. Cables.	(6)	4314
1873.4	316.4	High Rock, view 70 yards west on blue-blazed trail		4460
1871.6	318.2	Sams Gap, US 23, I-26	35.9529,-82.5606 P (pg. 35)	3725

Standing Bear
Tobes Creek Rd
Pigeon River
Green Corner Rd
Waterville Rd
32
Davenport Gap
Big Creek Ranger Station (1.3E)
828.486.5910

240.3 Green Corner Rd
Standing Bear Farm (0.1W) 423.487.0014 Open year-round, hosted by Maria. Bunk $20, Tenting $15PP and up, Cabin or treehouse $30PP. Reasonably-priced resupply, beer, cook-yourself meals. All stove fuel. Daypacks for slackpackers. Shuttles anywhere. Kennel service & dog shuttle for hike through Smokies, $250. Directions (see map): Green Corner Rd is unsigned gravel road 1.0 north of I-40, go west 200 yards to white farmhouse. Parking $5/car/day. Credit cards accepted. Mail: 4255 Green Corner Rd, Hartford, TN 37753.

273.4 NC 209, US 25/70 ***Hot Springs, NC*** 11.5% tax added to all Hot Springs lodging prices. **Trailfest Apr 21, 22**; Friday dinner $5 at the Comm. Center, activities all day, Sa & Su pancake b'fast $4.

Elmers Sunnybank Inn 828.622.7206 Located across from Dollar General, at 26 Walnut St. Traditional thru-hikers $25PP semi-private room, incl. linens, towel & shower. Gourmet organic vegetarian meals avail. No pets, no smoking, no cc. Historic Sunnybank Inn has offered hospitality to AT hikers since 1948. Staffed by former thru-hikers, the Inn offers an extensive library & well-equipped music room. Work exchange possible. Mail: PO Box 233, Hot Springs, NC 28743 ⟨www.sunnybankretreatassociation.org⟩

Hostel at Laughing Heart Lodge 828.206.8487 $20PP bunks, $25 semi-private, $30 single private, $45D private (one full-size bed). Open yr-round. All rooms include am coffee, shower & towel, movies, hiker kitchen, Wifi. Pets $5 in limted rooms. Tenting w/shower $10S $15D (one tent). Shower only $5. Laundry $5 incl. soap. Quiet time 10p-7a. Lodge rooms $100 include cont. b'fast, call/text 828.622.0165 to reserve. Mail: 289 NW Hwy 25/70, Hot Springs, NC 28743.

Iron Horse Station 866.402.9377 Hiker rate $65D. Restaurant, tavern and coffee shop. Serves L/D, and offers some vegetarian options. Live music Tu, We, Fr, Sa, Su. ⟨www.theironhorsestation.com⟩

Little Bird Cabins 828.206.1487 Rental cabin sleeps 6, incl. kitchenette. Reservations by phone or online. Pet fee $15. CC accepted. Open yr-round. littlebirdcabinrentals@gmail.com ⟨www.littlebirdcabinrentals.com⟩

Mountain Magnolia Inn 800.914.9306 Discount

hiker rates $75S $95D when rooms avail. incl. AYCE b'fast. Dinner Th-M, open to all. ⟨www.mountainmagnoliainn.com⟩

Creekside Court 828.206.5473 hiker rate (must ask) Su-Th $60S $80D, F-Sa $75S $100D, pets allowed. ⟨www.lodginghotspringsnc.com⟩

Hot Springs Resort & Spa 828.622.7676 Tenting $24 up to 4. Camping cabins (no TV, no linens, common bath/showers) tax-incl. prices; $55.88 sleeps 5, $73.76 sleeps 8. Pets $10. Motel-style room (linens, TV, some w/mineral water bath) $120-$300. Mineral water spa $20S before 6p; 3-person rate $38 before 6p, $43 after 6p. Camp store carries snacks & supplies; Massage therapy avail. CC accepted. ⟨www.nchotsprings.com⟩

Spring Creek Tavern 828.622.0187 Su-Th 11-10, Fr-Sa 11-11. 50 Varieties of beer, special AT burger, outdoor deck, live music Fr-Sa nights. 3 rooms for rent, call or book online. ⟨www.thespringcreektavern.com⟩

Alpine Court Motel 828.206.3444 Tax-incl. prices; $57S, $67D, $10EAP. Cabin $100/PN. Charges +fee if CC.

Smoky Mountain Diner 828.622.7571 M-Th 6a-8p; Fr-Sa 6:30a-8p; Su 6:30a-2p. Hiker special 12 oz burger.

ArtiSun Gallery 828.622.3573 Open 7 days 9-4. Coffee, baked goods, ice cream, AT hiker artwork. May use phone. FedEx/UPS Mail: 16 S. Andrews Ave, Hot Springs, NC 28743.

Visitor Center 828-622-9932 WiFi signal accessible outside after hours.

Hiker's Ridge Ministries Resource Center 812.201.7974 Open M-Sa 9-3, Mar 14 - May. Place to relax, coffee, drinks, snacks & restroom. ⟨www.hikersridge.com⟩

Bluff Mountain Outfitters 828.622.7162 daily 9-5 (seasonally 9-6) Full service outfitter, fuel/oz. Complete resupply, natural foods grocery & hiker foods. Free 20 min. computer/internet access, ask about WiFi. ATM & scale inside. Shuttles Franklin-Damascus & area airports & bus stations. SoBo hikers can print GSMNP permits. Ships UPS packages. Mail: (USPS) PO Box 114 Hot Springs, NC 28743 or (FedEx/UPS) 152 Bridge St. ⟨www.bluffmountain.com⟩

Hot Springs BBQ Grill & Pub 828.622.9400 Open Fri-Sun only.

Hot Springs Library 828.622.6584 Hikers Welcome! ⟨www.madisoncountylibrary.com⟩

■ **Glenda Dolbeare, LMT** 603-204-7893, will come to **Laughing Heart** for massage services.

289.7 Log Cabin Drive (dirt/gravel road)

Hemlock Hollow Inn & Paint Creek Cafe (0.7W) 423.787.1736 Open year-round. Go west on Log Cabin Dr. to paved Viking Mtn Rd. Bunkroom $25PP with linens, $20 without. Cabin for couples with linens $60. All rooms heated. Tent site $12PP. Pets $5. All stays include shower, free return ride to trail. Nonguest shower & towel for $5. Camp store stocked with long term resupply, some gear, cold drinks, foods, fruit, stove fuels. Cafe open 7 days in hiker season only; open off-season with call-ahead reservation. Shuttles available, slackpacking welcomed. Parking free for guests, fee for non-guests. WiFi availalbe for a fee. Credit cards accepted. Maildrop (ETA mandatory): 645 Chandler Circle, Greeneville, TN 37743. ⟨www.hemlockhollowinn.com⟩

310.0 Rector Laurel Road

Hiker Paradise 423.735.4437 NOBOs turn left on Rector Laurel Rd. Bunkroom $15PP, Tent $5PP. Shuttles & slackpacking for fee. To Erwin $20, Hot Springs $30, other destinations negotiable. Complete resupply (fuel & food). Laundry $5 for a small load. Pet friendly. Smoking & drinking area at campsites.

318.2 Sams Gap, US 23

Little Creek Cafe (2.8E) 828.689.2307 M-Th & Sa 6-2; F 6-8. Closed Su.

Wolf Creek Market (3.3E) Open M-F 6-2, Sa 7-2.

NoBo	SoBo	Feature	Elev
1869.8	320.0	Meadow	4429
1869.3	320.5	Street Gap, gravel road	4100
1869.1	320.7	Powerline	4161
1867.9	321.9	Low Gap, campsite downhill to west with piped spring	4300
1867.1	322.7	Spring	4645
1866.7	323.1	Powerline	4820
1865.6	324.2	Blue-blazed trail 100 yards west to water; bypass trail to east	5065
1865.5	324.3	Spring	5224
1865.3	324.5	Yellow-blazed trail to west	5374
1865.1	324.7	Big Bald, survey marker	5516
1864.5	325.3	Big Stamp, treeless saddle on ridge, bypass trail to east	5399
1864.2	325.6	Dirt road	5270
1863.9	325.9	**Bald Mountain Shelter** (0.1W) (10) 25.6◄18.9◄10.1◄►10.6►21.1►33.9 Spring on side trail to shelter. Cables.	5090
1863.7	326.1	Piped Spring (0.2W) on blue blazed trail	4984
1862.5	327.3	Little Bald (tree covered)	5220
1861.4	328.4	Spring	4393
1860.4	329.4	Whistling Gap, campsite	3883
1859.8	330.0	Trail 0.1E to High Rocks	4267
1858.7	331.1	Stream, two footbridges	3569
1858.2	331.6	Spivey Gap, US 19W, stream south of gap. 36.0319,-82.4202 P (0.5W) **(pg. 38)**	3200
1857.8	332.0	Ogelsby Branch, cross twice on footbridge	3555
1856.9	332.9	Stream.	3820
1856.7	333.1	Devils Creek Gap, dirt road	3769
1854.5	335.3	Stream.	3036
1854.4	335.4	Stream.	2998
1853.6	336.2	Stream.	3047
1853.3	336.5	**No Business Knob Shelter** Reliable water on AT 0.3S of shelter. (6) 29.5◄20.7◄10.6◄►10.5►23.3►32.4	3171

SoBo	NoBo	Feature		Elev
1850.9	338.9	Temple Hill Gap, Temple Hill Trail		2850
1848.8	341.0	Views to Erwin		2648
1847.1	342.7	River Rd, Unaka Springs Rd, **Erwin, TN** (3.8W). AT to east, crossing Nolichucky River on bridge	36.1042,-82.4467 P (pg. 38)	1673
1846.8	343.0	Railroad tracks		1706
1845.8	344.0	Side trail East to Nolichucky Gorge Campground before footbridge. Trail not signed	(pg. 39)	1729
1845.4	344.4	Footbridge, stream		1790
1845.0	344.8	Footbridge, stream		1910
1844.6	345.2	Stream.		2008
1844.3	345.5	Footbridge		2101
1844.1	345.7	Footbridge		2217
1842.8	347.0	**Curley Maple Gap Shelter,** water south of shelter 31.2◄21.1◄10.5◄►12.8►21.9►30.4	(14)	3063
1842.3	347.5	Spring		3219
1841.7	348.1	Stream		3319
1841.5	348.3	Stream		3302
1838.7	351.1	Indian Grave Gap, TN 395. Water 0.1E outside of curve in road.	36.1096,-82.3616 P (pg. 39)	3350
1838.2	351.6	Survey marker (USFS 381-28)		3704
1838.0	351.8	Powerline		3745
1837.6	352.2	USFS 230, Red Fork Rd (gravel)		3767
1835.3	354.5	Beauty Spot Gap, clearing. Parking to west, trail parallel to USFS 230 from here north to Deep Gap.	36.1163,-82.3372 P	4323
1834.8	355.0	Piped spring & campsites 100 yards west across USFS 230.		4115
1834.4	355.4	AT skirts Red Fork Rd		4559
1833.3	356.5	Unaka Mountain, dense spruce forest.		5180

1000 3000 5000
NoBo SoBo

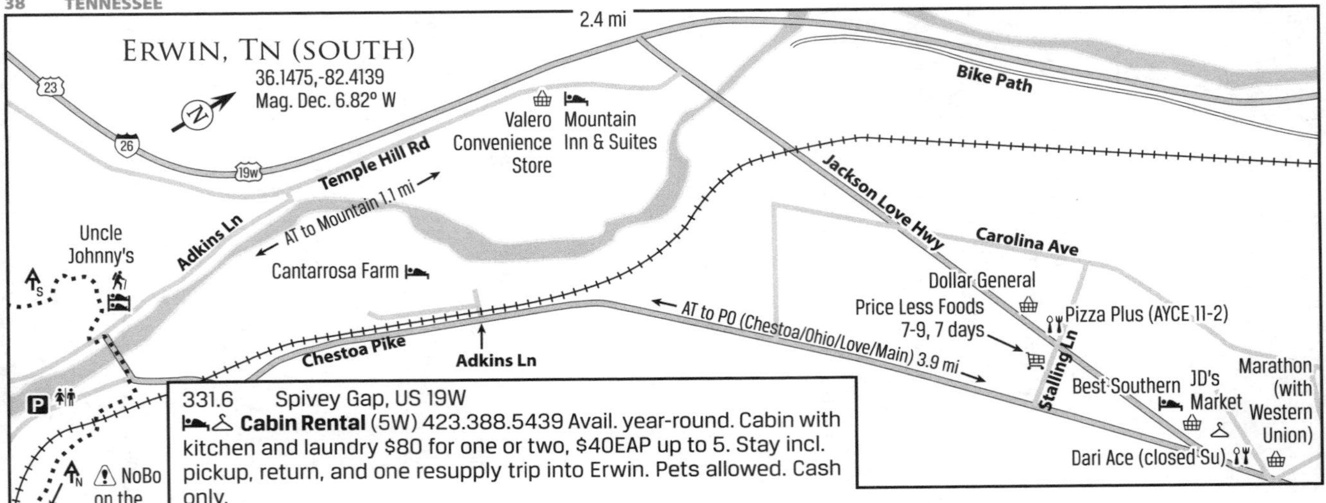

331.6 Spivey Gap, US 19W

Cabin Rental (5W) 423.388.5439 Avail. year-round. Cabin with kitchen and laundry $80 for one or two, $40EAP up to 5. Stay incl. pickup, return, and one resupply trip into Erwin. Pets allowed. Cash only.

342.7 River Rd, Unaka Springs Rd ***Erwin, TN 37650*** (Hostel & Cantarroso Farm near trail, town center 3.8W)

Uncle Johnny's Nolichucky Hostel & Outfitters 423.735.0548 Open yr-round only 60ft from the AT. 3 Free town shuttles/day for guests. Tenting $15PP (riverside-$17.50), incl. showers w/towel & soap (non-guest $5). Smart TV, WiFi, grills. 50' x 16' Covered hammock area w/individual lighting, electrical outlets & a 15' picnic table: $20PP. Hostel: $22PP, full linens $5. Fridge/m'wave/computer. Cabins w/AC & heat: reg/$25-$35PP, large Condo/Cabin: $65-$105. Laundry (multiple machines) $5. Dog friendly for socialized pets. Outfitter store. Shuttles/ slackpacking (fee). Parking $2-$3/day. Bike, kayak, tube, rafting trips. No charge for mail: 151 River Rd, Erwin 37650.

Cantarroso Farm 423.833.7514 0.9W from Chestoa Bridge. Open yr-round. Clean & quiet setting w/personal svc. Cabin $25PP (2-5), call for private rate. Upstairs suite $60S, $90D incl. access to full kitchen, private bath, balcony w/river view & large screen TV. Stay incl. P/U & return to Chestoa trail head, access to river, fishing gear, grill, coffee/tea, bed w/linens, shower w/soap & towel, use of fridge, m'wave, toaster oven & cooking gear. Add'l charge for laundry, town shuttles, slackpacking. No pets. Mail: 777 Bailey Lane, Erwin TN 37650 ⟨www.cantarrosofarm.com⟩

Mountain Inn & Suites 423.743.4100 Hiker rate $79.99S, $10EAP incl. b'fast buffet. No pets. Coin laundry. Hot tub (Apr-Oct) & swimming pool (Mem Day-Labor Day). Mail: 2002 Temple Hill Rd, Erwin TN 37650.

Super 8 423.743.0200, $49.99S, $59.99D, $10EAP, max 4, incl. b'fast, laundry, no pets. Mail: 1101 N

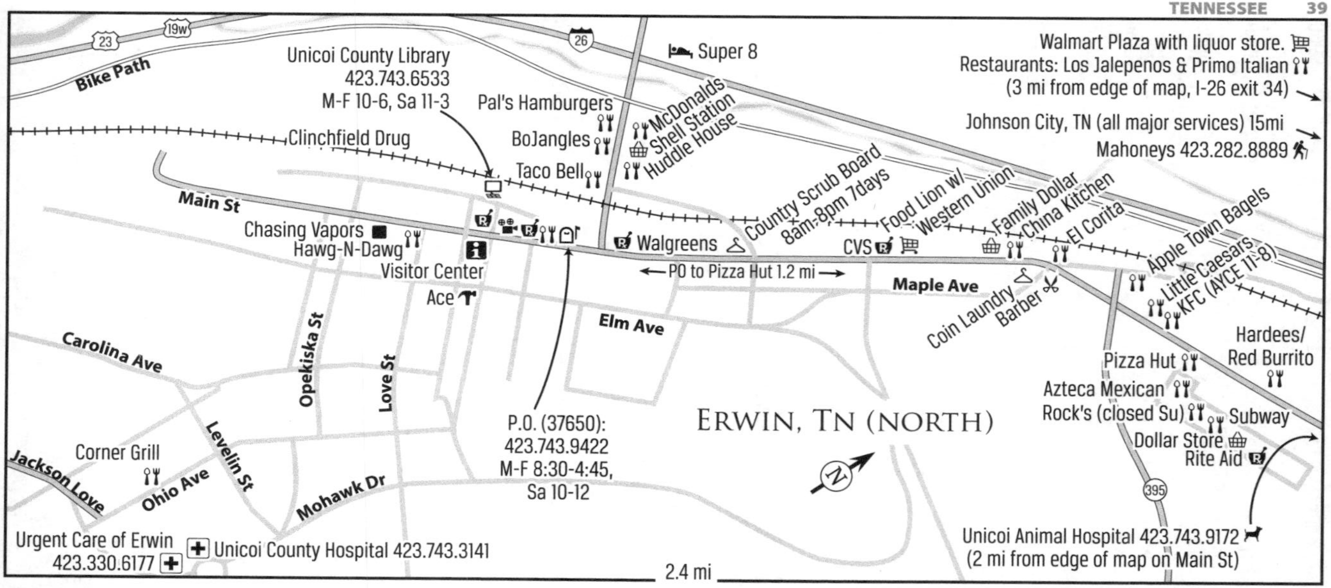

Erwin, TN (North)

Unicoi County Library 423.743.6533 M-F 10-6, Sa 11-3
Clinchfield Drug
Main St
Chasing Vapors
Hawg-N-Dawg
Visitor Center
Ace
Pal's Hamburgers
BoJangles
Taco Bell
McDonalds
Shell Station
Huddle House
Super 8
Walgreens
Country Scrub Board 8am-8pm 7days
Food Lion w/ Western Union
CVS
Family Dollar
China Kitchen
El Corita
Apple Town Bagels
Little Caesars
KFC (AYCE 11-8)
PO to Pizza Hut 1.2 mi
Maple Ave
Coin Laundry
Barber
Elm Ave
Carolina Ave
Opekiska St
Love St
Levelin St
Ohio Ave
Mohawk Dr
Jackson Love
Corner Grill
Bike Path
P.O. (37650): 423.743.9422 M-F 8:30-4:45, Sa 10-12
Walmart Plaza with liquor store.
Restaurants: Los Jalepenos & Primo Italian (3 mi from edge of map, I-26 exit 34)
Johnson City, TN (all major services) 15mi
Mahoneys 423.282.8889
Hardees/ Red Burrito
Pizza Hut
Azteca Mexican
Rock's (closed Su)
Subway
Dollar Store
Rite Aid
Unicoi Animal Hospital 423.743.9172 (2 mi from edge of map on Main St)
Urgent Care of Erwin 423.330.6177
Unicoi County Hospital 423.743.3141
2.4 mi

Buffalo St, Erwin TN 37650.

Best Southern 423.743.6438 Call for rates.

Primo's Italian Restaurant 423.543.8400 10:30a-9:30p. (near Unicoi Walmart) BYOB.

Shuttles by Tom 423.330.7416, 910.409.2509 Owners Tom (10-K) and Marie (J-Walker) Bradford, licensed and insured. Shuttles to all area trailheads, bus stations, airports, outfitters, etc.. from Springer-Harpers Ferry. ⟨www.hikershuttles.com⟩

Baker's Shoe Repair 423-743-5421 Also repairs jackets & packs

344.0 Side trail to:

Nolichucky Gorge Campground 423.743.8876, Tent or bunkroom (when avail.) $10, incl. shower. Cabin $80/up. Well-behaved pets okay. Small camp store. CC accepted. ⟨www.nolichucky.com⟩

351.1 Indian Grave Gap

Rock Creek Recreation Area (USFS) (3.3W) 423.638.4109 Tent site $12, Open May-Nov.

Poplar Creek Farmstay (5.4E) 828.688.1653 2BR Apt. Rental (sleeps 6), starting at $99. Room rentals (sleeps 2) avail. Nov-Mar. starting at $40 + $25 cleaning. 2 Night min. for both. Dogs under 40lbs; $25, over 45 lbs: $40. Laundry $2. Cable TV, WiFi, full kitchen, food items for sale on-site. Prising H20, Pets welcome. 10 Min from Indian Grave Gap in Poplar, NC. ⟨www.poplarcreekfarmstay.com⟩

1831.1 358.7 Low Gap, campsite, weak stream 0.1W 3900

1830.2 359.6 Footbridge, stream 4122
1830.0 359.8 **Cherry Gap Shelter** 33.9◄23.3◄12.8◄►9.1►17.6►22.8 . . . . . . (6) 3988
Spring 120 yards on blue-blazed trail behind shelter to the left.
1829.6 360.2 Unmarked trail crossing 3908

1828.6 361.2 Little Bald Knob, trail skirts summit 4337
1828.4 361.4 Stream. 4286

1826.9 362.9 Iron Mountain Gap, TN 107, NC 226 . . . . 36.1433,-82.2332 P (pg. 42) 3723

1825.6 364.2 Campsite, piped spring 0.1W from signpost near north end of clearing . . . 4023

1824.5 365.3 Rock pillar. 4434

1822.8 367.0 Greasy Creek Gap, campsite at gap, water 0.2W, ... (pg. 42) 4034
Greasy Creek Hostel 0.6E
1822.0 367.8 Campsite, weak spring 0.1W 4134

1820.9 368.9 **Clyde Smith Shelter** (1976) (0.1W) . . . . (10) 4496
32.4◄21.9◄9.1◄►8.5►13.7►15.6 Water 0.1 left of shelter, tent sites behind.

1819.7 370.1 Little Rock Knob, views to west, south of summit 4918
1819.4 370.4 Stream. 4749
Here north to Roan parking, NoBo trail bearing is compass south.
1818.6 371.2 Stream. 4375

1817.5 372.3 Hughes Gap, TN 1330, Hughes Gap Rd. . . . . 36.1368,-82.141 P 4040
1817.1 372.7 Water 50 yards east 4288

> **Golden ragwort – Small flower with yellow center and small floppy petals. "Field flower" that can create a sea of yellow.**

1814.5 375.3 Ash Gap, campsite at gap, water 0.1E 5350

1813.1 376.7 Toll House Gap,saddle between Roan . . . . 36.104,-82.1331 P 6212
High Bluff & Knob, 0.1E to parking, picnic area, open Mem day - Oct 1.
1813.0 376.8 Chimney (remnant) 6134
1812.4 377.4 **Roan High Knob Shelter** (0.1E) . . . . (15) 6193
30.4◄17.6◄8.5◄►5.2►7.1►25.1 Piped spring, highest shelter on AT.
1811.6 378.2 ⚠ NoBo: watch for AT turning west off of the wide treadway 5784

1811.0	378.8	Several footbridges, streams		5525
1810.9	378.9	Carvers Gap, TN 143, NC 261	36.1068,-82.1106	5512
		Access road to summit (1.9mi) open approx. Memorial day - Oct 1		
1810.2	379.6	Round Bald, 30 yards east to summit, views		5813
1809.4	380.4	Jane Bald, big rock slab, views back to Roan Mtn		5790
1808.8	381.0	Side trail 0.5E to Grassy Ridge Bald and views, AT to west.		5891
1808.6	381.2	Springs		5864
1807.9	381.9	Campsite to west		5373
1807.2	382.6	**Stan Murray Shelter**	(6)	5045
		22.8◄13.7◄5.2◄►1.9►19.9►29.5		
		Spring on blue-blazed trail opposite shelter.		
1805.3	384.5	**Overmountain Shelter** (0.3E) Yellow Mountain Gap.	(20)	4657
		15.6◄7.1◄1.9◄►18.0►27.6►35.8 Converted barn. Water on way to shelter.		
1804.3	385.5	Two intersections with old roadbed		5180
1804.1	385.7	Side trail 0.1E to Big Yellow Mountain		5271
1803.7	386.1	Little Hump Mountain, clearing		5459
1803.0	386.8	Piped spring, campsites to north and south		5177
1802.4	387.4	Bradley Gap, spring east 100 yards		4950
1801.8	388.0	Fence		5406
1801.5	388.3	Hump Mountain, Stan Murray plaque, NoBo have several false summits		5587
1800.7	389.1	Fence		5226
1800.1	389.7	Spring		5007
1799.8	390.0	Spring		4857
1799.1	390.7	Doll Flats, **NC-TN** border		4600
1798.8	391.0	Stone steps, view.		4321
1798.5	391.3	Spring west of trail, massive stone wall.		4085
1796.9	392.9	Stream.		3268
1796.7	393.1	Wilder Mine Group campsite, piped spring 150 yds north on A.T.		3111
1796.6	393.2	Apple House Tentsite	(1)	3052
1796.1	393.7	US 19E **Elk Park, NC** (2.4E) **Roan Mtn, TN** (3.5W)	(pg. 42)	2895
1795.9	393.9	Bear Branch Rd, streams north of road	36.1794,-82.0128	2900
1795.1	394.7	AT + Jeep Path, south end, stream.		3219
1794.7	395.1	AT + Jeep Path, north end		3434
1793.7	396.1	Open ridge with views to east and west		3766
1793.2	396.6	Isaacs Cemetery		3600
1792.8	397.0	Buck Mountain Rd, water at church 0.1E	36.204,-81.9975	3501
1792.5	397.3	Campbell Hollow Rd, streams south of road		3396
1792.2	397.6	Footbridge at bottom of ravine		3408
1791.8	398.0	Footbridge, stream		3432

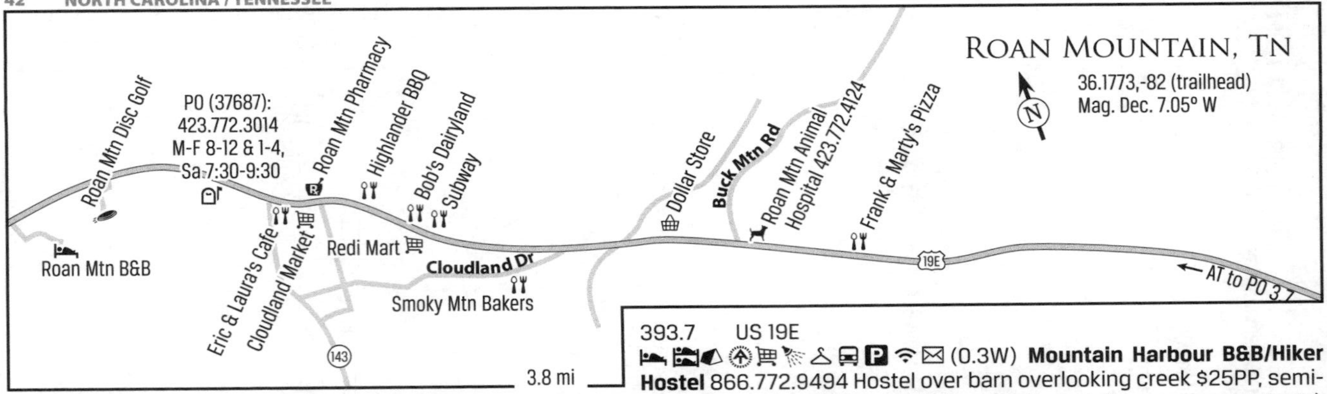

362.9 Iron Mountain Gap, TN 107, NC 226 ***Buladean, NC*** (4.1E)
Mountain Grill 828.688.9061 Cash only, M-Sa 11-8.

367.0 Greasy Creek Gap
(0.6E) **Greasy Creek Friendly** 828.688.9948 All room prices include tax: $10PP bunkhouse, $15PP/up indoor beds, $7.50PP tenting incl. shower. Shower w/out stay $3. Pets ok outside. Pup Shed (4 beds)-pets ok. Open yr-round (call ahead Dec-Feb), self serve during the Sabbath (sundown Fr to sundown Sa). Home cooked meals, incl. vegetarian options. Limited kitchen privileges. Store of goods for multi-day resupply incl. snacks, meals, Coleman/ alcohol/oz. Shuttles Hot Springs to Damascus. Parking $2/night. Free long distance calls w/in US. CC ok. Directions: take Old Woods Rd east (trail east, not compass east), follow curve to the left, then take the 1st right (should be going downhill all the way). Hostel is 1st house to the right. Mail: 1827 Greasy Creek Rd, Bakersville, NC 28705 ⟨www.GreasyCreekFriendly.com⟩

393.7 US 19E
(0.3W) **Mountain Harbour B&B/Hiker Hostel** 866.772.9494 Hostel over barn overlooking creek $25PP, semi-private king bed $55D, treehouse $75D, incl. linens, shower, towel, full kitchen, wood burning stove, video library. Tenting w/shower $10, non-guest shower w/towel $4, laundry w/soap $5. B'fast $12 when avail. B&B rooms $125-165 incl. b'fast, separate shower & fireplace, A/C, refrigerator, cable TV/DVD. Free white gas/ denatured alcohol. General Store on-site, open also to non-guests, sells fuel canisters & full resupply. Slackpack/long distance shuttles by arrangement. Secured parking $10/day or $2/day w/shuttle. Open year-round. Mail: (non-guests $5) 9151 Hwy 19E, Roan Mountain, TN 37687. ⟨www.mountainharbour.net⟩

Doe River Hiker Rest 575.694.0734 6M from 19E. 4 Pvt. rooms, 2S & 2D. $30PP incl. shower, laundry, linens, kitchen, PU/Rtn from 19E & town. Shuttle avail. Mail:275 Old Railroad Grade Rd, Roan Mtn, TN 37687. General Store. Cash, PayPal, CC. Pets OK.

Roan Mountain, TN 37687 (3.5W)

Roan Mountain Hiker Festival First annual event, May 5, 6 & 7th, Tent city $5, Farmer's Market, Live music, Vendors.

Roan Mountain B&B 423.772.3207 Yr-round, hiker friendly! Hiker rate $65S, $85D not incl. b'fast. Cafe close by. Free P/U & return at Hwy 19E & 5p shuttle to town. Pets ok w/prior approval. No alcohol, no smoking inside. Laundry $5. Shuttles & slackpacking Erwin to Watauga Lake. Section hiker parking. CC. ‹www.roanmtbb.com›

Eric & Laura's Cafe 423.481.1234, M-Sa, 6:30a-2p: Closed Su. See B&B for discount card.

Bob's Dairyland 423.772.3641 7 days, 6am-9pm

Smoky Mountain Bakers 423.957.1202 Tu-Sa 8-8, fresh bread, wood-fired pizza.

Frank & Marty's Pizza 423.772.3083, Tu, We, Sa, 4-9; Th, Fr, 11-9; Closed, Su & Mo.

Redi Mart 423.772.3032 M-Sa 8-10, Su 9-10.

Cloudland Market 423.772.3201 M-Sa 8-7.

Water Sources

Be aware of trail conditions before heading out, and tune in to advice from outfitters and other hikers. The trail gets rerouted, springs dry up, streams alter their course. Be prepared to deal with changes, particularly late in the season. Never carry just enough water to reach the next spring.

Elk Park, NC 28622 (see services on map)

Newland, NC (7E, 19E to NC 194)

The Shady Lawn Lodge 828.733.9006, Thru-hikers get 10% off regular room rates, which are approx. $80D ($5 extra on weekends). Free pickup & return when driver is avail. Laundry and restaurants nearby.

Banner Elk, NC

Harmony Hostel 828.898.6200 Clean & spacious w/semi-private sleeping areas, incl. linen, shower & communal kitchen. No bunkbeds. Laundry $5. Walk to restaurants in Banner Elk. Free shuttle from Hwy 19E at 3p & 6p for hostel guests, add'l shuttle services avail. for fee. Supply stop at Dollar General. Free b'fast incl. toast & jam, oatmeal, fruit, tea/coffee & boiled eggs (limit 2) on request. Section hiker parking. No smoking, no alcohol. Not the typical hiker hostel. $45.00 + tax/person.

406.4 Upper Laurel Fork. (0.3W) Blue-blazed side trail to hostel originates at the hand-railed footbridge. Follow side trail along creek (drinking creek water is not recommended).

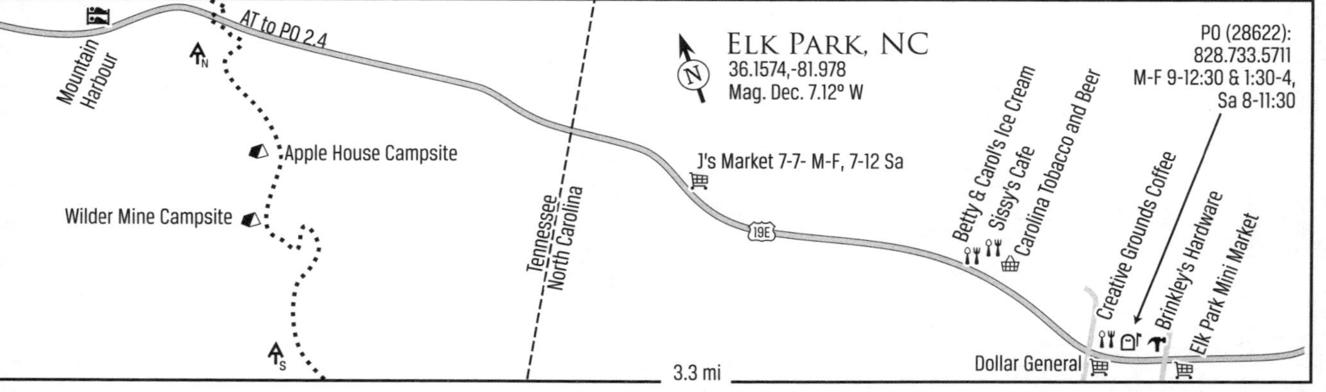

1790.7	399.1	Side trail 0.1E to Jones Falls		2985
1790.0	399.8	Campsite, Elk River 0.1E		2736
1789.6	400.2	Stream.		2697
1788.6	401.2	Stream (cross twice)		2831
1787.8	402.0	Footbridge, stream		3020
1787.4	402.4	Mountaineer Falls to west		3110
1787.3	402.5	**Mountaineer Shelter,** water 70 yards from shelter 25.1◄19.9◄18.0◄►9.6►17.8►26.4	(14)	3173
1786.5	403.3	Campsite to east		3244
1786.1	403.7	Slide Hollow Stream, footbridge		3348
1785.9	403.9	Roadbed.		3520
1785.7	404.1	Walnut Mountain Rd		3603
1784.8	405.0	Footbridge, stream (many in area)		3453
1784.0	405.8	Bench, view		3509
1783.4	406.4	Upper Laurel Fork, side trail to hostel	(pg. 43)	3314
1782.7	407.1	Footbridge, stream		3445
1782.5	407.3	USFS 293 (gravel), waterfall south on AT		3457
1781.7	408.1	Spring		3341
1781.5	408.3	Spring		3378
1781.1	408.7	Footbridge, stream		3436
1780.7	409.1	Hardcore Cascades.		3391
1779.9	409.9	Stream.		3633
1779.4	410.4	Campsite, several streams and footbridges		3563
1777.8	412.0	Rock outcropping, views		3933
1777.7	412.1	**Moreland Gap Shelter** 29.5◄27.6◄9.6◄►8.2►16.8►24.0 Water source long way downhill across from shelter.	(6)	3798
1775.5	414.3	Piped spring		3806
1775.1	414.7	Forest Service road		3773
1774.4	415.4	Trail skirts White Rocks Mountain		3977
1773.1	416.7	Trail to Coon Den Falls 0.8E downhill		3419
1772.0	417.8	Stream.		2849

SoBo	NoBo	Landmark		Elev
1771.6	418.2	Barn		2594
1771.4	418.4	Dennis Cove Rd, USFS 50, hostels	36.2643,-82.1231 P (pg. 46)	2491
1770.6	419.2	Footbridge	water	2427
1770.3	419.5	Switchback ⚠ Path straight ahead is high water bypass, reconnects at L.F. Shltr		2395
1770.1	419.7	Laurel Falls ⚠ Do not swim close to falls, there is a dangerous whirlpool	water	2120
1769.5	420.3	**Laurel Fork Shelter** 35.8◄17.8◄8.2◄►8.6►15.8►22.6	water, shelter (8)	2162
1769.1	420.7	Waycaster Spring, two footbridges over Laurel Fork	water	1983
1768.6	421.2	Side trail to **Hampton, TN** US 321 (1.0W) Hampton is west on 321.	**(pg. 47)**	1959
1766.0	423.8	Pond Flats, campsite, spring 0.1N on AT.	water, campsite	3693
1763.2	426.6	Campsite to east	campsite	2298
1762.9	426.9	NoBo: east on Shook Branch Rd	36.301660, -82.128085 **(pg. 47)**	2019
1762.8	427.0	US 321, **Hampton, TN** (2.6W) NoBo: turn west after crossing 321 **Shook Branch Recreation Area**, picnic area, sandy beach. No Camping.	36.3019,-82.129 P restrooms, trash, water **(pg. 47)**	1990
1761.3	428.5	Griffith Branch	water	2040
1760.9	428.9	**Watauga Lake Shelter** 26.4◄16.8◄8.6◄►7.2►14.0►21.6 Closed 4/15/16 due to bear activity. Not known when it will reopen. Cook away from shelter and properly store your food (bear pole).	water, shelter (6)	2063
1759.7	430.1	Watauga Dam, AT on road for 0.4 mi south & north of dam, sparsely blazed..		1975
1758.4	431.4	Wilbur Dam Rd	36.3288,-82.1115 P	2250
1755.4	434.4	Spring	water	3309
1753.7	436.1	**Vandeventer Shelter,** views 24.0◄15.8◄7.2◄►6.8►14.4►22.7 Water 0.3 mile down steep blue-blazed trail 0.1S of shelter.	views, water, shelter (6)	3564

SoBo NoBo 1000 3000 5000

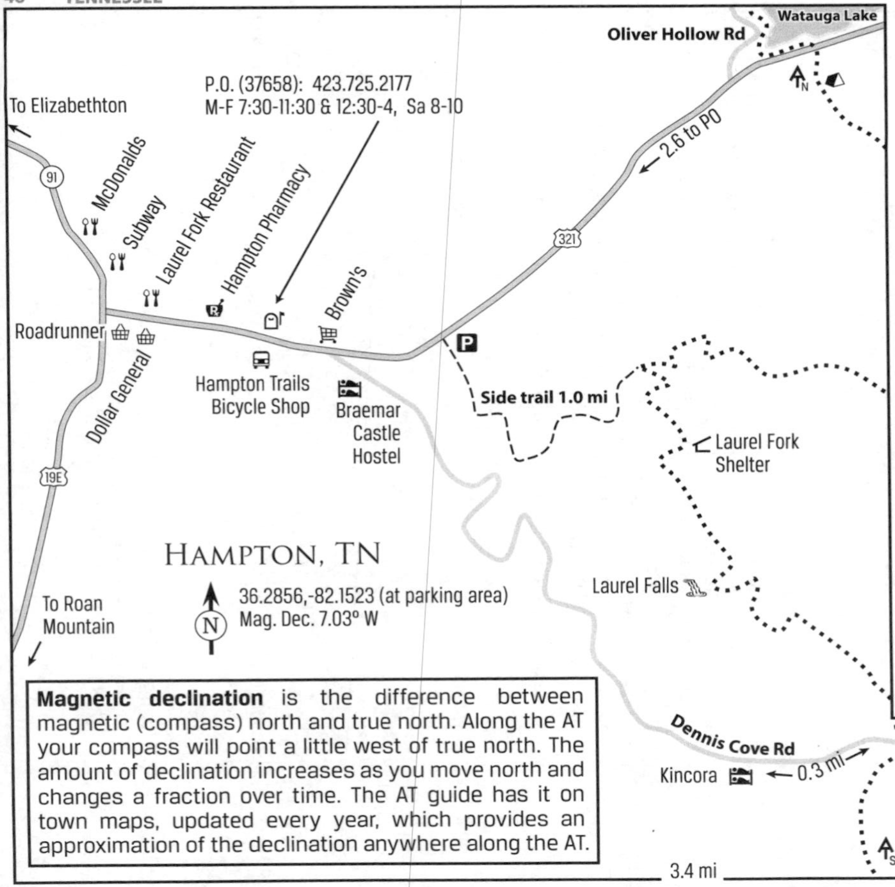

418.4 Dennis Cove Rd, USFS 50

(0.3W) **Kincora Hiking Hostel** 423.725.4409 Cooking facilities, laundry, $5/night suggested donation. No dogs, 3 night limit. Coleman/alcohol/oz. Long-time owner Bob Peoples is very active in trail maintenance; if you have interest in working on the trail, ask about opportunities. Mail (non-guest fee $5): 1278 Dennis Cove Rd, Hampton, TN 37658.

(0.4E) **Black Bear Resort** 423.725.5988 Open Mar 1 - Oct 31. Clean & spacious creekside resort w/ bunkroom $20, upper bunkroom $25, tenting $10PP. Cabin $50/$65 for up to 4 people, $15EAP, 6-person max. Courtesy phone, computer, movies (DVD) & free am coffee for all guests. Camp store w/ long-term resupply items (freeze-dried meals), snacks, sodas, pizza, beer, ice cream & food that can be prepared on-site w/ microwave/stove. Laundry $5. Fuel/oz & canister fuel. Pet friendly. CC accepted. Long & short distance shuttles. Parking free for section-hiking guests, $3/night for non-guests. Maildrops (nonguest fee $5): 1511 Dennis Cove Rd, Hampton, TN 37658. reserve@blackbearresorttn.com ⟨www.black resorttn.com⟩

HAMPTON, TN

36.2856,-82.1523 (at parking area)
Mag. Dec. 7.03° W

To Elizabethton
P.O. (37658): 423.725.2177
M-F 7:30-11:30 & 12:30-4, Sa 8-10
McDonalds
Subway
Laurel Fork Restaurant
Hampton Pharmacy
Brown's
Roadrunner
Dollar General
Hampton Trails Bicycle Shop
Braemar Castle Hostel
Side trail 1.0 mi
2.6 to PO
Oliver Hollow Rd
Watauga Lake
Laurel Fork Shelter
Laurel Falls
To Roan Mountain
Dennis Cove Rd
Kincora
0.3 mi
0.4 mi
Black Bear Resort
3.4 mi

Magnetic declination is the difference between magnetic (compass) north and true north. Along the AT your compass will point a little west of true north. The amount of declination increases as you move north and changes a fraction over time. The AT guide has it on town maps, updated every year, which provides an approximation of the declination anywhere along the AT.

421.2 Side trail to Hampton (1.0W) see ***Hampton, TN*** below

426.9 Shook Branch Rd
Boots Off Hostel & Campground 239.218.3904 Private room $50/2 persons. $15EAP. Bunkhouse $20 incl. linen & lockable storage. Cabin tent $20 1P, $15EAP. Tent/hammock $10PP incl. local shuttle, shower, c. b'fast. Laundry $5. Canoe & kayak rentals. Parking for fee. Non guests $5 shower, $5 maildrop, shuttle for fee. Dog friendly, call in advance. No dogs in bunkhouse.

427.0 US 321
(0.8E) **Dividing Ridge Campground** 423.957.0821, 1219 US Hwy 321. Hiker Friendly. Open most of the year, closed some in winter-call. Donations accepted. Shower, charging stations, TV in pavillion, wash tub. No arrival after 9p, pets okay.

Hampton, TN (2.6W)

Brown's Grocery & Braemar Castle Hostel 423.725.2411 423.725.2262 Open yr-round. Both operated by Sutton Brown; check-in at grocery to stay at the hostel or for shuttles. Store open M-Sa 8-6, closed Sunday. Store accepts CC; hostel is cash only. Pets ok. WiFi at hostel only.
Hampton Trails Bicycle Shop 423.725.5000 ⟨www.hamptontrails.com⟩ brian@hamptontrails.com
Doe River Taxi 423.297.1500 24 hrs. Caters to the AT of NE TN.

Elizabethton, TN (services 5 mi. north of Hampton)

Americourt 423.542.4466 $60 plus tax, up to 4 in room, incl. hot b'fast. Pets $25. Not avail. on race weekends. Mail: 1515 Hwy 19E, Elizabethton,TN 37643.
Little Caesars, Arbys, Lone Star Steakhouse
Food City, Ingles, Big Lots
State Line Drive-in 423.542.5422 Open seasonally F, Sa & Su.

⚠ Bear Interactions & Bear Canisters

Due to increasing bear/human interactions, the Appalachian Trail Conservancy strongly recommends the Use of Bear Canisters for food storage while overnight camping along the A.T. in GA, NC, & TN.

Bulter, TN

Iron Mountain Inn 423.768.2446 Yr-round. 10mi from Hampton. Call for p/u or for directions. Fee for p/u & return. B&B room incl. b'fast for $100S/$150D. Log cabin w/hot tub under the stars, $50PP, no b'fast. CC OK but w/5% fee. Free laundry. Shuttles from Watauga Lake to Damascus. Pets OK. Mail: c/o Woods, 268 Moreland Dr, Butler, TN 37640 ⟨www.creeksidechalet.net⟩

447.5 TN 91 1.9E to Sluder Rd hostel, 2.6E to Wallace Road campground, and 4.5E to ***Shady Valley*** (listed at US 421).
Switchback Creek Campground (2.6E) 407.484.3388 Apr 1 - Oct 31. 1.8E to Sluder Rd, turn right for 0.2mi, then right on Wallace Rd. 0.6mi to 570 Wallace Rd, Shady Valley, TN 37688. Cabin for two $40, campsite $12+tax, cash only. Showers, laundry, Wifi. Call for ride at TN91/Low Gap. Pets allowed for camping only.

454.0 Low Gap, US 421

Shady Valley, TN 37688 (2.7E)

M–F 8-12, Sa 8-10, 423.739.2073
Shady Valley Country Store & Deli 423.739.2325 Open year-round. May 1-Oct 31: M-F, 6-8; Sa, 8-8; Su, 9-6; Closes earlier in winter. Deli serves burgers & sandwiches. Coleman fuel.
Raceway Restaurant 423.739.2499 Open 7-8 all days except W 7-2 & Su 8-2.

Prices are subject to change, particularly at hotels. Prices published in this guidebook were given in fall of 2016 & often represent a significant discount for hikers. Businesses intend to keep these prices throughout 2017, but they are not obliged to do so.

SOBO	NOBO	Feature		Elev
1749.9	439.9	Campsite 0.1N, stream 100 yards east		3859
1748.6	441.2	Turkeypen Gap		3971
1747.7	442.1	Powerline		4092
1747.1	442.7	Spring		4000
1746.9	442.9	**Iron Mountain Shelter,** spring 0.3S on AT 22.6◄14.0◄6.8◄►7.6►15.9►35.6	(6)	4095
1745.6	444.2	Nick Grindstaff Monument		4090
1743.1	446.7	Footbridge, stream, bog bridges north of stream.		3580
1742.7	447.1	Roadbed.		3581
1742.3	447.5	TN 91. **Shady Valley, TN** (3.5E) South end of handicap-accessible trail.	36.4814,-81.9603 P (pg. 47)	3506
1741.5	448.3	North end of handicap-accessible trail		3608
1739.3	450.5	**Double Springs Shelter** 21.6◄14.4◄7.6◄►8.3►28.0►34.5 Spring 80 yards left of shelter. Rich Knob to south, Holston Mtn Trail to north.	(6)	4073
1737.7	452.1	Locust Knob		3615
1735.8	454.0	Low Gap, US 421 Piped spring on south side of road. **Shady Valley, TN** (2.7E)	36.5386,-81.9489 P (pg. 47)	3384
1734.4	455.4	Low stone wall on east side of AT		3574
1733.9	455.9	Double Spring Gap, campsite		3542
1733.5	456.3	Weak, muddy spring east side of AT		3657
1732.5	457.3	McQueens Knob, disused shelter 0.1N.		3900
1732.1	457.7	McQueens Gap, USFS 69	36.5743,-81.932 P	3680

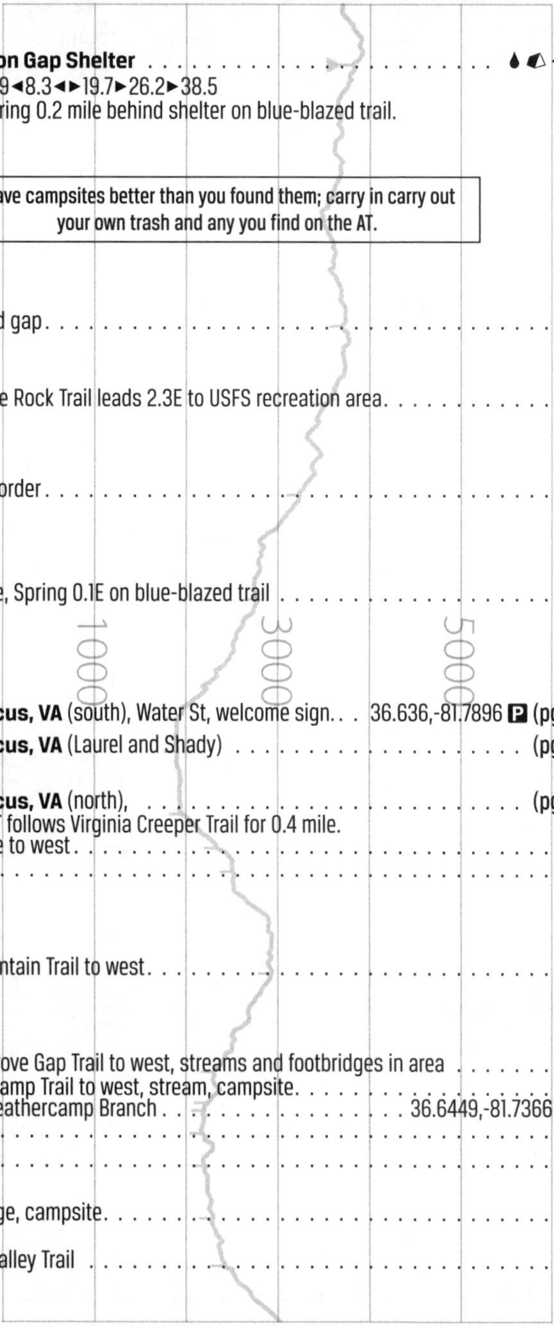

SoBo	NoBo	Feature		Elev
1731.0	458.8	**Abingdon Gap Shelter** 22.7◄15.9◄8.3◄►19.7►26.2►38.5 Piped spring 0.2 mile behind shelter on blue-blazed trail.	(5)	3780

Leave campsites better than you found them; carry in carry out your own trash and any you find on the AT.

SoBo	NoBo	Feature		Elev
1727.0	462.8	Unnamed gap		3667
1725.9	463.9	Backbone Rock Trail leads 2.3E to USFS recreation area.		3487
1724.5	465.3	**TN-VA** border		3210
1722.9	466.9	Campsite, Spring 0.1E on blue-blazed trail		2768
1721.1	468.7	**Damascus, VA** (south), Water St, welcome sign.	36.636,-81.7896 P (pg. 52)	1919
1720.6	469.2	**Damascus, VA** (Laurel and Shady)	(pg. 52)	1911
1719.7	470.1	**Damascus, VA** (north), US 58, AT follows Virginia Creeper Trail for 0.4 mile.	(pg. 52)	1974
1719.2	470.6	Campsite to west		2339
1718.8	471.0	Spring		2505
1717.3	472.5	Iron Mountain Trail to west		2913
1715.8	474.0	Beech Grove Gap Trail to west, streams and footbridges in area		2302
1715.3	474.5	Feathercamp Trail to west, stream, campsite.		2232
1715.2	474.6	US 58, Feathercamp Branch	36.6449,-81.7366 P	2200
1714.8	475.0	Stream.		2180
1714.4	475.4	Stream.		2205
1713.6	476.2	Footbridge, campsite		2287
1712.9	476.9	Taylors Valley Trail		2407

1711.3	478.5	**Saunders Shelter** (0.2W) 35.6◄28.0◄19.7◄►6.5►18.8►24.0. ☽💧⛺∠(8) Reliable spring on right behind shelter and down road.	3359
1710.9	478.9	North shelter side trail	3344
1709.0	480.8	Beartree Gap Trail, 3.0W to Beartree Recreation Area	3050
1708.9	480.9	Pond, campsite 💧⛺	3016
1708.3	481.5	Stream. 💧	2978
1707.8	482.0	Footbridge, stream 💧	2913
1707.3	482.5	AT + Creeper Trail (south end)	2688
1706.6	483.2	Luther Hassinger Memorial Bridge, 36.6494,-81.6724 P AT + Creeper Trail (north end), VA 728.	2781
1706.2	483.6	Stream. 💧	2813
1706.0	483.8	VA 859, Grassy Creek Rd (gravel)	2943
1705.8	484.0	Streams 💧	3034
1704.8	485.0	**Lost Mountain Shelter** ☽💧⛺∠(8) 34.5◄26.2◄6.5◄►12.3►17.5►24.2 Water source on trail to left of shelter.	3381
1703.7	486.1	US 58, footbridge, stream 36.6398,-81.6654 P ⊼ 💧	3160
1703.4	486.4	Stream, campsite 💧⛺	3231
1702.9	486.9	Spring 💧	3345
1702.7	487.1	Fence stile	3451
1702.4	487.4	VA 601, Beech Mountain Rd 36.6373,-81.6404 P 💧 Fence stile, 50 yards north of road is sign for spring to west.	3526
1701.9	487.9	Spring 💧	3707
1699.9	489.9	Buzzard Rock, Side trail west to Whitetop Mtn Rd, summit of Whitetop Mountain..	5080
1699.1	490.7	Piped spring on east side of trail 💧	5082
1699.0	490.8	Whitetop Mtn Rd, USFS 89 36.632,-81.6019 P 💧⛺ Campsites just after road.	5087
1698.3	491.5	Stream. 💧	5172
1696.6	493.2	VA 600, Elk Garden, views, spring south on AT 36.6462,-81.5832 P 📷 ☽💧	4448
1696.3	493.5	View, bench to west 📷	4582
1696.0	493.8	Fence, enter Lewis Fork Wilderness	4672
1694.5	495.3	Deep Gap, spring 0.1 south and north 💧	5015
1693.5	496.3	Brier Ridge	5215
1693.1	496.7	Spring 💧	5191
1692.6	497.2	Side trail 0.5W to Mt Rogers, Virginia's highest peak at 5,729 ft.	5430
1692.5	497.3	**Thomas Knob Shelter** 38.5◄18.8◄12.3◄►5.2►11.9►16.1 📷☽💧∠(16)	5413
1692.2	497.6	Campsite ⛺	5397

SoBo	NoBo	Feature		Elev
1691.5	498.3	Rhododendron Gap, Pine Mountain Trail to west		5398
1691.0	498.8	Wilburn Ridge Trail 0.1E to rock outcropping, view		5447
1690.7	499.1	Fatman Squeeze (rock tunnel)		5358
1690.0	499.8	Grayson Highlands State Park (south end), fence **Horse trail crosses AT.** No tenting in GHSP.	**(pg. 53)**	4999
1688.7	501.1	Massie Gap, 0.2E to parking area	**(pg. 53)**	4890
1688.1	501.7	GHSP boundary, two fence stiles		4595
1687.5	502.3	Stream.		4420
1687.3	502.5	**Wise Shelter** 24.0◄17.5◄5.2◄►6.7►10.9►20.1	(8)	4409
1687.2	502.6	East fork of Big Wilson Creek, footbridge, stream, fence stile Grayson Highlands State Park (north end)		4390
1686.8	503.0	Horse trail		4357
1685.3	504.5	Bearpen Trail		4662
1684.7	505.1	Stone Mountain, views		4820
1684.1	505.7	The Scales livestock corral. First Peak Trail to east, Crest Trail to west.	36.6697,-81.4872	4648
1682.9	506.9	Fence stiles, Pine Mountain Trail to west		4950
1681.1	508.7	Spring		4240
1680.6	509.2	**Old Orchard Shelter** 24.2◄11.9◄6.7◄►4.2►13.4►23.2 Water 100 yards on blue-blazed trail to right. Privy 50 yards behind shelter.	(6)	4066
1679.8	510.0	Old Orchard Trail		3782
1678.9	510.9	Fox Creek, VA 603 Footbridges and streams 0.1 to north and to south. 100 yards east to parking and porta-potty.	36.6966,-81.5066	3480
1677.3	512.5	Chestnut Flats, Iron Mountain Trail to west		4240
1676.4	513.4	**Hurricane Mtn Shelter** (0.1W) 16.1◄10.9◄4.2◄►9.2►19.0►26.0 Creek and tentsites opposite side of trail.	(8)	3788
1675.8	514.0	Hurricane Creek Trail 0.3W to USFS 84, AT to east		3451
1675.3	514.5	Spring		3146
1674.6	515.2	Powerline, stream just north on AT		3208
1674.1	515.7	Stream.		3004
1673.6	516.2	Stream.		2968
1673.3	516.5	Dickey Gap Trail to **USFS Hurricane Creek Campground** (0.7W) 276.783.5196 Tent site $16, shower $2. Open mid Apr-Oct. Restroom & shower.		2941
1672.5	517.3	Comers Creek (drinking not advised), footbridge, cascades.		3310

468.7 Water St, ***Damascus, VA***
Larry Conroy 276.206.1245, **Barbara Clark** 276.274.0907

469.2 Laurel and Shady

470.1 US 58

Trail Days ⟨www.traildays.us⟩ (May 19-21, 2017) is the largest event on the AT. Hiker reunion & talent show, presentations, music, contra dancing, & hiker parade. Many gear reps & retailers on-hand.

Dave's Place $21 per room per night for 1 or 2 persons, max stay 2 nights. All rooms private. Shower & towel w/out stay $3. No alcohol/pets/ smoking. Check-in at Mount Rogers Outfitters.

Crazy Larry's 276.475.7130 Hostel w/ A/C & heat $40. Shower, laundry & big b'fast incl. Shuttles for a fee. Reserv. suggested. Mail: 209 Douglas Dr, Damascus, VA 24236.

Hikers Inn 276.475.3788 $25 Bunks, Hostel Queen $50. Rooms in house & Airstream $75/$65; whole hostel $135/$100. Guest laundry $5. Run by Lee & Paul (2010 thruhiker "Skink"). A/C in all rooms. Smoking outside, dogs allowed in hostel & Airstream, cash/check/cc. Closed in winter.

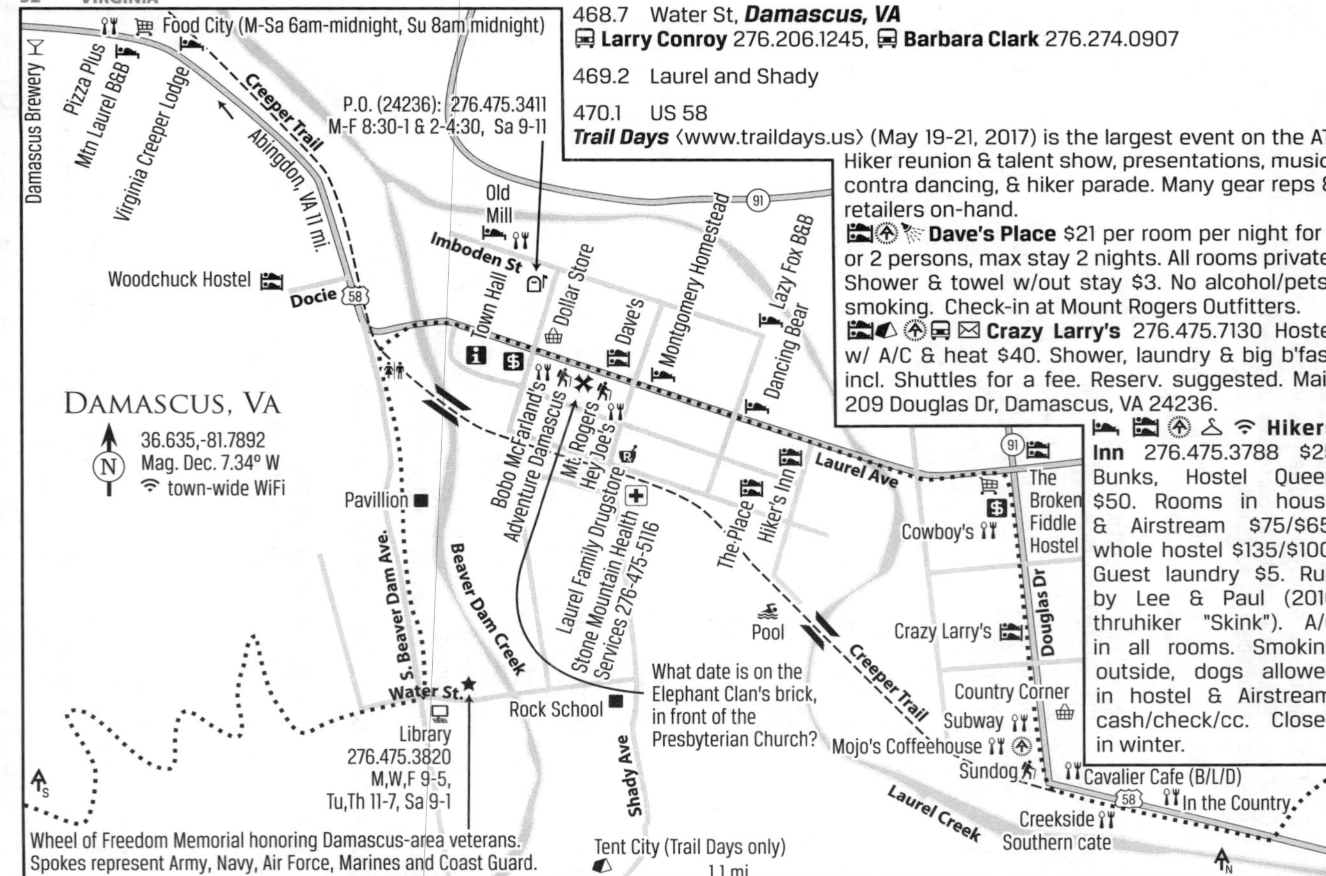

The Place 276.492.3983 Methodist Church-run bunkrooms, tenting, pavilion, guest only showers w/ towel & soap. Town clothes avail. Suggested donation $7. Seasonal caretaker, please help keep the bunkroom clean. No pets/alcohol/smoking on premises. 2 Night max unless sick/ injured. Check-in 10a-10p. Open early Mar - mid-Nov (depending on weather). No vehicle-assisted hikers except during Trail Days.

Woodchuck Hostel 406.407.1272. Yr- round bed w/linens $25. One private cabin $45S $55D. Teepee $15PP. Tent/hammock $12. Hot b'fast w/stay ($2 extra for tenter or hammocker). Laundry $5. Shower w/out stay $3. Kitchen privileges, common area, large yard, pavilion w/ gas grill. Dogs OK. Alcohol fuel/oz, cold drinks & snacks avail. Free shuttles to Food City, other shuttles by arrangement. No drugs/alcohol. CC w/ $2 fee. Mail: P.O.Box 752, Damascus Va. 24236

Appalachian Folk School 423.341.1843 Non-profit run by Warren Doyle (17 AT traverses) offers work-for-stay weeknights (M-Th) only (2-3 hrs/night) for all hikers who have a spiritual/poetic connection to the trail. Open Mar-Apr & mid Sep-mid Nov. Kitchen privileges, shower, wireless, laundry & rides to/from the AT between Rt. 321 (Hampton) & VA 603 (Fox Creek)- work for stay only. Located in Mountain City, TN.

The Broken Fiddle Hostel 276.608.6220 Located directly on the AT in Damascus. Offers 2 private rooms $45/2, $10 eap (Q bed & couch), 4 single beds in shared space $25PP, tent & hammock space $10PP. Tax incl. in all fees. Laundry $5, Shower w/o stay $3. Pets ok outside. Includes c. b'fast. Full kitchen use. Close to resupply & PO. Call for shuttle availability. CC accepted w/processing fee.

Lazy Fox B&B 276.475.5838 Yr-round $75/up incl. tax & b'fast. No CC. No pets/smoking. Guest Mail: PO Box 757, 133 Imboden St, Damascus, VA 24236.

Mountain Laurel Inn 276.492.6072

Montgomery Homestead Inn 276.492.6283 $75/up incl. laundry. No smoking/alcohol/pets. Open Mar-Oct, no CC. Mail (guest only): (USPS) PO Box 12, (FedEx/ UPS) 103 E. Laurel Ave, Damascus, VA 24236. mgmhomestead@gmail.com

Dancing Bear B&B 423.571.1830, $75/up incl. laundry. No smoking/alcohol/pets. Open Mar-Oct, No CC. Mail (guest only): (USPS) PO Box 12, (FedEx/ UPS) 103 E. Laurel Ave, Damascus, VA 24236.

Virginia Creeper Lodge 276.492.1143 $75/room hiker rate, $25EAP (most sleep 6). Shared kitchen, common area, satellite TV, pet friendly. Coin laundry. 702 N. Beaverdam Ave. Damascus, VA 24236.

Food City (0.5W on US 58) 276.475.3653, M-Sa 6a-12a; Su 7a-12a

Mt. Rogers Outfitters 276.475.5416 Full service backpacking store, fuel/oz. Shuttles, parking for section hikers $5/ day. Shower w/towel $3. Mail: PO Box 546, 110 W Laurel Ave, Damascus, VA 24236 ⟨www.mtrogersoutfitters.com⟩

Adventure Damascus 888.595.2453, 276.475.6262 ⟨www.adventuredamascus.com⟩ Caters to thru-hikers w/ backpacking gear, hiker foods, alcohol/Coleman/oz, other fuels, bike rentals, shuttles to area trailheads by arrangement, $3 showers, daily yr-round. USPS/UPS Mail: PO Box 1113, 128 W Laurel Ave, Damascus, VA 24236

Sundog Outfitter 276.475.6252 Backpacking gear & clothing, repairs, hiker food, Coleman/alcohol/oz, other fuels, shuttles to area trailheads by arrangement, open 7 days. Mail: PO Box 1113 or 331 Douglas Dr, Damascus, VA 24236 ⟨www.sundogoutfitter.com⟩

Library 276.475.3820, M,W,F 9-5, T,Th 11-7, Sa 9-1, internet 1 hr.

499.8 **Grayson Highlands State Park**

276.579.7092 Blue-blazed trail (0.5E) to parking; campground 1.5 mi. farther east on road. Park closed in cold weather; call ahead if possible. Camp store with courtesy phone, tent site w/ shower $21, shower only $5. May 1 - mid Oct.

501.1 Massie Gap

Grayson Highlands General Store & Inn 276.579.4602 3.2E of park entr. Good resupply, restaurant, motel rooms, ice cream shop, laundry, hiking/bouldering gear.

NoBo	SoBo	Description		Elev
1671.3	518.5	Dickey Gap, AT crosses VA 650 (gravel), east 50 yards to VA 16 (paved Sugar Grove Hwy), **Troutdale, VA**, 2.6 south on VA 16	**(pg. 58)**	3300
1670.4	519.4	Horse trail		3485
1669.7	520.1	Bobby's Trail (blue-blazed), campsite and spring (0.2E)	💧 ⛺	3698
1667.2	522.6	**Trimpi Shelter** (0.1E) 20.1◄13.4◄9.2◄►9.8►16.8►36.1	☽ 💧 ∠ (8)	2985
1666.4	523.4	Fence stiles 0.2 apart, cattle graze in area, close gates behind you		2684
1666.0	523.8	VA 672 (gravel)		2608
1665.1	524.7	VA 670, South Fork Holston River	36.7631,-81.4939 🅿	2450
1664.1	525.7	Stream, intermittent	◊	2602
1663.6	526.2	Campsite on west side of trail	💧 ⛺	2861
1661.2	528.6	VA 601 (gravel), limited parking	36.7994,-81.4575 🅿	3269
1659.7	530.1	Powerline		3318
1658.8	531.0	Footbridge, stream	💧	3011
1657.4	532.4	**Partnership Shelter,** showers, tenting not allowed near shelter 23.2◄19.0◄9.8◄►7.0►26.3►35.7 Can call for pizza from Visitor Center.	☽ 🚿 💧 ∠ (16)	3242
1657.2	532.6	VA 16, Mt Rogers Visitor Center **Sugar Grove, VA,** 24375 (3.2E), **Marion, VA** 24354 (5.9W)	36.8114,-81.4204 🅿 **(pg. 58)**	3220
1656.5	533.3	VA 622		3270
1653.2	536.6	USFS 86, Glade Mountain Rd. Private road, permission required, may not be suitable for passenger cars.	36.8348,-81.3708 🅿	3650

SoBo NoBo 1000 3000 5000

NoBo	SoBo	Feature		Elev
1651.9	537.9	Glade Mountain		4113
1650.9	538.9	Spring	💧	3513
1650.6	539.2	Stream.	💧	3287
1650.4	539.4	**Chatfield Shelter** 26.0◄16.8◄7.0◄►19.3►28.7►39.4	(6)	3173
1650.1	539.7	USFS 644 (dirt), streams to north and south	💧	3046
1649.8	540.0	Footbridge, stream	💧	2929
1649.5	540.3	Stream.	💧	2775
1648.8	541.0	Two powerlines		2698
1648.6	541.2	VA 615, Lindamood School Settlers Museum 0.1E (276.686.4401), parking avail. at farm. (Apr 1-Nov 15)	36.8708,-81.3577 P	2596
1648.1	541.7	VA 729		2537
1647.3	542.5	Fence stile		2708
1646.6	543.2	Middle Fork of the Holston River, footbridge, RR tracks just north of river	💧	2436
1645.8	544.0	VA 683, US 11, I-81, **Atkins, VA**	(pg. 59)	2420
1645.4	544.4	I-81 underpass		2419
1644.5	545.3	VA 617, Davis Cemetery	36.8973,-81.3691 P	2450
1643.9	545.9	Fence stile, end of field		2566
1643.7	546.1	Blue-blazed trail 0.1E to water at Davis Hollow	💧 ⛺	2539
1642.4	547.4	Davis Path campsite and privy, level ground for 1-2 shelters only.	⛺	2874
1640.2	549.6	Gullion (Little Brushy) Mountain		3300
1639.8	550.0	Virginia Horse Trail		3185
1639.1	550.7	Crawfish Trail to east, campsite and stream on AT south of here	💧 ⛺	2600
1638.1	551.7	Stream.	💧	3024
1637.4	552.4	Spring	💧	3347
1637.2	552.6	Tilson Gap, crest of Walker Mtn		3432
1636.4	553.4	Spring, fence	💧	2948
1635.7	554.1	VA 610, Old Rich Valley Rd. Fence stiles here and to south	(pg. 59)	2700
1634.9	554.9	Fence stile		2770
1634.3	555.5	VA 742, Holston River Bridge	💧	2474
1633.8	556.0	Stream.	💧	2518
1633.3	556.5	VA 42, O'Lystery Pavilion (private, do not use) Campsite just north of trail to parking area.	36.9833,-81.4064 P 💧 ⛺ (pg. 59)	2536

NoBo SoBo 1000 3000 5000

SoBo	NoBo	Feature		Elev
1632.3	557.5	Brushy Mountain		3200
1631.1	558.7	**Knot Maul Branch Shelter** (0.1W), water 100 yds to right of shelter on blue blaze trail. 6.1◄26.3◄19.3◄►9.4►20.1►33.6	☽ 💧 ⊏ (8)	2757
1630.4	559.4	Footbridge, stream	💧	2597
1629.7	560.1	Lynn Camp Creek, footbridge, campsite	💧 ⛺	2400
1628.6	561.2	Lynn Camp Mountain		3035
1627.4	562.4	Lick Creek, footbridge	💧	2268
1626.4	563.4	Stream.	◊	2318
1626.2	563.6	VA 625, USFS 222 (gravel)	37.0226,-81.4262 🅿	2326
1625.0	564.8	Stream.	◊	3096
1623.8	566.0	Chestnut Ridge, south end, start of clearing		3780
1623.5	566.3	Pond, spring at north end, best water source for Chestnut Knob Shelter	💧	3896
1622.7	567.1	Views from open ridgeline	📷	4177
1621.8	568.0	Spring 0.1E on unmarked roadbed	◊	4315
1621.7	568.1	**Chestnut Knob Shelter** 35.7◄28.7◄9.4◄►10.7►24.2►33.9 Stone shelter, fully enclosed with door.	☽ ⊏ (8)	4393
1620.3	569.5	Walker Gap, dirt road 100 yards south , piped spring.	37.0544,-81.3789 🅿 💧	3520
1619.3	570.5	Garden Mountain, rock outcropping		3869
1615.5	574.3	VA 623, **Hostel (4.0W) Call for shuttle**	37.077,-81.3071 🅿 **(pg. 60)**	3867
1614.5	575.3	Davis Farm Campsite (0.5W).	◊ ⛺	3850

SoBo NoBo 1000 3000 5000

SOBO	NOBO	Feature	Elev
1611.9	577.9	Stream (unreliable)	2889
1611.0	578.8	**Jenkins Shelter,** creek 100 yards north on AT. (8) 39.4◄20.1◄10.7◄►13.5►23.2►37.7	2400
1606.6	583.2	Laurel Creek, VA 615 (gravel) 37.1025,-81.2022 P Intersection with Trail Boss Trail. Campsite just north of road.	2450
1604.7	585.1	Trail Boss Trail to west	3099
1602.7	587.1	Views to west	2996
1601.8	588.0	Powerline	2721
1600.3	589.5	AT on gravel road from here north to US 52	3088
1599.7	590.1	US 52 (North Scenic Hwy), **Bland, VA** (2.5E), **Bastian, VA** (3W) **(pg. 60)**	2905
1599.3	590.5	AT crosses over I-77 on VA 612	2780
1598.9	590.9	VA 612 parking, Kimberling Creek, drinking discouraged 37.1389,-81.1266 P	2600
1597.5	592.3	**Helveys Mill Shelter** (0.3E) (6) 33.6◄24.2◄13.5◄►9.7►24.2►33.7 Water source 0.3 mile down switch-backed trail in front of shelter.	3121

Mountain Laurel - Shrub similar to the rhododendron. Grows five to ten feet high and blossoms with abundant cup-shaped white flowers.

518.5 Dickey Gap, VA 650, ***Troutdale, VA 24378*** (2.6E)
(2.6E) **Troutdale Church Hostel** 276.677.4092 bunkhouse with microwave, tenting, shower. Pets outside, no alcohol. Mar15-Nov15, donations appreciated. Hikers welcome to service in hiker attire. Pastor Ken Riggins. NO maildrops; 62 Sapphire Lane, Troutdale.
Fox Creek Store 4mi. South on Rt 16, M-F. 7-7; Sa, 7-6. Deli.

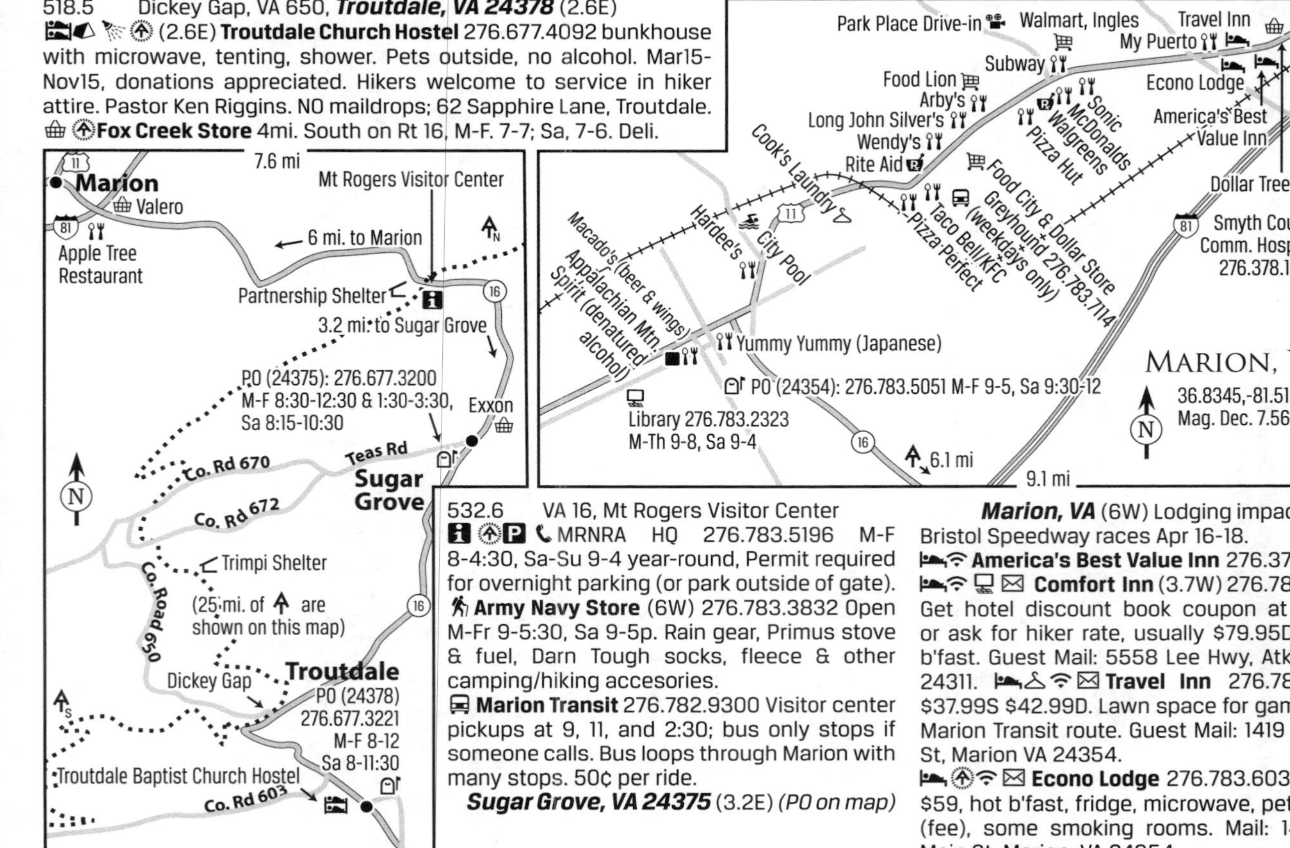

532.6 VA 16, Mt Rogers Visitor Center
MRNRA HQ 276.783.5196 M-F 8-4:30, Sa-Su 9-4 year-round, Permit required for overnight parking (or park outside of gate).
Army Navy Store (6W) 276.783.3832 Open M-Fr 9-5:30, Sa 9-5p. Rain gear, Primus stove & fuel, Darn Tough socks, fleece & other camping/hiking accesories.
Marion Transit 276.782.9300 Visitor center pickups at 9, 11, and 2:30; bus only stops if someone calls. Bus loops through Marion with many stops. 50¢ per ride.

Sugar Grove, VA 24375 (3.2E) *(PO on map)*

Marion, VA (6W) Lodging impacted by Bristol Speedway races Apr 16-18.
America's Best Value Inn 276.378.0481
Comfort Inn (3.7W) 276.783.2144 Get hotel discount book coupon at Exxon or ask for hiker rate, usually $79.95D. Cont. b'fast. Guest Mail: 5558 Lee Hwy, Atkins, VA 24311. **Travel Inn** 276.783.5112, $37.99S $42.99D. Lawn space for games. On Marion Transit route. Guest Mail: 1419 N Main St, Marion VA 24354.
Econo Lodge 276.783.6031 $49 - $59, hot b'fast, fridge, microwave, pets okay (fee), some smoking rooms. Mail: 1420 N. Main St, Marion, VA 24354.

Park Place Drive-In 276.781.2222 Walk-ins welcome. Has mini-golf, arcade & ice cream shop. Open seasonally.

544.0 VA 683, US 11, I-81, ***Atkins, VA 24311***
Intersection is between Atkins & Rural Retreat in the township of Groseclose.

Relax Inn
276.783.5811 $45S $50D, $5EAP (max 4), pets $10. Parking $3/day. Call for shuttle avail. Mail(guests limit 2 boxes, non-guest $5): Relax Inn, 7253 Lee Hwy, Rural Retreat, VA 24368.

The Barn Restaurant
276.686.6222 M-Sa 7-8, Su 7-3, 16oz hiker burger, Sunday buffet 11-2. Must leave pack outside. Parking for section hikers $5/day, $25/wk. Mail: 7412 Lee Hwy Rural Retreat, VA 24368.

Rambunny & Aqua 276.783.3754 Shuttle referrals & other help.

Skip 276.783.3604 By appt, covers Damascus to Pearisburg

554.1 VA 610, Old Rich Valley Rd

Quarter Way Inn (0.8W) 276.522.4603 tina@quaarterwayinn.com. Open April – June. Renovated 1910 farmhouse, run by 2009 thru-hiker Tina (Chunky) and husband, Brett. $30pp for indoor bunk with pillow, shower, towel, laundry, loaner clothes, & morning coffee. $40S $75D private room; $18pp tenting, includes same. Gourmet breakfast available for $12 when 3 or more request it. Resupply (snacks, fuel, Mountain House, pasta sides, oatmeal, etc.), pizza, pop & ice cream. Guests can enjoy movie library, free phone calls and sky chairs hanging from a giant Sycamore tree. Slackpacking from Marion/Partnership shelter and Atkins often available – call in advance. Parking $3/per day. Credit cards accepted. No dogs. ID required. ⟨www.quarterwayinn.com⟩

556.5 VA 42, O'Lystery Pavilion (private, do not use)

Appalachian Dreamer Hiker Hostel (2.5W) 276.682.4061 Call for pickup from VA42 or walk W approximately 2.0W from VA42 or VA610 crossing to Dotson Ridge Rd. Hostel is at the top of Dotson Ridge. Working farm - no pets allowed. Dinner and breakfast provided, laundry, WiFi. Photo ID required, must sign insurance release, anyone under 18 must be with parent (proof of relationship required) Limited resupply, shuttle to town (fee). Shuttle for slackpacking when time permits. Bunk room with 6 bunks, 2 baths limited tent sites with access to basement bath. No alcohol and no drugs. 2 night stay max. Check website for complete list of rules. $20 donation requested. Picks up from VA610/ Old Rich Valley Rd or VA 42. ⟨www.appalachiandreamerhikerhostel.com⟩

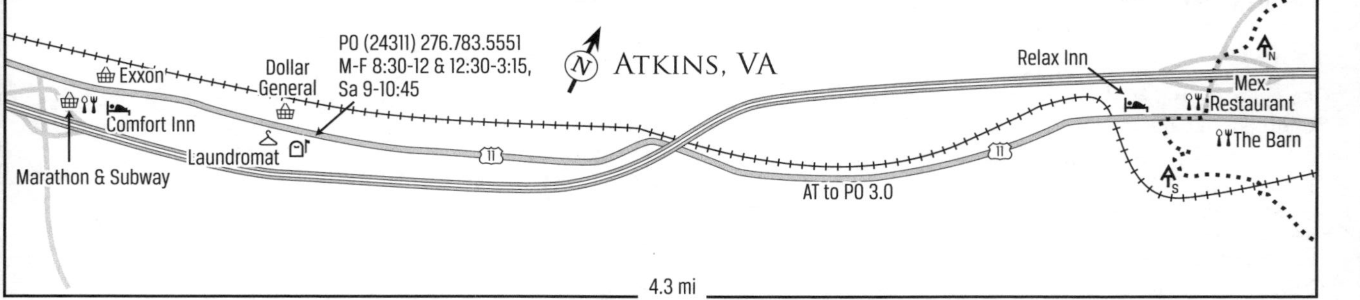

574.3 VA623

Saint Luke's Hostel (4.0W) 276.472.2150 yr-round. Call for free shuttle, it's hard to find. Tenting $15, Bunks $20. Private & semiprivate avail. Kitchen use, fuel avail. Maildrops guests only: 1404 Banks Ridge Rd. Burkes Garden, VA 24651

590.1 US 52, North Scenic Hwy, ***Bland, VA 24315*** (3E to PO or Citgo, 4E to hotel & restaurants)

M-F 8:30-11:30 & 12-4, Sa 9 -11, 276.688.3751

Big Walker Motel 276.688.3331 $66.13(1-2), $71.64(3-4), pets OK. Fridge & microwave. Guest Mail: (UPS) 70 Skyview Ln, Bland VA 24315, (USPS) PO Box 155, Bland VA 24315.

Days Inn Hostel 239.285.4583 Trailhead P/U (small fee) from 606, 608, 611, 615, Hwy52, Bunks $20, Private room $30. Hiker suite w/TV & laundry $45. Slackpacking avail, full kitchen, grill, limited resupply incl fuels. WiFi/ Sat. TV. Laundry $4. Alcohol ok. Maildrops to: c/o [hiker name] 2359 Byrnes Chapel Rd, Bland VA 24315

Subway, Dairy Queen

Grants Supermarket 276.688.0314 M-Sa 8-8, Su 10-7

Citgo, Bland Square Grill 276.688.3851 Open 7 days 6:30-7 year-round. Groceries, Canister fuel & Heet, Grill serves B/L/D.

Dollar General 7 days 8-10

Bland Family Clinic 276.688.0500 M-Tu, 10-6; Th, 9-5; F, 10-2; W clsd. Call ahead: sometimes closes early.

Bland County Library 276.688.3737 M & F, 10a-5p; Tu-Th, 10a-7p; Sa, 10a-2p. 697 Main Street.

Bubba's Shuttles 276.730.5869 barnes.james43@yahoo.com Shuttles from Damascus to Pearisburg & Roanoke Airport.

Bastian, VA 24314 (3W)

M-F 8-12, Sa 9:15-11:15, 276.688.4631

Pizza Plus 276.688.3332 Su-Th 11a-9p, F-Sa 11a-10p.

Bland Pharmacy 276.688.4204 M-F, 9a-5p; Sa, 9a-12p; clsd Su.

Bland County Medical Clinic 276.688.4331 M 8-6, Tu-Th 8-8, F 8-5, 12301 Grapfield Rd. ⟨www.blandclinic.com⟩

Trail Etiquette

Avoid using a cell phone anywhere within the trail corridor, especially in shelters or within earshot of other hikers. Turn ringer off.

When hikers approach one another on the trail, the uphill hiker has the right-of-way, but the rule is irrelevant. If a hiker is approaching, look for an opportunity to step aside, regardless of your position. Be aware of hikers approaching from behind, and step aside so that they may pass.

Take only as much shelter space as you need to sleep. Shelter spaces cannot be reserved for friends who have yet to arrive. If you bring alcohol to a shelter or campsite, do so discreetly. Soon after dark is bedtime for most hikers.

The AT is liberating, and outlandish behavior is part of AT lore. Be considerate; boisterous and erratic behavior may be unsettling to strangers stuck in the woods with you. Conversely, hikers seeking a serene experience should be aware that AT hiking is, for many, a social experience. Be tolerant. Stay flexible; be prepared to move on rather than trying to convince others to conform to your expectations.

Town Etiquette

Ask permission before bringing a pack into a place of business. Assume that alcohol is not permitted in hostels & campsites until told otherwise.

Don't expect generosity, and show appreciation when it is offered. If you are granted work-for-stay, strive to provide service equal to the value of your stay.

Respect hotel room capacities; hotel owners should know how many people intend to stay in a room. Try to leave hotel rooms as clean as a car traveler would. If a shower is available, use it.

APPALACHIAN TRAIL CONSERVANCY®

The ATC works with the National Park Service, 31 volunteer maintaining clubs, and multiple other partners to engage the public in conserving this essential American resource. Their website, www.AppalachianTrail.org, contains information about trail history and protection, hike planning, volunteer opportunities, and trail conditions. Please join or donate to the ATC.

Dispose of Waste Properly

- Pack it in; pack it out. Leave any donated items at hiker boxes in town rather than at campsites or shelters.
- Walk at least 100 feet (40 steps) away from shelters, water sources and campsites to dispose of urine, toothpaste, cooking water and strained dishwater, and to wash bodies, dishes or clothing. Minimize any use of soap.
- Use the privy only for human waste and toilet paper. Pack out disposable wipes and hygiene products.
- If there is no privy, walk at least 200 feet (80 steps) away from campsites, shelters, trails and water sources to bury feces in a hole 6 to 8 inches deep.
- Bury or carry out toilet paper.

Camping & Campfire Regulations

Camping & Campfire regulations along the A.T. change frequently. Many are addressed in The A.T. Guide. Please visit www.appalachiantrail.org/camping for comprehensive listing to familiarize yourself with camping and campfire regulations for the entire A.T.

ATC Voluntary Thru-hiker Registration

ATC's Voluntary Thru-hiker Registration helps prospective thru-hikers to choose start dates that best avoid the impacts of overcrowding. Section hikers, even though you will not register, make use of the information to avoid peak dates. ⟨http://appalachiantrail.org/home/explore-the-trail/thru-hiking⟩

Bear Interactions & Bear Canisters

Due to increasing bear/human interactions, the Appalachian Trail Conservancy strongly recommends the use of bear canisters for food storage while overnight camping along the A.T. in GA, NC, & TN. Recommended canisters: http://sierrawild.gov/bears/food-storage

Solid, non-pliable "bear canisters" are required if you camp in GA each year between Jarrard Gap & Neel Gap from March 1 to June 1.

Within the Great Smoky Mtn NP all food must be hung from cables; even food within bear canisters.

www.ApalachianTrail.org

Baxter State Park Permit Requirements

Stop at Monson Visitor Center (pg. 220) to preregister for their Baxter State Park permit and get important information you'll need to know about the 100mile wilderness.

Minimize Campfire Impacts

- Use stoves for cooking – if you need a fire, build one only where it's legal and in an existing fire ring. Leave hatchets and saws at home – collect dead and downed wood that you can break by hand. Burn all wood to ash.
- Do not try to burn trash, including foil, plastic, glass, cans, tea bags, food, or anything with food on it. These items do not burn thoroughly. They create noxious fumes, attract wildlife like skunks and bears, and make the area unsightly.
- Where campfires are permitted, leave the fire ring clean by removing others' trash and scattering unused wood, cold coals, and ashes 200 feet away from camp after the fire is cold and completely out.

SoBo	NoBo	Feature		Elev.
1590.9	598.9	VA 611 (gravel)	37.1453,-81.0094 P	2820
1590.6	599.2	Stream, unreliable	💧	2679
1589.5	600.3	Brushy Mountain		3101
1587.8	602.0	**Jenny Knob Shelter** (0.1E), spring 0.1 on blue blaze left of shelter 33.9◄23.2◄9.7◄►14.5►24.0►40.1	☽ 💧 ⊏ (6)	2668
1587.1	602.7	Stream.	💧	2328
1586.8	603.0	Stream, campsite.	💧 ⛺	2264
1586.6	603.2	Lickskillet Hollow, VA 608, footbridge	37.1569,-80.9614 P 💧	2200
1585.4	604.4	Powerline		2771

Rhododendron - 10-15 foot tall shrubs with broad waxy leaves. Grows in thick stands that the AT sometimes tunnels through. Flowers grow in large bouquets of ruffled pink.

SoBo NoBo 1000 3000 5000

SoBo	NoBo	Feature		Elev.
1581.4	608.4	Kimberling Creek, suspension bridge, drinking discouraged	💧	2025
1581.3	608.5	VA 606, parking to east **Trent's Grocery** (0.5W)	37.1757,-80.9083 P **(pg. 64)**	2041
1579.5	610.3	Dismal Falls Trail, 0.3W to waterfall, camping on side trail. Road on other side of falls sometimes brings visitors by car.	💧 ⛺	2343
1579.2	610.6	Stream, campsite.	💧 ⛺	2273
1577.8	612.0	Footbridge		2365
1577.6	612.2	Footbridge, stream	💧	2390
1577.3	612.5	Two streams	💧	2453
1576.7	613.1	Woods road		2585
1576.2	613.6	Streams, footbridge	💧	2528
1575.8	614.0	Footbridge, stream (2)	💧	2453
1575.6	614.2	Dismal Creek, gravel road, campsite, footbridge to north	💧 ⛺	2447
1575.4	614.4	Ribble Trail 3.0W connects with AT near Big Horse Gap		2452
1574.8	615.0	Center of one-mile stretch with at least 6 stream crossings by footbridge.		2477
1574.1	615.7	Clearing, side trail to west		2513
1573.9	615.9	Footbridge, stream (2)	💧	2516
1573.5	616.3	Dirt road		2580
1573.3	616.5	**Wapiti Shelter** (0.1E) 37.7◄24.2◄14.5◄►9.5►25.6►38.2	☽ 💧 ⊏ (5)	2603
1573.1	616.7	Stream.	💧	2651
1572.7	617.1	Stream.	💧	2802

SoBo	NoBo	Feature	Elevation
1572.0	617.8	Spring . . . 💧	3342
1570.7	619.1	View . . . 📷	3896
1568.4	621.4	Side trail 0.1E to radio tower, views from ledge in front of tower . . . 📷	4027
1567.8	622.0	Ribble Trail west, wide grassy path, reconnects with AT south of Wapiti Shelter . .	3800
1567.7	622.1	Big Horse Gap, USFS 103 ⚠ Sometimes confused with Sugar Run Gap, which is 1.5N. There is a short sign south of road, west of AT	3749
1566.5	623.3	Woods road . . .	3485
1566.1	623.7	Sugar Run Gap, Sugar Run Rd (gravel), bear left at fork for hostel (small sign on tree), hostel on right. **Woods Hole Hostel** (0.5E) . . . . (**pg. 64**)	3395
1564.7	625.1	View, 30 yards east. . . . 📷	3910
1563.9	625.9	Side trail to forest service road . . .	3557
1563.8	626.0	**Docs Knob Shelter,** reliable spring to left of shelter 33.7◄24.0◄9.5◄►16.1►28.7►32.6 . . . (8)	3541
1562.6	627.2	Spring . . . 💧	3399
1560.8	629.0	Spring . . . 💧	3150
1560.1	629.7	Powerline, view . . . 📷	3431
1558.0	631.8	View . . . 📷	3693
1557.9	631.9	Campsite and water (0.2W) from AT on Blue Blazed Trail . . . 📷	3693
1557.4	632.4	Angels Rest 0.1W to view. . . . 📷	3550
1556.2	633.6	Roadbed. . . .	2595
1555.5	634.3	Cross Ave (paved), VA 634, **Pearisburg, VA** (0.7E) . . . (**pg. 64**)	2010
1555.4	634.4	**Stream with small cascade** . . . 💧	1929
1554.4	635.4	Narrows Rd Parking Area, **Narrows, VA** (3.6W) . . . 37.3341,-80.7553 P	1603
1553.8	636.0	US 460, Senator Shumate Bridge, New River, Circle under north end of bridge. . .	1589

SoBo NoBo

1000 3000 5000

608.5 VA 606

Lickskillet Hostel 276.779.5457 (.8E) Church at corner of VA 608/42. Hostel owner is Mongo. Suggested donation $15, WiFi, daily shuttle to Bland. Not a party place. Mail for guests: 35 Price Ridge Rd, Bland, VA 24315

Dismal Falls Retreat (1.0W) 276.928.0450 Cabin rental, call for rates/reservations. Turn Rt on Dismal Creek Rd, just W of Trent's Grocery. 0.5M from VA606. Kitchen, pool table, Limited shuttle. ⟨www.rentmygetaway.com⟩

Trent's Grocery (0.5W) 276.928.1349 Yr-round, M-Sa, 7-8; Sun, 8-8. Deli w/pizza, hamburgers, hot dogs & more. Camping $6, shower $3, laundry $3. Coleman/alcohol/oz & canister fuel. CC OK. Soda machines outside. Shuttles. Mail: 900 Wilderness Rd, Bland, VA 24315.

Larry Richardson 540.921.4724 Shuttle range Bland to Pearisburg.

623.7 Sugar Run Gap, Sugar Run Rd

Woods Hole Hostel (0.5E) 540.921.3444 1880's Chestnut-log cabin discovered by Roy & Tillie Wood in 1986. Granddaughter, Neville, continues the legacy w/husband Michael, w/ emphasis on sustainable living through beekeeping, farming, organic gardening, pottery, yoga(free) & massage therapy. Directions: NoBo right on dirt rd at Sugar Run Gap (SoBo turn left). Bear left at fork, go downhill 0.5 mi, to hostel on right. Bunkhouse $18PP has mattresses, electricity & hot shower. Camping $12PP. Pet friendly. Indoor rooms: $30PP shared / $55 private (thru-hiker rate). Guests often invited to share communal meals. Dinner $14, b'fast $9. Free Shuttles for fee, computer access, laundry, smoothies, cheese, home roast coffee & baked goods. Coleman/alcohol/ oz, fuel canisters. CC or cash(discount). Guest mail: Woods Hole Hostel, 3696 Sugar Run Rd, Pearisburg, VA 24134. ⟨www.woodsholehostel.com⟩

634.3 Cross Ave (paved), VA634, ***Pearisburg, VA 24134*** (0.7E)

Angel's Rest Hiker Haven 540.787.4076 $10-35PP/ D. Day pass $5 (shower/laundry) Dogs $3. Private & shared rooms. Cable/ Netflix/DVD's. Shuttle. Slack Packing. Onsite Chiropractic & Acupuncture Svc. Thru-hiker discount. Maildrop: 200 Douglas Ln, Pearisburg VA, 24134

Holiday Motor Lodge 540.921.1551 Yr-round Lodge. Hostel open May 1-Sep 15. Prices incl. tax: $20 bunkroom w/WiFi, TV, pets free. Limited economy rooms $39, other rooms $50. $10 Pet fee. Pool. Mail: 401 N Main St, Pearisburg, VA 24134.

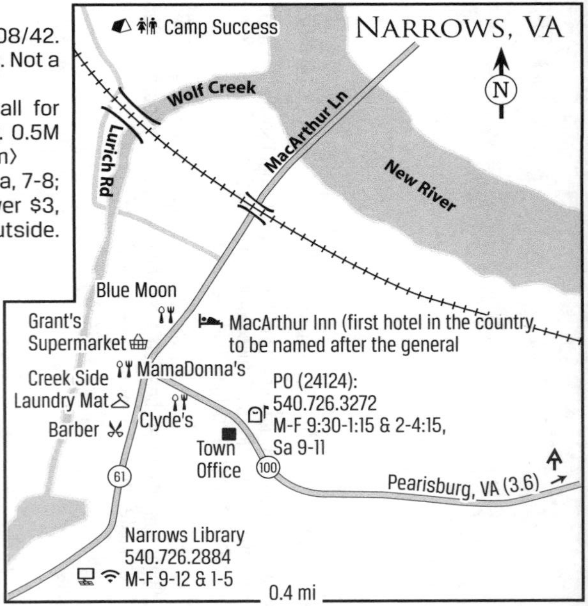

Holy Family Hostel 540.626.3337 Volunteer caretaker, Patrick Muldoon please do NOT call for a ride. Check-in directions posted. Suggested donation $10PP, 2 night max. Open Mar-Nov; otherwise call. Hot shower, fridge, grill. Keep hostel clean & noise down (church in residential area). Well behaved pets, no alcohol/drugs.

Plaza Motel 540.921.2591 $44S $55D incl. tax, no pets, CC ok. Mail: 415 N. Main St, Pearisburg, VA 24134.

Pearis Mercantile 540.921.2260 M-Sa 10-5:30 Selection of hiker foods, small gear items, fuel.

NARROWS, VA

Camp Success
N
Wolf Creek
Lurich Rd
MacArthur Ln
New River
Blue Moon
Grant's Supermarket
MacArthur Inn (first hotel in the country to be named after the general
Creek Side Laundry Mat
MamaDonna's
Barber
Clyde's
Town Office
PO (24124): 540.726.3272 M-F 9:30-1:15 & 2-4:15, Sa 9-11
61
100
Pearisburg, VA (3.6)
Narrows Library 540.726.2884 M-F 9-12 & 1-5
0.4 mi

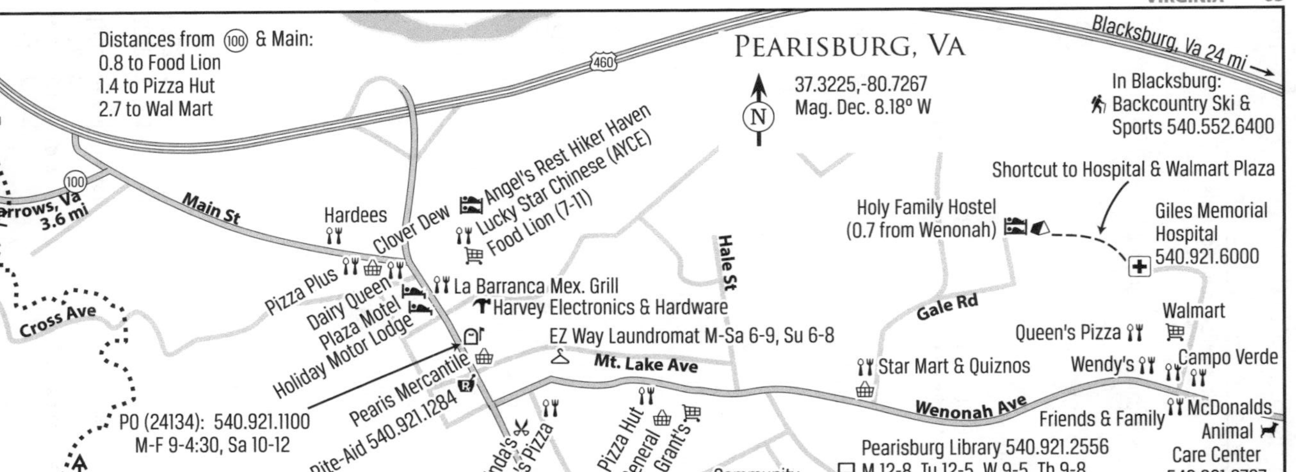

Don Raines 540.921.7433 ratface20724@aol.com Anytime, anywhere. Slackpacking avail.

Tom Hoffman 540.921.1184 gopullman@aol.com. Mid-range shuttles centered in Pearisburg.

Community Health Center 540.921.3502 M-F 8-4:30 Quick, low-cost healthcare, hikers welcome.

Harvey Electronics and Hardware 540.921.1456 M-F 9-5, Sa 10-4. Cell phones & supplies, canister fuel, alcohol/oz, tent repair kits.

Narrows, VA (3.6W on VA 100)

MacArthur Inn 540.726.7510 -Allen Neely. Hiker rooms $45 (sleeps 4) other rooms avail. Call for ride from Pearisburg area trailheads $5 round trip. Longer shuttles & slackpacking by arrangement. Free long distance phone, cable TV & WiFi, & use of kitchen. In center of town w/all services in walking distance. Shower $8. On-site restaurant serves dinner Th 5p-8p Mtn Music Jam 6:30-9p Mail: 117 MacArthur Ln, Narrows, VA 24124.

Camp Success Camping $5 tent/night, no showers. Check-in at Town Office 540.726.3020 M-F, 9-5. Call ahead for after-hrs arrivals or print permit from ⟨www.townofnarrows.org⟩.

Right Turn Clyde 540.921.7283 Th–Fr 6–10; Sa 3-10

Grants Supermarket 540.726.2303 M–Sa 8–9, Su 9–8

MamaDonna's 540-599-3508

655.9 **The Captain's**

Camping at 4464 Big Stony Creek Rd, 30 yds East of AT. Use zip line to cross the creek. This is not a hostel; do not enter the house. You may camp even when no one is home. Dogs bark but are friendly & are contained by an invisible electric fence. If it rains, you may stay on back porch. Hiker Feed two weeks after Trail Days.

1552.8	637.0	Landfill Rd (dirt), don't drink from stream	1587

✽ Fire Pink - Scarlet-colored flower with five snake-tongued petals.

1550.3	639.5	Cross Clendennin Rd (VA 641), follow Pocahontas Rd for 0.1mi	2190
1549.5	640.3	Powerline	2637
1549.3	640.5	Dirt road, Stream 💧	2685
1548.3	641.5	Piped spring (can go dry in late summer). ◊	3157
1547.7	642.1	**Rice Field Shelter** (0.1E) 40.1◂25.6◂16.1◂▸12.6▸16.5▸25.3 ☽ ⊏ (7) Stiles south & north. Unreliable water to left behind shelter 0.3 mile down hill.	3375
1547.1	642.7	Cell tower	3368
1546.6	643.2	Powerline, view 📷	3435
1546.1	643.7	Campsite west, water to east 💧 ⛺	3300
1542.6	647.2	Symms Gap, campsite to west. ⛺	3320
1541.6	648.2	Groundhog Trail to west	3421
1540.8	649.0	Campsite ⛺	3388
1540.0	649.8	Dickenson Gap	3300
1537.6	652.2	Allegheny Trail to west	3726
1535.7	654.1	Streams ◊	2964
1535.1	654.7	**Pine Swamp Branch Shelter** ☽ 💧 ⊏ (8) 38.2◂28.7◂12.6◂▸3.9▸12.7▸18.5	2532
1534.8	655.0	Stony Creek Valley, 0.1E to parking on VA 635. 37.4191,-80.6046 🅿	2381
1534.3	655.5	Stream. 💧	2400
1533.9	655.9	Camping at "The Captain's" place 30 yards east 💧 ⛺ (pg. 65)	2410
1533.7	656.1	Footbridge, stream 💧	2435

SoBo	NoBo	Feature		Elev
1532.7	657.1	Bridge over Stony Creek, VA 635, don't drink water from creek		2450
1531.7	658.1	Gravel road		3121
1531.4	658.4	Spring 100 yards east		3362
1531.2	658.6	**Bailey Gap Shelter** 32.6◄16.5◄3.9◄►8.8►14.6►21.0 Water 0.2S on AT, then east down blue-blazed trail.	(6)	3510
1530.2	659.6	Spring		3721
1528.6	661.2	Spring		3760
1527.5	662.3	VA 613 (gravel), Mountain Lake Rd		3950
1527.3	662.5	Wind Rock, view, campsite		4100
1526.5	663.3	Woods road		4054
1524.9	664.9	Lone Pine Peak		4026
1524.4	665.4	War Branch Trail to east		3507
1524.0	665.8	Spring		3267
1522.4	667.4	**War Spur Shelter,** spring north on AT 25.3◄12.7◄8.8◄►5.8►12.2►18.2	(6)	2361
1521.6	668.2	VA 632, cross Johns Creek on footbridge		2080
1521.5	668.3	Footbridge, stream, campsite		2058
1520.5	669.3	Spring		2627
1519.6	670.2	Rocky Gap, VA 601 (gravel)		3264
1519.0	670.8	Johns Creek Mountain Trail to west		3782
1517.8	672.0	Kelly Knob, view		3730
1516.6	673.2	**Laurel Creek Shelter** 18.5◄14.6◄5.8◄►6.4►12.4►22.5 Water 60 yards north of shelter junction and west of AT.	(6)	2798
1516.4	673.4	Stream		2753
1516.0	673.8	Piney Ridge		2614
1514.5	675.3	Pasture, several fence stiles		2227
1514.1	675.7	Footbridge, Sinking Creek, VA 42, **Newport, VA** (8.0E) "Trail east" is compass west (NoBo right, SoBo left to town).	(pg. 72)	2097
1513.3	676.5	VA 630 (paved), chimney, and footbridge close together		2145

5000
3000
1000
NoBo
SoBo

SoBo	NoBo	Feature	Icons	Elev
1512.9	676.9	Keffer Oak, largest oak tree on AT in south, over 18' around, over 300 yrs old Dover Oak along AT in NY is slightly larger.		2322
1512.5	677.3	Powerline		2526
1511.1	678.7	Powerline		3223
1510.4	679.4	Bruisers Knob		3417
1510.2	679.6	**Sarver Hollow Shelter** (0.4E) (2002) 21.0◄12.2◄6.4◄►6.0►16.1►29.7	☽ 💧 ∠ (6)	3402
1508.3	681.5	View	📷	3381
1508.0	681.8	View	📷	3354
1506.9	682.9	North end of ridge crest on Sinking Creek Mountain, Eastern Continental Divide West is old route of AT leading 2.5 miles to Old Hall Rd.		3368
1505.3	684.5	Stream.	💧	2703
1504.2	685.6	**Niday Shelter**, water on opposite side of AT 18.2◄12.4◄6.0◄►10.1►23.7►24.7	☽ 💧 ⛺ ∠ (6)	1988
1502.8	687.0	VA 621, Craig Creek Rd	37.3793,-80.25 🅿	1547
1502.3	687.5	Many footbridges crossing Craig Creek and feeder streams. within a mile north of road.	💧	1583
1499.8	690.0	Bench at southern crest of Brush Mountain		2988
1499.1	690.7	Audie Murphy Monument Murphy was most decorated American soldier of World War II. Monument on blue-blazed trail to west.		3100
1495.3	694.5	Footbridge, Trout Creek , VA 620 (gravel)	💧	1548
1494.9	694.9	Powerline		1749
1494.1	695.7	**Pickle Branch Shelter** (0.3E) 22.5◄16.1◄10.1◄►13.6►14.6►17.0 Tenting along trail to shelter. Water on steep trail 0.2 mile downhill from shelter.	☽ 💧 ⛺ ∠ (6)	1951
1493.1	696.7	View	📷	2392

NoBo	SoBo	Feature		Elev
1490.2	699.6	View	📷	2963
1489.9	699.9	Cove Mountain Trail 0.1E to Dragons Tooth (stone monolith), views.	📷	3020
1489.1	700.7	Lost Spectacles Gap		2520
1488.7	701.1	Rawies Rest, view	📷	2482
1488.5	701.3	View	📷	2307
1487.8	702.0	Scout Trail west to Dragons Tooth Parking	P	2039
1487.4	702.4	VA 624, Newport Rd	(pg. 72)	1810
1486.6	703.2	Footbridge taken out by flood. Must ford stream or rock hop.		1816
1486.1	703.7	Fence stile		1842
1485.8	704.0	VA 785, Blacksburg Rd		1790
1485.5	704.3	Footbridge, Catawba Creek, fence stile, treat water	💧	1770

The AT is mostly on National Park Service Land from Newport Rd to Mtn Pass Rd (roughly from Catawba through Troutville). Camping permitted only in designated locations (at the shelters, Lamberts Meadow Campsite and the Pig Farm Campsite).

NoBo	SoBo	Feature		Elev
1481.5	708.3	VA 311, **Catawba, VA** (1.0W) .37.3801,-80.0898 **2 porta potties in parking lot**	P (pg. 72)	1990
1480.9	708.9	Footbridge		2030
1480.5	709.3	**Johns Spring Shelter** (2003) 29.7◄23.7◄13.6◄►1.0►3.4►9.4 Unreliable spring 25 yrds left front of shelter.	(6)	1957
1480.1	709.7	Footbridge		2110
1479.5	710.3	**Catawba Mountain Shelter** (1984) Camping to north 24.7◄14.6◄1.0◄►2.4►8.4►22.8 Blue-blaze to water 100 yards from front of shelter.	(6)	2203
1477.8	712.0	McAfee Knob; excellent views, no camping.	📷	3197
1477.3	712.5	Powerline		2781
1477.2	712.6	Water to east, Pig Farm campsite, same water source as shelter		2682
1477.1	712.7	**Campbell Shelter** (1989), water 150 yards to left of shelter 17.0◄3.4◄2.4◄►6.0►20.4►26.6	(6)	2636
1474.0	715.8	Brickeys Gap, Lamberts Meadow Trail to east		2194

1472.2 717.6 Tinker Cliffs, 0.5 mile cliff walk, views back to McAfee Knob 3000

1471.7 718.1 Scorched Earth Gap, Andy Layne Trail to west 2600

1471.1 718.7 **Lamberts Meadow Shelter** 9.4◄8.4◄6.0◄►14.4►20.6►27.9 . (6) 2126
1470.8 719.0 Lamberts Meadow Campsite, Sawmill Run 2000
Footbridge, stream. North of footbridge an east trail rejoins AT at Brickeys Gap.

1468.6 721.2 Blue-blazed trail west to view 2217

1466.7 723.1 Angels Gap 1692
1466.4 723.4 Powerline 1840

1465.7 724.1 Hay Rock, view 1955

1464.5 725.3 Powerline, view 1920

1463.7 726.1 Powerline 1959

1462.9 726.9 Powerline 1386
1462.3 727.5 Powerline, railroad tracks, bridge 1165

1461.7 728.1 US 220, **Daleville, VA** . . . . (pg. 72) 1253

1460.5 729.3 I-81, trail passes under on VA 779 1400
1460.2 729.6 US 11, RR tracks, **Troutville, VA** (0.8W) . . . . 37.4045,-79.8895 P (pg. 72) 1300
1459.9 729.9 Fence stile 1497
1459.7 730.1 VA 652, Mountain Pass Rd 1450
1459.4 730.4 Fence 1521

1456.7 733.1 **Fullhardt Knob Shelter** (0.1E) . . . . (6) 2632
22.8◄20.4◄14.4◄►6.2►13.5►20.0 Water source can run dry if no recent rainfall. Treat water from cistern.

1453.9 735.9 Salt Pond Rd, USFS 191 2248

1453.1 736.7 Curry Creek, Curry Creek Trail to west 1572

1452.3 737.5 Stream. 1670

1451.0 738.8 Wilson Creek, Colliers Pit historical marker to north 1549
1450.5 739.3 **Wilson Creek Shelter** 26.6◄20.6◄6.2◄►7.3►13.8►20.8 . . . . (6) 1854
Reliable stream 0.3 mile downhill in front of shelter.
1450.0 739.8 Spring 2000

1448.1 741.7 Blackhorse Gap, dirt road, Blue Ridge Parkway (BRP) mile 97.7 to east 2404

1447.4 742.4 BRP 97.0, Taylors Mountain Overlook 2350

1445.6 744.2 BRP 95.3, Harveys Knob Overlook 2527

1443.9 745.9 Hammond Hollow Trail to west 2327

1443.2 746.6 **Bobblets Gap Shelter** (0.2W) 27.9◄13.5◄7.3◄►6.5►13.5►18.4 . . (6) 2086
If spring to left of shelter dry, look farther downstream.
1442.4 747.4 BRP 92.5, Peaks of Otter Overlook 2341

1441.8 748.0 BRP 91.8, Mills Gap Overlook 2450

1440.1 749.7 Bearwallow Gap, footbridge, stream, VA 43, 0.2E to BRP 90.9 . . . . . . **(pg. 76)** 2228
Buchanan, VA (5.0W)

1438.5 751.3 Cove Mountain 2720
1438.1 751.7 Little Cove Mountain Trail to east 2517

1436.7 753.1 **Cove Mountain Shelter** 20.0◄13.8◄6.5◄►7.0►11.9►17.2. . . . . (6) 1942
1436.5 753.3 View 1970

1435.0 754.8 Buchanan Trail 1790

1433.5 756.3 Cross Jennings Creek on VA 614 bridge . . . . . . 37.5291,-79.6225 P **(pg. 76)** 951
Swimming hole, campsites. **Buchanan, VA** (5.0W)
Bearing of NoBo AT in this area is more south than north.

675.7 VA 42, Sinking Creek, Trail "east" here is compass west.

(1.0W) **Sublett Place** 540.544.3099 Home and cottage for rent, prices seasonal. Ask for hiker rate. ⟨www.thesublettplace.com⟩

(1.0W) **Joe's Trees** 540.544.7303 Limited summer/fall hours (call ahead), 7 days Nov 18-Dec 17, closed Dec 18 thru Apr. Drinks, jerky, cheese, jams. ⟨www.joestrees.com⟩

Newport, VA 24128 (8E)

Store, post office and restaurant near intersection of 42 and 460.

M-F 8:15-11:30 & 12:30-3:15, Sa 9-11, 540.544.7415

Super Val-U 540.544.7702 Su-Th 6-10, F-Sa 6-10:30

702.4 VA 624, Newport Rd

(0.3E) **Four Pines Hostel** Owner Joe Mitchell. Yr-round hostel is a 3-bay garage w/shower; please leave a donation. Laundry: $3 wash/$3 dry. Pet friendly. Shuttles to/from The Homeplace Restaurant (Th-Su) & to Catawba Grocery. Longer shuttles for fee. Mail: 6164 Newport Rd, Catawba VA 24070.

Catawba Grocery 540.384.8050 West 0.3 mile to VA 311 & then left 0.1 mile to store, 7 days, 5:30a-10p. **Grill** serves b'fast, pizza, burgers, ice cream.

708.3 VA 311, ***Catawba, VA 24070*** (1W)

(1.0W) M-F 9-12 & 1-4, Sa 8:30-10:30, 540.384.6011

(1.4W) **Homeplace Restaurant** 540.384.7252 Th-F 4-8, Sa 3-8, Su 11-6, Popular AYCE family-style meals incl. drink and tax; $14 (two meats) $15 (three meats), $8 (kids 3-11).

728.1 US 220, ***Daleville, VA***

729.6 US 11, ***Troutville, VA***

Troutville Trail Days June 2-4, 2017 at Town Park. Free hiker dinner, gear, repair, live music, food, vendors, & 5K race.

Troutville Park & Fire Station Free camping at town park, no pets. Free laundry and showers at fire station.

Super 8 540.992.3000 $59.36 + tax, c. b'fast, pool, accepts major cc, no pets.

Howard Johnson Express 540.992.1234 $49.95 hiker rate, cont. b'fast. Game room and pool. Pets $10. Mail: 437 Roanoke Road, Daleville, VA 24083.

Comfort Inn 540.992.5600 hiker rate $52.99D, $10EAP, c. b'fast, pets $25.

Quality Inn 540.992.5335 $71/up, pets $25.

Holiday Inn Express 540.966.4444 $109-119, no pets. Mail: 3200 Lee Hwy, Troutville, VA 24175.

Red Roof Inn 540.992.5055

Motel 6 540.992.6700 $39.99D $6EAP, pets ok (no fee).

Three Li'l Pigs BBQ 540.966.0165 Open year-round, extended summer hours Monday-Thursday 11am-9:30pm, Friday-Saturday 11am-10:30pm, Sunday 11am-9pm, Hiker friendly, hand-chopped BBQ ribs and wings, large selection of beer, some locally-brewed. Thru-hikers get free banana pudding dessert (w/ meal purchase) Mid April to June 1.

Kroger Grocery Store and Pharmacy 540.992.4920 24hr, pharmacy M-F 8-9, Sa 9-6, Su 12-6.

Outdoor Trails 540.992.5850 Full service outfitter. White gas & denatured alcohol by oz. Computer for internet use, shuttler service. Open M-F 9-8, Sat 9-6 during hiking season (Apr 25-Jul 2); open M-F 10-8, Sat 10-6 the rest of the year. Mail: Botetourt Commons, 28 Kingston Dr, Daleville, VA 24083.

Homer Witcher 540.266.4849 Trail maintainer/2002 thru-hiker.

Flying Mouse Brewery 540.254.0636 Open Th 5-7, F 4-8, Sa 2-8, Su 1-5. Check ⟨www.flyingmousebrewery.com⟩ for beer tasting events. 0.4W to Precast Way, then right 0.1mi.

Roanoke, VA (13E)

A large city with an airport approx 13 miles from the AT.

(5E) **Gander Mountain** 540.362.3658, 8195 Gander Way.

(10E) **Sportsman's Warehouse** 540.366.9700, 3550 Ferncliff Ave NW. Full service outfitter w/full line of gear incl. fuel, frz-dried foods, boots, clothes & trekking poles.

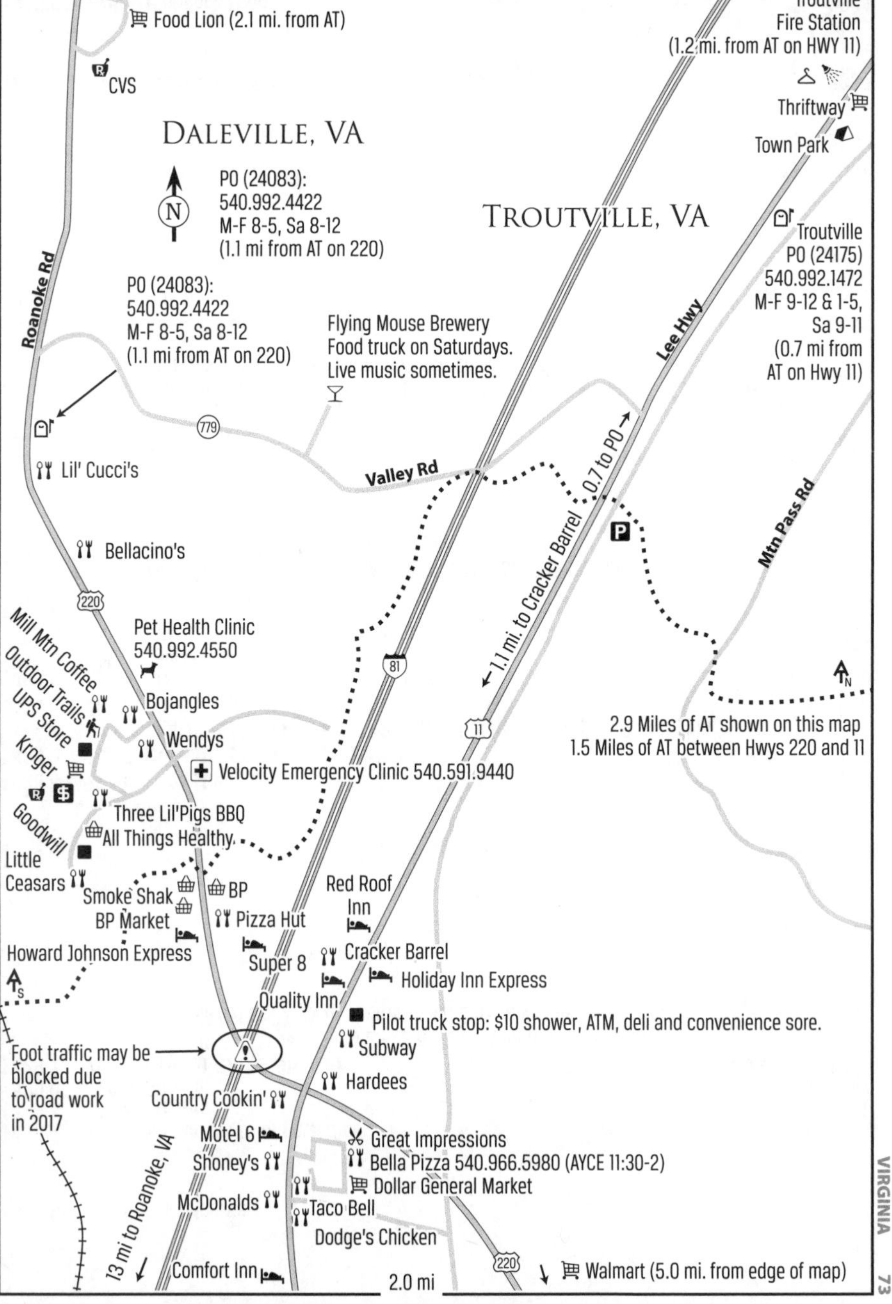
Food Lion (2.1 mi. from AT)
CVS
DALEVILLE, VA
PO (24083):
540.992.4422
M-F 8-5, Sa 8-12
(1.1 mi from AT on 220)
Troutville
Fire Station
(1.2 mi. from AT on HWY 11)
Thriftway
Town Park
TROUTVILLE, VA
Troutville
PO (24175)
540.992.1472
M-F 9-12 & 1-5,
Sa 9-11
(0.7 mi from
AT on Hwy 11)
Roanoke Rd
PO (24083):
540.992.4422
M-F 8-5, Sa 8-12
(1.1 mi from AT on 220)
Flying Mouse Brewery
Food truck on Saturdays.
Live music sometimes.
Lee Hwy
779
0.7 to PO
Valley Rd
Lil' Cucci's
Mtn Pass Rd
1.1 mi. to Cracker Barrel
Bellacino's
220
Pet Health Clinic
540.992.4550
Mill Mtn Coffee
Outdoor Trails
UPS Store
Kroger
Goodwill
Bojangles
Wendys
81
11
Velocity Emergency Clinic 540.591.9440
2.9 Miles of AT shown on this map
1.5 Miles of AT between Hwys 220 and 11
Three Lil'Pigs BBQ
All Things Healthy
Little
Ceasars
Smoke Shak
BP
BP Market
Red Roof
Inn
Pizza Hut
Howard Johnson Express
Super 8
Cracker Barrel
Holiday Inn Express
Quality Inn
Pilot truck stop: $10 shower, ATM, deli and convenience sore.
Foot traffic may be
blocked due
to road work
in 2017
Subway
Hardees
Country Cookin'
Motel 6
Great Impressions
Shoney's
Bella Pizza 540.966.5980 (AYCE 11:30-2)
Dollar General Market
McDonalds
Taco Bell
Dodge's Chicken
13 mi to Roanoke, VA
Comfort Inn
2.0 mi
220
Walmart (5.0 mi. from edge of map)

SOBO	NOBO	Feature		Elev
1431.9	757.9	Fork Mountain		2042
1430.7	759.1	Stream south of powerline		1239
1430.4	759.4	Stream		1271
1430.0	759.8	Stream		1192
1429.7	760.1	**Bryant Ridge Shelter** 20.8◄13.5◄7.0◄►4.9►10.2►22.6 Stream on trail to shelter. Blue-blazed trail 0.1N of shelter leads 0.5E to VA 714.	(20)	1277
1426.6	763.2	Campsite, 0.1W to spring (signed)		2937
1425.4	764.4	Floyd Mountain		3560
1424.8	765.0	**Cornelius Creek Shelter** (0.1E) 18.4◄11.9◄4.9◄►5.3►17.7►21.6 Water on trail to shelter. Privy behind shelter.	(6)	3114
1424.5	765.3	Stream		3027
1423.9	765.9	Black Rock Overlook, view 200' west		3450
1423.6	766.2	Footbridge, stream		3306
1423.3	766.5	Intersection with Cornelius Creek Trail		3224
1422.2	767.6	Apple Orchard Falls Trail 1.1W to 200' waterfall, 0.1E to Sunset Field, USFS 812 (Parkers Gap Rd) 0.1N on AT.		3351
1420.7	769.1	Apple Orchard Mountain, Federal Aviation Admin (FAA) tower, views		4225
1420.4	769.4	The Guillotine		4005
1419.8	770.0	BRP 76.3		3900
1419.5	770.3	**Thunder Hill Shelter** 17.2◄10.2◄5.3◄►12.4►16.3►25.1 Poor water source, tentsites north of shelter	(6)	3917
1418.5	771.3	Hunting Creek Trail, BRP 74.9		3594
1418.1	771.7	0.1E to BRP 74.7 Thunder Ridge Overlook		3501
1416.3	773.5	Harrison Ground Spring		3307
1415.7	774.1	Spring		2908
1414.8	775.0	Petites Gap, gravel road, BRP 71.0 to east		2369
1413.6	776.2	Highcock Knob,		3064

2000 3000 5000

1412.6 777.2 Marble Spring, campsite, spring 100 yards west 2349

1412.1 777.7 Sulphur Spring Trail south crossing 2456

(NoBo) Poor cell reception at US 501, consider calling ahead if you need ride.

1410.3 779.5 Gunter Ridge Trail, Hickory Stand 2650

1409.8 780.0 Sulphur Spring Trail north crossing 2588

1409.0 780.8 Big Cove Branch, stream 1890

1407.1 782.7 **Matts Creek Shelter,** Matts Creek Trail 2.5E to US 501 (6) 848
Ford knee deep Matts Creek to get to shelter 22.6◄17.7◄12.4◄►3.9►12.7►22.2

1406.3 783.5 AT parallels James River from here north for 1.0 mile, no camping 695

1405.1 784.7 James River footbridge, longest foot-use-only bridge on AT 678

1404.9 784.9 US 501, VA 130, **Big Island VA** (5.6E), **Glasgow VA** (5.9W) P (pg. 77) 680

1404.7 785.1 Lower Rocky Row Run Bridge, stream 679

1403.8 786.0 VA 812, USFS 36 (gravel) 37.6048,-79.3883 P 801

1403.4 786.4 Stream. 919

1403.2 786.6 **Johns Hollow Shelter** (6) 1021
21.6◄16.3◄3.9◄►8.8►18.3►23.9 Springs to left and right of shelter.

1401.2 788.6 Little Rocky Row Trail to west, view just north on AT 2416

1400.1 789.7 Big Rocky Row, view 2992

1398.6 791.2 Saddle Gap, Saddle Gap Trail. 2600

1397.5 792.3 Saltlog Gap, Saltlog Gap Trail (0.5W) 2573

1396.0 793.8 Bluff Mountain, Ottie Cline Powell monument, views 3372

1394.9 794.9 Punchbowl Mountain 2850

1394.4 795.4 **Punchbowl Shelter** (0.2W), spring front left of shelter (6) 2487
25.1◄12.7◄8.8◄►9.5►15.1►25.3

1394.0 795.8 BRP 51.7 Punchbowl Mtn Overlook, water north of road. 37.6738,-79.3347 P 2170
SoBo hikers must go right & uphill a few yards to find AT on other side.

1393.7 796.1 VA 607, Robinson Gap Rd (gravel), **Buena Vista, VA** (6.0W) 37.6761,-79.332 P 2100

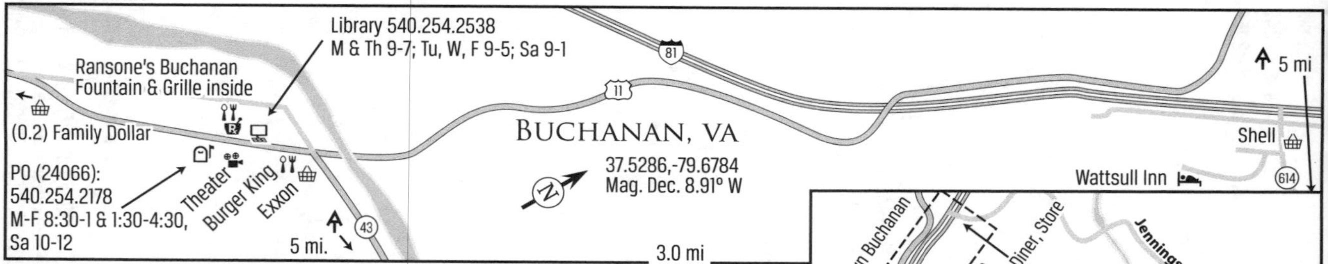

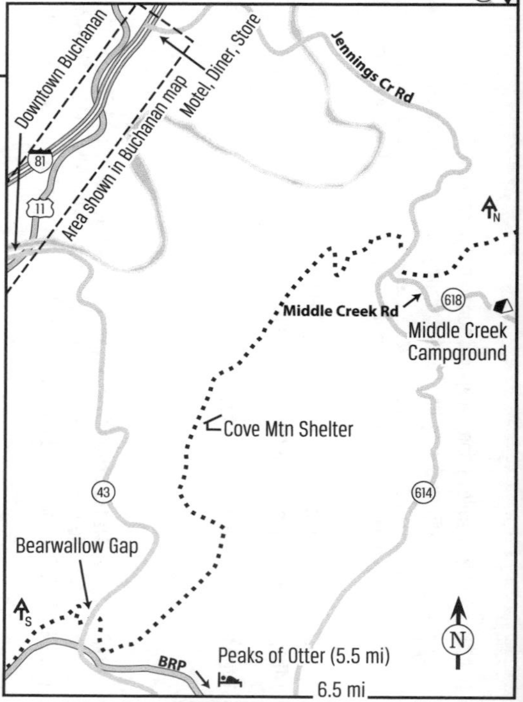

749.7 Bearwallow Gap, VA 43

(5.5E) **Peaks of Otter Lodge & Restaurant** 540.586.1081
Go 0.1E on to the Blue Ridge Parkway (the overpass), then follow Blue Ridge Parkway to the left 5.0 miles. Motel rooms $119 - $199, higher in October. Restaurant open for B/L/D. Sunday buffet brunch 11:30am-3:30pm. Some supplies at camp store. December-March days reduced to Friday-Suday (& lower lodging pricing). Camping managed separately, 540.586.7321, Open May 1 - October 30 2017, $16-19.

Buchanan, VA (5W) *Also see next entry.*

756.3 Jennings Creek (0.3E), VA 614 (Note: "Trail East" here is compass SW (see map). To go to campground, NoBos go right on VA 614, SoBos go left.

(1.2E) **Middle Creek Campground** 540.254.2550
Camping $12PP includes showers & pool; or $5.00 for just shower; Cabins $45/up, AC rec room w/couches, outlets, movies. Grill w/bacon cheeseburgers, milkshakes, nachos, wings & more. Resupply, fuel. Call for free shuttle to & from trailhead, signal strongest near parking area. Night registration available. If you'd rather walk, NoBos go right on 614 for 0.2 miles, then left 1 mile on 618. Guest Mail: 1164 Middle Creek Rd, Buchanan, VA 24066 ⟨www.middlecreekcampground.com⟩

Buchanan, VA (I-81 exit 168) (5W on VA 614)

Wattstull Inn 540.254.1551 Hiker rates starting $60+tax, pets $15. Contnental breakfast. Pool. Ask about shuttles. **Foot of the Mtn Cafe** on-site serving breakfast, lunch & dinner.

784.9 US 501, VA 130

Ken Wallace 434.609.2704 Range: Buchanan- Waynesboro.

Stanimal's Shuttle Service 540.290.4002 covers all of VA

Glasgow, VA 24555 (5.9W)

Town Hall 540.258.2246 Maintains shelter & Knick Field.

Bosses Grill & Lounge 540.258.3076 L/D, Pool table, dart boards

Glasgow Grocery Express 540.258.1818 M-Sa, 6-11:30p; Su, 8-11:30p. Coleman/alcohol/oz, canisters/heet.

Natural Bridge Animal Hospital (10.4W) 540.291.1444 M-F 8-6.

Gary Serra 757.681.2254 Gary has completed the AT twice in sections and is familiar with all trailheads. Pickups at Glasgow & Buena Vista trailheads. Shuttles along AT, to Roanoke, Lynchburg and Charlottesville airports, and to Amtrak station. Will do long-distance shuttles. Sells fuel canisters.

Big Island, VA 24526 (5.6E)

M-F 8:15-12 & 1-4, Sa 8-10, 434.299.5072

H&H Food Market 434.299.5153 7 days 5:30-9, B/L/D served 6:30-8, Mail: 11619 Lee Jackson Hwy, Big Island, VA 24526.

Big Island Family Medical Center 434.299.5951 M-Tu & Th-F 8:30-5. Closed Sa-Su.

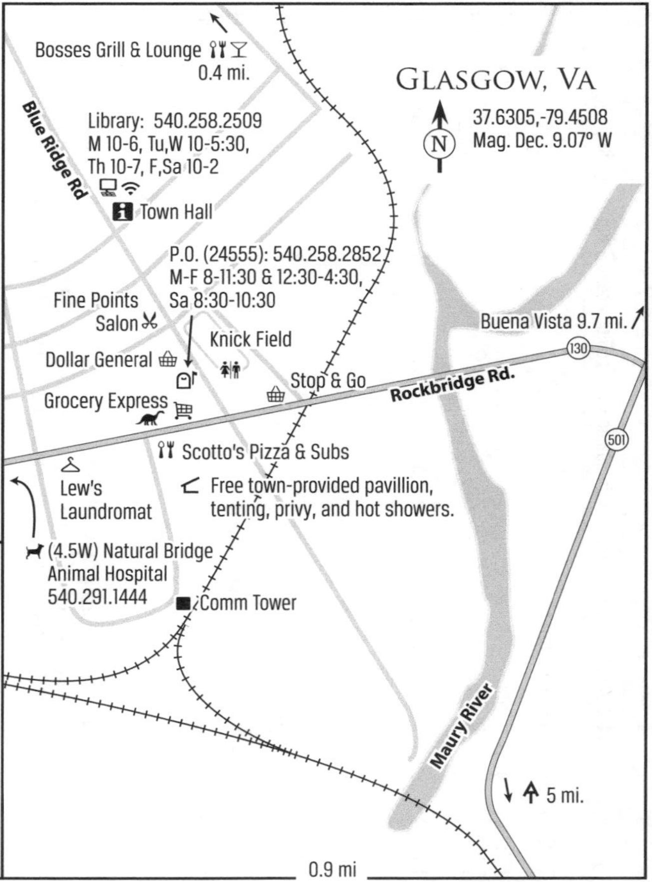

(SoBo) Poor cell reception at US 501, consider calling ahead if you need ride.

1391.8 798.0 Rice Mountain 2166

1391.2 798.6 Spring . . . . . . ♦ 1669

1390.8 799.0 Dirt road 1306

1389.9 799.9 Reservoir Rd (gravel), Pedlar River Bridge. . . . . . . 37.6705,-79.2845 P ♦ ⛺ 952
campsite 0.2S of road.

1388.2 801.6 Spring . . . . . . ♦ 1164

1387.4 802.4 Stream. . . . . . . ♦ 1116

1386.9 802.9 Swapping Camp Rd (gravel) 1286

1386.6 803.2 Stream. . . . . . . ♦ 1344

1384.9 804.9 **Brown Mountain Creek Shelter** . . . . . . ☽ ♦ ⛺ ∠ (6) 1358
22.2◄18.3◄9.5◄►5.6►15.8►22.4 Swimming hole. Camping opposite side of creek. In dry conditions, get water from Brown Mountain Creek south of shelter.

SoBo NoBo 1000 3000 5000

1383.1 806.7 US 60, **Buena Vista, VA** (9.3W) . . . . . . 37.7234,-79.2506 P **(pg. 80)** 2065

1382.2 807.6 USFS 507 (dirt) 2650

1380.3 809.5 Bald Knob, not actually bald 4059

1379.3 810.5 Hotel Trail, **Cow Camp Gap Shelter** (0.6E) . . . . . . ☽ ♦ ∠ (8) 3468
23.9◄15.1◄5.6◄►10.2►16.8►24.4
Water source on blue-blazed trail left of shelter before small stream crossing.

1378.1 811.7 Cole Mountain, views. . . . . . . 📷 4022

1376.8 813.0 Hog Camp Gap, USFS 48 (gravel), grassy meadow,. . . . . . ♦ ⛺ **(pg. 81)** 3503
many campsites. Signed spring just north of road crossing and 0.3 east.

1375.9 813.9 Tar Jacket Ridge, view . . . . . . 📷 3847

1374.6 815.2 Salt Log Gap, USFS 63, two gravel road crossings 3257

1373.4	816.4	USFS 246		3556
1372.9	816.9	Greasy Spring Rd, Lovington Spring Trail to west		3600
1371.0	818.8	Piney River north fork.		3482
1369.8	820.0	Elk Pond Branch		3714
1369.1	820.7	**Seeley-Woodworth Shelter** 25.3◄15.8◄10.2◄►6.6►14.2►20.4 Piped spring 0.1 mile downhill to right.	(8)	3806
1368.9	820.9	Stream.		3717
1368.0	821.8	Rock Spring, west 100 yards to campsite and spring		3517
1366.8	823.0	Spy Rock Rd (formerly Fish Hatchery Rd, unpaved)	**(pg. 81)**	3454
1366.4	823.4	Campsite, Spy Rock 0.1E, rock outcrop requiring scramble, view		3781
1364.2	825.6	Cash Hollow Rd		3280
1363.4	826.4	VA 826 (dirt road not easily passable). 0.5W to upper Crabtree Falls trailhead, parking area & privy. Falls Trail downhill 1.0 to major waterfall and 2.1 mi. to lower parking on VA 56 near **Crabtree Falls Campground.**	**(pg. 81)**	3350
1362.5	827.3	**The Priest Shelter** (0.1E) 22.4◄16.8◄6.6◄►7.6►13.8►29.6	(8)	3885
1362.0	827.8	The Priest, views on AT south of summit		4063
1360.4	829.4	View		2933
1358.9	830.9	Cripple Creek		1863
1357.7	832.1	VA 56, Tye River suspension bridge 37.8384,-79.0231 100 yards north, **Crabtree Falls Campground** (4.0W)	P **(pg. 81)**	970
1356.5	833.3	Roadbed.		1667
1356.0	833.8	Mau-Har Trail to west, rejoins AT to the south at Maupin Field Shelter		2019
1355.1	834.7	Stream.		1734
1354.9	834.9	**Harpers Creek Shelter** 24.4◄14.2◄7.6◄►6.2►22.0►34.7 Harpers Creek in front of shelter. Privy uphill.	(6)	1892

NoBo 5080 1000 3000 5000

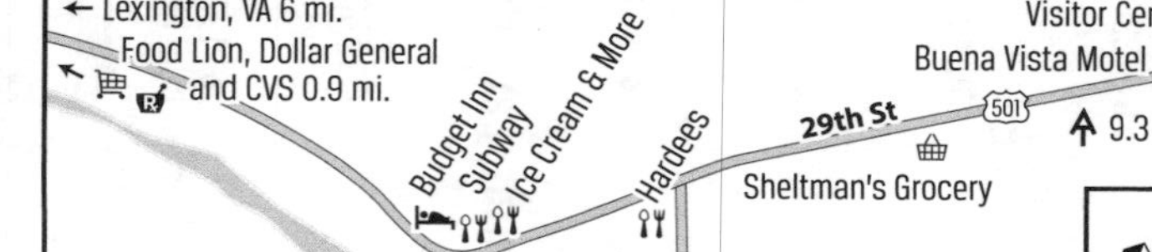

806.7 US 60

 (4.0W) **Three Springs Hostel Bunk & B'fast** Closed for renovations, possibly open Fall 2017 for SoBos. Check website for details. www.threespringshostel.com⟩

Buena Vista, VA 24416 (9.3W)

Glen Maury Park Campground 540.261.7321 AT hiker special $5 tentsite. Sometimes WFS. Free shower, even without stay, South end of town across river. Maury River Fiddlers Convention mid-June.

Buena Vista Motel 540.261.2138 $44-$79 $44-$79 Rooms have fridge & microwave, free local calls.

Budget Inn 540.261.2156 $59.95-$99.95, pets $10 and must use smoking room.

Amish Cupboard 540.264.0215 Deli, ice cream, jerky, tons of candy & dried foods. M-F, 10-7 (deli 10-6); Sa, 10-5:30. ⟨www.theamishcupboard.com⟩

Lewis Grocery 540.261-6826 7 days 9-9, short order grill w/ excellent burgers & salads.

Food Lion 540.261.7672, 7 days 7-10.

Maury Express 800.964.5707 M-F 8-6, Sa 10-4 Area bus makes hourly loop though BV & connects with a Lexington loop bus. 50¢ per board (exact change required).

Ken Hawkins 540.817.9640 Shuttle range Punchbowl Overlook (BRP 51.7) to Reeds Gap.

E's-y Rider Cab Company 540.461.2467, 540.461.1348 Open 24x7. Covers all of VA.

Edgewater Animal Hospital 540.261.4114 M-F 8-6, Sa 8-12

Regional Visitor Center 540.261.8004 Multi-day parking-must checkin during business hrs 9a-5p.

Lexington, VA 24450 (15W of Buena Vista)

Brierley Hill B&B 540.464.8421 relax@brierleyhill.com Open yr-round. Thru-hiker special $75PP for double occupancy room. Incl. b'fast, free laundry facilities & WiFi. Shuttle to/from the AT (Rt. 60) for add'l fee. No Pets. Mail: 985 Borden Rd, Lexington, VA 24450.

502 South Main B&B 540.460.7353 info@502southmain.com. Yr-round "Thru-hiker special" $150/night for up to 3 people. Round trip to AT (Rt. 60) $10PP, free laundry, hearty b'fast. Restaurants & shops nearby. No pets/smoking. CC. Mail: 502 S. Main St, Lexington VA 24450

Walkabout Outfitter (24.3W) 540.464.4453 M-Sa 10-5:30, Su 12-5 Full service outfitter owned by Kirk Miller (Flying Monkey '99). Fuel canisters.

813.0 Hog Camp Gap, USFS 48

Three Springs Hostel (1.5W) See listing at US 60, pg. 80.

823.0 Spy Rock Rd ***Montebello, VA 24464***

2.4W to post office, general store. Go downhill on gravel road 1.1W to parking area on Fish Hatchery Rd. Watch for right turn 0.5 from AT, and watch for blue blazes. Follow F.H. Road (turn right at intersection) 0.9mi. to Crabtree Falls Hwy (VA 56). Go left on VA 56 0.4 miles to post office.

M-F 10-2, Sa 10-1, 540.377.9218

Montebello Camping & General Store 540.377.2650 Store open year-round 8-6 (summer 8-8, winter 9-5) camping & laundry Apr 1 - Oct 31. Thru-hiker rate on tentsite $14(1 person), $21(2), $28(3 or more) sometimes has fuel/oz.

Earl Arnold 540.377.2119 Shuttles James River to Rockfish Gap. earlarnold@aol.com.

826.4 VA 826 (3.7 miles to Crabtree Falls Campground: 0.5W on 826 to Meadows parking area, 1.0 on blue-blaze trail to top of falls, 1.7 to bottom of falls, and 0.5 right on US 56.)

832.1 VA 56, Tye River (4W to Crabtree Falls Campground)

Crabtree Falls Campground 540.377.2066 ⟨www.crabtreefallscampground.com⟩ Cabins $50 four people, camping $26/site(2 tents). Laundry, free shower even w/o stay. Trail foods and snacks, ice cream, sodas. stove fuel. Mail (shoebox size or smaller): 11039 Crabtree Falls Hwy, Tyro, VA 22976.

841.1 Maupin Field Shelter

Royal Oaks Cabins 540.943.7625 (1.7W) Cabin (hiker rate) $50D M-Th, $70D F-Su, $15EAP, up to 4. Tenting $20 up to two. Cabin & tenting both include WiFi, shower w/towel. From Maupin Field Shelter, follow Jeep Rd behind shelter west 1.2mi to the Blue Ridge Pkwy (first paved road). Turn left on BRP for 0.5mi to Love Rd (814). Turn right for 100 yds to Royal Oaks. Call for shuttle from Reeds Gap. Country Store open yr-round M-Sa, 10-6; Su, 12-6; (snacks, sodas, canned food) & deli on-site. royaloaksresort@gmail.com

842.8 Reeds Gap, Rte 664 - 5.0E to pub, 2.8W (S on BRP) to Royal Oaks (listed previously)

Devils Backbone Brewpub 434.361.1001 On Rte. 664 at intersection w/Patrick Henry Hwy (151). 7 Days 7a-9p, till 10p F-Su. Serves B/L/D. Hikers welcome to camp on-site for free. Pickup rarely avail, but morning return ride often provided ⟨www.dbbrewingcompany.com⟩

DISPOSE OF WASTE PROPERLY ⟨www.appalachiantrail.org/LNT⟩

- Pack it in; pack it out. Leave any donated items at hiker boxes in town rather than at campsites or shelters.
- Walk at least 100 feet (40 steps) away from shelters, water sources & campsites to dispose of urine, toothpaste, cooking water & strained dishwater, & to wash bodies, dishes or clothing. Minimize use of soap.
- Use the privy only for human waste and toilet paper. Pack out disposable wipes and hygiene products.
- If there is no privy, walk at least 200 feet (80 steps) away from campsites, shelters, trails and water sources to bury feces in a hole 6 to 8 inches deep. Bury or carry out toilet paper.

NOBO	SOBO	Feature	Elev
1353.4	836.4	View	2778
1353.0	836.8	Chimney Rock, view	3164
1351.6	838.2	Three Ridges Mountain	3959
1350.8	839.0	Hanging Rock Overlook, view	3499
1348.7	841.1	**Maupin Field Shelter** (6) (pg. 81) 20.4◄13.8◄6.2◄►15.8►28.5►41.5 Piped spring behind shelter. Privy to right of shelter on unmarked path. Mau-Har Trail northern intersection. Jeep road leads 1.4mi. to BRP.	2746
1347.0	842.8	Reeds Gap, VA 664, BRP 13.6 in view to west 37.9016,-78.9853 (pg. 81)	2650
1346.5	843.3	Three Ridges Overlook, BRP 13.1 .37.907,-78.9795	2700

Staying in or within 100 yards of any single AT shelter south of Waynesboro is limited to 3 nights in a 30-day period. This also applies to Davis Farm and Davis Path Campsites.

NOBO	SOBO	Feature	Elev
1344.3	845.5	Stream	2607
1343.5	846.3	Rock Point Overlook, view to west	2791
1342.7	847.1	Cedar Cliffs, view	2800
1342.2	847.6	Dripping Rock, BRP 9.6, spring .37.9411,-78.9369	2950
1341.9	847.9	Laurel Springs Gap, spring	2849
1341.0	848.8	Side trail 0.3W to Humpback picnic area	3215
1340.2	849.6	Campsite, view	3529
1339.4	850.4	Humpback Mountain	3628
1338.4	851.4	Trail 0.2W to view at The Rocks	3263
1336.7	853.1	Spring	2520
1335.7	854.1	Spring	2335
1335.6	854.2	Side trail 0.2W to Humpback Gap, BRP 6.0	2328
1334.7	855.1	Glass Hollow Overlook, view to east	2250
1334.3	855.5	Side trail 1.3W to Humpback Visitor Center 37.9692,-78.8974	2290
1334.2	855.6	Albright Loop Trail to west	2225

SOBO NOBO 1000 3000 5000

1332.9 856.9 **Paul C. Wolfe Shelter** 29.6◂22.0◂15.8◂▸12.7▸25.7▸38.9 . . . . . (10) 1574
Mill Creek 50 yards in front of shelter. Waterfall with pool 100 yards.

1332.1 857.7 Small cemetery 1860

1331.4 858.4 Cabin ruins, chimney 2068

1331.1 858.7 Spring 2048

1329.8 860.0 Stream 1873

1328.9 860.9 Stream 1735

1327.9 861.9 US 250 + Blue Ridge Pkwy . . . . . 38.0311,-78.8591 **(pg. 86)** 1917
Rockfish Gap, **Waynesboro, VA** (3.7W), I-64 overpass, south end of Skyline Dr.

1326.9 862.9 Shenandoah National Park (SNP) . . . . . **(pg. 88)** 2221
Entrance station and self-registration for overnight permits.

1324.2 865.6 Skyline 102.1, McCormick Gap 2450

1322.9 866.9 Bears Den Mountain, communication towers, tractor seats 2885

1322.4 867.4 Skyline 99.5, Beagle Gap 38.0729,-78.7935 2550

1321.6 868.2 Little Calf Mountain 2917

1320.9 868.9 Calf Mountain 2989

1320.2 869.6 **Calf Mountain Shelter** (0.3W) . . . . . (0.2W) (6) 2668
34.7◂28.5◂12.7◂▸13.0▸26.2▸34.4 Spring on way to shelter. Bear pole.

1319.7 870.1 Powerline 2293

1319.6 870.2 Spring 2285

1319.2 870.6 Gravel road 0.1W to Skyline 96.9, Jarman Gap 2248

1319.0 870.8 Spring, just south of woods road 2143

1317.4 872.4 Skyline 95.3, Sawmill Run Overlook 2200

1316.0 873.8 Turk Mountain Trail to west. 2657

1315.8 874.0 Skyline 94.1, Turk Gap. 38.129,-78.7849 2600

1313.8 876.0 Skyline 92.4 3009

1313.5 876.3 Wildcat Ridge Trail east to Skyline 92.1 . . . . . 38.1484,-78.7746 P 2914

> ✿ Turks Cap Lily - Petals of this down-facing large flower curl back to form a bun shape (Turk's cap). Common color is flame orange and yellow, speckled with brown dots.

1310.8 879.0 Skyline 90.0, spur trail to east leads to Riprap parking area. . . . . . P 2752

1310.4 879.4 Riprap Trail branches to west 2980

1309.7 880.1 Skyline 88.9. 2615

1307.9 881.9 Skyline 87.4, Black Rock Gap, Paine Run Trail. . . . . . 38.2066,-78.7496 P 2321

1307.7 882.1 Skyline 87.2 2379

1307.2 882.6 **Blackrock Hut** (0.2E) 41.5◄25.7◄13.0◄►13.2►21.4►33.8 . . . ☽ 💧 ⛺ ∠ (6) 2743

1306.8 883.0 Trayfoot Mountain Trail to west 3076

1306.7 883.1 Blackrock, views from summit, which is skirted by the AT . . . . . 📷 3092

1306.1 883.7 Blackrock parking area. . . . . . 38.2222,-78.7332 P 2923

1305.6 884.2 Skyline 84.3. 2800

1305.5 884.3 Jones Run parking . . . . . 38.2301,-78.7263 P 2790

1304.9 884.9 Two trails west to Dundo Campground (primitive, reserved for group use) 2753

1304.2 885.6 Skyline 82.9, Browns Gap . . . . . 38.2404,-78.7109 P 2576

1303.6 886.2 Big Run Loop Trail to west 2829

1303.3 886.5 Skyline 82.2. 2795

1302.8 887.0 West to Doyles River Parking Overlook, Skyline 81.9 . . . 38.2468,-78.6948 P 📷 2854

1302.0 887.8 Doyles River Traill, west to Skyline 81.1, ... 38.2542,-78.683 P 💧 2860
east to Doyles River Cabin (locked), 0.3E to spring, 1.2E to falls

1301.2 888.6 Trail to Loft Mtn amphitheater 3171

1301.1 888.7 Trail to **Loft Mtn Campground** (go here if camping). . . . . . 💧 ⛺ (pg. 89) 3259

1300.5 889.3 Trail to **Loft Mtn Campground** . . . . . 💧 ⛺ (pg. 89) 3289

1300.1 889.7 Powerline 3238

1299.9 889.9 Trail to **Loft Mtn Store** (in view to west). . . . . . (pg. 89) 3159

1298.7 891.1 Frazier Discovery Trail 0.3W to **Loft Mtn Wayside** 3291

1298.6 891.2 Frazier Discovery Trail to west 3299

1297.7 892.1 Trail to 0.5W to **Loft Mtn Wayside** (flatter than FDT), Ivy Creek spring 0.1W . . 💧 2974

1297.1 892.7 Cross Ivy Creek . . . . . 💧 2560

1296.4 893.4 View to west . . . . . 📷 2949

1295.6 894.2 West to Skyline 77.5, Ivy Creek Overlook . . . . . P 📷 2876

1294.0 895.8 **Pinefield Hut** (0.1E), Skyline Dr (0.1W). . . . . . ☽ 💧 ⛺ ∠ (6) 2474
38.9◄26.2◄13.2◄►8.2►20.6►32.1 Spring on trail to shelter and 50 yards behind. Both unreliable. Campsites uphill, beyond shelter.

SoBo	NoBo	Location		Elev
1293.8	896.0	Skyline 75.2, Pinefield Gap	38.2902,-78.6419 P	2590
1293.0	896.8	Weaver Mountain		2876
1291.9	897.9	Skyline 73.2, Simmons Gap Simmons Gap ranger station on paved road 0.2E from where AT crosses Skyline. Water avail. at pump outside buildings.	💧	2250
1289.1	900.7	View east to Powell Gap Hollow	📷	2587
1288.6	901.2	Skyline 69.9, Powell Gap		2294
1287.0	902.8	Skyline 68.6, Smith Roach Gap		2600
1285.8	904.0	**Hightop Hut** (0.1W), reliable spring 0.1 from shelter 34.4◄21.4◄8.2◄►12.4►23.9►34.8	💧 (8) (6)	3183
1285.3	904.5	Spring east of AT	💧	3521
1285.1	904.7	View to west from flank of Hightop Mtn	📷	3514
1283.7	906.1	Skyline 66.7	38.3449,-78.5531 P	2650
1282.7	907.1	Stream.	💧	2507
1282.4	907.4	Skyline 65.5, Swift Run Gap, **Elkton, VA** (6.4W) Bridge over US 33, access road north of bridge 0.1W to phone, water (treat), SNP self-registration	💧 📞 **(pg. 89)**	2367
1280.8	909.0	Saddleback Mtn Trail to east		3022
1279.8	910.0	Trail 0.3E to spring, no camping	💧	2956
1279.3	910.5	South River Picnic Area 0.1W. Falls Trail to east.	38.3817,-78.5192 P (0.1W) 🚻 💧	2893
1278.9	910.9	South River Fire Road		2881
1277.3	912.5	Baldface Mountain		3624
1276.1	913.7	Spring, Pocosin Cabin (locked), Parking on Skyline.	38.4136,-78.4897 P 💧	3150
1276.0	913.8	Trail west to parking on Skyline	P 💧	3158
1274.2	915.6	West to **Lewis Mtn Campground & Cabins**	💧 (pg. 89)	3443
1274.1	915.7	West to **Lewis Mtn Campground**	38.4372,-78.479 P 💧 (pg. 89)	3393

861.9 Rockfish Gap

Afton Mountain Visitor Center 540.943.5187 Open most days 9-5. Info on town services & trail angels. Many lodging facilities offer free pickup/return from here. Long-term parking okay; leave contact info & return date.

Inn at Afton 540.942.5201 Hiker rate $40+tax, pets allowed. Some restaurants deliver here.

(0.5W on 250) **Colony House Motel** 540.942.4156 $42-70+tax, pets $10, some snacks sold on-site, rooms have micro & fridge. Ask about tenting on-site. Mail: 494 Three Notched Mtn Hwy, Waynesboro, VA 22980.

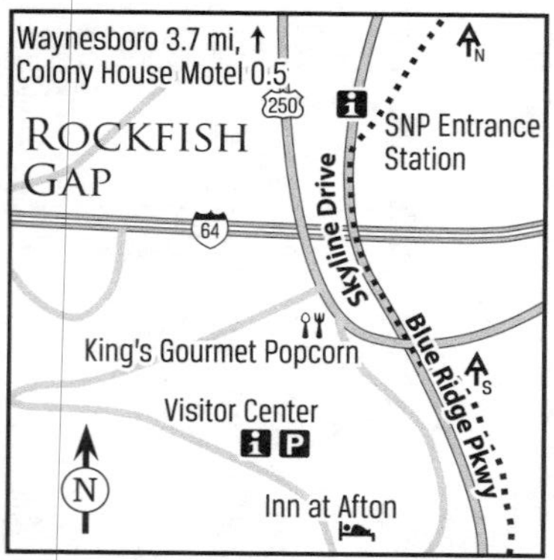

Waynesboro 3.7 mi, ↑
Colony House Motel 0.5
250
ROCKFISH GAP
64
Skyline Drive
SNP Entrance Station
King's Gourmet Popcorn
Blue Ridge Pkwy
Visitor Center
Inn at Afton
N
S

King's Gourmet Popcorn 7 days, 10a-7p. Clsd Christmas & Thanksgiving. Hot dogs, sodas, coffee, pork rinds, kettle corn, & gourmet popcorn. CC OK.

Waynesboro, VA 22980 (4.5W on I-64)

Hiker Fest On June 10, gather at Heritage on Main at 11a for food and a movie. Camping area has pavillion, grill and solar charger; shower at nearby YMCA.

YMCA 540.942.5107 Free camping & showers. Use of YMCA facilities $10. Check-in at front desk, need photo ID.

Stanimal's 328 Hostel (4.5W) 540.290.4002 AdamStanley06@gmail.com $30 hiker-only hostel incl. P/U & return to trail, mattress w/clean linens, shower w/towel, soap, laundry. Large private area including sunroom & finished basement, laptop, WiFi & DVDs. Fridge, freezer & m'wave. Snacks, drinks, & ice cream for sale. Discounted slackpacking for multinight guests. Located in residential area but only 2 blocks from grocery & restaurants. Please respect noise level. Hikers are required to call ahead & speak w/owner prior to staying. Owned by Adam Stanley AT '04, PCT '10.

Grace Hiker Hostel Supervised Lutheran Church hostel open May 22-Jun 17, clsd Su nights. 2-Night limit! Please do not call the church office. Check-in 5-8p, check-out 9a; hikers staying over may leave packs. Cots in air-conditioned Fellowship Hall, showers, internet, big-screen TV & DVD, hiker lounge w/kitchenette, snacks & b'fast foods. 20 hiker max. No pets, smoking, drugs, alcohol, firearms or foul language. Donations gratefully accepted. Congregation cooks free dinner Thu nights followed by optional vespers service.

Tree Streets Inn 540.949.4484, $85S/D, incl. b'fast, pool, snacks, no pets. Free pickup/return from Rockfish Gap w/stay. Maildrops (preregistered guests only): 421 Walnut Ave, Waynesboro, VA 22980.

Belle Hearth B&B 540.943.1910 $105D, (seasonal higher). Includes breakfast, pool, pickup and return. No smoking, no alcohol, no pets. Maildrop (guests only): 320 S. Wayne Ave, Waynesboro, VA 22980 ⟨www.bellehearth.com⟩

Quality Inn 540.942.1171 Hiker rates $65.99S $70.99D + tax, $10EAP (max 2), pets $10. Incl. c. b'fast.

Heritage on Main 540.946.6166 Hiker-friendly sports bar, beer, burgers, salads. M-Th 11am-12am, F,Sa 11-1am. Live music W&Sa, trivia Th.

Weasie's Kitchen 5:30a-8p M-F; 5-2 weekends.

Ming Garden

Rockfish Gap Outfitters 540.943.1461 M-Sa 10a-6p; Su 12p-5p; Full service outfitter, Coleman/alcohol/oz, other fuels, shuttle info. Frz-dried foods. Located between town & trail; ask your ride to stop on the way. No aqua blaze.

DuBose Egleston 540.487.6388 "Yellow Truck" shuttles Roanoke to Harpers Ferry (fee).

Ace Hardware 540.949.8229 Canister & Coleman fuel. Alcohol/oz.

Front Royal Outdoors 540.635.5440 Offers aquablaze options ranging from Port Republic to Snickers Gap; make arrangements from Waynesboro. Will store gear while you're on the river. Avail. Mar 15-Jun 30 (thru Oct 31 for SoBos). Please learn the rules for camping on the river.

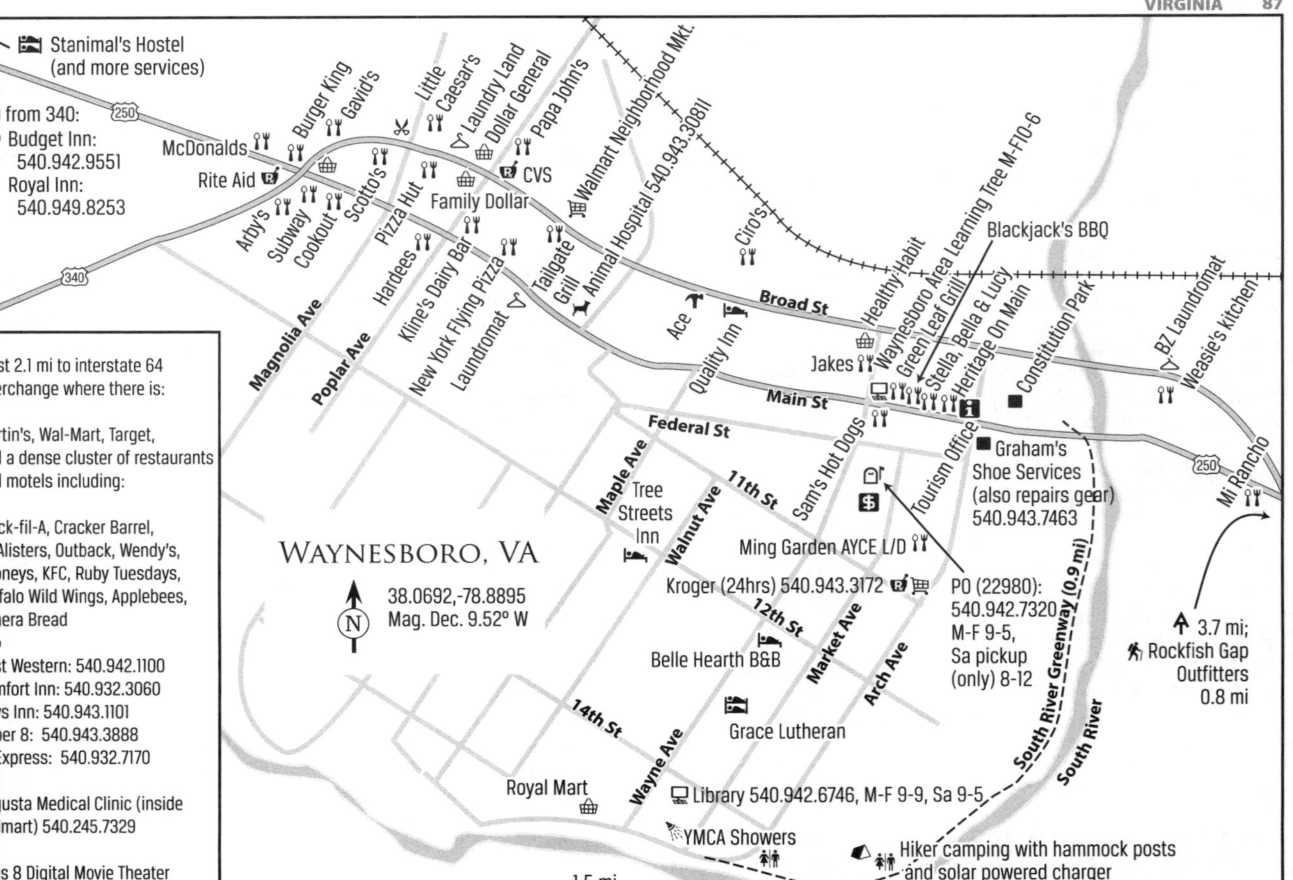
Stanimal's Hostel (and more services)
0.9 from 340:
Budget Inn: 540.942.9551
Royal Inn: 540.949.8253
250
340
McDonalds
Rite Aid
Burger King
Gavid's
Arby's
Subway
Cookout
Scotto's
Pizza Hut
Little Caesar's
Laundry Land
Dollar General
Papa John's
CVS
Family Dollar
Hardees
Kline's Dairy Bar
New York Flying Pizza
Laundromat
Tailgate Grill
Animal Hospital 540.943.3081
Walmart Neighborhood Mkt.
Ace
Quality Inn
Ciro's
Broad St
Main St
Healthy Habit
Jakes
Waynesboro Area Learning Tree M-F10-6
Green Leaf Grill
Stella, Bella & Lucy
Heritage On Main
Blackjack's BBQ
Constitution Park
BZ Laundromat
Weasie's kitchen
Mi Rancho
Magnolia Ave
Poplar Ave
Federal St
Maple Ave
Tree Streets Inn
Walnut Ave
11th St
Sam's Hot Dogs
Tourism Office
Graham's Shoe Services (also repairs gear) 540.943.7463
Ming Garden AYCE L/D
Kroger (24hrs) 540.943.3172
PO (22980): 540.942.7320 M-F 9-5, Sa pickup (only) 8-12
12th St
Market Ave
Arch Ave
Belle Hearth B&B
Grace Lutheran
14th St
Wayne Ave
Royal Mart
Library 540.942.6746, M-F 9-9, Sa 9-5
YMCA Showers
Hiker camping with hammock posts and solar powered charger
South River Greenway (0.9 mi)
South River
3.7 mi; Rockfish Gap Outfitters 0.8 mi
WAYNESBORO, VA
N
38.0692,-78.8895
Mag. Dec. 9.52° W
1.5 mi
West 2.1 mi to interstate 64 interchange where there is:
Martin's, Wal-Mart, Target, and a dense cluster of restaurants and motels including:
Chick-fil-A, Cracker Barrel, McAlisters, Outback, Wendy's, Shoneys, KFC, Ruby Tuesdays, Buffalo Wild Wings, Applebees, Panera Bread
Best Western: 540.942.1100
Comfort Inn: 540.932.3060
Days Inn: 540.943.1101
Super 8: 540.943.3888
HI Express: 540.932.7170
Augusta Medical Clinic (inside Walmart) 540.245.7329
Zeus 8 Digital Movie Theater

Shenandoah National Park (SNP)

540.999.3500 | www.nps.gov/shen | Emegency line: 800.732.0911

Backcountry Permits are required for overnight hikes within the park. There is a $10 per hiker fee for the Park entry permit and a fine for not having one. Permits are available from self-registration sites at the south and north entrance of the AT into SNP, from any park visitor center, or by mail (see contact information above).

Concrete 4"x4" signposts are used to mark intersections. Information is stamped into an aluminum band at the top of the post.

What is known as a "shelter" on most of the AT is called a "hut" in Shenandoah, and three-sided day-use-only structures are called "shelters." When overnighting in the park, please use the huts or designated campsites, which are usually near the huts.

Backcountry stay is limited to 14 consecutive nights; two at any one location. If you cannot tent in a designated campsite, follow LNT principles of dispersed camping. Tenting at a new location is limited to one night and must be:

- 20 yards from the trail (preferably out of view).
- One quarter mile from any park facility (roads, campgrounds, lodges, visitor centers, and picnic areas).
- 10 yards from any water source.
- 50 yards from other camping parties, building ruins, or "no camping" signs.
- Not within designated "no camping" locations.

Groups are limited to 10. Campfires are only permitted at pre-constructed fire rings at the huts. Pets must be leashed.

Lodges and campgrounds are typically full on weekends. A small number of unreserved walk-in tentsites are avail. on a first-come, first-served basis at all campgrounds except Lewis Mtn.

Delaware North Companies Parks & Resorts 877.247.9261 ⟨www.GoShenandoah.com⟩ operates the Skyland Resort, Big Meadows Lodge and Lewis Mountain Cabins, gift shops & camp stores and restaurants within Shenandoah National Park; many readily accessible from the trail.

The Park Service operates campgrounds. Call 877.444.6777 or visit ⟨www.recreation.gov⟩ to reserve campsites. All campsites accommodate 2 tents and up to 6 persons. All except Mathews Arm have coin operated laundry and showers. Many facilities are closed November-May and all are closed December-March.

Yellow Cab of the Shenandoah 540.692.9200 serves all of SNP (24/7). Pet friendly, accepts CC.

If You Plan to be a 2000-Miler

The ATC recognizes hikers who have completed the trail, all at once or in sections, with a "2000-miler" certificate. Your name will be printed in the Spring issue of ATC's member magazine, *AT Journeys*, and listed on ATC's website. The honor system application states that conditional bypasses and reroutes are acceptable and that "Issues of sequence, direction, length of time or whether one carries a pack are not considered." The number "2,000" is used out of tradition, and does not imply that hiking less than the full mileage qualifies. Feel free to set your own agenda on the AT, but if 2000-miler recognition is important to you keep in mind that the application will ask if you "have made an honest effort to walk the entire Trail."

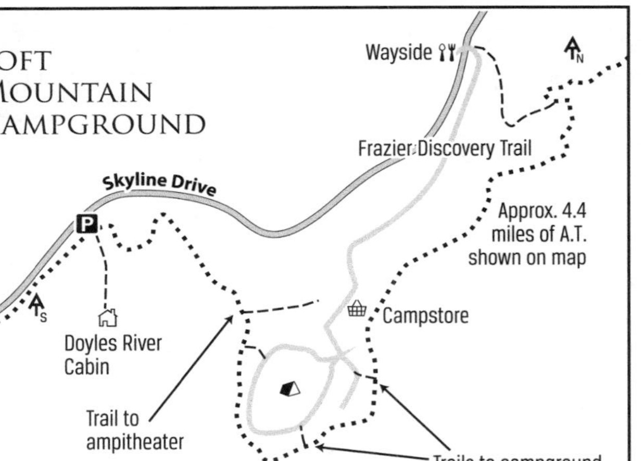

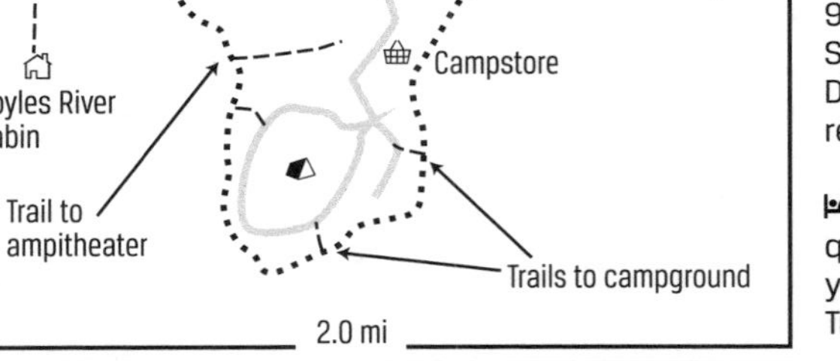

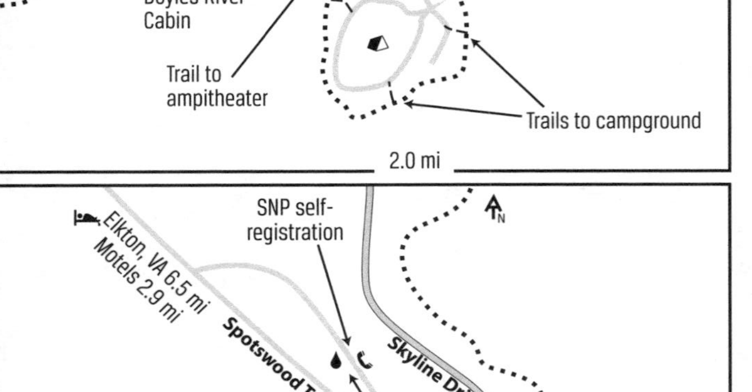

888.7, 889.3 Loft Mountain Campground

889.9 Loft Mountain Wayside

Loft Mountain Campground Campsites $15. AT skirts the campground, & several short side trails lead to campsites & the camp store. Showers, laundry & long term resupply available from camp store. Open early-May to late-Oct.

Loft Mountain Wayside 1.1 miles from camp store, serves B/L/D, short-order menu. Open early-Apr - mid-Nov, daily 9-7.

907.4 US 33, Swift Run Gap. US 33 is also known as Spotswood Trail. The AT crosses over US 33 on the Skyline Drive. North of the bridge, take access road to the west to reach US 33.

(2.9W):

Country View Motel 540.298.0025 Room with 1 queen bed $75, two queen beds $91. No charge for laundry, but you must have detergent. Mail for guests: 19974 Spotswood Trail, Elkton, VA 22827.

(3.2W):

Swift Run Camping 540.298.8086, $20 campsite, laundry, pool, and snack bar, open year-round.

Bear Mountain Grocery 540.298.9826, M-F 5am-8pm, Sa 6–8, Su 8-7.

(6.5W): ***Elkton, VA 22827***

M-F 8:30-4:30, Sa 9-11, 540.298.7772

Food Lion

Pizza Hut, several fast-food restaurants

Rite Aid

915.6, 915.7 Lewis Mountain Campground

Lewis Mountain Campground & Cabins 540.999.2255, 877.247.9261 Campsites $17, small bunkhouse, cabin rates seasonal. Open Mar31 - Nov 5. Camp store open same dates, Su-Th 9-6, F-Sa 9-7. Reservations 877.247.9261.

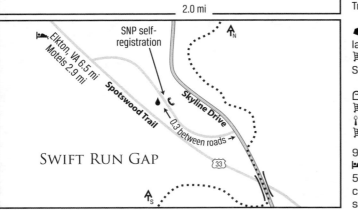

1273.4	916.4	**Bearfence Mountain Hut** (0.2E; 0.1 on gravel rd, 0.1 on side trail) 33.8◄20.6◄12.4◄►11.5►22.4►26.8	P (6) (6)	3198
1272.7	917.1	Bearfence Mountain Loop Trail, two intersections 0.2 mile apart, views 0.1E		3548
1272.2	917.6	Skyline 56.4, Bearfence Mtn Trail, parking 0.1W	38.4524,-78.4669 P	3390
1270.8	919.0	Skyline 55.1, Bootens Gap	38.4675,-78.4573 P	3243
1270.3	919.5	Laurel Prong Trail to east		3536
1269.9	919.9	Hazeltop		3812
1268.0	921.8	Skyline 52.8, Milam Gap, parking to east	38.4988,-78.4457 P	3300
1267.4	922.4	Spring, No camping in Big Meadows clearing within sight of Skyline Dr		3270
1266.9	922.9	Tanners Ridge Rd (gravel), cemetery		3318
1266.3	923.5	Lewis Spring & Road, Lewis Falls 0.5W Gravel road 0.2E to Skyline, then left 0.2 to **Big Meadows Wayside**	38.4524,-78.4669 P (pg. 92)	3330
1265.8	924.0	Rock outcropping, view		3637
1265.4	924.4	Trail to **Big Meadows Lodge,** Lewis Falls 0.5W	(pg. 92)	3558
1265.0	924.8	Trail east to **Big Meadows Campground**	(pg. 92)	3546
1264.8	925.0	David Spring 20 yards west		3490
1264.6	925.2	Stream		3369
1263.8	926.0	Fishers Gap, Skyline 49.3 to east, maintenance road		3050
1263.6	926.2	Franklin Cliffs, view		3035
1262.5	927.3	Trail to Spitler Knoll parking, 4 cars	38.5482,-78.4138 P	3250
1261.9	927.9	**Rock Spring Hut** (0.2W) 32.1◄23.9◄11.5◄►10.9►15.3►28.4 Locked cabin in front.	(9) (8)	3509
1261.6	928.2	Trail east to Hawksbill Mountain, no camping anywhere above 3600′		3619
1260.6	929.2	Hawksbill Gap, parking to east	38.5629,-78.3825 P	3361
1260.1	929.7	Stream, trail to Crescent Rock Overlook, parking to east	P	3429
1259.3	930.5	Spring		3323
1258.4	931.4	Spring		3436
1258.1	931.7	Skyland stables, service road	38.5867,-78.3834 P	3550
1257.5	932.3	Trail to **Skyland Resort & Restaurant** (0.1W)	P (pg. 92)	3760
1257.4	932.4	Skyland service road north	38.5926,-78.376 P	3699
1256.9	932.9	Trail to Stony Man Summit (0.2W) Highest point on the AT in SNP		3837
1256.3	933.5	Little Stony Man Cliffs, overlook to west		3582
1256.1	933.7	Passamaquoddy Trail		3428
1255.8	934.0	Spur trail to parking	38.6059,-78.3664 P	3254
1255.4	934.4	Stony Man Overlook	38.6123,-78.3625 P	3093
1255.0	934.8	Nicholson Hollow Trail		3109
1254.8	935.0	Crusher Ridge Trail		3173
1254.2	935.6	Corbin Cabin Trail		3122

NOBO	SOBO	Feature		Elev
1253.8	936.0	Powerline		3304
1253.1	936.7	Pinnacles Picnic Area & Parking, restrooms, water from faucet		3410
1252.9	936.9	East to Skyline 36.4, side trail to Jewell Hollow Overlook		3359
1252.6	937.2	Leading Ridge Trail to west.		3379
1252.0	937.8	The Pinnacle		3730
1251.0	938.8	**Byrds Nest #3 Hut,** spring 0.4E on service road 34.8◄22.4◄10.9◄►4.4►17.5►28.0	(8)	3266
1250.6	939.2	View		3343
1250.3	939.5	Meadows Spring Trail to east	(0.3E)	3354
1249.7	940.1	Overlook, Mary's Rock to west		3423
1248.8	941.0	Spring		2853
1248.0	941.8	Trail to Panorama RR parking, powerline	38.6605,-78.3221	2340
1247.8	942.0	US 211, Thornton Gap, **Luray, VA** (9W)	**(pg. 92)**	2239
1247.7	942.1	Skyline 31.2		2327
1246.6	943.2	**Pass Mountain Hut** (1939) (0.2E) 26.8◄15.3◄4.4◄►13.1►23.6►31.7 2 bear poles, 2 privies, and 8 tent sites. Piped spring 15 yards behind shelter.	(8)	2789
1245.8	944.0	Pass Mountain		3052
1244.7	945.1	Beahms Gap Overlook, parking to east		2490
1244.3	945.5	Spring to west		2436
1243.4	946.4	Neighbor Mtn Trail, Byrds Nest #4 day use picnic area.	(0.5E)	2675
1239.7	950.1	Stream, Jeremys Run Trail		2238
1239.2	950.6	**Elkwallow Wayside** (and Gap) 0.1E on side trail or on Skyline 23.9 Grill B/L/D, limited groceries, vending outside, 9-7 Early April-Early Oct. Frost-free pump at picnic area south of wayside.		2480
1238.5	951.3	Range View Cabin (locked) 0.1E	(0.1E)	2969
1237.7	952.1	Skyline 21.9, Rattlesnake Point Overlook		3083
1237.1	952.7	Tuscarora Trail to **Mathews Arm Campground** (0.7W) Primitive campground open May-Oct; no services. Tent sites $14.		3400
1236.7	953.1	Skyline 21.1, Hogback parking		3350
1236.4	953.4	Skyline 20.8, Hogback Overlook		3350
1235.2	954.6	Skyline 19.7, Little Hogback parking 50 yards east		3019
1235.1	954.7	Little Hogback Mountain, view		3050
1234.5	955.3	Skyline 18.8		2795

923.5 Lewis Spring Rd (See map for easiest access)

924.4 Big Meadows Lodge

Big Meadows Lodge Open mid-May thru mid-Nov. Lodge rooms, cabins & suites, reservations required. Some pet-friendly rooms. B:7:30-10a, L:12-2p, D:5:30-9p. **Tap Room** M-F 4-11p; Sa-Su 2-11p.

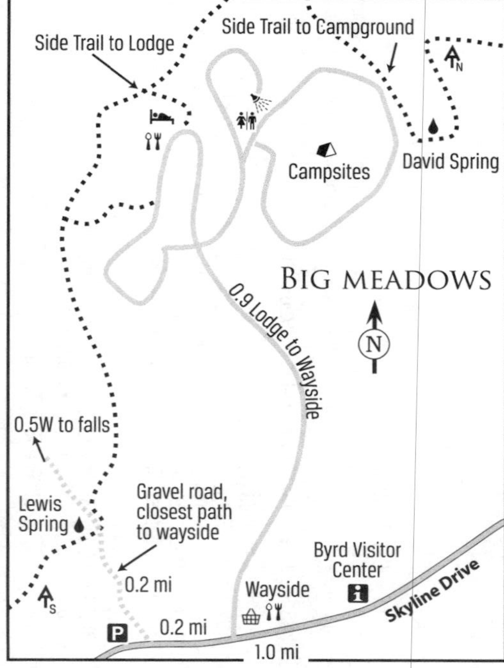

Big Meadows Wayside B/L/D, Fuel/oz at gas station. Open mid-Mar to mid-Nov check dates.

924.8 Big Meadows Campground 540.999.3231

$20/tent site, 6 persons/site, self-register after hrs. Coin laundry & showers. Open mid-Mar thru mid-Nov. Check dates.

932.3 Side trail to Skyland

Skyland Resort & Restaurant 540.999.2212 End of Mar - Dec 1. Check dates. Rates seasonal, reservations required. Dining room hours B: 7:30-10:30, L: 12-2:30, D: 5:30-9, nightly entertainment. **Tap Room** 2-10:30. Snack foods & sodas sold at gift shop & vending machines.

942.0 US 211, Thornton Gap

(4.5W on US 211) to **Brookside Cabins & Restaurant** 540.743.5698 ⟨www.brooksidecabins.com⟩ $85-$200 cabins open year-round, range in size (2-6 persons). A few have kitchen & hot tub, no TV or phone. Restaurant AYCE F-M, closed Dec-Mar.

(5.3W) **Yogi Bear's Jellystone Park** 540.743.4002 Cabins $63-$528 for 4-15, summer wkend 2-night min/3 on holiday wkend (rates may change). Tentsites $37-75, 2-night min. Open late Mar-late Nov. Pets at tentsites & some cabins. Stays incl. free water slide, paddle boat, mini golf. Mem-Labor Day snack shop w/hamburgers, hot dogs, pizza. Coin laundry, camp store, pool. Guest only showers.

(6.9W) **Days Inn** 540.743.4521 $89.95-$109.95D, $10EAP, cont. B, pets under 50 lbs $15, pool.

Luray, VA 22835 (9W) Farmer's market held on Saturdays.

Open Arms at the Edge of Town 540.244.5652 Call/text for avail. Open yr-round, w/in a mile of town. Bunkroom $30PP, camping $15PP w/shower & kitchen privileges. B'fast/soda/snacks for sale on-site. Laundry $5/load. Free guest P/U & dropoff at Thornton Gap. Guest Mail: 1260 E Main St, Luray, VA 22835

South Court Inn B&B 540.843.0980 Discounted rate for hikers $100S/D when rooms avail., incl. big b'fast. No pets, smoking outside only. Wir sprechen Deutsch.

Cardinal Inn 888.648.4633 Hiker rate: winter $55, summer $75. No pets.

Budget Inn 540.743.5176 $69.95D/up, $79.95D/up Weekends, $10EAP, pets $10. Mail (non-guests pay $10): 320 W. Main St, Luray, VA 22835.

Luray Caverns Motels 540.743.4536, 888.941.4531 East & West buildings, standard room- Su-Th $75; F-Sa $95. 20% discount coupon on food at Luray Caverns. No pets. Mail w/reservation: 831 W. Main St, Luray, VA 22835

Best Western 540.743.6511 Call for rates, pets $20.

Woodruff House B&B 540.843.3200 ⟨www.woodruffhousebandb.com⟩

Mimslyn Inn 540.743.5105 $169/up, Speakeasy on-site M-Th 3p-10p; Fr-Sa 3p-11p; Su 2p-10p. Dinner 4-11p, full bar, W-F entertainment. ⟨www.mimslyninn.com⟩

Rock Tavern River Kamp 540.843.4232 Tentsites $45 for 4 incl. showers, Yurt $110 (4 person), luxury cabins hold up to 10. Call in advance for availability ⟨www.massanuttensprings.com⟩

Appalachian Outdoors Adventures 540.743.7400 Full-service outfitter, Coleman/alcohol/oz, canisters, Dr. Bonner's/oz, frz-dried foods. M-Th 10-6, F-Sa 10-8, Su 1-5. Mail: 2 West Main St, Luray, VA 22835.

Visitor Center 540.743.3915 daily 9-5. 5mi. north of town on Shenandoah River

Main Street Barber Shop 540.244.2815 Hiker friendly walk in haircuts for men & women $7.50 incl. beard trim. Closed We & Su.

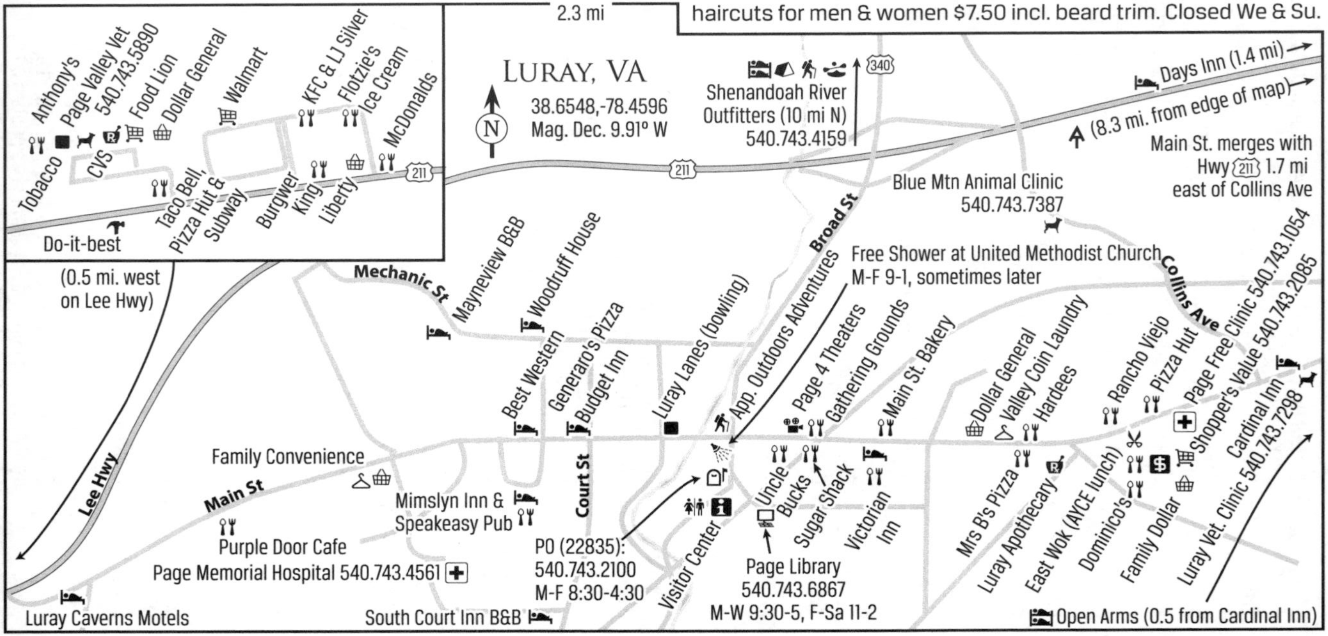

LURAY, VA
38.6548,-78.4596
Mag. Dec. 9.91° W
2.3 mi
Anthony's
Page Valley Vet 540.743.5890
Food Lion
Dollar General
Walmart
KFC & LJ Silver
Flotzie's Ice Cream
McDonalds
Tobacco
CVS
Taco Bell, Pizza Hut & Subway
Burgwer King
Liberty
Do-it-best
Shenandoah River Outfitters (10 mi N) 540.743.4159
Days Inn (1.4 mi)
(8.3 mi. from edge of map)
Main St. merges with Hwy 211 1.7 mi east of Collins Ave
Blue Mtn Animal Clinic 540.743.7387
Broad St
Free Shower at United Methodist Church M-F 9-1, sometimes later
Collins Ave
(0.5 mi. west on Lee Hwy)
Mechanic St
Mayneview B&B
Woodruff House
Best Western
Generaro's Pizza
Budget Inn
Luray Lanes (bowling)
App. Outdoors Adventures
Page 4 Theaters
Gathering Grounds
Main St. Bakery
Dollar General
Valley Coin Laundry
Hardees
Rancho Viejo
Pizza Hut
Page Free Clinic 540.743.1054
Shopper's Value 540.743.2085
Cardinal Inn 540.743.7298
Lee Hwy
Family Convenience
Main St
Mimslyn Inn & Speakeasy Pub
Court St
Uncle Bucks
Sugar Shack
Victorian Inn
Mrs B's Pizza
Luray Apothecary
East Wok (AYCE lunch)
Dominico's
Family Dollar
Luray Vet. Clinic 540.743.7298
Purple Door Cafe
Page Memorial Hospital 540.743.4561
PO (22835): 540.743.2100 M-F 8:30-4:30
Visitor Center
Page Library 540.743.6867 M-W 9:30-5, F-Sa 11-2
Luray Caverns Motels
South Court Inn B&B
Open Arms (0.5 from Cardinal Inn)

SoBo	NoBo	Location	Elev
1233.5	956.3	**Gravel Springs Hut** (0.2E), spring en route to shelter ☽ 💧 ⛺ (8) 28.4◂17.5◂13.1◂▸10.5▸18.6▸24.1	2635
1233.3	956.5	Skyline 17.7, Gravel Springs Gap 38.7678,-78.2335 P	2666
1232.5	957.3	View west 📷	3068
1232.2	957.6	South Marshall Mountain	3212
1231.7	958.1	Skyline 15.9, parking to west. P	3050
1231.0	958.8	North Marshall Mountain, view 📷	3368
1230.0	959.8	Hogwallow Flat	2959
1229.5	960.3	Skyline 14.2, Hogwallow Gap 38.7898,-78.1887 P	2739
1227.8	962.0	Skyline 12.3, Jenkins Gap, parking to east. 38.8065,-78.1808 P	2339
1226.9	962.9	Compton Springs 💧	2700
1226.5	963.3	Compton Peak	2909
1225.7	964.1	Skyline 10.4, Compton Gap parking 38.8236,-78.1706 P	2434
1223.9	965.9	Compton Gap Tr ("VA 610/Chester Gap" post) **Front Royal Hostel** (0.5E) **(pg. 98)**	2350
1223.7	966.1	SNP permit self-registration station.	2334
1223.0	966.8	**Tom Floyd Shelter** 28.0◂23.6◂10.5◂▸8.1▸13.6▸18.1 ☽ 💧 ⛺ (6) bear pole, trail behind shelter and side trails north on AT lead to water.	1943
1222.1	967.7	Trail 0.4W to N. Virginia 4H Center, parking. P 🚻 **(pg. 98)**	1371
1221.5	968.3	VA 602, stream south of road. 💧	1083
1220.1	969.7	US 522, **Front Royal, VA** (3.5W) 38.878,-78.1507 P **(pg. 98)**	950
1219.8	970.0	US 522 (east trailhead) **Mountain Home Cabbin** (0.1E) 🛏 **(pg. 98)**	974
1219.3	970.5	Bear Hollow Creek 💧	1076
1218.2	971.6	Woods road	1558
1216.8	973.0	CCC Rd.	1800
1216.7	973.1	Sealock Spring, Mosby Campsite. Named after Colonel John Mosby 💧 ⛺	1749
1216.0	973.8	Powerline	1653
1214.9	974.9	**Jim & Molly Denton Shelter** Porch, chairs, solar shower. ☽ 🚿 💧 ⛺ (8) 31.7◂18.6◂8.1◂▸5.5▸10.0▸18.4 bear pole, piped spring 100 yards south. ✖ PVC pipe on outer wall of shower has printing on it. What city name is in red?	1326

SoBo NoBo 1000 3000 5000

SoBo	NoBo	Feature	Elev
1213.9	975.9	Stream.	1048
1213.8	976.0	VA 638, powerline to south	1070
1213.1	976.7	Ridgetop clearing, bench, view	1437
1211.9	977.9	VA 55 (John Marshall Hwy), Manassas Gap 38.9092,-78.0533 P **(pg. 98)** RR tracks to south, AT passes under I-66 on Tuckers Lane.	800
1211.7	978.1	Tuckers Lane parking, Footbridge, stream 38.9113,-78.053 P	817
1210.4	979.4	Stone wall	1415
1209.4	980.4	**Manassas Gap Shelter** (0.1E) (1939) (6) 24.1◄13.6◄5.5◄►4.5►12.9►19.8 Bear Pole. Reliable spring downhill to right of shelter on side trail. Blue-blazed trail south of shelter leads 0.9W to VA 638.	1669
1208.1	981.7	Spring	1721
1207.4	982.4	Trico Tower Trail 0.3W to comm tower, parking on VA 638 38.9536,-78.0270 P	2080

Trillium – Three-petal flower set upon three leaves. White and pink varieties are plentiful in the southern Appalachians.

SoBo	NoBo	Feature	Elev
1204.9	984.9	**Dicks Dome Shelter** (0.2E) 18.1◄10.0◄4.5◄►8.4►15.3►29.5 (4) Whiskey Hollow Creek in front of shelter (treat water). Stream on AT 75 yards north of shelter side trail.	1397
1204.5	985.3	Powerline	1607
1203.9	985.9	Spring	1753
1203.7	986.1	Signal Knob parking on VA 638 / Fire Trail Rd 0.1W. 38.9852,-77.9997 P	1837
1202.9	986.9	Boundary to Sky Meadows State Park.	1832
1202.6	987.2	Bench, 1.7E to **Sky Meadows State Park Visitors Center** 800.933.7275 Open W-Su 8-5, restrooms, soda machine, 12 sites & primitive group camping, $9PP, reservation required, campers must arrive before dusk.	1801
1201.8	988.0	View 0.4E on Ambassador Whitehouse Trail	1578
1200.2	989.6	Two footbridges, streams	888
1200.1	989.7	Ashby Gap, US 50/17	945
1199.9	989.9	Trail 0.1E to parking on VA 601, Blueridge Mtn Rd 39.0157,-77.962 P	1080
1198.7	991.1	Stream.	1137
1198.1	991.7	Stream.	1034
1197.8	992.0	Trail west to Myron Glaser Cabin (locked)	1127
1197.3	992.5	Stream.	997
1196.9	992.9	Fishers Hill Trail to west	1093
1196.5	993.3	**Rod Hollow Shelter** (0.1W) 18.4◄12.9◄8.4◄►6.9►21.1►36.7 (8) Piped spring left of shelter. Stream on AT south of side trail.	891
1196.1	993.7	Stream, Fishers Hill Trail to west, south end of The Roller Coaster 13.5 miles of tightly packed ascents and descents.	802
1194.8	995.0	Spring at Bolden Hollow	843

1193.2 996.6 Footbridge, Morgan Mill Stream, campsite 775

1192.7 997.1 VA 605, Morgan Mill Rd (gravel) . . . . . . 39.0721,-77.912 P 1047

1192.0 997.8 Stream. 1010

1191.1 998.7 Buzzard Hill, AT east of summit 1251

1190.5 999.3 Two streams 804

1189.6 1000.2 **Sam Moore Shelter** (1990) 19.8◄15.3◄6.9◄►14.2►29.8►33.9 . (6) 904
Springs in front of shelter and to the left. Several tent sites to left of shelter.

1189.1 1000.7 Campsite 1289

1188.3 1001.5 Spout Run Ravine, stream 709

1187.1 1002.7 Footbridge, stream, campsite 60 yards north on AT 830

1186.6 1003.2 Bears Den Rocks, **Bears Den Hostel** (0.2E), view north on AT . . . . **(pg. 98)** 1265

1186.0 1003.8 Snickers Gap, VA 7 & 679 (Pine Grove Rd) . . . . 39.1153,-77.8475 P **(pg. 99)** 1000
If parking lot is full, vehicles parked on either shoulder will be towed

1185.2 1004.6 Stream. 802

1183.8 1006.0 Stream. 856

1183.5 1006.3 **VA-WV** border 1146

1183.3 1006.5 Raven Rocks, Crescent Rock 0.1E, view 1252

1183.1 1006.7 Campsite 1365

1182.7 1007.1 The Roller Coaster (north end); 13.5 miles of ascents and descents 1134
Sand Spring to west, good water source, Devils Racecourse boulder field to north

1179.8 1010.0 Wilson Gap 1380

1178.6 1011.2 Two trails 0.2E to **Blackburn AT Center** . . . . . . 39.1877,-77.7978 P **(pg. 99)** 1650

1176.9 1012.9 Laurel Springs, boardwalk 1449

1175.9 1013.9 Buzzard Rocks 1518

1175.4 1014.4 **David Lesser Memorial Shelter** (0.1E) . . . . . . (6) 1421
29.5◄21.1◄14.2◄►15.6►19.7►24.7 Overflow camping area below shelter.
Spring 0.2 mile downhill from shelter.

1174.1 1015.7 Roadbed 1321

1172.4 1017.4 Keys Gap, WV 9, markets 0.3E or W . . . . 39.2616,-77.7625 P (pg. 102) 911

1170.9 1018.9 Powerline 916

1170.2 1019.6 Campsite 1125

1168.5 1021.3 **VA-WV** border, Loudoun Heights, Loudoun Heights Trail to east 1117
No camping or fires from Loudoun Heights Trial thru Potomac River

1167.9 1021.9 WV 32, Chestnut Hill Rd 580

1167.0 1022.8 US 340, north end Shenandoah River Bridge ⚠ No hitchhiking on 340 . **(pg. 102)** 319

1166.7 1023.1 Side trail to **Appalachian Trail Conservancy** (0.2W) . . . . **(pg. 102)** 434

1166.3 1023.5 Jefferson Rock, view north to Potomac and Shenandoah Rivers 432

1166.1 1023.7 **Harpers Ferry, WV**, High Street . . . . 39.3165,-77.7558 P **(pg. 102)** 274

1165.8 1024.0 Potomac River, Byron Memorial Footbridge, **WV-MD** border. North of 246
river turn east on C&O Canal Towpath. No camping on AT section of towpath.

1164.7 1025.1 Pass under Sandy Hook Bridge (US 340) 248

MD Guidelines: camp only at designated campsites where tent symbols are shown). Alcohol not permitted on AT lands in MD.

1163.2 1026.6 C&O Canal Towpath north end, RR tracks, US 340 underpass . . . . **(pg. 104)** 246
From Keep Tryst Rd: **Knoxville, MD** (1.0W), **Brunswick, MD** (2.5E)

1162.6 1027.2 Weverton Rd . . . . .39.333,-77.6832 P 371

1161.9 1027.9 Trail east to Weverton Cliffs, view 859

1159.8 1030.0 **Ed Garvey Shelter** . . . . (12) 1083
36.7◄29.8◄15.6◄►4.1►9.1►16.6 Water on steep 0.4 mile trail in front of shelter.
2 tent sites north & south of shelter.

1158.0 1031.8 Brownsville Gap, roadbed 1063

1156.1 1033.7 Gapland Rd, Gathland State Park, War Correspondents . . . . **(pg. 104)** 950
Monument. Frost-free spigot by restrooms. No camping, No fires, no trash cans.

1155.7 1034.1 **Crampton Gap Shelter** (0.3E)(1941) . . . . (6) 1163
33.9◄19.7◄4.1◄►5.0►12.5►20.7 Intermittent spring 0.1S on AT.
NoBo: consider bringing water from Gathland SP in dry season (June-Sept).

SoBo NoBo 1000 3000 5000

965.9 Compton Gap Trail (post label "VA 610/Chester Gap")

Front Royal Terrapin Station Hostel (0.5E) 540.539.0509 At the last northbound concrete post in SNP, the AT turns left. NoBos go straight, follow Compton Gap Trail 0.5 mi. to paved road. Hostel is first home on left on paved road. Owned by Mike Evans, ‹gratefulgg@hotmail.com›. Enter in back through marked gate. Open Apr 17-July 5, 2017. Hikers only, picture ID required, bunk only $25, shower w/soap & shampoo $3, laundry $3. One night hiker special $30 includes bunk, shower, laundry, pizza & soda. $50 Two-night special also includes slackpack and 2nd night but not 2nd dinner. All visits include free town shuttle. Other shuttles for fee. WiFi, charging stations, TV, library, music, room to chill. Reservations recommended. No dogs. Mail for overnight guests: 304 Chester Gap Rd, Chester Gap, VA 22623.

Mobile Mike's 540.539.0509 shuttles and more (Mike Evans).

967.7 Side trail to:

Northern VA 4H Center (0.4W) 540.635.7171 ‹www.nova4h.com/appalachian-trail› Swimming pool Mem-Labor Day, shower $1, concession stand. Free parking up to 30 days, register on-line or check-in at office. Donations graciously accepted.

969.7, 970.0 US 522 (Remount Road) ***Front Royal 22630*** (4W)

Visitor Center 540.635.5788 7 days, 9-5pm. Hiker goodie bags, hiker box, pack storage. Cold drinks AT Maps for sale. Trolly from trailhead to town runs in Spring.

Mountain Home Cabbin 540.692.6198 MountainHomeAT@gmail.com. Renovated "Cabbin" at historic home of Lisa & Scott "Possible" AT'12 Jenkins, 3471 Remount Rd (US 522). SoBos: Go straight to Rte 522 (Gate 7 sign) and turn left. NoBos: At US 522 trailhead, cross road, continue on AT for .3 mi. parallel to 522. When trail turns left/north from 522, go right to Gate 7 sign by road. Both: From "Gate 7" sign on 522, go east 120 yards. Mountain Home is first driveway on left with long stone wall east of AT. Cabbin is first small red brick building. Open year-round, call/email ahead suggested, drop-ins OK. 4 single, 2 double beds. $25PP includes bed, fresh linens, shower, hiker clothes, hiker box, breakfast, WiFi, some cell, and town shuttle for dinner and resupply. Laundry $3. Pizza, ice cream, snacks and fuel for sale on site. All are welcome to lemonade, cookies, water. Faucet on SW corner of Cabbin. Max 1 dog per night for $5. Parking $3/day for non-guests. Mail: 3471 Remount Rd., Front Royal, VA 22630.

Quality Inn 540.635.3161 $69, $10EAP (up to 4) incl. c. b'fast Pets $15. Pool. If you need ride back to AT in the morning, let them know at check-in. **Thai Restaurant** onsite. Mail: 10 Commerce Ave, Front Royal, VA 22630.

Parkside Inn 540.631.1153 Clean, hiker friendly: $50-75 w/ mini fridge & microwave. Trail pickup/drop-off when avail.

Woodward House B&B 540.635.7010 Hiker rate $110D+tax w/b'fast, pickup & return to trail. Open year-round. CC accepted.

Super 8 540.636.4888 10% hiker discount, pets $10.

Scottish Inn 540.636.6168 $50/up, pets $10.

Budget Inn 540.635.2196

Lucky Star Lounge L/D variety, some vegetarian, live music.

Front Royal Trolly Pick-ups 2x daily at Rt 522 & AT crossing, May 15-Jul 15. M-F, 9:50a & 2:20p; Sa-Su, 2:20 & 5:20. 50 cents PP, drop off anywhere on Trolley route. Drivers may leave early. Please arrive 10 min prior.

977.9 VA 55, Manassas Gap, ***Linden, VA 22642*** (1.2W)

M-F 8-12 &1-5, Sa 8-12, 540.636.9936, packages held only 15 days.

Apple House Restaurant 540.636.6329 Tu-Su 7-8, M 7-5 year-round. Hiker specials, supplies and rides sometimes avail.

Monterey Convenience Store 540.636.6791 Su-W 5-8; Th-Sa 5-9

The Giving Tree 540.686.6261 M-Sa 10-7; Su 10-5, Arbor Day-Christmas Eve. Local produce, ice cream, meat, dairy & more.

1003.2 Bears Den Rocks

Bears Den Hostel 540.554.8708 A castle-like stone lodge, ATC owned & PATC operated. Bunk $20PP, tenting $12PP incl. full house privileges. Hiker Special: Bunk, laundry(5p-9p), pizza, soda & pint of Ben & Jerry's ice cream $30PP. All stays include shower & self-serve pancake b'fast. CC OK. Hiker room w/TV, shower, Internet & sodas, accessible all day by entering

a mileage code at the hostel door. Upper lodge, kitchen, camp store & office open 5-9p daily. Check-out 9a. Slackpacking & shuttles may be avail. during summer. Parking $3/day. Hosts the **Northern Ruck Jan 27, 28, 2017**. No drugs/alcohol anywhere on property. Pets welcome, but not allowed inside. Mail can be picked up during office hrs: Bears Den Hostel, 18393 Blue Ridge Mountain Rd, Bluemont, VA 20135. ⟨www.bearsdencenter.org⟩
✖What is the Pennsylvania license plate number?

1003.8 Snickers Gap, VA 7 & 679 (Pine Grove Rd). AT crosses VA 7 at intersection w/Pine Grove Rd. Take P.G. Rd. to restaurants. Take VA 7 0.8E, then right on route 734 for PO.

Bluemont, VA 20135

(1.7E) M-F 10-1 & 2-5, Sa 8:30-12, 540.554.4537

Horseshoe Curve Restaurant (0.3W) 540.554.8291 Tu-W 5-11; Th-Su 12-11. Live bands F & Sa. Good pub food. Su 12-9.

Pine Grove Restaurant (0.9W) 540.554.8126 M-Sa, 7-8; Su, 7-2. Welcomes hikers, b'fast served all day.

The Village Market 540.955.8742 Open 11a-8p Mo-Sa. Hiker friendly. Pizza, sandwiches & more. Fuel by oz. Limited shuttle to/or delivery from store to trail, Bear's Den or Blackburn Trail Th & Fr eve, all day Sa ⟨thevillagemarket.webs.com⟩

1011.2 Side trails, both (0.27E) to:
Blackburn AT Center 540.338.9028. PATC caretaker on-site. Hiker bunks in small cabin w/wood-burning stove. On porch of main building: logbook, donation box, pay phone, & electrical outlets to charge devices. Solar shower on lawn, water from hose, picnic tables. Open year-round.

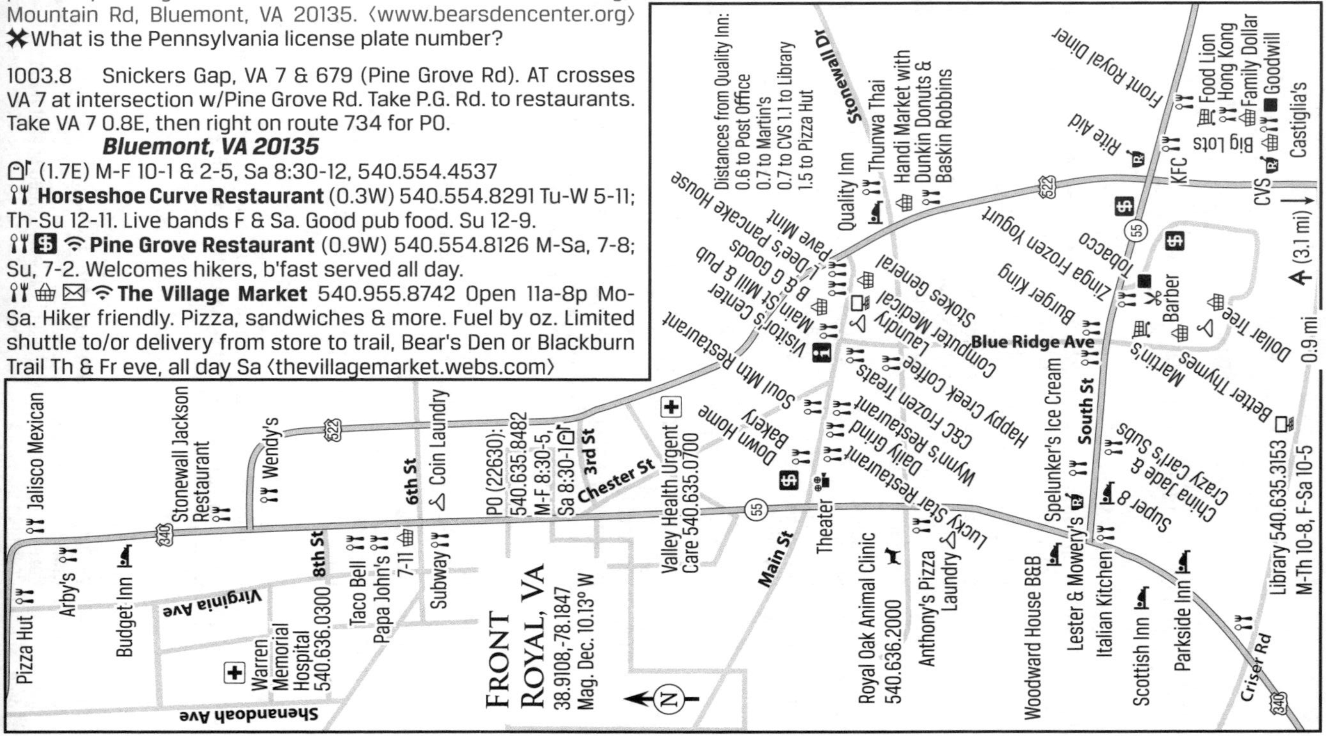

FRONT ROYAL, VA
38.9108,-78.1847
Mag. Dec. 10.13° W

Distances from Quality Inn:
0.6 to Post Office
0.7 to Martin's
0.7 to CVS 1.1 to Library
1.5 to Pizza Hut

PO (22630): 540.635.8482 M-F 8:30-5, Sa 8:30-10
Valley Health Urgent Care 540.635.0700
Warren Memorial Hospital 540.636.0300
Royal Oak Animal Clinic 540.636.2000
Library 540.635.3153 M-Th 10-8, F-Sa 10-5

Pizza Hut
Jalisco Mexican
Arby's
Budget Inn
Stonewall Jackson Restaurant
Wendy's
Taco Bell
Papa John's
7-11
Subway
Coin Laundry
Stonewall Dr
Quality Inn
Thunwa Thai
Handi Market with Dunkin Donuts & Baskin Robbins
Pave Mint
L Dee's Pancake House
B & G Goods
Main St Mill & Pub
Visitor's Center
Soul Mtn Restaurant
Down Home Bakery
Stokes General
Computer Medical
Laundry
Happy Creek Coffee
C&C Frozen Treats
Wynn's Restaurant
Daily Grind
Lucky Star Restaurant
Theater
Anthony's Pizza
Laundry
Woodward House B&B
Lester & Mowery's
Spelunker's Ice Cream
Italian Kitchen
Scottish Inn
Parkside Inn
Super 8
China Jade & Crazy Carls Subs
Burger King
Zinga Frozen Yogurt
Tobacco
Barber
Martin's
Dollar Tree
Better Thymes
Front Royal Diner
Rite Aid
KFC
Big Lots
Food Lion
Hong Kong
Family Dollar
Goodwill
Castiglia's
CVS
(3.1 mi)
0.9 mi
Blue Ridge Ave
South St
Main St
Chester St
3rd St
6th St
8th St
Virginia Ave
Shenandoah Ave
Criser Rd
N

1153.1 1036.7 Spring 0.5E, trail to Bear Spring Cabin (locked) 1437

1152.5 1037.3 White Rock Cliff, view. 1579
1152.3 1037.5 Lambs Knoll 50 yards west to tower, view 1733

1151.2 1038.6 Lambs Knoll tower road (paved) 1347

1150.7 1039.1 **Rocky Run Shelters** (0.2W) 24.7◄9.1◄5.0◄►7.5►15.7►20.6 (6)(16) 982
Left fork on side trail to better water source & old shelter. Right to new shelter.

1149.7 1040.1 Fox Gap, Reno Monument Rd (paved), **South Mountain Creamery** (2E). 1068

1148.9 1040.9 **Dahlgren Backpack Campground** 980
Large tenting area, picnic tables, restrooms; no fee. Note proximity to road.

1148.6 1041.2 Turners Gap, US Alt 40, restaurant 0.1W, 39.4840,-77.6198 P **(pg. 104)** 1080
Boonsboro, MD (2.5W)

1147.3 1042.5 Monument Rd 1256
1147.0 1042.8 Washington Monument State Park, picnic tables, 39.4977,-77.6208 P 1358
parking near entry, restrooms adjacent to visitor center.
1146.7 1043.1 Washington Monument (0.1W) 1550
1146.4 1043.4 Powerline 1311

1144.6 1045.2 Boonsboro Mountain Rd, residential area. 1297
1144.3 1045.5 Bartman Hill Trail 0.6W to Greenbrier SP **(pg. 104)** 1394
1143.9 1045.9 I-70 footbridge, US 40, 39.5353,-77.6035 P **(pg. 105)** 1239
Parking north end of footbridge 0.1E. Also cross Boonsboro Mtn Rd south of hwy.

1143.2 1046.6 **Pine Knob Shelter** (0.1W) (1939), south end of loop trail (5) 1378
16.6◄12.5◄7.5◄►8.2►13.1►22.7 Piped spring next to shelter.

1141.6 1048.2 Annapolis Rocks to west, campsite (0.2W) (13) 1756
Caretaker on site. Tentsites near outstanding overlook. No fires.

1140.6 1049.2 Black Rock Cliffs to west 1779
1140.2 1049.6 Black Rock Creek 1597
1140.0 1049.8 **Pogo Memorial Campsite** 1500
Campsite east of AT, spring 100 yards west. Thurston Griggs Trail to west.

Poison Ivy - Vine that can grow as ground cover or that can cling to trees or other brush. Stems redden toward the end and terminate with 3 pointed-oval leaves.

1135.2 1054.6 Wolfsville Rd, MD 17, **Smithsburg, MD** (1.5W) **(pg. 105)** 1340
1135.0 1054.8 **Ensign Cowall Shelter** (1999) 20.7◄15.7◄8.2◄►4.9►14.5►16.9 (8) 1384
Boxed spring, somewhat stagnant, south between shelter & road.
1134.8 1055.0 Powerline 1500

1133.7 1056.1 Foxville Rd, MD 77, **Smithsburg, MD** (1.7W) . . . 1590

1132.5 1057.3 Spring . . . 1325
1132.3 1057.5 Powerline . . . 1345
1131.9 1057.9 Warner Gap Hollow, stream, Warner Gap Rd (gravel, AT to west). . . . 1150

1131.2 1058.6 Little Antietam Creek . . . 1075
1131.1 1058.7 Raven Rock Rd, MD 491. . . . 1062
1130.8 1059.0 Raven Rock Cliff, view 100 yards east . . . 1288
1130.1 1059.7 **Raven Rock Shelter** (0.1W) (2010), Ritchie Rd (0.6E) . . . (16) 1647
20.6◄13.1◄4.9◄►9.6►12.0►13.2 Two story shelter.
Water on opposite side of AT (0.3E) on steep side trail.

1128.3 1061.5 Ends of High Rock Loop Trail 0.2 apart . . . 39.6948,-77.5232 1795
0.1E from either end to view and parking. Parking gated from dusk till 8am.
1.7 from parking area to Pen Mar Park via Pen Mar Rd.

1125.5 1064.3 Pen Mar County Park . . . 39.7164,-77.5072 **(pg. 109)** 1321
Cascade, MD (1.4E), **Waynesboro, PA** (2.1W to Walmart, downtown 4.5)
1125.2 1064.6 **MD-PA** border, RR tracks, Mason-Dixon Line . . . 1250
1125.1 1064.7 Pen Mar Rd . . . 1240
1124.6 1065.2 Falls Creek, footbridge, campsite . . . 1068
1124.1 1065.7 Buena Vista Rd . . . 1290

1122.9 1066.9 Old PA 16. . . . 1278
1122.6 1067.2 Footbridge, stream, PA 16, . . . 39.7414,-77.4905 **(pg. 109)** 1200
Blue Ridge Summit, PA (1.2E)
1122.4 1067.4 Mentzer Gap Rd, NoBo: turn west . . . 1250
1122.0 1067.8 Rattlesnake Run Rd (gravel) . . . 1378

1120.5 1069.3 **Deer Lick Shelters** 22.7◄14.5◄9.6◄►2.4►3.6►10.2 . . . (2x5) 1406
Spring 10 yards north on AT or (0.2E) on blue-blazed trail.
1120.2 1069.6 Pipeline clearing . . . 1489
1119.6 1070.2 Dirt road . . . 1378

1118.3 1071.5 Orange-blazed Chickadee Snowmobile Trail . . . 909
1118.1 1071.7 **Antietam Shelter** (1940) . . . (6) 889
16.9◄12.0◄2.4◄►1.2►7.8►13.4 Better to get water from Old Forge Park 0.1N
1118.0 1071.8 Old Forge Picnic Area, Old Forge Rd . . . 39.8005,-77.4793 898
1116.9 1072.9 **Tumbling Run Shelters** . . . (2x4) 1082
13.2◄3.6◄1.2◄►6.6►12.2►19.6 Piped water 75 yards right of shelter.

1115.6 1074.2 Chimney Rocks, view to east. . . . 1900

1017.4 Keys Gap, WV 9

(0.3E) **Sweet Springs Country Store** 540.668.9067, 540.668.7123, 703.622.7526 (Matt or Nathan) Run by a Twelve Tribes spiritual community. Offers WFS, meals, shower, laundry. P/U & return from Bears Den, Blackburn Trail Center, Keys Gap, Harpers Ferry. Grocery & outfitter nearby. Mail: 37091 Charles Town Pike, Hillsboro, VA 20132

(0.3W veer left at intersection) **Mini-Mart & Torlone's Pizza**

(2.0E) **Stoney Brook Organic Farm & Hostel** 703.622.7526, 571.442.2834 (Matt or Nathan) Run by a Twelve Tribes spiritual community. WFS, meals, shower, laundry. Pickup/return from Bears Den, Blackburn Trail Ctr, Keys Gap, Harpers Ferry. Grocery & outfitter close. Mail: 37091 Charles Town Pike, Hillsboro, VA 20132

1022.8 US 340, Shenandoah River Bridge

Go west on 340 to Clarion Inn Harpers Ferry, KOA, or Charles Town; E to Frederick. NoBos stay on AT for better access to Harpers Ferry.

Econo Lodge 304.535.6391 $109-139 (peak rate midsummer), 10% hiker discount, hot b'fast bar, no pets.

(1.2W) **Harpers Ferry KOA** 304.535.6895 7 Days. 7a-10p/summer, 9a-5p/winter. Camping $45/up, cabins $95/up, both prices for 2 persons, $8EAP. Coin laundry on-site, shower only $5. Cafe has limited hours.

(1.3W) **Clarion Inn Harpers Ferry** 304.535.6302 Call for rates. Used to be the Quality Inn. Newly remodeld rooms. **Whitehorse Tavern** on-site. 10% discount for hikers.

Charles Town, WV 25414 (6W) All major services.

Walmart with grocery and pharmacy 304.728.2720

Jefferson Urgent Care 304.728.8533 M-F 8-8, Sa-Su 8-5

Winchester Foot & Ankle 304.725.0084

Jefferson Animal Hospital 304.725.0428

Frederick, MD 21701 (20E) All major services.

1023.1 Side Trail to ATC HQ (0.2W)

ATC HQ 304.535.6331 Open yr-round daily 9–5. Closed Thanksgiving, Christmas & New Year's. If you're thru-hiking or hiking the entire trail in sections, have your photo taken for the album; a postcard version of this photo may be purchased (1st one free for ATC members). Hiker lounge, register, scale, cold & hot drinks inside, along w/hats, shirts, maps, all ATC publications. Coleman/alcohol/oz for donation. Info board on front porch. Mail: (USPS) PO Box 807 or (FedEx/UPS) 799 Washington St, Harpers Ferry, WV 25425 ⟨www.appalachiantrail.org⟩.

1023.7 ***Harpers Ferry, WV 25425*** *(more services on map)*

Teahorse Hostel 304.535.6848 0.5W of ATC $35 per bunk + tax incl. waffle b'fast. Laundry $6. No pets, alcohol or smoking. Open for check in 3p-9p. For availability & reservations: www.teahorsehostel.com. Shuttle range Thornton Gap to Duncannon & Dulles Airport. For shuttle call 304.506.2890.

The Town's Inn 304.932.0677 Private room $110-$160 up to 4 persons. One pet room. Hostel $35PP. Laundry $5, shuttles $1/mile, no maildrops, Visa/MC OK. Dining 6a-10p daily yr-round. Shop stocked for hiker resupply. ⟨www.TheTownsInn.com⟩

Harpers Ferry Hostel (in Knoxville, MD see pg. 102)

Guide Shack Cafe 304.995.6022 Veteran owned. Locally roasted coffee, espresso, teas, sandwiches, soup, chili, baked goods, granola & ice cream. Hiker resupply offered spring 2017. Gear up, climb the bouldering wall & strategize your next adventure.

The Outfitter at Harpers Ferry & Harpers Ferry General Store 888.535.2087 Full service outfitter w/good selection of shoes & trail food. Shuttle referrals. Open daily 10–6. Mid-Mar thru Dec. Seasonal hrs otherwise.

Harpers Ferry National Historical Park 304.535.6029 $10 per vehicle entrance fee, parking up to 2 weeks (must register). Free shuttle bus to lower town (starts-9a). Gates open 8a-dusk.

HostelHiker.com 202.670.6323 Shuttles from Thorton Gap to Pen-Mar Park. To/from DC, Dulles & Baltimore Airports.

Mark "Strings" Cusic 304.433.0028 mdcusic@frontier.com Shuttle range Rockfish Gap to Duncannon.

Pan Tran 304.263.0876 Route to Charles Town (Walmart) M-F 9:05, 10:42, 12:03, 1:24, 3:00, and 4:45 $2.50 each way.

Locust Valley Bible Church 240.469.1584 Offers rides to/from church services. Lunch provided when possible. P/U from

H.F. High St. to Monument Rd. Give as much notice as possible, 1-2 days appreciated.

Amtrak 800.872.7245 "Capitol Limited" daily HF to Wa. DC Union Station 11:31a-1:05p (depart-arrive), DC to HF 4:05-5:16p. $13 ea way.

■ **Caring Hands Chiropractic & Massage** 301.371.3922, 240.344.0066 Dr Jenny Foster. Call/text ahead for appointment. Try for beginning of zero days for max benefit. Ride may be possible from Harpers Ferry or a road crossing in MD.

Maryland Rail Commuter Service (MARC) 410.539.5000 "Brunswick Line" M-F to Washington DC Union Station departs 5:25a, 5:50a & 6:50a, returns 4:25p, 5:40p & 6:20p. $14 ea way ⟨www.mta.maryland.gov/marc-train⟩

HARPERS FERRY, WV

39.325,-77.739
Mag. Dec. 10.5° W

PO (25425) 304.535.2479:
M-F 8-4, Sa 9-12

Canal House
Anvil
Teahorse Hostel
Washington St
Guide Shack Cafe
Bolivar-HF Library
304.535.2301
M,Tu,F,Sa 10-5:30
W,Th 10-8
Polk St
7-11
Country Cafe
7-3, 7 days
Union St
Econo Lodge
Laurel Lodge
Mena's Italian (closedM)
Fillmore St
ATC
← From ATC to AT 0.6 →
Side Trail to ATC HQ
Potomac St
Railroad Station
Amtrack: Chicago ⟨⟩ DC
MARC: Martinsburg ⟨⟩ DC
Potomac River
"Lower Town"
(see inset)
Jefferson Rock
Shenandoah St
340
← Charles Town (all major services) 6.7 from AT
← Clarion Inn Harpers Ferry (1.3W)
KOA
Harper's Ferry National
Historic Park-parking
and shuttle
Shoreline Rd
Frederick, MD 21 mi →
Washington, DC 68 mi →
Chestnut Hill Rd
1.8 mi

High St
Hannah's BBQ
Potomac St
Church St
Scoops Ice Cream
General Store &
Outfitter at HF
Coffee Mill
Town's Inn & Sundry Store
Coach House Grill & Bar
Cannonball Deli
Confectionaries
Lower Town

Origin of town names:
Harpers Ferry - Potomac ferry service operated by Robert Harper.
Charles Town – Founded by Charles Washington, brother of George.
Frederick, MD - Frederick Calvert, 6th Baron Baltimore.

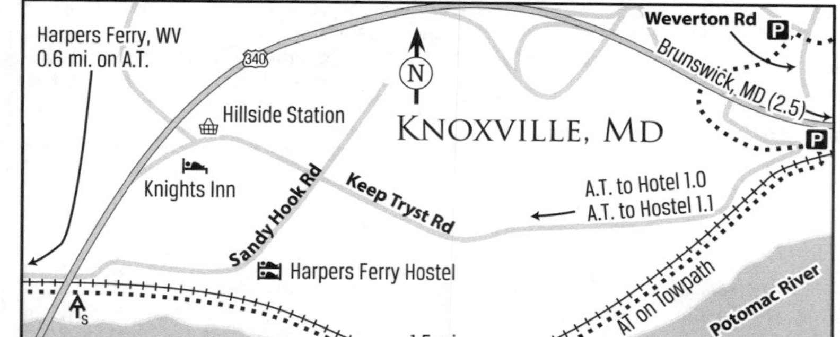

1026.6 US 340, Keep Tryst Rd, ***Knoxville, MD, 21758*** (1W)
HI Harpers Ferry Hostel 301.834.7652 ID required for any stay. Discounted thru hiker rate $22.40 incl. tax, shower, internet & WiFi, linens, A/C & heat, make-your-own b'fast & dinner. Call for trail angel help with rides. Laundry $4. Tenting $10PP incl. outside shower, porta-potty, WiFi, soda machine and phone charging on back porch. Fire pits & grill on lawn. Inside Access Fee of $5PP incl. b'fast, inside showers. Service dogs okay inside, otherwise dogs on leash allowed only if tenting. Store with hiker snacks inside and there is often free food. Complimentary meals on Tu, Fr, & Sa. Netflix movies avail. No drinking. Non-guest parking $5/day. Check-in 5-10p, check-out 10a. Open May 1–Nov 15 for individuals, year-round for groups. Mail: 19123 Sandy Hook Rd, Knoxville, MD 21758 ⟨www.hiusa.org⟩.

Knights Inn 301.660.3580 $59.99/KNG-2, $69.99/DBL-2, $89.99/ DBL-3, $99.99/DBL-4 incl. fridge, m'wave, cont B. Hiker laundry $5. ADA defined service animals are welcome at this hotel.

Hillside Station 301.834.5300 Convenience store with pizza, wings, and more. M-Sa 6-9, Su 7-7.

Brunswick, MD 21716 (2.5E from Keep Tryst Rd)

M-F 8-4:30, Sa 9-12, 301.834.9944

Wing N' Pizza Shack 301.834.5555 Delivers to HF Hostel.

1033.7 Gathland SP
(0.4W) **Maple Tree Campground** 301.432.5585 $30 tentsite for up to 4 persons, $10EAP. Campstore has candy bars, sodas, batteries & m'wavable food. Open Yr-round. On Townsend Rd which is to the right as you exit the park. ⟨www.TheTreehouseCamp.com⟩

1041.2 Turners Gap, US Alt 40
(0.1W) **Old South Mountain Inn** 301.432.6155 Tu–F 5-close, Sa 4-close, Su brunch 10:30-1:30, dinner 2-close. Men, no sleevless shirts. Please shower first. Dining reservations preferred. Outside dining on the patio now avail. ⟨www.oldsouthmountaininn.com⟩

Boonsboro, MD (2.5W)

Vesta Pizzeria 301.432.6166 Pickup or delivery. Open 11a daily. Delivery after 4p wkdays, all day wkends.

Mountainside Deli & Ice Cream 301.432.6700 M-F 6-8, Sa 8-8, Su 11-6. Cash only.

Cronise Market Place M-F 9-7, Sa 9-6, Su 12-6.

Turn the Page Book Store Café 301.432.4588

Crawfords 301.432.2903 M-F 6:30-8:30, Sa 6:30-6:30. Limited supplies.

Marcy's Laundry Center 301.491.5849 M-Su 5:30 a-10 p.

1045.5 Bartman Hill Trail (0.6W) to:
Greenbrier State Park 301.791.4767 Open 8a to Sunset. Camping 1st Fr of Apr to last wkend in Oct. $5 Entrance fee waived if camping or if you walk in on Bartman Trail. Prices listed as MD resident/nonresident. Tent sites w/showers $26-30, higher wkends/holidays. Pets allowed at Dog Wood. Avail. Mem Day-Labor Day: lunch concession stand, lake swimming, row boat & paddle boat rentals.

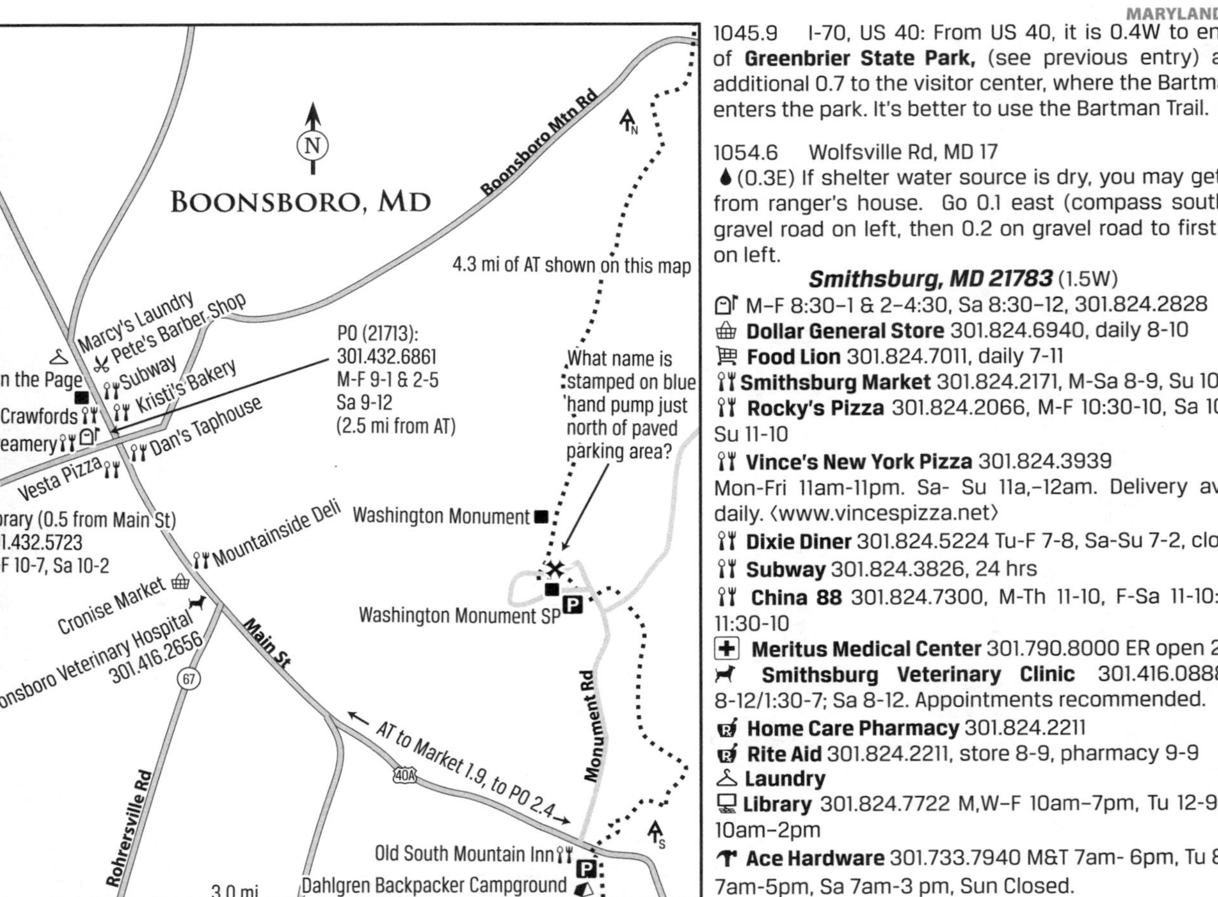

1045.9 I-70, US 40: From US 40, it is 0.4W to entrance of **Greenbrier State Park,** (see previous entry) and an additional 0.7 to the visitor center, where the Bartman Trail enters the park. It's better to use the Bartman Trail.

1054.6 Wolfsville Rd, MD 17

(0.3E) If shelter water source is dry, you may get water from ranger's house. Go 0.1 east (compass south) to a gravel road on left, then 0.2 on gravel road to first house on left.

Smithsburg, MD 21783 (1.5W)

M–F 8:30–1 & 2–4:30, Sa 8:30–12, 301.824.2828

Dollar General Store 301.824.6940, daily 8-10

Food Lion 301.824.7011, daily 7-11

Smithsburg Market 301.824.2171, M-Sa 8-9, Su 10-9

Rocky's Pizza 301.824.2066, M-F 10:30-10, Sa 10:30-11, Su 11-10

Vince's New York Pizza 301.824.3939
Mon-Fri 11am-11pm. Sa- Su 11a,–12am. Delivery available daily. ⟨www.vincespizza.net⟩

Dixie Diner 301.824.5224 Tu-F 7-8, Sa-Su 7-2, closed M.

Subway 301.824.3826, 24 hrs

China 88 301.824.7300, M-Th 11-10, F-Sa 11-10:30, Su 11:30-10

Meritus Medical Center 301.790.8000 ER open 24/7

Smithsburg Veterinary Clinic 301.416.0888 M-F 8-12/1:30-7; Sa 8-12. Appointments recommended.

Home Care Pharmacy 301.824.2211

Rite Aid 301.824.2211, store 8-9, pharmacy 9-9

Laundry

Library 301.824.7722 M,W–F 10am–7pm, Tu 12-9pm, Sa 10am–2pm

Ace Hardware 301.733.7940 M&T 7am- 6pm, Tu & W & F 7am-5pm, Sa 7am-3 pm, Sun Closed.

1114.7	1075.1	Pipeline clearing	1916
1113.6	1076.2	Powerline	2027
1112.9	1076.9	Snowy Mountain Rd	1703
1112.3	1077.5	Swamp Rd, **South Mountain, PA** 17261 (1.0E) (pg. 109)	1560
1111.9	1077.9	PA 233, **South Mountain, PA** 17261 (1.2E) (pg. 109)	1605

⚠ Many springs in PA run dry in June, July & August.

1110.3	1079.5	**Rocky Mountain Shelters** (0.2E)(1989) ☽ 💧 ⛺ ⊏ (2x4) 10.2◄7.8◄6.6◄►5.6►13.0►19.2 Piped spring 0.5 mile on trail to road, then right 75 yards.	1662
1107.3	1082.5	US 30, **Fayetteville, PA** (3.5W). 39.9059,-77.4786 🅿 **(0.6E)****(pg. 110)** Overnight parking SW corner of US 30 & Pine Grove Rd, check-in at park HQ.	960
1106.9	1082.9	Side trail to **Caledonia State Park**, pool area (pg. 110)	934
1106.1	1083.7	Locust Gap Rd, Valley Trail to west	1334
1104.7	1085.1	**Quarry Gap Shelters** (1935) 13.4◄12.2◄5.6◄►7.4►13.6►24.5 ☽ 💧 ⛺ ⊏ (2x4)	1471
1104.4	1085.4	Footbridge, stream 💧	1542
1104.0	1085.8	Hosack Run Trail to east	1819
1103.2	1086.6	5-way gravel road intersection	1984
1102.4	1087.4	Powerline	1867
1102.0	1087.8	Woods road	1986
1100.7	1089.1	Middle Ridge Road	2070
1100.1	1089.7	3 Points (intersecting gravel roads), campsite to north	1961
1099.7	1090.1	PATC Milesburn Cabin (locked), spring 100 yards west 💧 ⛺	1681
1099.4	1090.4	Ridge Rd (gravel), campsite north of road ⛺	1907
1098.6	1091.2	Rocky Knob Trail (orange-blazed)	1902
1098.0	1091.8	Powerline, campsite to north ⛺	1913
1097.3	1092.5	**Birch Run Shelter** (2003) stream 75 yards north on AT ☽ 💧 ⛺ ⊏ (8) 19.6◄13.0◄7.4◄►6.2►17.1►25.2	1800
1097.2	1092.6	Footbridge, stream 💧	1783
1096.0	1093.8	Shippensburg Rd 39.9972,-77.405 🅿	2040
1094.9	1094.9	Dead Woman's Hollow Road (gravel), **AT Midpoint** (2017) The A.T. north of Dead Woman's Hollow Road may be temporarily rerouted for short durations. Hikers should observe signage & follow any reroutes as directed.	1954

1094.1	1095.7	Side trail to Michener Cabin (locked)	(0.3E)	1850
1093.5	1096.3	Woods road		1849
1092.2	1097.6	Woodrow Rd (gravel), campsite 0.1N		1779
1091.7	1098.1	Stream.		1538
1091.2	1098.6	Sunset Rocks Trail to east, rejoins AT to north		1318
1091.1	1098.7	**Toms Run Shelter** (1936)	(4)	1302
		19.2◄13.6◄6.2◄►10.9►19.0►37.2 Water behind shelter		
1090.9	1098.9	Stream.		1272
1089.9	1099.9	Michaux Rd		1330
1089.0	1100.8	Toms Run, footbridge, stream. Sunset Rocks Trail to east.		1020
1087.8	1102.0	PA 233 (paved), NoBo on road 0.1W, veer right on road into park		899
1087.5	1102.3	**Pine Grove Furnace SP, AT Museum** 40.0317,-77.3054 P	(pg. 110)	872
1087.0	1102.8	Fuller Lake, free showers, snack bar 11-7 daily Mem-Labor Day		841

No camping within one mile of PGF SP; camping within the park only at designated (paid) campsites. No overnight sleeping in pavilions.

1085.1	1104.7	Campsite		1251
1084.9	1104.9	Pole Steeple Trail to west		1300
1083.9	1105.9	Campsite		1370
1081.7	1108.1	Roadbed		1049
1081.4	1108.4	Trail to **Mountain Creek Campground** (0.7W) steep	(pg. 110)	1015
1080.3	1109.5	Spring 50 yards west on marked trail		725
1080.2	1109.6	**James Fry (Tagg Run) Shelter** (0.2E), campsite west of AT	(9)	699
		24.5◄17.1◄10.9◄►8.1►26.3►33.6 Spring uphill from shelter; water 0.2E farther.		
1079.8	1110.0	Pine Grove Rd (paved)		664
1079.6	1110.2	Stream		639
1079.2	1110.6	⚠ Cross RR tracks; sharp east turn for NoBo, west for SoBo		633
1079.0	1110.8	PA 34, Hunters Run Rd, **Store & Deli** (0.2E) 40.0777,-77.1945 P **(0.1E)**	(pg. 110)	625
1077.0	1112.8	PA 94, **Mt Holly Springs, PA** (2.5W)	(pg. 111)	880
1076.7	1113.1	Sheet Iron Roof Rd, campground 0.4W 40.093,-77.1641 P	(pg. 111)	773
1076.3	1113.5	Footbridge, stream, campsite		687
1076.0	1113.8	Footbridge, stream		671
1075.6	1114.2	Old Town Rd (gravel)		736
1075.0	1114.8	Rock maze		1186

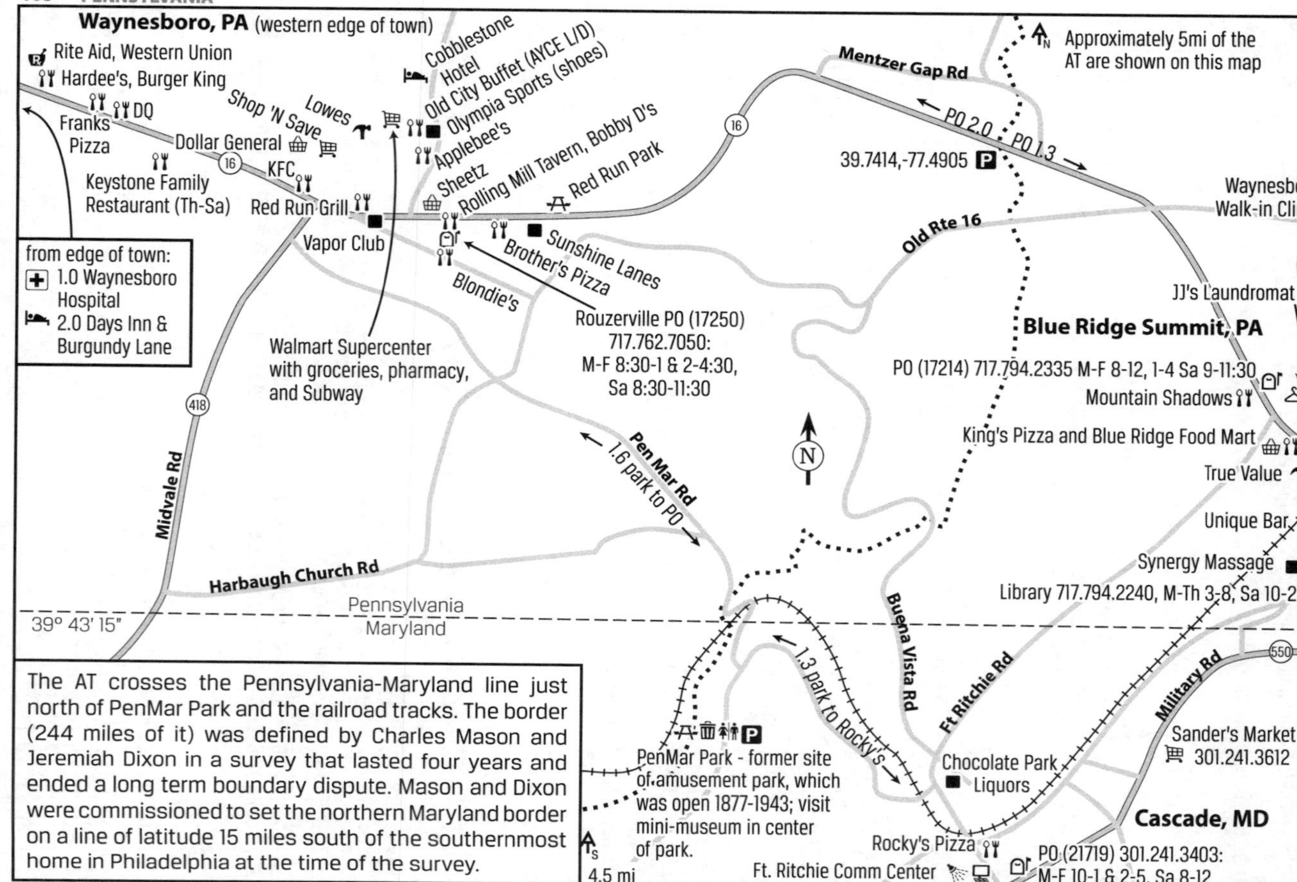

The AT crosses the Pennsylvania-Maryland line just north of PenMar Park and the railroad tracks. The border (244 miles of it) was defined by Charles Mason and Jeremiah Dixon in a survey that lasted four years and ended a long term boundary dispute. Mason and Dixon were commissioned to set the northern Maryland border on a line of latitude 15 miles south of the southernmost home in Philadelphia at the time of the survey.

1064.3 **Pen Mar County Park** Open first Su in May to last Su in Oct. Vending & water; no camping. Restrooms locked when park closed. Bobby D's & other pizza places deliver. Pen Mar Rd passes in front of park, east of AT. Rouzerville PO is nearest to the AT. If intending to walk to town, do so from AT/Pen Mar Rd intersection 0.3N of park. Services avail. in multiple directions from the park & from PA 16. See map and listings for options.

Dennis Sewell 301.241.3176 PU from Harpers Ferry to Pine Grove Furnace SP, will PU Baltimore AP. Dogs OK.

Waynesboro, PA 17214

Mason-Dixon Appalachian Trail Outdoor Festival Sa, Jun 17, 2017 at Red Run Park, 12143 Buchanan Trail E, 10-4

Cobblestone Hotel 717.765.0034 Hiker Discount. $80/up +tax, incl. hot b'fast, pool, hot tub.

Bobby D's Pizza 717.762.0388

Also: Olympia Sports large selection of running shoes.

2.0W of Walmart:

Burgundy Lane B&B 717.762.8112 $90-105D w/ full b'fast, free laundry & shuttle to trailhead or town stop. Longer shuttles for fee. Mail: 128 W Main St, Waynesboro, PA 17268.

Days Inn 717.762.9113 $59S, $69D, $5EAP. C b'fast, $10 pet fee, laundry next door.

Nina Murphy Shuttle Service 703.946.9404 Shuttle service for Waynesboro, VA, Dulles & Reagan National AP, & SNP.

Waynesboro Hospital 717.765.4000 501 E Main St.

Wayne Heights Animal Hospital 717.765.9636

Cascade, MD (1.4E on Pen Mar/High Rock Rd)

Sanders Market M–Sa 8:30–8, open till 9pm Tu and Sa.

Ft Ritchie Comm Center 301.241.5085 Showers, computer access, M-Th 6-9, F 6-6, Sa 9-5, Su 9:30-4.

1067.2 PA 16 ***Blue Ridge Summit, PA 17214*** (1.2E)

Unique Bar & Grill 717.794.2565 live music.

Dollar General (1.2E) 717.296.1576 8a-10p

Waynesboro Walk-in Clinic 717.762.1700 M-F 8-5

Synergy Massage 877.372.6617 Will P/U & Return to trail. Free showers, hot tub & pool. Massage by apt. as low as $30.

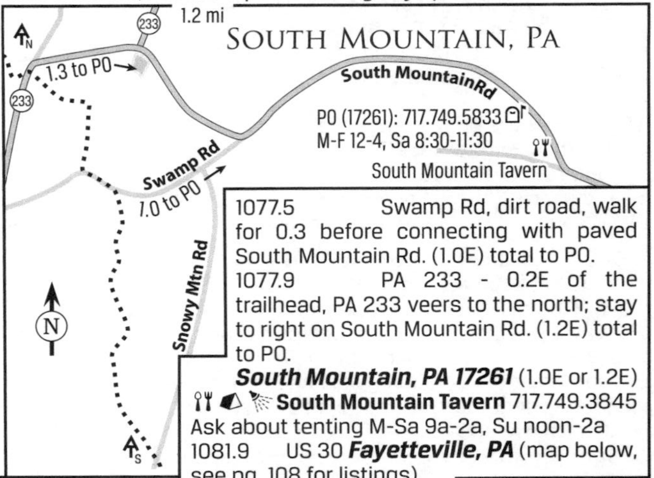

SOUTH MOUNTAIN, PA

1.2 mi
1.3 to PO
South Mountain Rd
PO (17261): 717.749.5833
M-F 12-4, Sa 8:30-11:30
South Mountain Tavern
Swamp Rd
1.0 to PO
Snowy Mtn Rd

1077.5 Swamp Rd, dirt road, walk for 0.3 before connecting with paved South Mountain Rd. (1.0E) total to PO.

1077.9 PA 233 - 0.2E of the trailhead, PA 233 veers to the north; stay to right on South Mountain Rd. (1.2E) total to PO.

South Mountain, PA 17261 (1.0E or 1.2E)

South Mountain Tavern 717.749.3845 Ask about tenting M-Sa 9a-2a, Su noon-2a

1081.9 US 30 ***Fayetteville, PA*** (map below, see pg. 108 for listings)

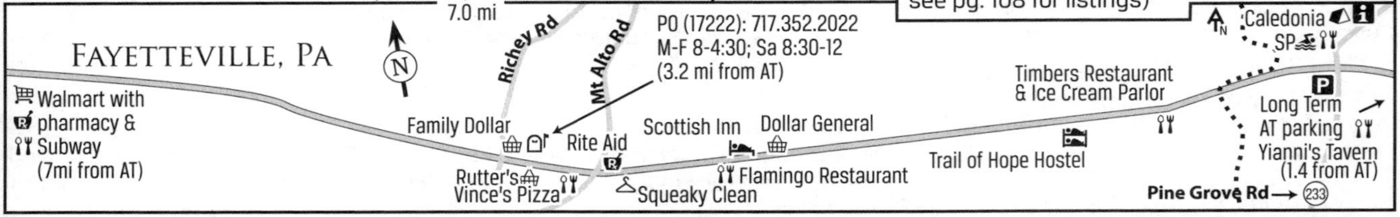

FAYETTEVILLE, PA

7.0 mi
Richey Rd
Mt Alto Rd
PO (17222): 717.352.2022
M-F 8-4:30; Sa 8:30-12
(3.2 mi from AT)
Walmart with pharmacy & Subway (7mi from AT)
Family Dollar
Rite Aid
Rutter's
Vince's Pizza
Scottish Inn
Dollar General
Flamingo Restaurant
Squeaky Clean
Timbers Restaurant & Ice Cream Parlor
Trail of Hope Hostel
Caledonia SP
Long Term AT parking
Yianni's Tavern (1.4 from AT)
Pine Grove Rd → 233

1082.5 US 30 ***Fayetteville, PA*** (see map pg. 107)

Trail of Hope Hostel 717.360.1481, 717.352.2513 $22 bunk or $12 camping. Coin laundry, use of kitchen, resupply incl. white gas/denatured/oz & canisters. Mail: 7798 Lincoln Way E, Fayetteville, PA 17222

Scottish Inn and Suites 717.352.2144, 800.251.1962 $59S, $69D, $15 pets. $5PP for pickup or return to trail. $10 for ride to Walmart. Coin laundry. Guest Mail: 5651 Lincoln Way East, Fayetteville, PA 17222

Timbers Restaurant & Ice Cream Parlor (0.4W) 717.401.0605 Charging station, snacks, fuels, hiker/pet friendly. Maildrop: 8228 Lincoln Way, Fayetteville, PA 17222

Rutters Convenience store with WiFi and deli.

Flamingo Restaurant 717.3528755 Excellent lrg b'fast

Vince's Pizza 717.401.0096

Freeman's Shuttle Service 717.491.2460 Front Royal to DWG. Slackpacking Pen Mar to Duncannon.

1082.9 Side trail to **Caledonia State Park**

Caledonia SP 717.352.2161 Open Mar 15 - Dec 15. Pool & snack bar open Memorial-Labor Day, 11-7, 7 days, weather permitting. Campsites avg. $30, pets free, $4.50 senior (62) discount. $4 shower or $5 shower & pool. Check-in at office for long term parking. Free local-call phone outside office. Some campsites under renovation winter 2016.

Gary Grant Shuttles 717.706.2578 Can shuttle individuals and groups ranging from Caledonia SP to Duncannon, to local resupply (Walmart), Greyhound and Amtrak stations. Slackpacking, fuel on-hand.

1102.3 **Pine Grove Furnace State Park** (see map)

Pine Grove Furnace State Park 717.486.7174 From end of Dec to end of Mar on weekdays only; open 7 days rest of year. Campsites start at $23 weekdays, $25 weekends, $2 off for PA residents. Dogs allowed in some sites. Restrooms throughout park. Check w/park office before parking overnight; cars can be left for up to two weeks in lot compass south of Museum (interior of park). Beach/swimming area at Fuller Lake $ Laurel Lake.

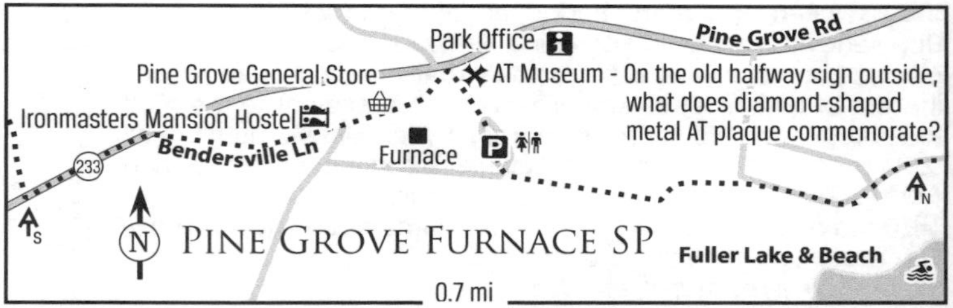

Ironmasters Mansion Hostel 717.486.4108 $25PP or $35PP incl. pizza dinner & b'fast (45/meal add'l);. 5-9p check-in, 9a check-out; closed 9a–5p & Tu nights. Call/email for reservations. Laundry $3. Open Apr 1-Oct 31; sometimes closed for special events. Mail: Ironmasters Hostel, 1212 Pine Grove Rd, Gardners, PA 17324, ironmasterspinegrove@gmail.com.

Pine Grove General Store 717.486.4920 Open daily 8am-7pm mid-May - Labor Day; weekends only mid-Apr - mid-May and Labor Day - Oct. Cold drinks, selection of hiking food, canister fuel, fuel/oz, socks, toiletries. Short-order grill. Soda machine outside. Home of ***half gallon challenge.***

A.T. Museum 717.486.8126 Hikers welcome to bring food to eat outside & relax. Artifacts and photos of past hikers, signs from Springer & Katahdin. Sells halfway patch & bandana. Open Mar 25-April 30 weekends only 12-4; May 7-July 16 daily 9-4; July 17-Aug 20 daily 12-4; Aug 23- Oct 29 W-Sun 12-4 **Hiker Festival** Jun 3. **Fall Festival** Oct 21-22. ⟨www.atmuseum.org⟩

1108.4 Side trail (0.7W) to campground

Mountain Creek Campground 717.486.7681 Open Apr-Nov, cabins $55+ tax, tentsites $28. Either holds 2 adults/4 children. Camp store has sodas & ice cream, short-order grill on weekends.

1110.8 PA 34, Hunters Run Rd,

Green Mtn Store (0.2E) 717.486.4558 M-F 7am-8pm, Sa 8-8, Su 9-6. Good selection of hiker foods, prepared foods, ice cream, canister fuel, heet.

1112.8 PA 94 ***Mt. Holly Springs, PA 17065*** (2.5W) 5mi farther to 81 interchange w/ Walmart & movies at Carlisle Commons.
M–F 8-1 & 2-4:30, Sa 9-12, 717.486.3468
Holly Inn, Restaurant & Tavern 717.486.3823 $50S, $55D $5EAP, free ride to/from AT, $5 round trip from Pine Grove Furnace SP. Fri live music, Sa karaoke, Sun open mic., Restaurant Su-Th 11:30-9, F-Sa 11:30-10.
Sheetz, Dollar General, Family Dollar
J & K Hi Hat Restaurant 717.323.0473 b'fast, lunch, dinner. closed Tu.
Subway, **Sicilia Pizza**
Holly Pharmacy 717.486.5321
Dollie's Laundromat

1113.1 Sheet Iron Roof Rd
Deer Run Campground (0.4W) 717.486.8168 Tent w/shower $10, cabin $75+tax.

1121.6 PA 174, ***Boiling Springs, PA 17007***
Free campsite & privy, see bottom right corner of map. RR tracks pass near campsite.
Allenberry Resort 800.430.5468 Call for Hiker Rates. Restaurant/Bar Tu-Su. Store open daily (snacks, beer & toiletries). Pool (in season), cc ok. $5 fee for Mail, call before sending: 1559 Boiling Springs Rd, Boiling Springs, PA 17007 ⟨www.allenberry.com⟩
Gelinas Manor 717.258.6584 Room w/shared BA $99D/up. No pets, no packs inside. Full b'fast at 8:30. Laundry $6/load. CC OK. Maildrops w/reservation: MUST say "in care of Gelinas Manor", 219 Front St, Boiling Springs, PA 17007. ⟨www.gelinasmanor.com⟩
Red Cardinal B&B 717.245.0823 Prices seasonal, queen BR incl. full b'fast, P/U & Ret from Boiling Springs (2mi away). No pets/smoking.
Karn's Quality Foods 717.258.1458 Daily 7–10.
Lakeside Food Mart 717.241.6163 ATM inside.
Boiling Springs Animal Hospital 717.258.4575 M,W 8-7:30, Tu,Th-F 8-6, Sa 8-1
Anile's Ristorante & Pizzeria 717.258.5070 L/D subs, pizza. Daily 11-10.
Boiling Springs Tavern 717.258.3614 L/D 11:30-2, 5-9, closed Su-M.
Boiling Springs Pool 717.258.4121 Mem. Day-Labor Day, M-Su 11-7, $2 hot shower. If you want to swim, visit ATC Regional Office for $3 off the $12 admission.
TCO Outdoors 610.678.1899 canister fuel & small hiking items.
Mike's Shuttle Service 717.497.6022
ATC Mid-Atlantic Regional Office 717.258.5771 Wkdays 8-5. Spigot on south side of building, may be off in winter. Staff & bulletin board provide info on trail conditions. Small shop w maps. Fuel/oz for donation.

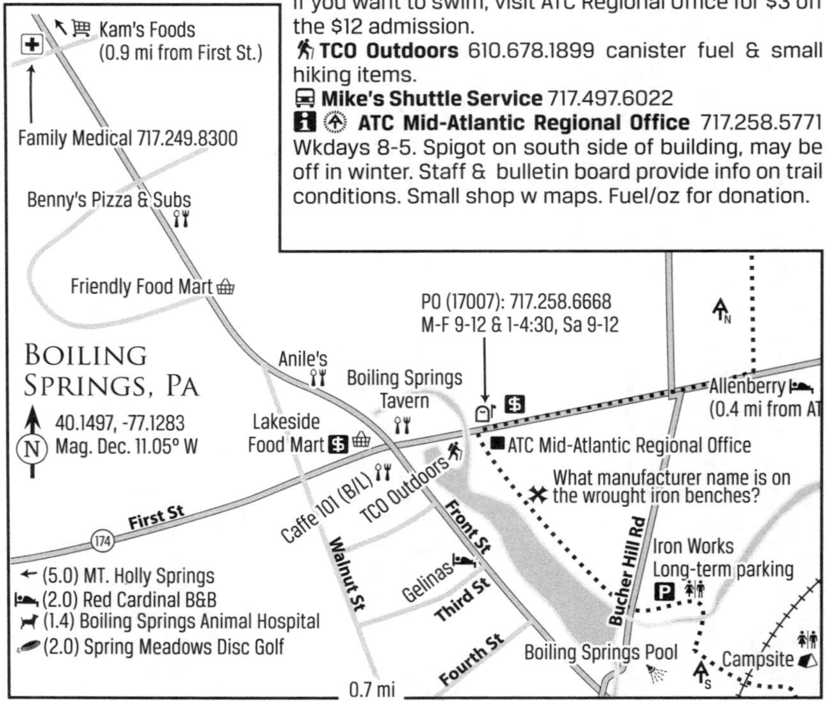

BOILING SPRINGS, PA
40.1497, -77.1283
Mag. Dec. 11.05° W
Kam's Foods (0.9 mi from First St.)
Family Medical 717.249.8300
Benny's Pizza & Subs
Friendly Food Mart
Anile's
Boiling Springs Tavern
Lakeside Food Mart
PO (17007): 717.258.6668
M-F 9-12 & 1-4:30, Sa 9-12
Allenberry (0.4 mi from AT)
ATC Mid-Atlantic Regional Office
What manufacturer name is on the wrought iron benches?
Caffe 101 (B/L)
TCO Outdoors
First St
Front St
Walnut St
Gelinas
Third St
Fourth St
Bucher Hill Rd
Iron Works Long-term parking
Boiling Springs Pool
Campsite
174
← (5.0) MT. Holly Springs
(2.0) Red Cardinal B&B
(1.4) Boiling Springs Animal Hospital
(2.0) Spring Meadows Disc Golf
0.7 mi

1074.6	1115.2	Rock maze	1097
1074.2	1115.6	Whiskey Spring Rd, reliable water from spring ●	830

> No camping & No Campfires in Cumberland Valley between Alec Kennedy & Darlington Shelters, except at backpackers campsite south of Boiling Springs.

1072.2	1117.6	Little Dogwood Run, campsite, orange-blazed trail 1.7E to BSA campground	870
1072.1	1117.7	**Alec Kennedy Shelter** (0.2E), spring behind shelter is unreliable (7) 25.2◂19.0◂8.1◂▸18.2▸25.5▸33.8	950
1071.2	1118.6	Center Point Knob, original AT midpoint, White Rocks Trail 0.4E to view	1060
1069.8	1120.0	Cornfield, south end	562
1069.3	1120.5	Leidigh Dr	553
1068.6	1121.2	Backpacker's Campsite (nearby railroad tracks can be noisy)	514
1068.4	1121.4	Bucher Hill Rd, get permit from ATC office to park overnight 40.1478,-77.1241 P	501
1068.2	1121.6	PA 174, First Street, ATC Mid-Atlantic Regional Office (pg. 111) **Boiling Springs, PA**	500
1066.7	1123.1	Stone wall	627
1066.1	1123.7	PA 74, York Rd 40.1731,-77.1211 P	573
1065.1	1124.7	Lisburn Rd	547
1064.6	1125.2	Byers Rd	556
1064.5	1125.3	Footbridge, stream	505
1064.1	1125.7	Trindle Rd, PA 641, kiosk 40.195,-77.1083 P (pg. 116)	540
1062.9	1126.9	Ridge Rd, Biddle Rd (pg. 116)	471
1062.4	1127.4	Old Stone House Rd, footbridge, stream	474
1061.7	1128.1	Appalachian Dr	525
1061.4	1128.4	PA Turnpike (I-76) overpass	498
1060.8	1129.0	Railroad tracks	478
1060.2	1129.6	US 11, **Carlisle, PA** (0.5W) (pg. 116)	490
1059.3	1130.5	Pass over I-81 on Bernheisel Rd	485
1058.7	1131.1	Fence stile (two)	465
1057.9	1131.9	Conodoguinet Creek, footbridge alongside road 40.2598,-77.1037 P **Scott Farm Trail ATC Crew HQ** Open May-Oct, picnic table, no camping. The AT u-turns, passes under bridge, and heads north.	389
1056.8	1133.0	Sherwood Drive, parking to east 40.274,-77.0995 P Many footbridges, streams north and south of this road.	397
1055.9	1133.9	PA 944 tunnel	480

1055.0 1134.8 Piped spring where AT crosses overgrown dirt road . . . 718
NoBo planning stay at Darlington Shelter consider getting water here.
1054.3 1135.5 View . . . 1102
1054.0 1135.8 Darlington Trail, Tuscarora Trail . . . 1246
1053.9 1135.9 **Darlington Shelter** (0.1E) 37.2◄26.3◄18.2◄►7.3►15.6►22.3 . . . (5) 1221
(2005) Unreliable water on blue-blazed trail in front of shelter. Taj Mahal privy.

1052.3 1137.5 Gravel road . . . 725
1052.0 1137.8 Millers Gap Rd (paved) . . . 684
1051.7 1138.1 PA 850. . . . 40.3218,-77.0781 P 673

1050.2 1139.6 Service road. . . . 761
1050.0 1139.8 Footbridge, stream . . . 852

1049.2 1140.6 Pipeline, view, trail very rocky from here north to PA 274 . . . 1319

1047.5 1142.3 Blue-blazed trail 0.4W to service road . . . 1259

1046.6 1143.2 **Cove Mountain Shelter** (0.2E)(2000) . . . (8) 1274
33.6◄25.5◄7.3◄►8.3►15.0►33.0 Spring 0.1 mile on steep side trail.

SoBo NoBo 1000 3000 5000

1044.6 1145.2 Hawk Rock, view . . . 1052

1043.9 1145.9 Old trail to west, AT turns east (uphill for NoBo) . . . 516
1043.5 1146.3 Inn Rd, trail very rocky from here south to pipeline. . . . 380
1043.0 1146.8 PA 274, pass under US 11/15 . . . 385
1042.6 1147.2 **Duncannon, PA**, High St + Broadway . . . **(pg. 116)** 393

1041.5 1148.3 Juniata River, bridge . . . 366

1040.8 1149.0 Susquehanna River . . . 40.396,-77.0085 P 376
North end of Clarks Ferry Bridge, US 22/322, railroad tracks
1039.9 1149.9 View . . . 655

1038.5 1151.3 Susquehanna Trail to west. . . . 1190
1038.3 1151.5 **Clarks Ferry Shelter** (0.1E)(1993) . . . (8) 1211
33.8◄15.6◄8.3◄►6.7►24.7►38.1 Reliable piped spring just beyond shelter.
1038.0 1151.8 Powerline . . . 1331

Nov. 15 - Dec15 (except Sundays): On state gamelands (much of the A.T. between Susquehanna River & Delaware Water Gap) everyone is required to wear at least 250 square inches of fluorescent orange material on the head, chest & back combined, or a fluorescent orange hat, and must be visible for 360º.

1035.4 1154.4 Powerline . . . 1225

SOBO	NOBO	Feature		Elev
1034.5	1155.3	PA 225	40.4119,-76.9299 P	1247
1033.9	1155.9	Powerline		1282
1032.5	1157.3	Table Rock, view		1333
1031.6	1158.2	**Peters Mtn Shelter** (1994) 22.3◄15.0◄6.7◄►18.0►31.4►35.5 Weak spring 0.3 mile steeply downhill from shelter (300 rock steps).	(16)	1169
1030.6	1159.2	Victoria Trail. ⚠ See State Game Lands guidelines pg. 115		1196
1030.0	1159.8	Whitetail Trail		1316
1028.9	1160.9	Kinter View		1320
1027.5	1162.3	Shikellimy Trail 0.9E to parking area	40.4377,-76.8198 P	1165
1026.5	1163.3	Campsite		1369
1025.2	1164.6	Spring 100 yards east on side trail		700
1024.9	1164.9	PA 325, Clarks Creek north of road	40.4515,-76.7762 P	550
1024.6	1165.2	Spring		606
1024.5	1165.3	Henry Knauber Trail to east		685
1023.2	1166.6	Spring		1251
1021.6	1168.2	Horse-Shoe Trail to east		1650
1020.9	1168.9	Rattling Run		1504
1018.3	1171.5	Yellow Springs Trail		1365
1018.2	1171.6	Clearing with trail register, camping Yellow Springs Village Site, old coal mining settlement (0.7W).		1450
1017.3	1172.5	Spring		1395
1016.1	1173.7	Sand Spring Trail west to "The General"		1361
1015.9	1173.9	Cold Spring Trail to east		1400

NoBo	SoBo	Feature	Coordinates / Services	Elev.
1013.7	1176.1	Spring, campsite		1080
1013.6	1176.2	**Rausch Gap Shelter** (0.3E) 33.0◄24.7◄18.0◄►13.4►17.5►32.6.	(6)	1063
1013.1	1176.7	AT on gravel road for 0.2 mile, bridge over Rausch Creek		904
1012.8	1177.0	Cemetery to west		860
1012.6	1177.2	Stony Creek, footbridge		827
1011.5	1178.3	Second Mountain		1362
1009.8	1180.0	Field		650
1009.5	1180.3	Cross two roads: Greenpoint School Rd, then PA 443		575
1008.9	1180.9	Pass under PA 72 and cross PA 443 Stream, campsite south of PA 72	40.4821,-76.5506 P	483
1007.5	1182.3	Swatara Gap, PA 72, **Lickdale, PA** (2.1E)	(pg. 120)	480
1007.1	1182.7	I-81, AT passes underneath		450
1006.8	1183.0	Gravel road		615
1002.9	1186.9	Abandoned powerline overlook, view		1386
1000.2	1189.6	**William Penn Shelter** (0.1E)(1993) 38.1◄31.4◄13.4◄►4.1►19.2►33.9 Water and tent sites 0.1W on blue-blazed trail.	(16)	1409
998.1	1191.7	PA 645, Waggoners Gap Rd **Pine Grove, PA** (3.4W)	40.5066,-76.3768 P (pg. 120)	1219
996.9	1192.9	Fisher Lookout, view		1310
996.2	1193.6	Kimmel Lookout, view		1362
996.1	1193.7	PA 501, **501 Shelter** (0.1W)(1975) 35.5◄17.5◄4.1◄►15.1►29.8►38.9 **Pine Grove, PA** (4.2W), **Bethel, PA** (4.1E)	40.5125,-76.3444 P (pg. 121)	1444
995.6	1194.2	Trail to Pilger Ruh (Pilgrims Rest), spring to east, Applebee Campsite to west.		1450

1000 3000 5000

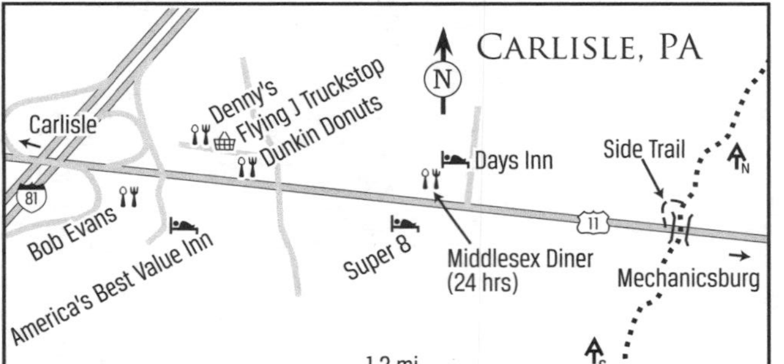

1125.7 Trindle Rd

1126.9 Ridge Rd

Pheasant Field B&B (0.5W) 717.258.0717 $135/up, free pickup & return w/stay, big b'fast, laundry for fee, behaved pets ok. Call from Trindle Rd, or from Ridge Rd, go 0.25W to Hickory Town Rd, turn left on road, B&B on right.

1129.6 US 11 (Carlisle Pike), ***Carlisle, PA 17013*** (0.5W to hotels)

The AT passes over the highway on a footbridge. A side trail down to the road is at the northwest corner of the overpass. Hotels run short of rooms (and go up in price) every other weekend when there is a car show.

Days Inn 717.245.2242 Hiker rate $55.95, cont B, pets $20.

Super 8 Motel 717.249.7000 $54.99S, $59.99D, cont. b'fast, $10 pet fee. Guest Mail: 1800 Harrisburg Pike, Carlisle, PA 17013.

Americas Best Value Inn 717.249.7775 $49.99/up + tax, cont B, $15 pet fee.

Flying J Truckstop 717.243.6659, 24hrs. Store, diner, pizza by the slice, showers $12 incl. towel, laundry.

Appalachian Running Company 717.241.5674 good selection of trail running shoes, shoe fitting, rides sometimes available.

Mechanicsburg, PA 17050 (5.0E)

Large city with an abundance of services, most notably: **CVS** (3.0E), **Giant Food** (4.3E), **Walmart** (4.6E), **Appalachian Brewing Co** (4.9E), **Wegmans** (5.4E) **Park Inn** (7.0E) 717.697.0321 restaurant & bars on-site.

1147.2 High St, ***Duncannon, PA 17020***

Doyle Hotel 717.834.6789, $25S, $35D, $10EAP + tax, bar serves L/D. Pool Table. Coleman/alcohol/oz and canister fuel. Accepts Visa/MC/Disc. Mail: (USPS/UPS) 7 North Market Street, Duncannon, PA 17020.

Stardust Motel 717.834.3191 $45S, $55D Sometimes pickup/return rides avail. No pets.

Red Carpet Inn 717.834.3320 $55S, $60D + tax. pickup and return from Duncannon for $10.

Riverfront Campground 717.834.5252 Site & shower $5PP, check-in daylight till dark. Shuttles. Note proximity of RR tracks.

Sorrento Pizza 717.834.5167

Goodies 717.836.6300 B'fast 6am-11am

Ranch House Restaurant 717.834.4710 B/L/D, near Stardust Motel has dinner buffet F-Sa, b'fast on weekends.

Lumberjack's Kitchen 717.834.9099 Near Red Carpet Inn M-Th L/D, F-Sun B/L/D

Mutzabaugh's Market 717.834.3121 Hiker-friendly, open 7 days 6am-10pm. Pickup/return to Doyle 4pm daily.

Rite Aid 717.834.6303 next door to market.

Pilot Travel Plaza 717.834.3156, Open 24/7 $12 showers.

Cove Mountain Animal Hospital 717.834.5534

■ **Christ Lutheran Church** Free hiker dinner Wednesdays in June & July 5pm-7pm. On Plum St + Church St one block west of High St.

Presbyterian Church 717.834.5815 Library w/internet access W 1-4, Sa 10-2.

Store 34 M-F 12-6, Sa 10-2. High speed internet $3/30 min, $5/hr

Trail Angel Mary 717.834.4706 2 Ann St, Duncannon, PA 17020

Blue Mountain Outfitters 717.957.2413 8mi south in Maryville, PA

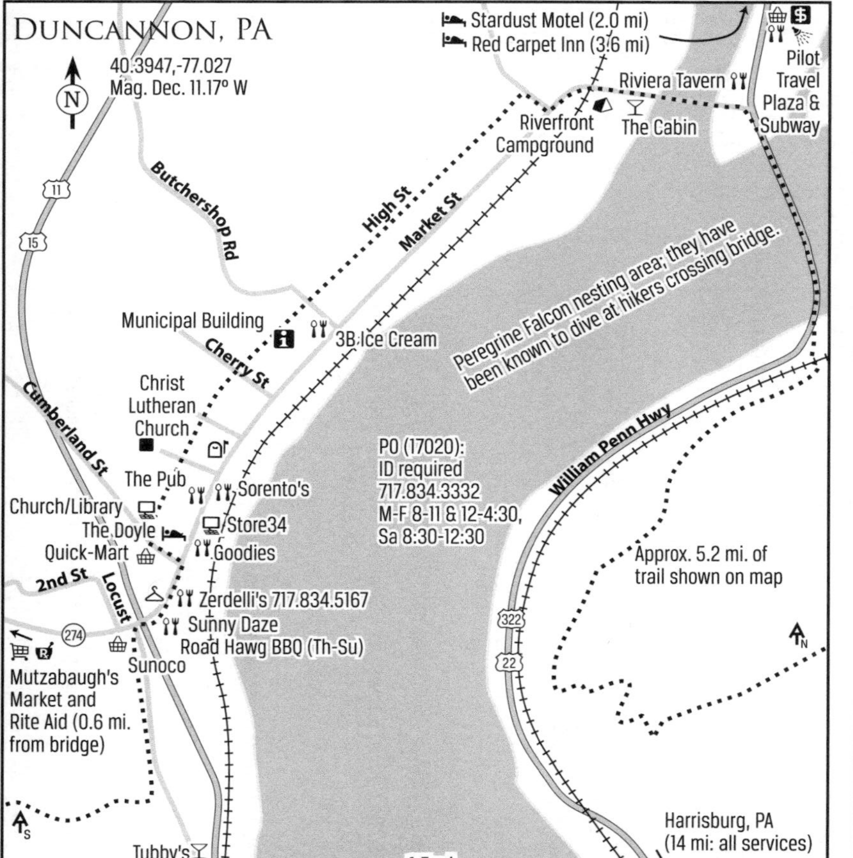

The AT is on **State Game Lands** in PA from north of Peters Mtn Shelter to Wind Gap, with the exception of small patches of land, mostly near major road crossings. Watch for posted regulations.

Primitive one-night camping is allowed:

- Only by hikers starting and ending at different locations.
- Within 200 feet of the AT, and
- 500 feet from water sources, trailheads, road crossings, and parking areas.
- Only small campfires are allowed, and only when the wildfire danger is less than "high."

Allentown, Bake Oven Knob Darlington, Cove Mtn, and Rausch Gap Shelters are on State Game Lands.

"Appalachee" is the name of an Indian tribe that once populated northwest Florida. Sixteenth century Spanish explorers used variants of the name to describe a region extending into the southern end of the mountain range. The place name, now morphed into "Appalachian," stuck to the mountains and moved north, leaving behind the flatlands where it originated.

SoBo	NoBo	Landmark		Elev
993.0	1196.8	Round Head, Shower Steps Trail, campsite to south on AT. Side trail to view.		1500
991.0	1198.8	Overlook, view.		1404
990.6	1199.2	⚠ NoBo: AT turns east, Boulderfield Trail to west (straight ahead)		1271
990.5	1199.3	Hertline Campsite and picnic table		1200
989.8	1200.0	Pipeline, road paralleling pipeline, cross twice, then parallel to AT		1516
987.1	1202.7	Fort Dietrich Snyder Monument	(0.2W)	1474
986.8	1203.0	PA 183, Rentschler Marker on side trail 30 yards north of road	(pg. 125)	1423
986.3	1203.5	Game Commission road (gravel)	40.5273,-76.2148 P	1479
985.5	1204.3	Black Swatara Spring 0.3E		1567
982.9	1206.9	Eagles Nest Trail to east		1601
981.7	1208.1	Sand Spring Trail 0.2E to spring		1510
981.0	1208.8	**Eagles Nest Shelter** (0.3W)(1988), spring on trail to shelter 32.6◄19.2◄15.1◄►14.7►23.8►31.2	(8)	1580
979.1	1210.7	Shartlesville-Cross Mtn Rd (overgrown dirt road).		1450
976.4	1213.4	Phillips Canyon Spring (unmarked, unreliable)		1500

974.4 1215.4 State Game Land Rd 1417

973.8 1216.0 Pipeline clearing, AT crosses multiple times 1413

972.2 1217.6 Schuylkill Trail 2.4E to Hamburg, parking 0.1N . . . . 40.5796,-76.0267 P 564
972.0 1217.8 **Port Clinton, PA**, Broad St + Penn St . . . . (pg. 125) 430
971.7 1218.1 PA 61, Blue Mtn Rd, **Hamburg, PA** (1.7E) . . . . (pg. 125) 490

969.2 1220.6 Spring to west, campsite 1184

968.0 1221.8 Minnehaha Spring, frequently dry 1361

966.6 1223.2 Reservoir Rd, stream north on AT . . . . 40.5896,-75.9443 P 878
Parking 0.3E only with permission from Hamburg Borough 610.562.7821 M-F 8-5.
966.3 1223.5 **Windsor Furnace Shelter** (0.1W)(1972) . . . . (8) 848
33.9◄29.8◄14.7◄►9.1►16.5►26.5 No swimming, creek south of shelter.
965.6 1224.2 Blue-blazed trail to **Blue Rocks Campground** (1.5E) . . . . (pg. 125) 997

964.7 1225.1 Pulpit Rock, 30 yards west to privy at Pulpit Rock Astronomical Park. 1582
No camping or fires.

962.9 1226.9 Yellow-blazed trail to **Blue Rocks Campground** (1.5E) . . . . (pg. 125) 1594
962.5 1227.3 The Pinnacle, 0.1E to panoramic view, no camping or fires 1615

960.8 1229.0 Furnace Creek Trail to west 1444
960.6 1229.2 Gold Spring, no camping or fires 1372

959.9 1229.9 Blue-blazed trail 1.5W reconnects with AT near Windsor Furnace Shelter 1402
959.6 1230.2 Pinnacle Spur Trail to west 1394

959.0 1230.8 Panther Creek, dependable 1090

958.1 1231.7 Parking lot 0.4E on side trail . . . . 40.6255,-75.9535 P 832

957.2 1232.6 Hawk Mountain Rd, **Eckville Shelter** (0.2E) . . . . . (6) (pg. 125) 692
38.9◄23.8◄9.1◄►7.4►17.4►24.2 Enclosed bunkroom, tent platforms, flush toilet, spigot at side of caretaker's house.
956.7 1233.1 Footbridge, stream, campsite north on AT 564

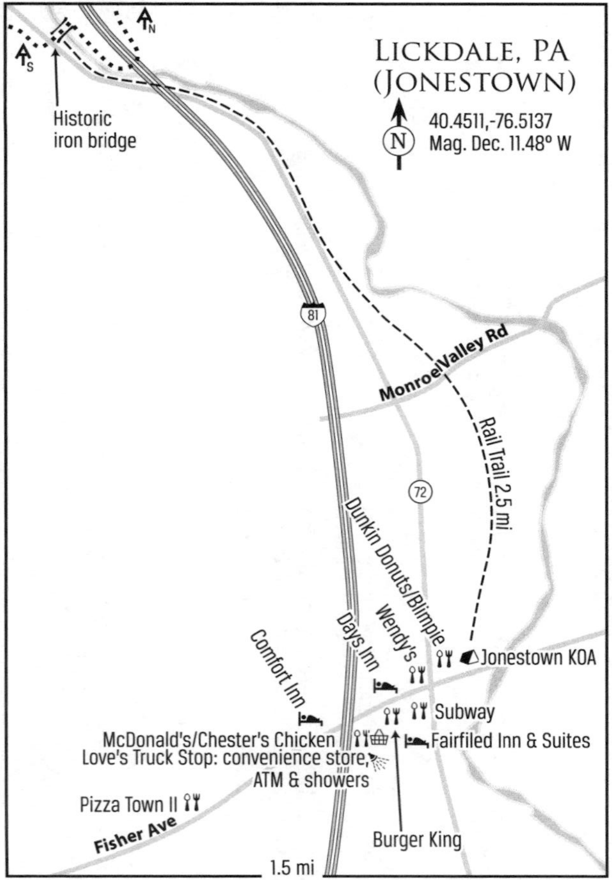

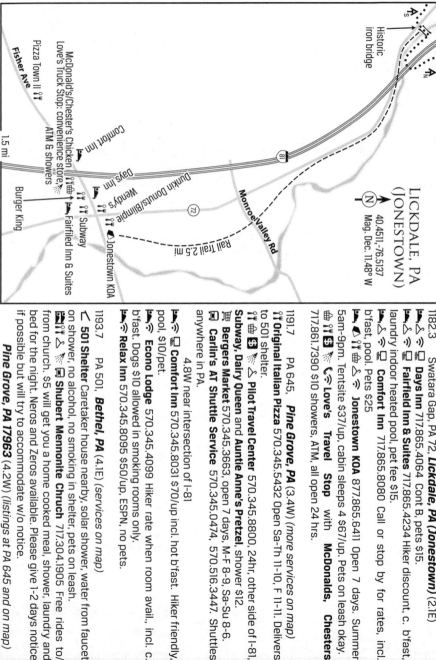

1182.3 Swatara Gap, PA 72, ***Lickdale, PA (Jonestown)*** (2.1E)

Days Inn 717.865.4064 Cont B, pets $15.

Fairfield Inn & Suites 717.865.4234 Hiker discount, c. b'fast, laundry indoor heated pool, pet fee $15.

Comfort Inn 717.865.8080 Call or stop by for rates, incl. b'fast, pool. Pets $25

Jonestown KOA 877.865.6411 Open 7 days. Summer 5am-9pm. Tentsite $37/up, cabin sleeps 4 $67/up. Pets on leash okay.

Love's Travel Stop with **McDonalds, Chesters** 717.861.7390 $10 showers, ATM, all open 24 hrs.

1191.7 PA 645, ***Pine Grove, PA*** (3.4W) *(more services on map)*

Original Italian Pizza 570.345.5432 Open Sa-Th 11-10, F 11-11. Delivers to 501 shelter.

Pilot Travel Center 570.345.8800, 24hr, other side of I-81, **Subway, Dairy Queen** and **Auntie Anne's Pretzel**, shower $12.

Bergers Market 570.345.3663, open 7 days, M-F 8-9, Sa-Su 8-6.

Carlin's AT Shuttle Service 570.345.0474, 570.516.3447. Shuttles anywhere in PA.

4.8W near intersection of I-81

Comfort Inn 570.345.8031 $70/up incl. hot b'fast. Hiker friendly, pool, $10/pet.

Econo Lodge 570.345.4099 Hiker rate when room avail., incl. c. b'fast. Dogs $10 allowed in smoking rooms only.

Relax Inn 570.345.8095 $50/up, ESPN, no pets.

1193.7 PA 501, ***Bethel, PA*** (4.1E) *(services on map)*

501 Shelter Caretaker house nearby, solar shower, water from faucet on shower, no alcohol, no smoking in shelter, pets on leash.

Shubert Mennonite Chruch 717.304.1905 Free rides to/from church. $5 will get you a home cooked meal, shower, laundry and bed for the night. Neros and Zeros available. Please give 1-2 days notice if possible but will try to accommodate w/o notice.

Pine Grove, PA 17963 (4.2W) *(listings at PA 645 and on map)*

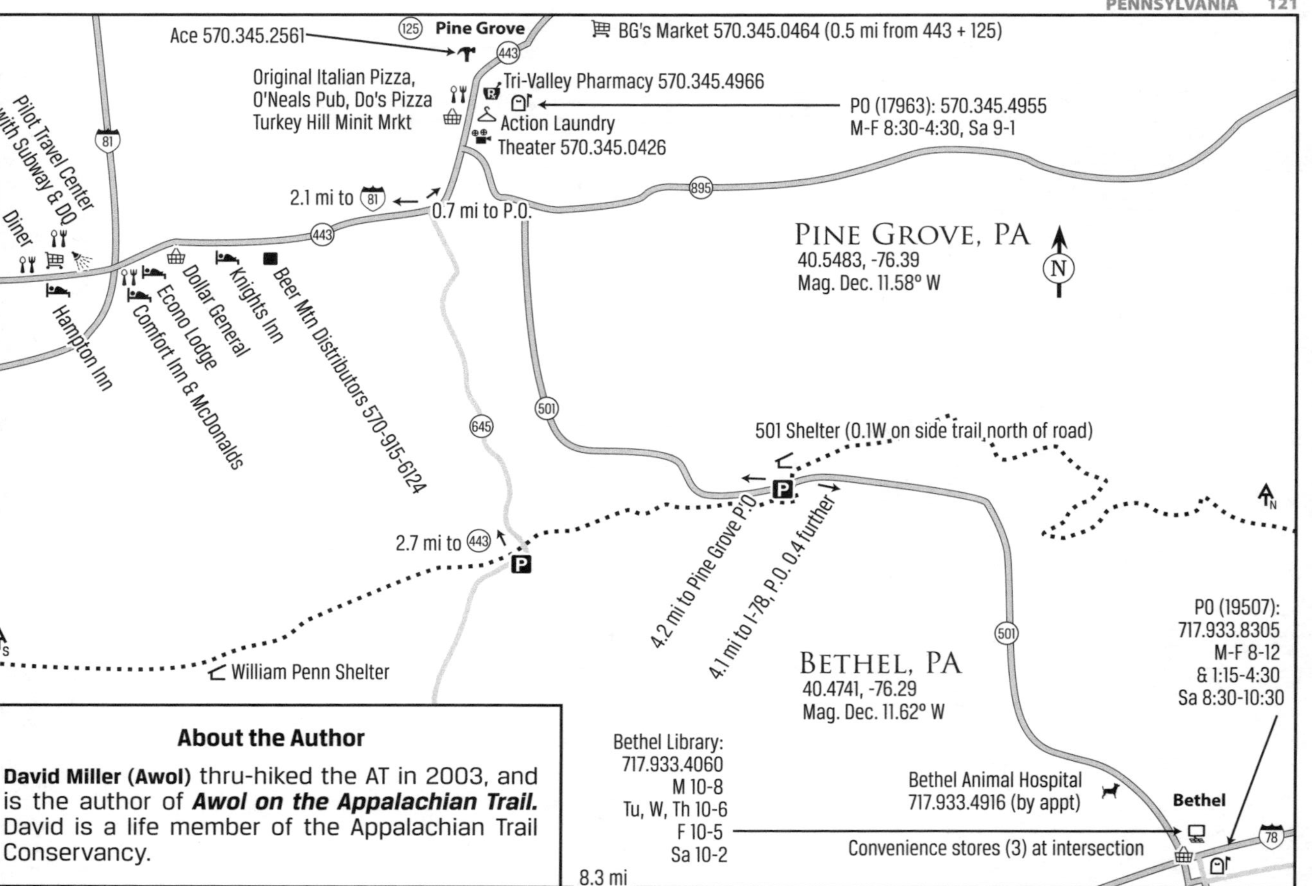

About the Author

David Miller (Awol) thru-hiked the AT in 2003, and is the author of ***Awol on the Appalachian Trail.*** David is a life member of the Appalachian Trail Conservancy.

955.3 1234.5 Hawk Mtn Trail to west 1364

954.2 1235.6 Dans Pulpit, trail register. 1615

953.6 1236.2 Dans Spring 0.1E 1558

951.0 1238.8 Tri-County Corner, ⚠ AT to west. 1524

949.8 1240.0 **Allentown Hiking Club Shelter** (1997) . . . . (8) 1488
31.2◄16.5◄7.4◄►10.0►16.8►33.5
Unreliable spring downhill in front of shelter 0.2 mile, another 0.1 farther.

949.5 1240.3 Springs to east; Blue 100 yards, Yellow 0.3 mi 1331

947.9 1241.9 Fort Franklin Rd (gravel) . . . . 40.6943,-75.8419 P 1350

946.0 1243.8 Trail 0.2W to restaurant (closer to AT + PA 309) 1356

945.7 1244.1 PA 309, Blue Mountain Summit . . . . 40.7072,-75.8086 P **(pg. 125)** 1360

943.9 1245.9 Powerline, New Tripoli Campsite 0.2W. 1431

942.8 1247.0 Knife Edge, view 1560

942.3 1247.5 Bear Rocks, view 1544

940.8 1249.0 Bake Oven Knob Rd (gravel) . . . . 40.7446,-75.7386 P 1450

940.4 1249.4 Bake Oven Knob. 1560

939.8 1250.0 **Bake Oven Knob Shelter** (1937) . . . . (6) 1387
26.5◄17.4◄10.0◄►6.8►23.5►37.2
Trail in front leads downhill to multiple water sources, more reliable farther down.

937.4 1252.4 Lehigh Furnace Gap, Ashfield Rd, Comm tower . . . . 40.7696,-75.6949 P 1320
Piped spring 0.5E on Ashfield Road, spring is on the right side of road.

936.3 1253.5 South Trail 0.3E to view. 1590

SoBo NoBo 1000 3000 5000

934.7 1255.1 North Trail (scenic route) to west, TV tower, AT is over Lehigh Valley Tunnel 1488
934.2 1255.6 Tower access road 1461

933.2 1256.6 North Trail (scenic route) to west 1065
933.0 1256.8 **George W. Outerbridge Shelter** (1965) Reliable piped spring 0.1N . . (6) 948
24.2◄16.8◄6.8◄►16.7►30.4►61.6
932.5 1257.3 Lehigh River south bank, PA 873, **Slatington, PA** (2.0E) . . . . . . **(pg. 128)** 422
932.0 1257.8 PA 248/145 traffic light, **Walnutport, PA** (2.0E) . . . . . . **(pg. 128)** 481
931.9 1257.9 Superfund Trailhead, **Palmerton, PA** (1.5W) . . . 40.7832,-75.6041 P **(pg. 128)** 492
Water 0.4W on blue-blazed trail to Palmerton.
931.0 1258.8 Superfund Detour south end 1420

Rocky, steep trail from Lehigh Gap. Deforested ridge due to zinc smelting from 1898-1980. Remedial activities associated with the revegetation of Blue Mountain are currently being conducted near the A.T. between Lehigh Gap & Little Gap as part of the Palmerton Zinc Pile Superfund Site. A.T. Hikers advised to stay on the A.T. & not use the road.

928.4 1261.4 High metallic content spring 0.1W (unmarked 40.8050,-75.5568) 1380
emergency water source, drinking not recommended.
928.2 1261.6 Superfund Detour north, powerline 1368
360 view from pile of rocks east of trail near power line tower.
927.1 1262.7 Little Gap Rd, **Danielsville, PA** (1.5E) . . . . . . 40.8062,-75.5346 P **(pg. 129)** 1100
926.7 1263.1 Tower access road (gravel) 1343

SoBo NoBo 1000 3000 5000

923.3 1266.5 Dirt road, powerline. 1571

922.3 1267.5 Delps Trail to east, ... (0.4E) 40.8092,-75.4512 P (0.7E) 1580
Campsite near trail intersection, unreliable spring 0.4E

920.7 1269.1 Stempa Spring 0.6E, reliable 1559

919.8 1270.0 Smith Gap Rd (paved) . . . . . . 40.8255,-75.4143 P **(pg. 130)** 1540

916.3 1273.5 **Leroy A. Smith Shelter** (0.2E)(1972) . . . . . . (8) 1456
33.5◄23.5◄16.7◄►13.7►44.9►51.5 Water 0.2 mile down blue-blazed trail; second source 0.2 mile farther. Piped spring 0.5 mile down service road.
916.1 1273.7 Powerline 1489

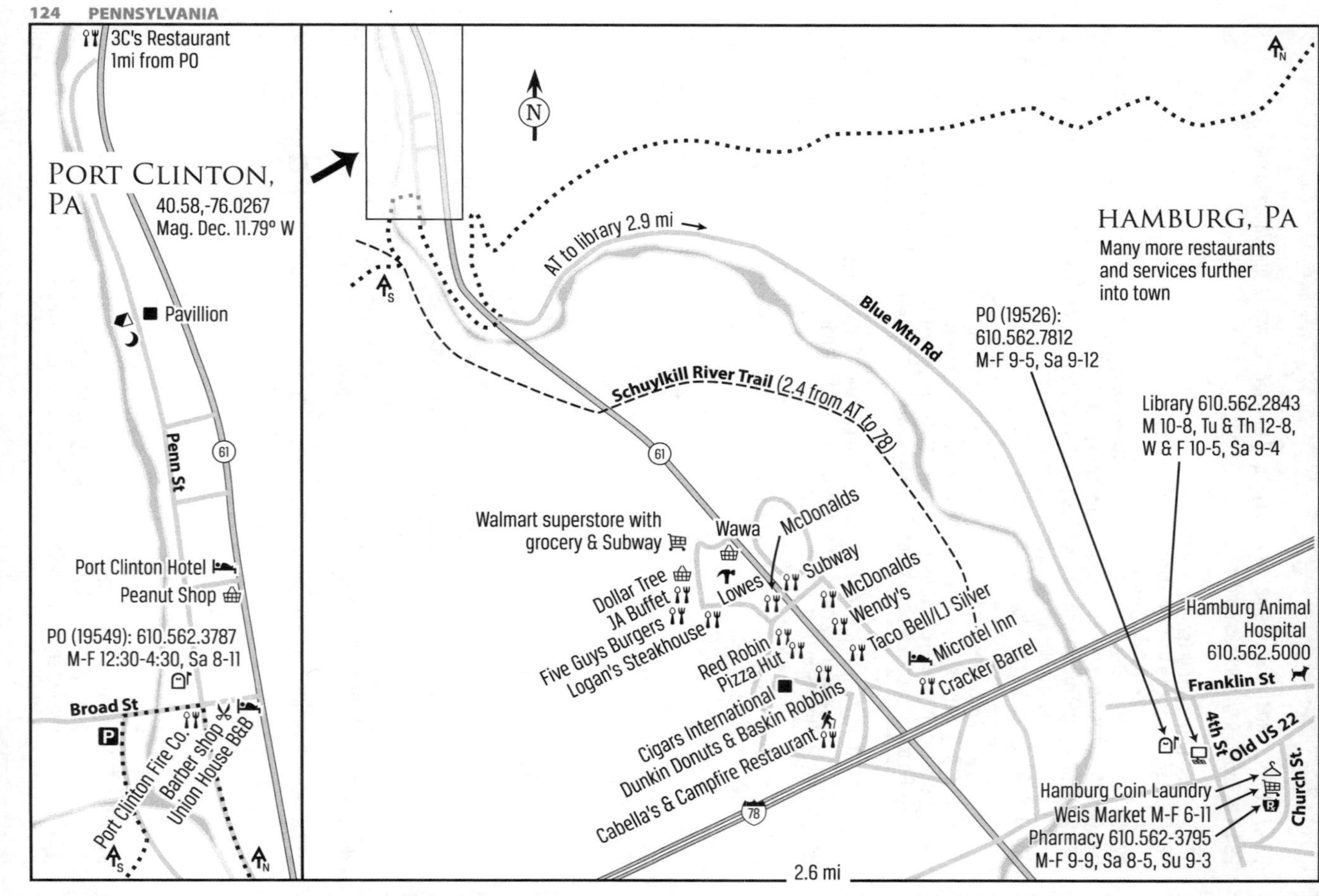
3C's Restaurant
1mi from PO
PORT CLINTON, PA
40.58,-76.0267
Mag. Dec. 11.79° W
Pavillion
Penn St
61
Port Clinton Hotel
Peanut Shop
PO (19549): 610.562.3787
M-F 12:30-4:30, Sa 8-11
Broad St
Port Clinton Fire Co.
Barber shop
Union House B&B
N
HAMBURG, PA
Many more restaurants
and services further
into town
AT to library 2.9 mi
Blue Mtn Rd
Schuylkill River Trail (2.4 from AT to 78)
PO (19526):
610.562.7812
M-F 9-5, Sa 9-12
Library 610.562.2843
M 10-8, Tu & Th 12-8,
W & F 10-5, Sa 9-4
Walmart superstore with
grocery & Subway
Wawa
McDonalds
Dollar Tree
JA Buffet
Five Guys Burgers
Logan's Steakhouse
Lowes
Subway
McDonalds
Wendy's
Taco Bell/LJ Silver
Microtel Inn
Cracker Barrel
Red Robin
Pizza Hut
Cigars International
Dunkin Donuts & Baskin Robbins
Cabella's & Campfire Restaurant
78
Hamburg Animal
Hospital
610.562.5000
Franklin St
4th St
Old US 22
Church St.
Hamburg Coin Laundry
Weis Market M-F 6-11
Pharmacy 610.562-3795
M-F 9-9, Sa 8-5, Su 9-3
2.6 mi

1203.0 PA 183

Rock 'n Sole Hostel 570.617.6432 Smoke free drug free family operation. A/C or heated bunkspace $40 incl. dinnner & b'fast, hot outdoor shower, sink & chemical privy. P/U & return 183 trail head. One daily resupply run to Dollar General. Options incl. laundry, maildrops, shuttle to Cabela's, Walmart & Yuengling Brewery tour. Slack packers & non-guest maildrops welcome. Contact for scheduling & shuttle cost.

1217.8 Broad St, Penn St ***Port Clinton, PA 19549***

Port Clinton Hotel 610.562.3354, 888.562.2626 Call for prices. Laundry/dining. $10 deposit for room key & towel, limited rooms avail. Open Tu-Su 11-9; Please shower before dining. CC OK.

Union House B&B 610.562.3155 after 5pm 610.562.4076 Open F-Su. Reservations avail. during week upon request.

3C's 610.562.5925 Open daily 6a-2p.

Port Clinton Fire Co 610.562.5499 Technically membership only; ask about visiting as a guest. Open 3p-past midnight.

The Peanut Shop 610.562.0610 Su-F 10-6, Sa 10-8 Soda, candy, dried fruit, trail mixes, ATM.

Pavilion Tenting max 2 nights, no car camping or drive-ins.

Port Clinton Barber Shop Hikers welcome to hang out, coffee, cookies & phone charging.

1218.1 PA 61, Blue Mtn Rd, ***Hamburg, PA 19526*** (1.7E)

Microtel Inn 610.562.4234 **Pappy T's Pub & Lounge** on-site. Call/stop by for hiker rate, incl. cont. b'fast. Mail (for guest w/reservation): 50 Industrial Dr, Hamburg, PA 19526

Cabela's 610.929.7000 M-Sa 8-9; Su 9-8. Largest Cabela's store in the world w/250,000 sq. ft. of retail space. Hiking gear, canister fuel. Pickup from trailhead if staff is avail. **Campfire Restaurant** Inside Cabela's serves 11a-5p, closes a little earlier than the store.

Hamburg Coin Laundry 610.562.4890

Hamburg Animal Hospital 610.562.5000 M-Th 9-7; F 9-5; Sa 9-11 by appt.

Barta Bus Service 610.921.0601 Routes within Hamburg $1.95 per boarding, stops at Cabellas. ⟨www.bartabus.com⟩

Pottsville, PA 17901 (15W, compass north on PA 61)

Yuengling Brewery 570.628.4890 America's oldest brewery. Tours M-F 10a-1:30p; Sa 11a-1p. Closed-toe shoes required.

1224.2 Blue-blazed trail to campground
1226.9 Yellow-blazed trail to campground

Blue Rocks Campground 610.756.6366 Tentsite $30/up, cabin $55/up accommodates 2 adults, 2 children. Showers & laundry. Pets allowed in campground, but not cabins. Open year-round w/limited days Nov-Mar. **Woody's Filling Station** open F-Su seasonally. Sells burgers, shakes, etc. Camp store (sodas, candy bars, snacks) closed Dec-Mar. CC accepted.

1232.6 Hawk Mountain Rd, 1.6W to Hawk Mountain Sanctuary.

Common Ground Farm & Retreat 610.756.4070, 50 Acre organic farm. Hiker discount $99/2-persons incl. b'fast, P/U & return from Eckville Shelter, laundry. Call about other trailheads. Slackpacking, parking for section hikers, longer shuttles for a fee. Mtn bike avail. for ride to store. Yr-round, no drugs/alcohol. CC OK. Mail w/reservation: 333 New Bethel Church Rd, Kempton, PA 19529

1244.1 PA 309

Blue Mountain Summit B&B 570.386.2003 $95–$125D incl. b'fast. 7 days by appt. No pets. Ok to get water at spigot at SW corner of building. Please be respectful of non-hiker guests at B&B & restaurant; OK to hang out in back. Please don't loiter in front or hang clothes to dry. Camping w/permission, no fires. Ask about shuttles. Dining (summer) Th 12-9; F 12-10; Sa 11-9; Su 11-8; (after Thanksg.) Th 4-9; F-Su same as summer. Live music on Fr. CC OK. Guest maildrop (call 1st): 2520 W Penn Pike, Andreas, PA 18211.

914.4	1275.4	Pipeline		1487
912.7	1277.1	Hahns Overlook, view		1450
911.9	1277.9	Powerline		1107
911.7	1278.1	PA 33, **Wind Gap, PA** (1.0E)	40.8607,-75.2928 P (pg. 130)	980
909.6	1280.2	Private road (gravel)		1591
906.0	1283.8	Campsite		1628
905.3	1284.5	Wolf Rocks bypass trail south end to west. Spring 100 yards west (treat)		1584
904.9	1284.9	Wolf Rocks, view		1623
904.3	1285.5	Wolf Rocks bypass trail north end to west.		1539
903.2	1286.6	Fox Gap, PA 191 (paved).	40.9354,-75.1969 P	1400
902.6	1287.2	**Kirkridge Shelter** 37.2◄30.4◄13.7◄►31.2►37.8►43.6 Tap 0.1 mi behind shelter, off in winter.	(6)	1440
902.3	1287.5	Campsite, view		1490
900.7	1289.1	Totts Gap, gravel road, powerline to south		1300
900.4	1289.4	Pipeline		1382
900.1	1289.7	Roadbed.		1401
898.7	1291.1	Mt Minsi		1461
897.7	1292.1	Lookout Rock, view		800
897.5	1292.3	Stream.		760
896.9	1292.9	Council Rock		536
896.8	1293.0	Turn east on gravel road		575
896.4	1293.4	Hiker parking lot	40.9798,-75.142 P	498
896.2	1293.6	PA 611, **Delaware Water Gap, PA**	(pg. 134)	386
895.9	1293.9	**PA-NJ** border, I-80, Delaware River Bridge west bank		278

894.9 1294.9 Kittatinny Visitor Center 40.9720,-75.1261 290
NoBo: cross under I-80 and turn left.
894.5 1295.3 Parking, V.C. is preferred for overnight parking. 40.9701,-75.1287 295
✖What name, stamped in cursive, is on (non-functioning) pump?
894.2 1295.6 Dunnfield Trail to east, reconnects with AT at Sunfish Pond (4 mi) 445

893.0 1296.8 Holly Spring Trail 950

New Jersey Guidelines: No campfires. Camping only at designated shelter areas and campsites, with some exceptions as posted.

890.9 1298.9 Backpacker Campsite, Douglas Trail to west, water south of camp 1327
No fires, use bear boxes/poles, leash dogs.
890.1 1299.7 Sunfish Pond south end, no swimming or camping. 1382

889.5 1300.3 Sunfish Pond north end, rock sculptures 1384

888.6 1301.2 Stream. 1452

887.9 1301.9 Powerline 1565
887.8 1302.0 Kittatinny Mountain, rocky summit 1532
887.2 1302.6 Kaiser Trail to west 1416

SoBo NoBo 1000 3000 5000

885.4 1304.4 Camp Rd (gravel), footbridge . . . . 41.033,-75.004 (pg. 134) 1109
Mohican Outdoor Center (0.3W)

884.2 1305.6 Rattlesnake Swamp Trail, view. 1475

883.3 1306.5 Catfish Lookout Tower, picnic table below the tower 1565

882.7 1307.1 Rattlesnake Spring on dirt road about 17 yards west of AT. 1260
882.4 1307.4 Stream. 1249
882.2 1307.6 Millbrook-Blairstown Rd (paved) 41.0595,-74.9636 1270
Millbrook Village (1.1W) historical park with picnic area.
881.9 1307.9 Swamp 1252
881.6 1308.2 Powerline 1384

879.5 1310.3 Campsite 1487

878.4 1311.4 Blue Mtn Lakes Rd, pump disabled, water 0.1E on road 1350
No camping in zone from 0.5 mile south of road to 3 mi. north of road.

876.3 1313.5 Side trail leads 0.5E to Crater Lake. No camping. 1447

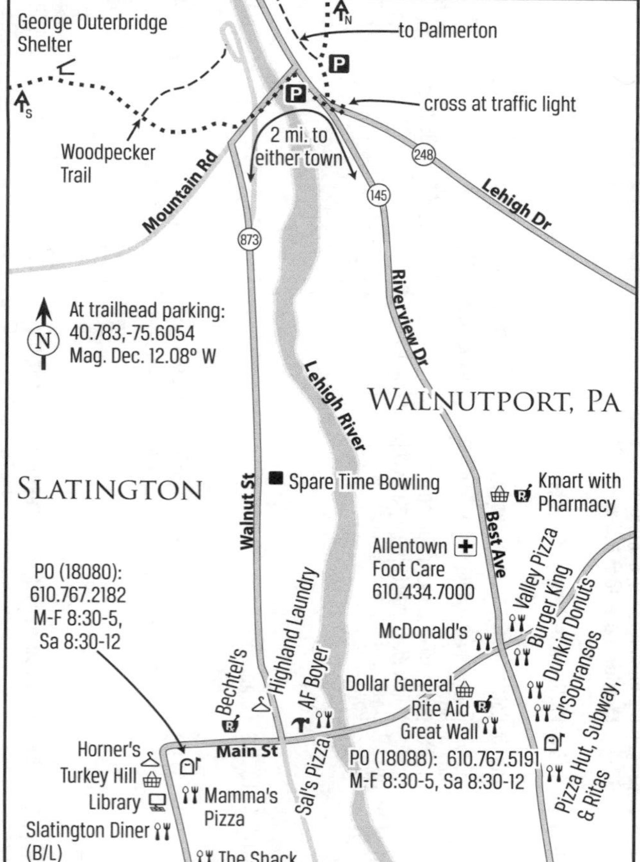

1257.3 Lehigh River, PA 873, ***Slatington, PA 18080*** (2E)

Bechtel's Pharmacy 610.767.4121 Open M-F 9-8, Sa 9-2.

Slatington Library 610.767.6461 M,W: 9-7, Tu 9-3, F 9-5, Sa 8-2.

1257.8 PA 248/145, ***Walnutport, PA 18088*** (2E)

Kmart 610.767.1812, Open daily 8-10, pharmacy hours slightly shorter. Grocery section only has dry goods (no produce).

Valley Pizza Family Restaurant 610.767.9000 L/D, delivers.

St Luke's Family Practice Center 610.628.8922 Open M-F.

Rite Aid Pharmacy 610.767.9595

Blue Ridge Veterinary Clinic 610.767.4896 ⟨www.blueridgeveterinary.com⟩ Call before coming.

1257.9 Superfund Trailhead

Palmerton, PA 18071 (1.5W)

Town Ordinance: Pets must be kept on leash.

Sunny Rest Resort 610.377.2911 ***Clothing optional*** resort 2 miles outside of town, rides sometimes avail. Weekdays: hotel rooms $118-209, camping $75, day visit $46-$56/couple. Prices higher on weekends. Mention trail guide for 20% discount. Addt'l discount for 18-35 y/o. Restaurant (B/L/D), nightclub, two heated pools, pool bar, hot tub, volleyball, nature trails, 425 Sunny Rest Rd, Palmerton, PA. Open May-Sep.

Bert's Restaurant 610.826.9921 Open 7a-8p 7 days, WiFi avail. in restaurant, ask about overnight stay and shower.

Palmerton Hotel Restaurant 610.826.5454 Dining Su-Th 4-10, F-Su 11-10.

Country Harvest 610.824.3663 8am-9pm 7 days.

Tony's Pizzeria 610.826.6161 L/D, no delivery.

Joe's Place 610.826.3730 L/D, deli sandwiches.

Little Gap Animal Hospital 610.826.2793 (3.5W) from town.

Towne Laundry 5am-7pm 7 days.

Brenda 484.725.9396 Call for pricing. Shuttles ranging from local to bus terminals & airports.

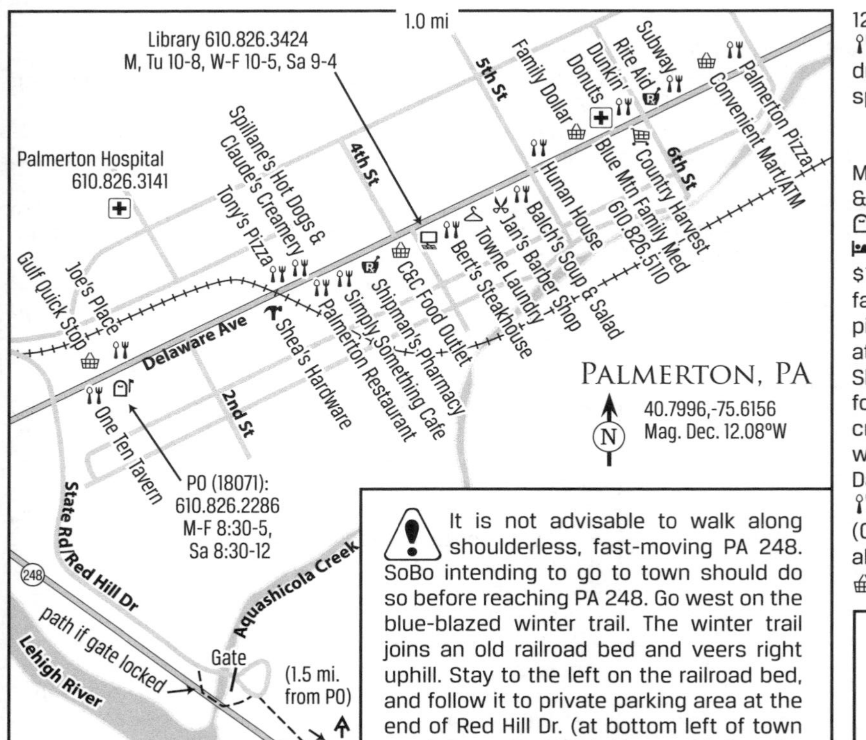

It is not advisable to walk along shoulderless, fast-moving PA 248. SoBo intending to go to town should do so before reaching PA 248. Go west on the blue-blazed winter trail. The winter trail joins an old railroad bed and veers right uphill. Stay to the left on the railroad bed, and follow it to private parking area at the end of Red Hill Dr. (at bottom left of town map). Cross Red Hill bridge and follow the road into town. If the bridge is gated or access is denied, hop the guardrail to PA 248, cautiously cross Aquashicola Creek on the 248 bridge, then hop the guardrail again to return to Red Hill Drive. The total distance to town is 1.5W miles on level ground.

1262.7 Little Gap Rd

Slopeside Pub & Grill 0.2W & 0.5mi up driveway. Hikers welcome to water from outside spigot. Grill hours: F-Sa 11:30-11; Su-Th 11:30-10.

Danielsville, PA 18038 (1.5E on Blue Mountain Dr, then left on Mountainview Dr to PO & B&B.)

M-F 9:30-1 & 2-4:30, Sa 8-12, 610.767.6882

Filbert B&B 610.428.3300 $100S, $150D + tax. Hosted by Kathy in Victorian farmhouse with A/C incl. full country b'fast. Will pickup at Little Gap (no charge). Fee for pickup at PA 309, Lehigh Gap, Smith Gap, or Wind Gap. Slackpacking possible DWG-Port Clinton. Parking for section hikers. Call ahead for reservations, no credit cards. Laundry for a fee. Italian restaurant will deliver. Guest only Mail: 3740 Filbert Dr, Danielsville, PA 18038. ⟨www.filbertbnb.com⟩

Blue Mountain Restaurant & Ice Cream (0.8E) 610.767.6379 B/L/D Tu-Su, closed M. Ask about overnighting.

Miller's Market (1.0E) 610.767.6671

Water Sources

Be aware of trail conditions before heading out, and tune in to advice from outfitters and other hikers. The trail gets rerouted, springs dry up, streams alter their course. Be prepared to deal with changes, particularly late in the season. Never carry just enough water to reach the next spring.

1270.0 Smith Gap Rd (Point Phillips Rd)

Home of John "Mechanical Man" and Linda "Crayon Lady" Stempa (1.0W, blue blazes on telephone poles) 610.381.4606, eponym of the spring 0.7 mile south. Hikers welcome to water from spigot at rear of house (no need to call) and to use outside shower during daylight hours. Pet friendly, ask about dog sitting. Please sign register. For-fee shuttles ranging from Lickdale (Swatara Gap) to Delaware Water Gap, safe place to park your car. ***Only with permission***, $10 camp or stay in garage with hot shower & towel, ride to Kunkletown included, and ride back to trail; call in advance. Sodas $1. Ask about stoves, fuel & maildrops.

(2.7E) **Evergreen Lake** 610.837.6401 East 1.7 on Smith Gap Road, then left one mile on Mountain Road. Tenting $30 for up to 2 adults, 2 children. Snack shop, laundry, free showers.

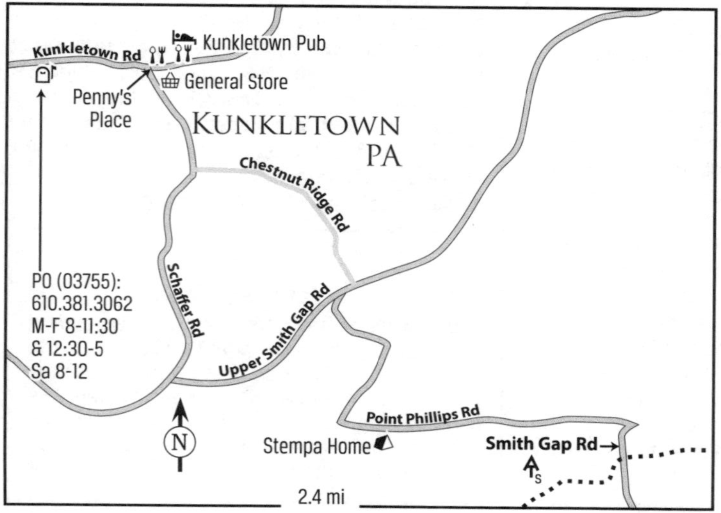

Kunkletown, PA 18058 (3.0W) See map: west on Smith Gap Rd/Point Phillips Rd for 2 mi to stop sign, right on Lower Smith Gap Rd for 100 yards, left on Chestnut Ridge Rd for 0.9 mi to Kunkletown Rd.

Kunkletown Pub 610.895.4255 Room $50/up, 10% discount on meals (L/D). Pool table. Meal delivery possible, $50 min. order.

Penny's Place 610.381.5350, 7 Days. Pub food & beer; good place to meet up with helpful locals. Free pool for hikers. Sells *The A.T. Guide*.

General Store 610.381.2887 Good selection of packaged foods, deli, ice cream. Summer hours 6:30-8:30 (till 7:30 in winter).

1278.1 PA 33

(4W) **Creature Comforts** 610.381.2287, 24/7 emergency care.

Wind Gap, PA 18091 (1E)

M–F 8:30–5, Sa 8:30–12, 610.863.6206

Travel Inn 717.885.3101 $59.99D weekdays, $69.99D weekends. Room for 4 $69.99 weekdays, $79.99 weekends.

Red Carpet Inn 610.863.7782
All stays include continental breakfast.

Giant Food Store 610.863.8635 24hr, deli w/salad bar.

K-Mart with pharmacy

Beer Stein 610.863.8338 Serves L/D wings, seafood.

Sal's Pizza 610.863.7565, delivers.

Hong Kong Chinese 610.863.9309 L/D buffet.

CVS 610.863.5341

Priority Care 610.654.5454 Walk-in clinic 7 days 8-8.

Slate Belt Family Practice 610.863.3019

WGM Taxi 570.223.9289

Gap Theatre 610.863.3094 Mostly used for concerts.

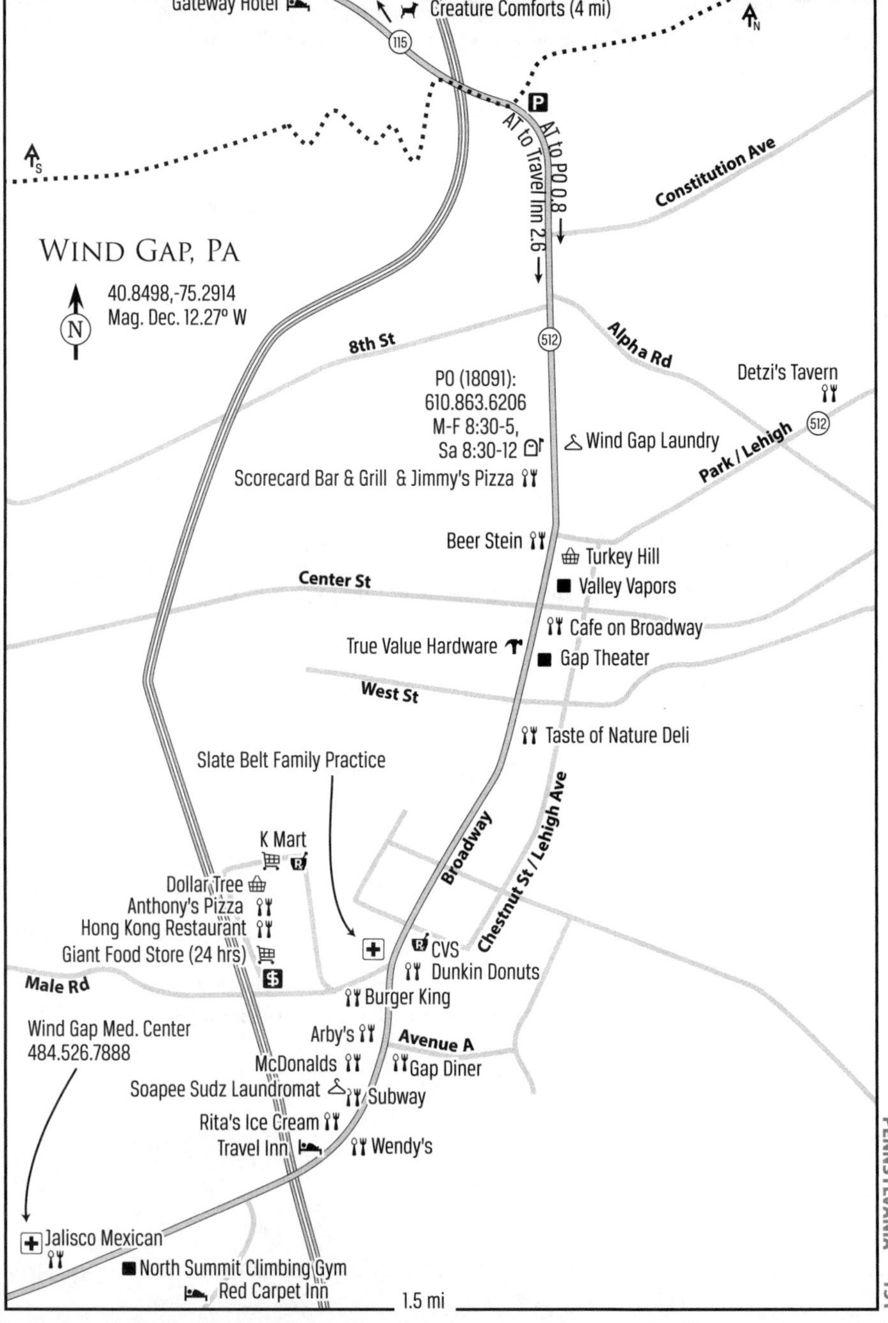
Gateway Hotel
Creature Comforts (4 mi)
115
AT to PO 0.8
AT to Travel Inn 2.6
Constitution Ave
WIND GAP, PA
40.8498,-75.2914
Mag. Dec. 12.27° W
N
8th St
512
Alpha Rd
Detzi's Tavern
PO (18091):
610.863.6206
M-F 8:30-5,
Sa 8:30-12
Wind Gap Laundry
Park / Lehigh
Scorecard Bar & Grill & Jimmy's Pizza
Beer Stein
Turkey Hill
Center St
Valley Vapors
Cafe on Broadway
True Value Hardware
Gap Theater
West St
Taste of Nature Deli
Slate Belt Family Practice
Broadway
Chestnut St / Lehigh Ave
K Mart
Dollar Tree
Anthony's Pizza
Hong Kong Restaurant
Giant Food Store (24 hrs)
CVS
Dunkin Donuts
Male Rd
Burger King
Wind Gap Med. Center
484.526.7888
Arby's
Avenue A
McDonalds
Gap Diner
Soapee Sudz Laundromat
Subway
Rita's Ice Cream
Travel Inn
Wendy's
Jalisco Mexican
North Summit Climbing Gym
Red Carpet Inn
1.5 mi

875.3 1314.5 Buttermilk Falls Trail, campsites to the north 1557

874.0 1315.8 Campsite 1293
873.6 1316.2 Rattlesnake Mountain 1492
873.3 1316.5 Spring 1365

871.4 1318.4 **Brink Shelter** (0.2W)(2013) 61.6◄44.9◄31.2◄►6.6►12.4►15.0 .... (8) 1229
Bear box. Close to road. Water 100 yards to right of old shelter site.

870.2 1319.6 Jacobs Ladder Trail 1374

868.4 1321.4 Powerline 1260

867.8 1322.0 US 206, Culvers Gap, **Branchville, NJ** (3.4E) .... **(pg. 134)** 935
867.5 1322.3 Sunrise Mountain Rd (paved) 41.1797,-74.788 972

865.9 1323.9 Culver Fire Tower (locked) 1543

864.9 1324.9 Stony Brook Trail 1.0W to free showers at Stony Lake ...... **(see map pg. 133)** 1344
864.8 1325.0 **Gren Anderson Shelter** (0.1W) .... (0.1W) (8) 1333
51.5◄37.8◄6.6◄►5.8►8.4►13.0 Spring to left of shelter and downhill 70 yards.

863.4 1326.4 Tinsley Trail 1446

862.4 1327.4 Sunrise Mountain, no camping at pavilion 41.2195,-74.7182 1653

861.7 1328.1 Roadbed 1451

860.7 1329.1 Stream (slow outflow from pond), treatment recommended 1384

859.0 1330.8 **Mashipacong Shelter** 43.6◄12.4◄5.8◄►2.6►7.2►19.6 Close to road. (8) 1410
Spring (0.6N) on red-blazed Iris Trail. Sometimes water left in bear box.
858.8 1331.0 Deckertown Turnpike 41.2523,-74.6895 1322

857.9 1331.9 Three intersections with red-blazed trail 1418

856.4 1333.4 **Rutherford Shelter** (0.4E) 15.0◄8.4◄2.6◄►4.6►17.0►28.5 .. (6) 1488
Spring 100 yards before shelter on connecting trail. Slow stream. Bear box.
856.1 1333.7 View 1481

NoBo	SoBo	Landmark	Elev
854.6	1335.2	Intersection with blue-blazed trail.	1601
853.7	1336.1	Iris Trail 0.2E to parking on NJ 23	1504
853.5	1336.3	NJ 23 . . . 41.3026,-74.6678 P (pg. 135)	1500
		High Point State Park Headquarters, **Port Jervis, NY** (4.4W)	
852.5	1337.3	Wooden tower, 0.3W to beach & concessions Mem-Labor Day 12-6	1701
852.3	1337.5	Green-blazed trail 0.3W to 220' tower atop highest point in NJ	1607
851.8	1338.0	**High Point Shelter** (0.1E) 13.0◄7.2◄4.6◄►12.4►23.9►36.0. (8)	1298
		Streams on both sides of shelter. Road to privy to right of shelter. Bear box.	
850.5	1339.3	Greenville Rd, County 519 (paved)	1100
849.6	1340.2	Courtwright Rd (gravel), stream on AT 0.1 south of road	986
849.1	1340.7	Streams	959
848.5	1341.3	Fergerson Rd (gravel), east 20 yards on road.	874
847.9	1341.9	Gemmer Rd (paved)	732
847.6	1342.2	Stream.	702
847.2	1342.6	Two footbridges, streams	606
846.9	1342.9	Goodrich Rd (paved)	625
846.7	1343.1	Pond	672
846.4	1343.4	Murray property 0.2W, gravel driveway . . . (pg. 138)	653
846.0	1343.8	Goldsmith Lane (gravel)	672
845.6	1344.2	Unionville Rd (paved), County Rd 651 . . . (pg. 138)	610
845.4	1344.4	Quarry Rd	616
844.7	1345.1	Lott Rd, **Unionville, NY** (0.7W) . . . (pg. 138)	590

Camp only in designated sites; fires only in campsite fire rings. Hitchhiking is illegal in NY.

NoBo	SoBo	Landmark	Elev
843.6	1346.2	NJ 284, **Unionville, NY** (0.7W), stream N of rd . 41.2885,-74.5524 P (pg. 138)	437
843.2	1346.6	Lower Rd (Oil City Rd).	528
842.7	1347.1	Carnegie Rd, NoBo: follow road 0.2W	415
842.4	1347.4	State Line Rd, NoBo: follow road 0.5E	423
842.2	1347.6	Wallkill River, parking. . . . 41.2877,-74.534 P	410
841.9	1347.9	AT + State Line Rd north end. NoBo: turn east into Wallkill Reserve	405
841.1	1348.7	90 degree turn on Wallkill perimeter	387
840.7	1349.1	90 degree turn on Wallkill perimeter	399
839.9	1349.9	Liberty Corners Rd (paved).	440
839.8	1350.0	Water to west	516
839.4	1350.4	**Pochuck Mtn. Shelter** (0.1W) 19.6◄17.0◄12.4◄►11.5►23.6►37.9 . (6)	884
		Bear box. Spigot at vacant house at foot of Pochuck Mountain.	
838.6	1351.2	View	1111
837.8	1352.0	Pochuck Mountain	1147
837.3	1352.5	Lovemma Lane (gravel).	880
837.1	1352.7	Stream.	794
836.7	1353.1	County Rd 565, **Glenwood, NJ** (1.1W), stream south of road . . . (pg. 138)	720
		SoBos planning to stay at Pochuck Mtn Shelter should get water here.	

1293.6 PA 611, ***Delaware Water Gap, PA 18327***

Church of the Mountain Hiker Center 570.476.0345 or 570.992.3934 Bunkroom, showers, overflow tenting, rides to Stroudsburg when avail. Donations encouraged. 2-night max. No drive-ins, no parking, no laundry. Phone numbers of persons who can help are posted in the hostel.

Pocono Inn 570.476.0000 $65 weekdays, $69 F & Sa + tax. No pets.

Deer Head Inn 570.424.2000 $90/up weekdays, $120/up weekends. No pets, no TV. Restaurant & lounge open to all. Live music Th-Su, hiker attire okay.

Watergap Country Club 570.476.4653 $80D Su-Th, $120D Fr-Sa. Shower, Laundry, no pets or tank-tops. Pool Tiki-bar.

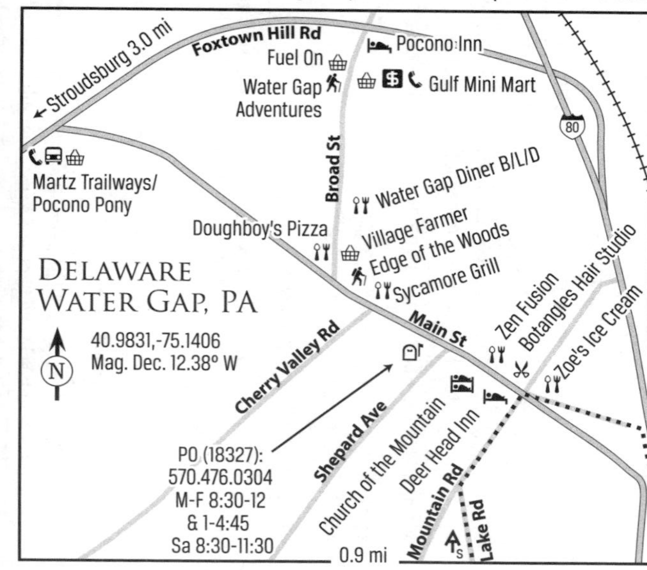

Village Farmer & Bakery 8a-8p daily. Hot dog & slice of pie $2.95. B'fast sandwiches, salads, sandwiches. CC min. $10.

Doughboy's Pizza 570.421.1900 Open 7 days in summer.

Edge of the Woods Outfitters 570.421.6681 Full line of gear, trail food, footwear. Coleman/alcohol/oz. Shuttles from Little Gap to Bear Mtn. Open 7 days, Memorial - Labor Day. Mail: (FedEx/UPS only) 110 Main St, Delaware Water Gap, PA 18327.

Water Gap Adventures 570.424.8533 Open Apr-Oct.

Kenny's Ole Dawg Shuttle 570.534.7539 Boiling Springs, PA to Jervis, NY.

Pocono Pony 570.839.6862 Runs on 2hr-loop through Stroudsburg, $1.50 per boarding.

Martz Trailways 570.421.3040 $66.50 NYC roundtrip.

Pocono Cab 570.424.2800

WGM Taxi 570.223.9289

Stroudsburg, PA 18360 (3.5W)

Large town with all services, incl. **Walmart** (24hrs w/pharmacy) supermarket, motels, laundry, and movie theater.

Dunkleberger's Sports 570.421.7950 M-Th 9-6, F 9-7, Su 9-5

1304.4 Camp Road

Mohican Outdoor Center (0.3W) 908.362.5670 Thru-hiker rates (change expected in 2017). Bunkroom $34.50PP, tenting $13 + tax. Shower/towel for tenters or w/o stay $5. Campfires only in designated areas. Welcome center & camp store hrs in peak season: Su-Th 8-7; F 8-9; Sa 8-8; Open 9-5 in winter (Nov-Apr). Water avail. at lodge or at spigot near garage across the street. Deli sandwiches, sodas, candy, Coleman/alcohol/oz & hiker supplies (footwear, packs, socks, poles). Operated by the AMC. Mail: 50 Camp Mohican Rd, Blairstown, NJ 07825 <www.outdoors.org/lodging/mohican/>

Knight Riders Taxi and Limo 908.850.4450

1322.0 US 206, Culvers Gap

Stokes SP 973.948.3820 Tentsites 2mi from SP office near Rte 206; cabins 4mi away. Tentsite 1-6 persons $25/up, cabins: $65/up. $5 lower for NJ residents. $5 Trans.

fee/stay. Free showers at Stony Lake Mem-Columbus Day, accessible from Stony Brook Trail.

Forest Motel 973.948.5456 $69S $79D + tax, pets $20, laundry $20. Guest Mail: 104 Rte 206 N, Branchville, NJ 07826.

Cobmin Ridge Motel 973.948.3459, 973.652.0780 $59/up.

Sunrise Appalachian Trail Deli 973-948-0045 Open 6-6 w/coffee, cold drinks, b'fast & deli sandwiches. Hiker friendly; ok to charge electronics, get water, use WiFi & bathroom. Mail: 15 Rte 206 S. Sandyston, NJ 07826

Stokes Steakhouse 973.948.3007 Beer, burgers, fish & chips, WiFi & charging outlets. Hrs: Fr 4p-10p, Sa-Su 3p-10p. Closed in winter.

Gyps Tavern Hikers welcome to inside or lakeside seating, charging outlets, economical food choices & packaged goods to go. Open L/D.

Jumboland Diner B/L/D, $2.99 b'kfast. Th dinner buffet.

(1.5E) **Dale's Market** 973.948.3078 M-F 6-9, Sa-Su 7-9

Branchville, NJ 07826 (3.4E)

M–F 8:30–5, Sa 8:30–1, 973.948.3580

1336.3 NJ 23

High Point State Park Headquarters 973.875.4800 Office open year-round 9am-4pm, Mem-Labor Day extended hours F&Sa 8-8. Bathrooms inside, water spigot outside. Overnight parking 0.25E. **Sawmill Lake Camping Area** 2.5 mile from HQ, tentsites $20 NJ resident/$25 non-resident plus $5.50 walk-in fee. Mail: 1480 State Rte 23, Sussex, NJ 07461.

(1.5E) **High Point Country Inn** 973.702.1860 $89.99D + tax, pets $10, no room phone. Laundry $7. Free P/U & return to trail from NJ 23, longer shuttles for a fee. Guest Mail: 1328 NJ 23, Wantage, NJ 07461

Port Jervis, NY 12785 (4.4W)

Days Inn 845.856.6611 $79.95D/up + tax, $10EAP, cont B. Guest Mail: 2247 Greenville Turnpike, Port Jervis, NY 12771.

Village Pizza 973.293.3364 M-S 10:30a-11p, Su 10-11

Shop Rite Market, **Price Chopper**

Rite Aid 845.856.8342, **Medicine Shoppe** 845.856.6681

Bon Secours Community Hospital 845.858.7000

Tri-States Veterinary Medical 845.856.1914

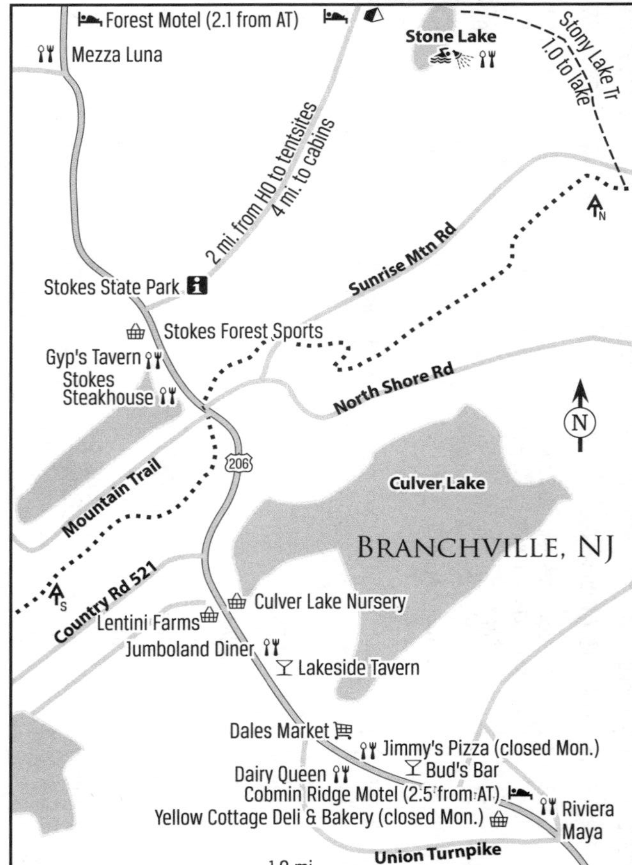

836.0	1353.8	Roadbed	764
835.2	1354.6	County Rd 517, **Glenwood, NJ** (1.1W) 41.2357,-74.4805 P (pg. 138)	428
834.5	1355.3	Pochuck Creek suspension footbridge. Boardwalk over swamp for (0.6S) and (0.2N) of footbridge.	394
833.8	1356.0	Canal Rd. 41.2266,-74.469 P	410
833.6	1356.2	Footbridge, Wawayanda Creek 💧	401
832.9	1356.9	NJ 94, **Vernon, NJ** (2.4E) 41.2193,-74.4551 P (pg. 139)	450
831.9	1357.9	Spring, climb up south side of mtn known as "stairway to heaven" 💧	973
831.5	1358.3	Pinwheels vista 0.1W, Wawayanda Mountain, side trail 0.8E to views 📷	1340
830.6	1359.2	Footbridge, stream 💧	994
829.8	1360.0	Barrett Rd (paved), **New Milford, NY** (1.8W) (pg. 139)	1140
828.7	1361.1	Cross stream on Iron Mountain Rd 💧	1060
827.9	1361.9	**Wawayanda Shelter** (0.1W). (6) 28.5◄23.9◄11.5◄►12.1►26.4►31.7 Water from park 0.1N and 0.2E.	1194
827.7	1362.1	Wawayanda State Park (0.2E) 41.1981,-74.3975 P 💧	1149
827.4	1362.4	Warwick Turnpike 41.2014,-74.3916 P (pg. 140)	1140
826.9	1362.9	Footbridge, stream 💧	1107
826.0	1363.8	Long House Dr / Brady Rd 41.1955,-74.3715 P	1115
824.9	1364.9	Long House Creek, footbridge 💧	1085
824.1	1365.7	Ernest Walter Trail (yellow-blazed) to east	1342
823.8	1366.0	**NJ-NY** border, State Line Trail 1.0E to **Lakeside, NJ**. 0.1N on AT is Zig Zag Trail to west.	1385
823.4	1366.4	Prospect Rock, highest point on AT in NY. Views of Greenwood Lake to east 📷	1433
822.5	1367.3	Furnace Brook 💧	1157
822.2	1367.6	Ladder	1250

⚠ NJ: No campfires allowed. Camping is limited to shelters and official campsites

820.8	1369.0	Cascade Brook 💧	1185
819.9	1369.9	Village Vista Trail, 0.8E to Greenwood Lake	1283

⚠ Despite the unimposing profile, rocks, abrupt ups & downs make this section challenging.

818.3	1371.5	Powerline	1199
817.8	1372.0	NY 17A, **Bellvale, NY** (1.6W) 41.2443,-74.2869 P (pg. 140) **Greenwood Lake, NY** (2.0E)	1180
817.2	1372.6	Pipeline clearing	1242
816.5	1373.3	Eastern Pinnacles, short bypass trail to west 📷	1213
816.3	1373.5	Brook 💧	1045

816.1	1373.7	Cat Rocks, view		1091
815.8	1374.0	**Wildcat Shelter** (0.2W) 36.0◄23.6◄12.1◄►14.3►19.6►22.8 Spring in front of shelter.	(8)	1070
814.5	1375.3	Highlands Trail		762
814.3	1375.5	Lakes Rd (paved), 0.1N powerline, footbridge and stream		680
814.0	1375.8	Fitzgerald Falls		733
812.7	1377.1	Allis Trail, Sterling Fire Tower 5.0E		1255
812.0	1377.8	Mombasha High Point		1280
810.9	1378.9	Boardwalk, pond		912
810.8	1379.0	West Mombasha Rd, stream just north on AT	41.2693,-74.2146 P	933
809.9	1379.9	Buchanan Mountain		1142
809.1	1380.7	East Mombasha Rd (paved)		840
808.8	1381.0	Little Dam Lake, stepping stones over creek		768
807.7	1382.1	Orange Turnpike	41.2695,-74.181 P (0.5E)	780
807.0	1382.8	Arden Mountain		1180
806.7	1383.1	Sapphire Trail		1120
806.3	1383.5	View		1040
805.9	1383.9	NY 17, **Southfields, NY** (2.1E), **Harrriman, NY** (3.7W)	**(pg. 141)**	550
805.5	1384.3	AT on Arden Valley Rd for 0.4 mile, Passes over NY State Thruway 87, crosses thru parking area north of bridge.	41.2649,-74.1544 P **(pg. 141)**	594
804.2	1385.6	Island Pond Rd (gravel) 0.1E to pond		1008
803.6	1386.2	Lemon Squeezer, Arden-Surebridge Trail to east		1088
803.3	1386.5	Island Pond Mountain		1298
802.9	1386.9	New York Long Path 52.0E to Manhattan		1055
802.2	1387.6	Surebridge Brook		1092
801.6	1388.2	AT joins Red Dot Trail (south end)		1341
801.5	1388.3	**Fingerboard Shelter** 37.9◄26.4◄14.3◄►5.3►8.5►40.7 Spring downhill to left unreliable. Water at Lake Tiorati 0.5E on Hurst Trail.	(8)	1348
800.9	1388.9	Fingerboard Mountain		1322
800.4	1389.4	Arden Valley Rd (paved), Tiorati Circle (0.3E)	41.2646,-74.1544 P **(pg. 141)**	1196
799.7	1390.1	Woods road		1027
798.3	1391.5	Footbridge, stream		836
798.2	1391.6	Seven Lakes Dr		850

1343.4 Murray property driveway
Private cabin open for the use of long distance hikers as it has been for nearly 20 yrs, tenting, well water, shower & privy. If you feel the need to change your brain chemistry this is probably not your stop, but serious hikers welcome. Maintain control of your dog near the mules, they are territorial. No groups please.

1344.2 Unionville Rd, County Rd 651

1345.1 Lott Rd

1346.2 NJ 284 ***Unionville, NY*** PO is 0.5W from any road crossing.
Village Office 845.726.3681 Tenters check-in at office or at Horler's.
Wit's End Tavern 845.726.3956 Darts, pool table. Open 7 days noon-midnight or later. Great ribs, burgers, wings.
Horler's Store 845.726.3210 M–Sa 6–8, Su 7–7, short-order grill open M-F 6:30-3, Sa-Su 7-1.

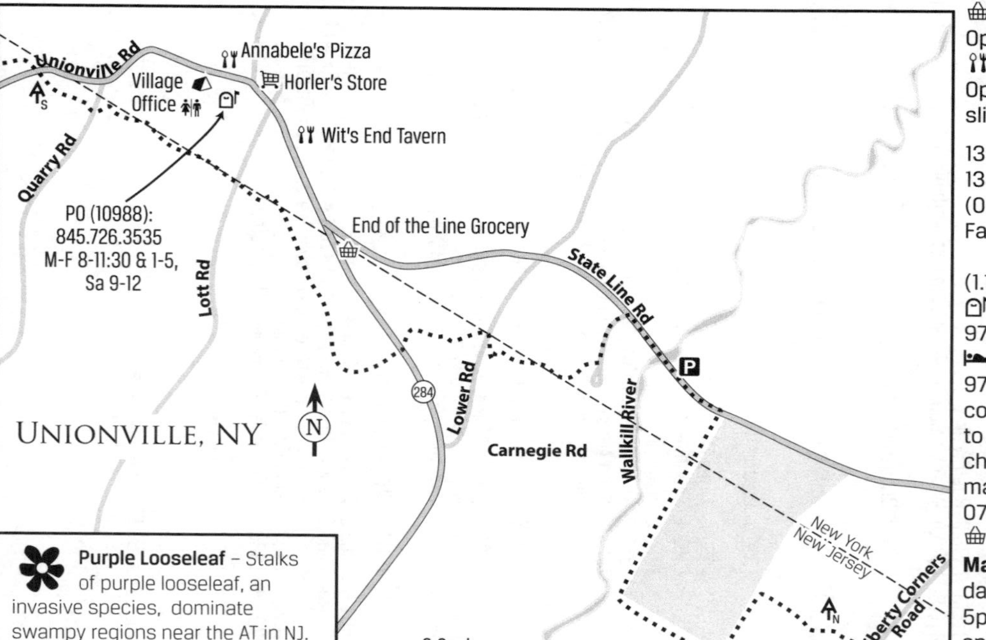

Purple Looseleaf – Stalks of purple looseleaf, an invasive species, dominate swampy regions near the AT in NJ.

State Line Deli 845.683.1566 Open x7, 6a-8p
Annabel's Pizza 845.726.9992 Open x 7, 11a-10p burgers, pizza by slice. ⟨www.annabelspizza.com⟩

1353.1 County Rd 565
1354.6 County Rd 517
(0.9W to PO and Pochuck Valley Farm)

Glenwood, NJ 07418
(1.1W from either road)
M-F 7:30–5, Sa 10–2, 973.764.2616
Apple Valley Inn 973.764.3735 $145-$160 + tax, incl country b'fast, no pets, shuttles to CR 517 & 565 w/stay. Gourmet chocolate store on site. Guest only mail: PO Box 302, Glenwood, NJ 07418.
Pochuck Valley Farms Market & Deli 973.764.4732 Open daily M–F 6am–6pm, Sa–Su 6am–5pm. B/L, produce, bakery. Water spigot and restroom.

1356.9 NJ 94

Living Word Church 973.809.3576 Free rides to/from church and resupply. Free showers and laundry. Free accommodations for Neros and Zeros. Pickup at RT 94 Vernon, NJ, Warwick TPK near Wawayanda St. Pk, Long House Rd. NY/NJ Border,and RT 17A Bellvale near creamery. Please call w/ as much advance notice as possible. Will try to accommodate w/o notice.

Rickey Farm/ Rickey Ministries 973.699.4950 WFS and shower or $10 per day campsite/shower. This is an event venue. Please call in advance in advance if possible.

Heaven Hill Farm (0.1W) 973.764.5144 Summer hrs daily 9–7, Su until 6. Ice cream, bakery, seasonal fruit & vegetables, picnic tables. ⟨www.heavenhillfarm.com⟩

(0.2E) **Mitch's Roadside Grill** Hot dog stand open 11-6 Apr-Oct. "The Best" Hot dogs, sodas. Shaded picnic tables, good place from which to hitch.

Appalachian Motel (1.2E) 973.764.6070 $70-110D, $10EAP. Call for ride. Pets $20. Laundry $10. Mail (guests only): 367 Route 94, Vernon, NJ 07462.

Vernon, NJ 07462 (2.4E)

Acme Market 973.764.5350 M-Sa 6-midnight, Su 6-10, **Starbucks** inside.

Vernon Urgent Care 973.209.2260 1.0 mile beyond hostel, M–F 8–8, Sa–Su 9–5.

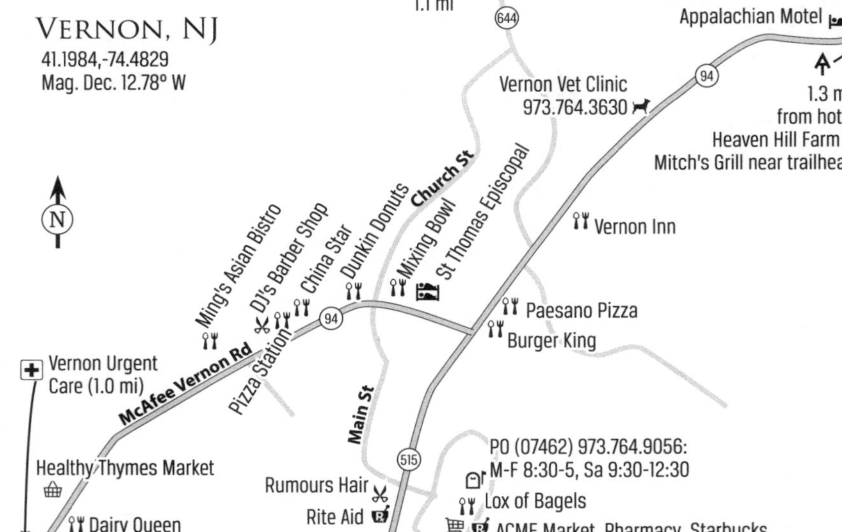

New Milford, NY (2.7W from NJ 94, see listings at Barrett Rd.)

1360.0 Barrett Rd

New Milford, NY 10959 (1.8W) 1.6W on Barret Rd, then right 0.2 on NJ 94 to shoe store and post office.

M-F 8:30-12:30, Sa 9-11:30, 845.986.3557

Sneakers to Boots 845.986.0333 Open M-F 10-6, Sa 10-5, Su 11-2 Shoes by Merrell, Keen, Oboz and others, merino wool socks. 314 Rt 94 South.

Be Prepared

Prepare for extreme weather, hazards, and emergencies – especially the cold – to avoid impacts from searches, rescues, and campfires.

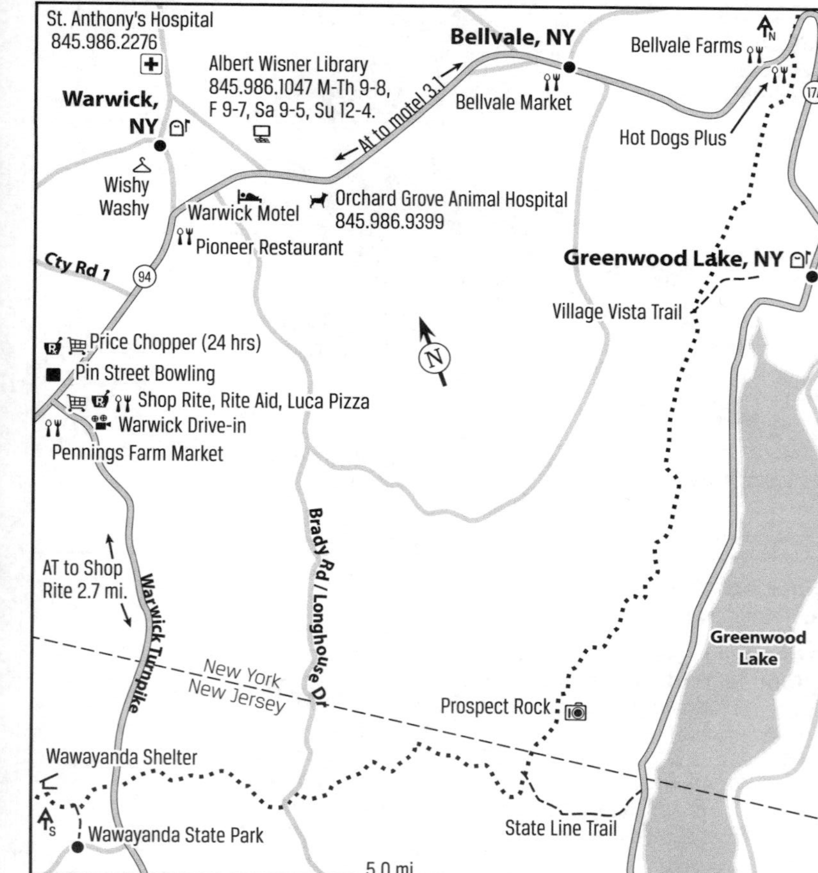

1362.4 Warwick Turnpike

Warwick, NY 10990

2.7W to NY 94, 1.5N on NY 94 to downtown with many restaurants, post office & library.

M–F 8:30–5, Sa 9–4, 845.986.0271

Meadow Lark Farm B&B 845.651.4286 Weeknights $75S/D or $99 for 3-person room, incl. b'fast. Rate is higher on Fri-Sa nights. Tenting $15 incl. shower & b'fast. All major CC, pets welcome. Shuttles covering NJ & NY, $1 per round-trip mile; free parking for section hikers. ⟨www.meadowlarkfarm.com⟩

Pennings Farm Market Local prod, Pub & Grill

Warwick Drive-In Theatre 845.986.4440 Walk-ins welcome. $10 adults, $6 kids & seniors.

Wishy Washy 845.987.5000

1372.0 NY 17A

Hot Dog Plus Open seasonally Tu-Sa 10:30-3:30.

Bellvale Farms 845.988.1818 Homemade ice cream, water from hose, electronic charging station. Ask about parking.

Bellvale, NY 10912 (1.6W)

Bellvale Market 845.544.7700, M-F 7-7; Sa 7-6; Su 7-4.

Greenwood Lake, NY 10925 (2E)

Anton's on the Lake 845.477.0010 Thru-hiker rate, 2-night min. Per night: Su-Th $80S/D, F-Sa $125/up. CC accepted, rooms w/whirlpool avail, no pets or smoking, small laundry loads only, swimming, paddle boats & canoe. Free shuttle & slackpack w/ stay. Longer shuttle for fee. Open year-round. Guest only Mail: (USPS) PO Box 1505, (FedEx/ UPS) Waterstone Rd, Greenwood Lake, NY 10925 ⟨www.antonsonthelake.com⟩

Breezy Point Inn 845.477.8100 $85+tax RM w/2 double beds, no pets, no smoking, L/D dining daily. Closed Jan. Guest Mail: (UPS/FedEx) 620 Jersey Ave, Greenwood Lake, NY 10925.

Greenwood Lake Taxi 845.477.0314 ⟨www.greenwoodlaketaxi.com⟩

Warwick, NY 10990 4.5W to downtown area, see map & more listings on pg. 138.

Warwick Motel (3.1W from NY 17A) 845.986.6656.

Night Owl Taxi 845.662.0359 Shuttles from Greenwood Lake 8a - 4p.

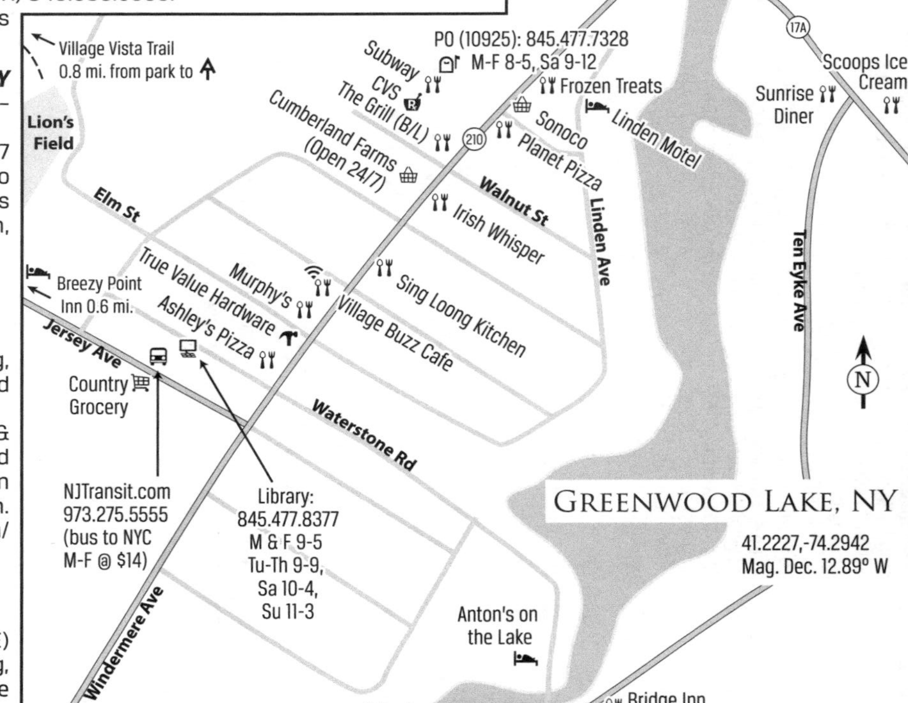

1383.9 NY 17 ***Southfields, NY 10975*** (2.1E) M-F 10–12 & 1–5, Sa 8:30–11:30, 845.351.2628

Tuxedo Motel 845.351.4747 $54.50S, $59.50D, $10EAP. No pets, no cooking. Food delivery options. Accepts Visa/MC. Mail: 985 Route 17 South, Southfields, NY, 10975.

Valero 0.1 west of PO.

Harriman, NY 10926 (3.7W)

Lodging, groceries, restaurants & more.

1384.3 Arden Valley Rd parking,
✖Brown and yellow sign has what word in quotes?

Harriman Shuttle Runs Sa, Su & holidays w/ pickup here at 11:43 and Tiorati circle at 11:40. Connects to town of Southfields and Tuxedo Train Station. $5 per ride. ⟨www.myharriman.com/harriman-shuttle-bus/⟩

Stony Point Center (see pg. 142)

1389.4 Arden Valley Rd (Tiorati Circle)
Lake Tiorati Beach (0.3E) 845.429.8257, 9-7 daily mid Jun-mid Aug, wkends only spring & fall. Restrooms, free showers, vending machine, swimming.

796.2	1393.6	**William Brien Memorial Shelter** 31.7◄19.6◄5.3◄►3.2►35.4►44.4. (8) Unreliable spring-fed well 80 yards down blue-blazed trail to right of shelter. Yellow-blazed Menomine Trail to east.	1075
795.3	1394.5	AT joins Red Dot Trail (north end)	914
794.9	1394.9	Black Mountain, views, can see NY City skyline	1192
794.1	1395.7	Palisades Parkway, busy 4-lane divided hwy. NY City 34E. Visitor center in median 0.4W, soda & snack machines. ⚠ Watch blazes next 3mi. north.	680
793.8	1396.0	Beechy Bottom Brook, footbridge, parking 0.8W	610
793.0	1396.8	**West Mountain Shelter** (0.6E) 22.8◄8.5◄3.2◄►32.2►41.2►49.0. (8) Views of Hudson River & NYC.	1221
792.3	1397.5	Views from ridge of West Mountain	1137
791.2	1398.6	Seven Lakes Dr	610
790.6	1399.2	Perkins Memorial Dr	794
788.8	1401.0	Bear Mountain, Perkins Memorial Tower, 41.3112,-74.0072 Vending machines, view of NYC skyline.	1305
788.2	1401.6	Perkins Memorial Dr (south end of 0.3 mi. roadwalk)	1001
786.9	1402.9	Bear Mountain State Park, Hessian Lake 41.313,-73.989 (pg. 144)	190
786.5	1403.3	Tunnel under US 9, Trailside Museum, bear cage is lowest point on AT (pg. 144)	177
786.0	1403.8	Bear Mountain Bridge, Hudson River, **Fort Montgomery, NY** (1.8W) (pg. 144)	200
785.5	1404.3	NY 9D, Bear Mountain Bridge north end	198
784.8	1405.0	Camp Smith Trail, 0.6E to Anthonys Nose, views of Hudson River	727
783.8	1406.0	Hemlock Springs Campsite	503
783.6	1406.2	Manitou Rd (gravel). 41.3296,-73.9533	460
782.6	1407.2	Osborne Loop Trail to west (blue-blazed)	774
782.2	1407.6	Curry Pond Trail to west (yellow-blazed)	857
781.2	1408.6	Osborne Loop Trail to west (blue-blazed)	862
780.7	1409.1	Carriage Connector Trail to west (yellow-blazed).	513
780.2	1409.6	US 9 + NY 403, **Peekskill, NY** (4.5E) (pg. 145)	400
779.9	1409.9	Old Highland Turnpike (paved)	461
779.6	1410.2	Franciscan Way (paved), **Graymoor Spiritual Life Center** (0.4E) (pg. 145)	540
779.5	1410.3	Two gravel roads	466
777.7	1412.1	Blue-blazed trail 0.1W to Denning Hill	900
776.9	1412.9	Old Albany Post Rd (gravel), Chapman Rd.	607

775.9 1413.9 Canopus Hill. 813
775.3 1414.5 Brook 395
775.2 1414.6 Canopus Hill Rd (paved) . . . . (pg. 145) 420

774.2 1415.6 South Highland Rd (paved), stream north side of road. 570

773.4 1416.4 Stream. 655

772.7 1417.1 Catfish Loop Trail (red-blazed) 941

771.5 1418.3 Dennytown Rd (paved), Three Lake Trail to west 41.4206,-73.8689 860
Water on side of pump building, open late-Apr-Oct.
771.3 1418.5 Catfish Loop Trail to east (red-blazed) 814

769.9 1419.9 Sunken Mine Rd (gravel), stream to north. 800

768.7 1421.1 Three Lakes Trail 986

767.8 1422.0 NY 301, Canopus Lake, **Clarence Fahnestock SP** (1.0E). . . . . **(pg. 145)** 920
767.2 1422.6 Fahnestock Trail to west 1101

NoBo: Upon reaching the park, AT turns left through playground then follows path at edge of lake.

765.8 1424.0 Green-blazed trail to lake, **Clarence Fahnestock SP** (0.2E) . . . **(pg. 145)** 998
View of the lake from AT north of this intersection.
765.0 1424.8 Stream 1023

763.6 1426.2 Shenandoah Mountain, view, painted 911 Memorial Flag. 1282
763.2 1426.6 Long Hill Rd (gravel) 1018
762.7 1427.1 Powerline 1000
762.1 1427.7 Shenandoah Tenting Area 0.1W, hand pump 900
761.7 1428.1 Brook 758
760.9 1428.9 Bridge over brook. 355
760.8 1429.0 Hortontown Rd, ... 41.5141,-73.7918 (6) **(pg. 145)** 357
RPH Shelter (1982) 40.7◄35.4◄32.2◄►9.0►16.8►25.6 Treat pump water.
760.5 1429.3 Footbridge, stream, Taconic State Pkwy underpass 529

757.3 1432.5 Hosner Mountain Rd, footbridge, stream (do not drink, farm upstream) 500

1402.9 Bear Mountain State Park, ***Bear Mountain, NY 10911***

1403.3 **Trailside Museum and Zoo** 845.786.2701 Open 10-4:30; no charge for hiking through. No dogs. Lowest elevation on the AT (124') is within the park. If closed, or if you have a dog, use bypass (see map).

1403.8 Bear Mountain Bridge, ***Fort Montgomery, NY 10922*** (1.8W)
Going into town? Consider passing through zoo first; hours are limited.
Bear Mountain Inn 845.786.2731 $149/up+tax, cont b'fast. Dining options: **1915, Blue Tapas & Hiker Cafe** in the inn, seasonal concession lakeside.
Bear Mountain Bridge Motel 845.446.2472 $75D and up, no pets, accepts Visa/MC, pickup/return to trail (park, zoo, or bridge) with stay. Wir sprechen Deutsch. Guest Mail: PO Box 554, Fort Montgomery, NY 10922.
Stony Point Center (8E) 845.786.5674 Call x100 7:30am-6pm or register on-line ⟨www.stonypointcenter.org/AT⟩ use code "ATHike" for discount: $50S wkdays, $80S wkends $10EAP up to 3. Incl. b'fast. Drug free 35 acre retreat with farm and pottery workshop. Shuttle from Rec Area $10 ea. way for up to 9 passengers. Buffet lunch $10, dinner $15. 1 acre-farm. Clean, simple rooms, no TV, common use bathrooms. Laundry $3. Fuel/oz and some hiker foods. Parking for section hikers, slackpacking Arden Valley Rd to Graymoor. Mail w/ reservation: 17 Cricketown Rd. Stony Point, NY 10980.
Overlook Lodge 845.786.2731 $149/up +tax, cont b'fast, some pet rooms.
Foodies Pizza 845.839.0383 B/L/D

Highland Falls, NY (3.8W)
Fairbridge Inn & Suites 845.446.9400 $85D, cont b'fast. Pets $15.
Dunkin' Donuts, and many other restaurants
My Town Marketplace 845.446.3663
Rite Aid 845.446.3170
Highland Falls Library 845.446.3113 M, Th-F 10-5, Tu 10-7, W 10-8, Sa 10-2.

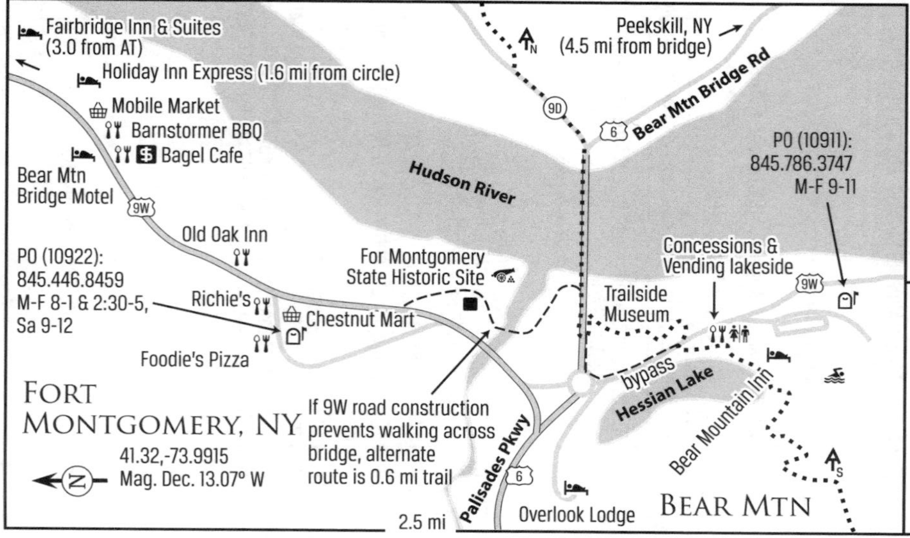

Fort Montgomery State Historic Site

Side trail starting from end of bridge guardrail 0.6W passes through Revolutionary War fort for which the town is named. The side trail is roughly the same length as the roadwalk but is more interesting. View the Hudson River bridge down the barrel of a cannon.

1409.6 US 9, NY 403
Stadium Sports Bar (0.8E) daily 11:30-10, closed M Jan-Feb.

Peekskill, NY 10566 (4.5E) large town
M–F 9–5, Sa 9–4, 914.737.6437

1410.2 Franciscan Way
Graymoor Spiritual Life Center (0.4E) 845.424.2111 Hikers permitted to sleep (free) at monastery's ball field picnic shelter Mar-Nov. Has water, privy & shower. Follow signs & blue-blazes; stay left at both forks in the road.

1414.6 Canopus Hill Rd
(1.6E) **Putnam Valley Market** 845.528.8626 Directions: 0.3E on Canopus Hill Rd, right on Canopus Hollow Rd for 0.1 mi, left on Sunset Hill Rd for 1.2 mi. Pizza, hot food from the grill, ATM, open M-Sa 6–9, Su 6-7.

1422.0 NY 301, Canopus Lake (1E to SP)
1424.0 Side trail entry (0.2E to SP beach)
Clarence Fahnestock State Park 845.225.7207, 800.456.2267 Open mid-Apr to mid-Dec. Thru-hikers get one free night of camping. Concession at beach open wkends only Mem Day - June; open daily July - Labor Day. Hours M-Sa 9-5, Su 9-6.

1429.0 Hortontown Rd, **RPH Shelter** (Ralph's Peak Hiker Cabin) Trail work weekend following July 4.
Pizza delivered after 4pm only by **Carlo's Pizza Express** 845.896.6500 and **Gian Bruno's** 845.227.9276.

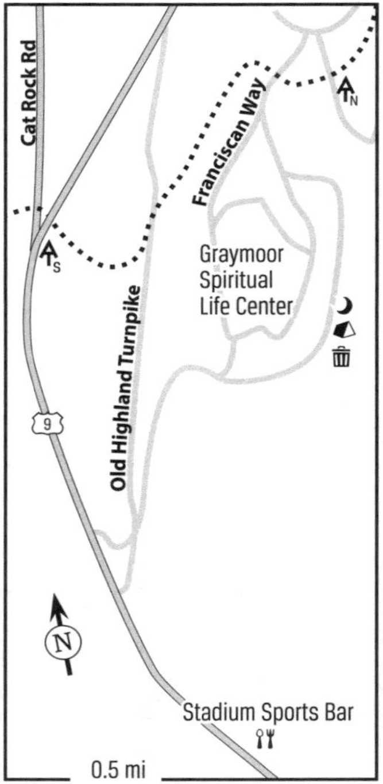

1434.1 NY 52
(0.4E) **Mountaintop Market Deli** 845.221.0928 Open daily 5–8, ATM, pay phone inside, welcome to water from faucet on side of building & electric outlets. Camping allowed nearby.
Danny's Pizzeria 845.223.5888 pizza by the slice.

Stormville, NY 12582 (1.9W)
M–F 8:30–5, Sa 9–12, 845.226.2627

1441.3 NY 55
(1.5W) Pleasant Ridge Plaza with:
Pleasant Ridge Pizza 845.724.3444 Open 7 days for L/D.
A&A Deli 845.452.4040
(1.2W) **Total Care Pharmacy** 845.724.5757. Open M-F 9-8, Sa 9-3

Poughquag, NY 12570 (3.1W)
M–F 8:30–1 & 2-5, Sa 8:30–12:30, 845.724.4763
Pine Grove Motel 845.724.5151 $70S $75D, + tax, no pets, accepts Visa/ MC/Disc.
Great Wall 845.724.5387, **Clove Valley Deli & Café** 845.227.1585
Beekman Pharmacy 845.724.3200
Beekman Animal Hospital 845.724.8387

Pawling, NY (4.0E, see pg. 148)

1446.5 County Rd 20, West Dover Rd
Dover Oak north side of road, largest oak tree on AT. Girth 20′ 4″ and estimated to be over 300 years old.

Pawling, NY 12564 (3.1E, see pg. 148)

Prices are subject to change, particularly at hotels. Prices published in The A.T. Guide were given in fall of 2016 & often represent a significant discount for hikers. Businesses *intend* to keep these prices throughout 2017, but they are not obliged to do so.

755.7 1434.1 NY 52, **Stormville, NY** (1.9W) . . . . . 41.541,-73.7328 🅿 (pg. 145) 800

755.1 1434.7 Stream, footbridge . . . . . 💧 837

754.5 1435.3 AT on Old Stormville Mountain Rd for 0.1 mile 971
754.3 1435.5 AT on Stormville Mountain Rd for 0.1 mile, crosses over I-84 950
754.1 1435.7 Grape Hollow Rd 955

752.8 1437.0 Side trail 0.6W to Indian Pass 1170

751.9 1437.9 Mt Egbert 1329
751.8 1438.0 **Morgan Stewart Shelter** . . . . . ☽ 💧 ⛺ (6) 1311
44.4◂41.2◂9.0◂▸7.8▸16.6▸20.6

750.7 1439.1 Depot Hill Rd, parking 0.1W. . . . . . 41.5715,-73.6807 🅿 1230

748.9 1440.9 Railroad track, Whakey Lake Stream . . . . . 💧 684
748.8 1441.0 Old Route 55 699
748.5 1441.3 NY 55, **Poughquag, NY** (3.1W) . . . . . 41.5897,-73.6592 🅿 (0.1W) (pg. 145) 720
748.2 1441.6 Beekman Uplands Trail to west 762

747.4 1442.4 Footbridge, stream (more streams in this area) . . . . . 💧 703
747.1 1442.7 Nuclear Lake south end, loop trail to east (yellow-blazed). 752

746.2 1443.6 Nuclear Lake north end, loop trail to east 775
745.8 1444.0 Beekman Uplands Trail to west 875

744.9 1444.9 Footbridge, swampy area . . . . . 💧 1045
744.6 1445.2 Penny Rd 1131
744.3 1445.5 West Mountain . . . . . 📷 1200
744.0 1445.8 **Telephone Pioneers Shelter** (0.1E), shelter trail crosses stream . . ☽ 💧 ⛺ (6) 902
49.0◂16.8◂7.8◂▸8.8▸12.8▸21.2 If dry, get water from residence 0.7N.
743.3 1446.5 County Rd 20, West Dover Rd, **Pawling, NY** (3.1E) . . . . . 💧 ✲ (pg. 145) 565

741.2 1448.6 Footbridge, stream, boardwalk from here north to RR track . . . . . 💧 463
740.9 1448.9 NY 22, **Appalachian Trail RR Station** . . . . 41.5938,-73.5871 🅿 🗑 (pg. 150) 480
Wingdale (4W), **Pawling** (2.6E) hot dog stand often here in summer, deli 0.6E
740.7 1449.1 Hurd Corners Rd, wooden water tower . . . . . 💧 480
740.0 1449.8 Stream to west . . . . . 💧 591

739.2 1450.6 Hammersly Ridge 1060
739.0 1450.8 Red Trail 1006
738.5 1451.3 Yellow Trail to east 938
738.2 1451.6 Red Trail to east. 972
738.1 1451.7 Green trail west, Red Trail east. 986

737.2 1452.6 Pawling Nature Reserve to east 900

736.2	1453.6	Stream		799
735.6	1454.2	Leather Hill Rd (gravel), stream to south		750
735.2	1454.6	**Wiley Shelter** 25.6◄16.6◄8.8◄►4.0►12.4►19.7 pump 0.1N.	(treat) (6)	701
735.0	1454.8	Duell Hollow Rd		557
734.7	1455.1	Footbridge, stream		437
734.0	1455.8	**NY-CT** border, Hoyt Rd	41.6418,-73.5208 P	400
733.7	1456.1	Side trail to parking, brook to north		429
733.4	1456.4	CT 55, **Gaylordsville, CT** (2.5E) **Wingdale, NY** (3.3W)	41.6447,-73.5193 P **(pg. 151)**	445
732.2	1457.6	Ten Mile Hill, Herrick Trail to east		1000
731.2	1458.6	**Ten Mile River Shelter** (0.1E) 20.6◄12.8◄4.0◄►8.4►15.7►25.7. Water (hand pump) to left. Group campsites across river and up trail to left.		277
731.1	1458.7	Ten Mile River, Ned Anderson Memorial Bridge		260
729.9	1459.9	Bulls Bridge Rd (paved) + Schaghticoke Rd AT on Schaghticoke Rd (gravel) 0.3 mile	41.6756,-73.5102 P **(pg. 151)**	366
728.7	1461.1	**CT-NY**		1027
728.1	1461.7	View to west from exposed slab of rock, many good sitting boulders.		1205

Campfires prohibited in CT. Camping only in designated sites.

726.7	1463.1	**NY-CT**, stream to north		1223
726.4	1463.4	Indian Rocks, view to east		1249
725.7	1464.1	Schaghticoke Mountain Campsite & privy 0.1W, stream on AT		904
724.9	1464.9	Stream.		988
723.8	1466.0	Thayer Brook		914
722.8	1467.0	**Mt Algo Shelter** 21.2◄12.4◄8.4◄►7.3►17.3►28.6		638
722.5	1467.3	CT 341, Schaghticoke Rd, **Kent, CT** (0.8E)	**(pg. 152)**	350
722.4	1467.4	Macedonia Brook		335
721.9	1467.9	Numeral Rock Trail to east		801
719.7	1470.1	Skiff Mountain Rd (paved), stream to south		771
719.0	1470.8	Calebs Peak		1124
718.7	1471.1	St. Johns Ledges, steep stone steps down to Housatonic River		883
717.8	1472.0	River Rd south end, NoBo: turn west on road for 0.8 mile		382
717.0	1472.8	Kent Rd to west		428
716.8	1473.0	River Rd north end		389

715.5	1474.3	**Stewart Hollow Brook Shelter** (0.1W). (6) 19.7◄15.7◄7.3◄►10.0►21.3►28.7 Footbridge over SH Brook.	398
714.9	1474.9	Stony Brook, campsite to west	414
713.4	1476.4	Footbridge, stream	452
713.1	1476.7	River Rd 41.8057,-73.395 P	460
712.9	1476.9	Dawn Hill Rd (paved)	583
712.2	1477.6	Silver Hill Campsite 0.1E, pavilion, water from pump is a great source, 35-40 pumps needed to start water flow	926
711.4	1478.4	CT 4, **Cornwall Bridge, CT** (0.9E) (pg. 153) High water bypass 0.5E on CT 4, then left on unpaved Old Sharon Rd for 0.5 mi.	700
711.2	1478.6	Old Sharon Rd (gravel), Guinea Brook south of road	756
711.1	1478.7	Breadloaf Trail 0.1E, view	944
710.0	1479.8	Hatch Brook	880
709.8	1480.0	Pine Knob Loop Trail 1.0E to Housatonic Meadows State Park	1005
709.1	1480.7	Another intersection with Pine Knob Loop Trail to east	1044
708.8	1481.0	Caesar Rd, Caesar Brook Campsite, stream to north	798
707.3	1482.5	Stream.	879
706.7	1483.1	Carse Brook, footbridge	810
706.6	1483.2	West Cornwall Rd, **West Cornwall, CT** (2.2E), **Sharon, CT** (4.7W) (pg. 153)	849
706.3	1483.5	Pass through cracked boulder similar to Lemon Squeezer.	1175
705.5	1484.3	**Pine Swamp Brook Shelter** (6) 25.7◄17.3◄10.0◄►11.3►18.7►19.9	1087
704.6	1485.2	Mt. Easter Rd	1150
704.0	1485.8	Woods road	1291
703.8	1486.0	Woods road	1287
703.1	1486.7	Sharon Mountain Campsite 0.1W, stream nearby.	1134
702.3	1487.5	Hang Glider View	1103
700.2	1489.6	Belters Campsite 0.2W, view.	746
699.9	1489.9	US 7, CT 112	520
699.5	1490.3	US 7, parking, bridge over Housatonic River 41.9327,-73.3635 P (pg. 154)	518
698.9	1490.9	Mohawk Trail 0.5E to view	565
698.3	1491.5	Warren Turnpike, footbridge, stream to north	535
697.5	1492.3	Water St parking. **Falls Village, CT**(0.3E) 41.9558,-73.3675 P (pg. 154)	559
697.2	1492.6	Iron Bridge (Amesville Bridge) over Housatonic River	533
696.8	1493.0	Housatonic River Rd, AT crosses road twice 0.2 mi. 41.9623,-73.374 P apart. In between are two short trails east to views of great falls.	626

696.3	1493.5	Spring	808
694.9	1494.9	Mt Prospect	1475
694.2	1495.6	**Limestone Spring Shelter** (0.5W), road 0.25 farther (6)	1304
		28.6◄21.3◄11.3◄►7.4►8.6►17.0	
694.1	1495.7	Rands View (field)	1250
693.6	1496.2	Giants Thumb	1293
692.8	1497.0	Stream.	1038
690.5	1499.3	AT on US 44 for 0.2W	700
690.2	1499.6	AT on Cobble Rd 0.2E, **Salisbury, CT** (0.5W). (pg. 154)	706
689.8	1500.0	Undermountain Rd (paved) **Salisbury** (0.8W). 41.9941,-73.42685 P (pg. 154)	720
689.6	1500.2	Stream.	828
688.5	1501.3	Streams (multiple)	1110
687.7	1502.1	Lions Head Trail 0.5W to Bunker Hill Rd	1496
687.5	1502.3	Lions Head, view, bypass trail to west	1729
686.8	1503.0	**Riga Shelter,** spring. Tent platform behind shelter (6)	1646
		28.7◄18.7◄7.4◄►1.2►9.6►9.7	
686.2	1503.6	Ball Brook Campsite, stream.	1720
685.6	1504.2	**Brassie Brook Shelter,** stream 20 yards north on AT (6)	1733
		19.9◄8.6◄1.2◄►8.4►8.5►22.8	
685.1	1504.7	Undermountain Trail 1.9E to CT 41	1834
684.9	1504.9	Bear Mountain Rd to west	1920
684.6	1505.2	Bear Mountain, rock observation tower, view. North side steep & rocky.	2316
684.2	1505.6	Unmarked trail 0.6W to Mt Washington Rd	1806
684.0	1505.8	Paradise Lane Trail to east, **CT-MA** border 50 yards north (not marked)	1694
683.8	1506.0	Sages Ravine Campsite to west	1527
683.4	1506.4	Sages Ravine, Misplaced border sign at footbridge.	1474
		AT parallel to stream for 0.3 mile, swimming holes.	
682.1	1507.7	Laurel Ridge Campsite 0.1W, spring to south	1608
681.9	1507.9	Stream.	1686

Massachusetts: Fires at designated sites (fireplace/ring) only. Camping permitted only at designated sites.

680.1	1509.7	Mt Race, views along ridgeline for 0.6S	2365
679.0	1510.8	Race Brook Falls Trail 0.3E to campsite	1950
678.3	1511.5	Mt Everett	2602
677.6	1512.2	Guilder Pond Picnic Area, Mt Everett Rd	2081
677.2	1512.6	**The Hemlocks Shelter** (0.1E) 17.0◄9.6◄8.4◄►0.1►14.4►19.7 (10)	1916
677.1	1512.7	**Glen Brook Shelter** (0.1E) 9.7◄8.5◄0.1◄►14.3►19.6►21.4	1941

Pawling, NY (east from NY 55, County Rd 20, or NY 22. If coming from NY 55, veer left on Old Rte 55)

Edward R. Murrow Memorial Park Town allows hikers to camp in park, one night only. One mile from the center of town, park offers lake swimming, no pets.

Vinny's Deli 845.855.1922, **Gaudino's Pizzeria** 845.855.3200, **Mama Pizza II** 845.855.9270, **Great Wall** 845.855.9750

McGrath Restaurant 845.855.0800 L/D.

Pawling Free Library Closed Sundays in July and August.

Martin and Donna 845.505.1671 or 845.546.1832. Nights & weekends only. Shuttle range RPH Shelter to Kent, CT.

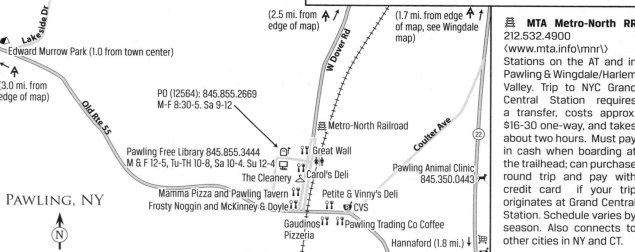

1448.9 NY 22, **Appalachian Trail Railroad Station**

Native Landscapes & Garden Center 845.855.7050 Open daily 9-5, please do not loiter after hours. Owner Pete Muroski is hiker-friendly. Free outside shower, charging, use of restrooms. Drinks, snacks, freeze-dried meals and canister fuel sold at the garden center. Mail: 991 Route 22, Pawling, NY 12564.

Tony's Deli (0.6E) 845.855.9540 sandwiches, salads, soda machine outside. Open daily 5am–midnight. Ask about camping.

MTA Metro-North Railroad (see info box on this page)

Pawling, NY (2.5E)

Wingdale, NY 12594 (4W)

Dutchess Motor Lodge 845.832.6400, 914.525.9276 $85S+tax. Ride for a fee when avail. A/C, free long distance, guest laundry $7, one pet room. Mail: 1512 Route 22, Wingdale, NY 12594.

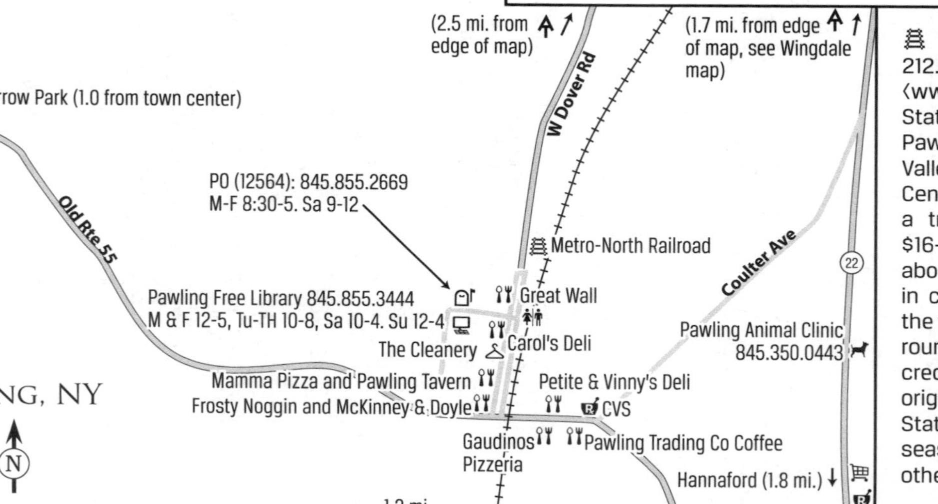

MTA Metro-North RR 212.532.4900 ⟨www.mta.info\mnr\⟩ Stations on the AT and in Pawling & Wingdale/Harlem Valley. Trip to NYC Grand Central Station requires a transfer, costs approx. $16-30 one-way, and takes about two hours. Must pay in cash when boarding at the trailhead; can purchase round trip and pay with credit card if your trip originates at Grand Central Station. Schedule varies by season. Also connects to other cities in NY and CT.

1456.4 CT 55, ***Gaylordsville, CT 06755*** (2.5E to bridge and country store, 0.6 further south to PO and diner)
M-F 8-1 & 2-5, Sa 8-12, 860.354.9727
Gaylordsville Diner 860.210.1622 B/L/D.
Wingdale, NY (3.3W) see map

1459.9 Bulls Bridge Rd, Schaghticoke Rd
(0.4E) To covered bridge with view of the Housatonic cascading down the backside of a dam. The one-lane bridge was built in 1842. Wooden bridges are covered to protect the wood deck and trusswork from the elements.
0.2 beyond bridge:
Country Market Fruit, ice cream, soda. M-Sa 5:30-7, Su 6:30-6.
Bulls Bridge Inn 860.927.1000 M-Th 5-9, F 5-9:30, Sa 12-9:30, Su 12-9. American cuisine (dinners $10-26), casual atmosphere, bar.

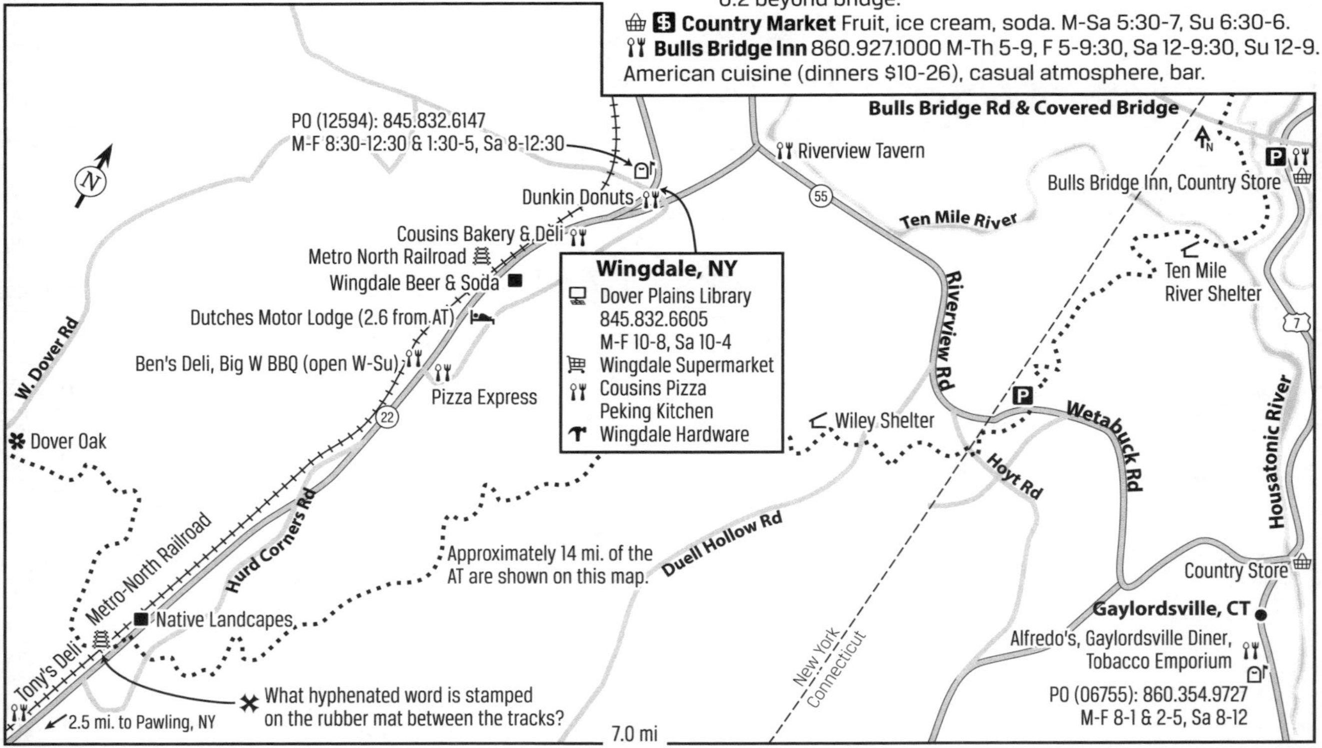

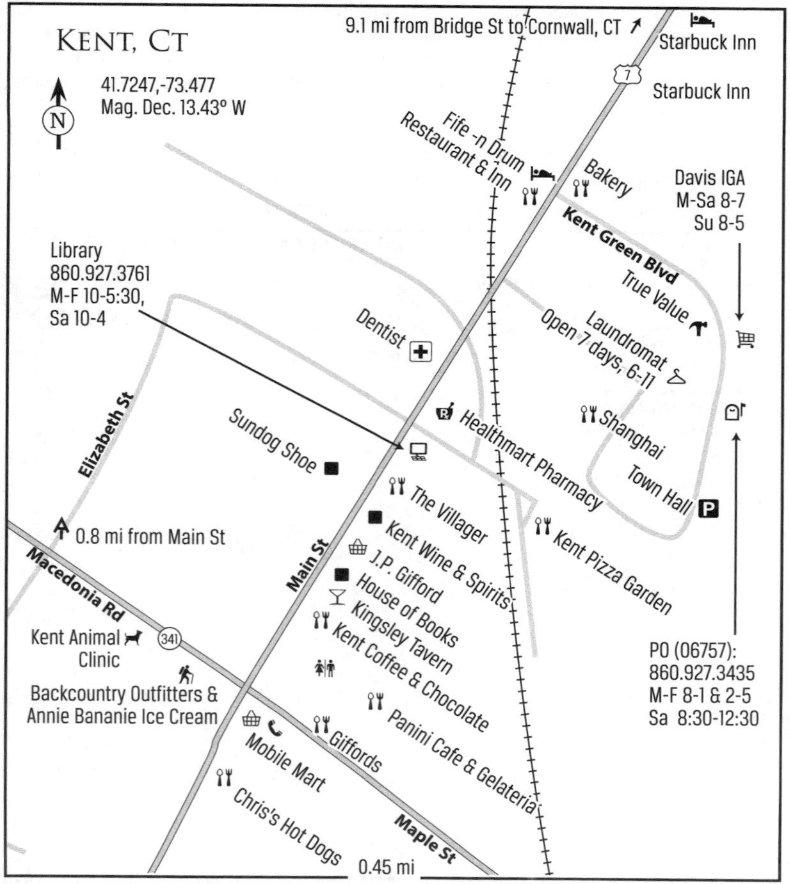

1467.3 CT 341, Schaghticoke Rd
Kent, CT 06757 (0.8E) (***15% lodging tax***)

Fife 'n Drum Inn & Restaurant 860.927.3509 Hiker room rates $140D+tax wkdays, $170D+tax wkends, $25EAP+tax, no pets. Front desk closed Tu, so make prior arrangements for Tu night stays. Guest Mail: (USPS) PO Box 188 or (FedEx/UPS) 53 N Main Street, Kent, CT 06757. ⟨www.fifendrum.com⟩

Cooper Creek B&B 860.927.4334 Hiker rate Su-Th $110D+tax. Weekend rates $145-200+tax. 2.5mi. north of town on US 7. Shuttles to/from Kent w/stay, slackpacking and longer shuttles for a fee.

Starbuck Inn 860.927.1788 $207D/up + tax, incl. full b'fast & afternoon tea. Sometimes discounted mid-week, accepts credit cards, no pets.

Newbury Inn 203.775.0220 About 20 miles from Kent, Gaylordsville, or Pawling (1030 Federal Rd, Brookfield, CT 06804). $79 +tax. $10EAP, cont. b'fast.

Backcountry Outfitters 860.927.3377 M–Sa, 9–6; Su, 10–4. Summer hours extended till 8p weekdays; 9p Fr & Sa; 6p, Su. Sells stamps, ships Priority Mail. Fuel/oz, canisters, selection of gear. **Annie Bananie Ice Cream & Grill** inside has hot dogs, coffee, snacks, barrels of candy, chocolates. Shuttles anywhere. Mail: 5 Bridge St, Kent, CT 06757. ⟨www.bcoutfitters.com⟩

JP Gifford B'fast sandwiches, salads, bakery, coffee and supplies.

■ **Sundog Shoe** 860.927.0009 10% hiker discount on footwear (Salomon, Merrell, High-Tech, Keen), socks (Darn Tough), Dirty Girl Gaiters and footbeds (Superfeet, Power Step).

■ **House of Books** UPS services, open daily 10-4:30.

1478.4 CT 4, ***Cornwall Bridge, CT 06754*** (0.9E)

Hitching Post Motel 860.672.6219 $65/up weekdays, $85/up weekends. Pets $10, laundry $5, shuttles $2/mi. Guest Mail: 45 Kent Road, Cornwall Bridge, CT 06754.

The Amselhaus 860.248.3155 $85S, $100D, $50EAP. 2-3 BR apartments include laundry, sat. TV, local & long-distance phone. Rides avail. Located behind carpet store, check-in at grey house next door to apartments. Mail: C/O Robin Vogel, 7 River Rd South, Cornwall Bridge, CT 06754.

Housatonic Meadows State Park 860.672.6772 Camping and Cabins 1.3 mi. north of town on US 7. Campsite $17 for CT residents, $27 nonresidents, $3 walk-in fee for first night. Cabins $50 CT residents, $60 nonresidents w/2 night min. No hammocks. Open mid-May to Oct, registration at main cabin by gate, no alcohol.

Cornwall Inn 860.672.6884 Su-Th $129D + tax, incl. cont. b'fast. Weekends 10% hiker discount. 2.2 miles south on US 7. Pickup/return to trailhead and other shuttles for a fee. Seasonal pool & hot tub. Pet fee. Maildrops with reservation.

Housatonic River Outfitters 860.672.1010 Some hiker gear, Aquamira. ⟨www.dryflies.com⟩

Cornwall Package Store (0.9E) 860.672.6645 M-Sa 10-7, Fri 10-8, Su 11-3. Water spigot outside. Stopping to sign their register can be refreshing.

1483.2 West Cornwall Rd

Bearded Woods Bunk & Dine 860.480.2966 Will pickup from W. Cornwall Rd., Falls Village or Salisbury. See details on pg 154.

West Cornwall, CT 06796 (2.2E)

M–F 8:30–12 & 2–4:30, Sa 9–12, 860.672.6791

Wandering Moose Café 860.672.0178

Sharon, CT 06069 (4.7W)

M–F 9:30–4:30, Sa 9:30–12:30, 860.364.5306

Sharon Farm Market 860.397.5161

Sharon Hospital 860.364.4228

Sharon Pharmacy 860.364.5105

Stacked Kitchen

Minimize Campfire Impacts

- Use stoves for cooking – if you need a fire, build one only where it's legal and in an existing fire ring. Leave hatchets and saws at home – collect dead and downed wood that you can break by hand. Burn all wood to ash.
- Do not try to burn trash, including foil, plastic, glass, cans, tea bags, food, or anything with food on it. These items do not burn thoroughly. They create noxious fumes, attract wildlife like skunks and bears, and make the area unsightly.
- Where campfires are permitted, leave the fire ring clean by removing others' trash and scattering unused wood, cold coals, and ashes 200 feet away from camp after the fire is cold and completely out.
- Read more of the Leave No Trace techniques developed for the A.T. at www.appalachiantrail.org/LNT

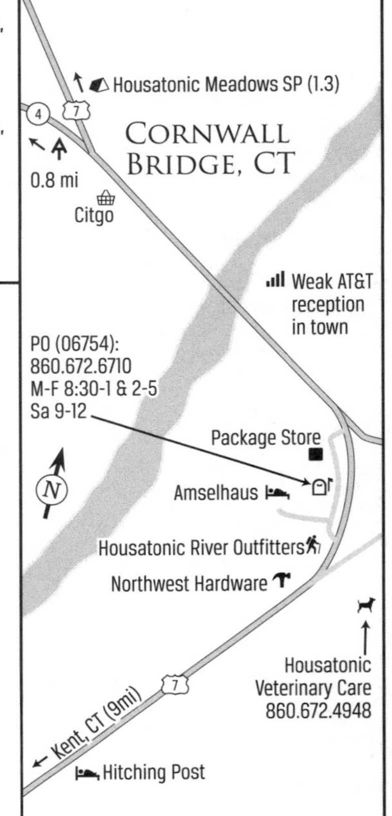

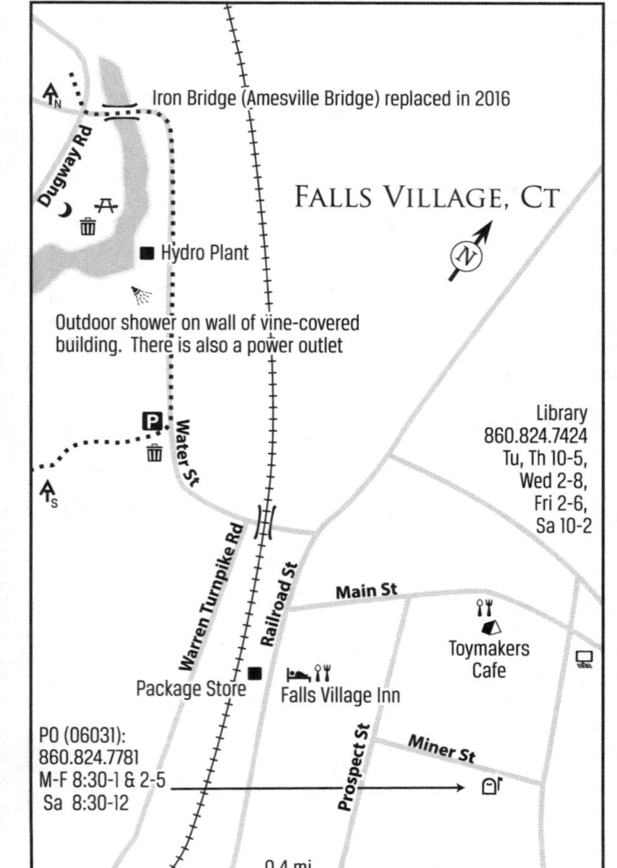

1490.3 US 7, bridge over Housatonic River

Bearded Woods Bunk & Dine 860.480.2966 Hudson & BIG Lu offer accommodations in their home to hikers $45pp. Includes: clean bunk w/linens, shower w/amenities, communal laundry, loaner clothes. Hearty b'fast, shuttle to/from trail & local PO. Cash only. Reservations recommended call or text Hudson for pick up from: W. Cornwall Rd, Falls Village or Salisbury between 1-6P. Resupplies: stove fuel & Aquamira. Pizza, drinks, snacks & ice cream avail. for purchase. Free slackpacking between W. Cornwall Rd & Salisbury w/second night stay. Longer shuttles for fee. Not a party place, no pets. Open May 1- Sep 1 (closed We.) Limited service may be available outside those dates. ⟨www.beardedwoods.com⟩

1492.3 Water Street Parking Area ***Falls Village, CT 06031***

Toymakers Café 860.824.8168 Thursday-Sunday (Th–F, 7–2; Sa–Su, 7–4) free tent sites, no trees for hammocks, hiker friendly, knock on upstairs door if closed. Cash only.

Falls Village Inn 860.824.0033 $239/up, restaurant & bar.

1499.6 Cobble Rd (0.5W)

1500.0 Undermountain Rd (0.8W) ***Salisbury, CT 06068***

Maria McCabe 860.435.0593 Beds in home $35PP incl. shower, use of living room, shuttle to coin laundry, cash only. Guest Mail: 4 Grove Street.

Vanessa Breton 860.435.9577 860.248.5714 Beds in home $40PP, pets $5, laundry $5. Shuttle range 100 mi. Street address is 7 The Lock Up Rd, but send mail to PO Box: PO Box 131, Salisbury, CT 06068 ($5 fee for non-guests)

White Hart Inn 860.435.0030 Rooms $245/up.

LaBonne's Market M–Sa 8–7, Su 8-6pm. Grocery, deli, bakery, pizza.

Town Hall 860.435.5170 M-F 8:30-4 Hikers welcome to use bathrooms and phone (local calls only).

Lakeville, CT *(2.0 mi. south of Salisbury)*

Boathouse 860.435.2111 Sports bar/restaurant

Mizza's Pizza 860.435.6266

Washboard Laundromat Behind Mizza's

Gary Monk (trail name "Blaze") counted every white blaze he passed during his 2002 northbound thru-hike. There were 80,900. I wouldn't tell anyone about getting lost.

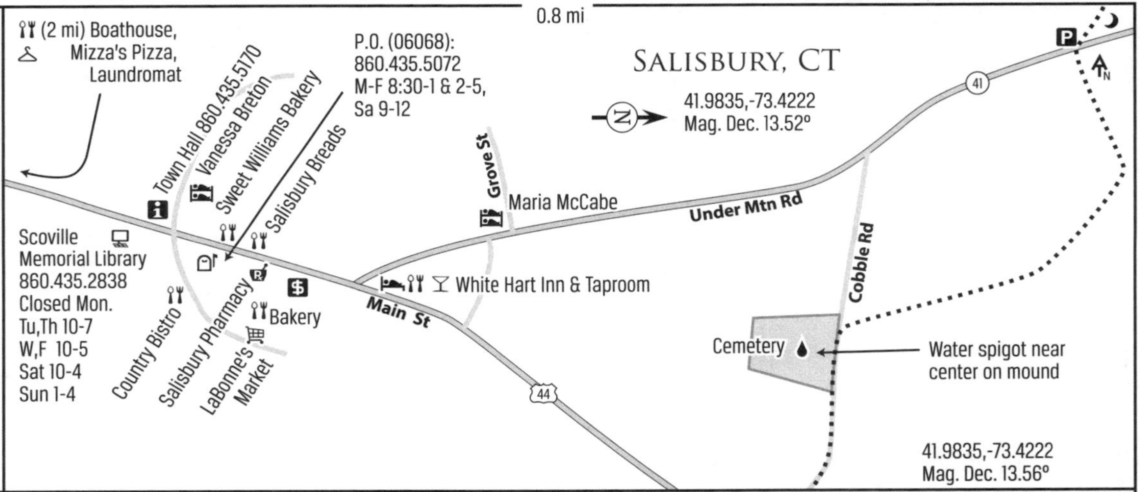

1513.3 Elbow Trailhead to MA 41

Racebrook Lodge 413.229.2916 ⟨www.rblodge.com⟩ Rates lowest off-season (Nov-May). M-Th $85-$160, F-Su $115-170. Stay incl. b'fast. Pets $15/night. **Stagecoach Tavern** on-site open Th-Su for dinner. Accepts Visa/MC/Disc, open year-round.

1517.0 MA 41 ***South Egremont, MA 01258*** (1.2W)

M–F 8:15–12 & 12:30–4, Sa 9–11:30, 413.528.1571

(0.1W) **ATC New England Regional Office** 413.528.8002 in Kellogg Conservation Center. Water from hose, picnic table, 2 charging outlets, no camping/parking.

Egremont Market 413.528.0075 Market & deli 6:30am-7pm 7 days (6pm in winter). Ice cream, trail mix, sodas.

Mom's Country Cafe 413.528.2414 B'fast/Lunch restaurant open 6:30-3 every day and 5-9pm F-Su. B'fast all day, free coffee refills, outdoor water spigot, hikers welcome.

Camping & Campfire Regulations

Many of the camping & campfire regulations along the Appalachian Trail are addressed in The A.T. Guide. However these regulations change frequently. Please visit www.appalachiantrail.org/camping for the most current and comprehensive listing so you may familiarize yourself with the most current regulations for the entire Appalachian Trail.

NoBo	SoBo	Feature	Coordinates / Services	Elev
676.5	1513.3	Elbow Trail 1.5E to MA 41 near **Racebrook Lodge**	(pg. 155)	1752
675.5	1514.3	Mt Bushnell		1847
674.4	1515.4	Jug End, view		1469
673.7	1516.1	Jug End Rd, unreliable piped spring 0.2E	42.1444,-73.4316 P	875
672.8	1517.0	MA 41, **South Egremont, MA** (1.2W)	(pg. 155)	810
671.8	1518.0	Footbridge, stream (2 close together)		711
671.2	1518.6	Footbridge, stream		694
671.0	1518.8	Sheffield Egremont Rd, Shays Rebellion Monument	42.1471,-73.3867 P	700
670.2	1519.6	Gravel road		742
669.9	1519.9	West Rd (paved)		703
669.2	1520.6	US 7, RR to south, soda vending 0.2E at repair shop **Sheffield, MA** (3.0E), **Great Barrington, MA** (3.0W)	(pg. 158)	675
669.0	1520.8	Footbridge, stream		664
668.3	1521.5	Housatonic River, cross on Kellogg Rd Bridge	42.144,-73.3595 P	659
667.9	1521.9	Boardman St		706
666.5	1523.3	June Mtn		1252
666.3	1523.5	Homes Rd (paved)		1150
665.7	1524.1	Footbridge, spring at bottom of cleft		1526
665.3	1524.5	East Mountain, view		1737
664.9	1524.9	Woods road		1789
662.8	1527.0	Ice Gulch, **Tom Leonard Shelter** 22.8◄14.4◄14.3◄►5.3►7.1►21.1 Campsite overlooking ravine north of shelter. Stream 0.2 on path to left or 0.3 on path to right.	(10)	1561
661.7	1528.1	Lake Buel Rd (paved), parking area with kiosk	42.1745,-73.294 P	1088
660.8	1529.0	MA 23 (paved) **East Mountain Retreat Center** (1.0W)	42.1844,-73.2907 P (pg. 159)	1050
659.6	1530.2	Blue Hill Rd (paved), Stony Brook Rd		1550
658.9	1530.9	Beartown Mtn Rd, Benedict Pond, 0.5W on blue-blazed trail to **Beartown State Forest,** beach, picnic area, phone, tent sites $10.		1598
658.7	1531.1	Benedict Pond Loop Trail to west, footbridge and stream east of AT		1624
658.2	1531.6	The Ledges		1820
657.8	1532.0	Stream.		1634
657.5	1532.3	**Mt Wilcox South Shelters** 19.7◄19.6◄5.3◄►1.8►15.8►24.6 Old shelter 0.1E (6), newer shelter 0.2E (12).	(5) (6/12)	1819

656.6 1533.2 Stream (several) 1830
656.5 1533.3 Pond, Swann Brook outlet at south end 1820

655.7 1534.1 **Mt Wilcox North Shelter** (0.3E) . . . . (10) 2067
21.4◄7.1◄1.8◄►14.0►22.8►31.6
655.0 1534.8 Motorcycle path 1833
654.9 1534.9 Beartown Mountain Rd, NoBo: turn east 1796
654.5 1535.3 East Brook, footbridge, more streams north and south 1716

651.9 1537.9 Fernside Rd / Jerusalem Rd (gravel) 1200
651.6 1538.2 Shaker Campsite to east; platforms, bear box, water north on AT 947

649.9 1539.9 Cobble Hill 1279
649.7 1540.1 Jerusalem Rd (paved), **Tyringham, MA 01264** (0.6W) . . . . (pg. 159) 1128
Water 0.1W on left side of road, water also outside of P.O. 0.6W.
649.2 1540.6 Three streams crossed by footbridges 1001
648.6 1541.2 Main Rd (paved), **Tyringham, MA** (0.9W) . . . . 42.2354,-73.1945 P (pg. 159) 995
Water, parking to west.

SoBo NoBo 1000 3000 5000

647.0 1542.8 Baldy Mtn 1921
646.8 1543.0 Webster Rd (gravel) 1800
646.2 1543.6 Knee-Deep Pond to west 1689

645.2 1544.6 Spring on side trail 0.1W 1781

644.4 1545.4 Goose Pond Rd (gravel) . . . . 42.2743,-73.1838 P (0.1E) 1650
644.0 1545.8 Cooper Brook, footbridge 1564
643.5 1546.3 Signed trail junction 1727
⚠ NoBo: this is not the side trail to Upper Goose Pond Cabin.

642.3 1547.5 Higley Brook, footbridge, Upper Goose Pond to west 1495
641.8 1548.0 Old chimney 1480
641.7 1548.1 **Upper Goose Pond Cabin** (0.5W) . . . . (pg. 159) 1552
21.1◄15.8◄14.0◄►8.8►17.6►34.5

640.5 1549.3 MA Turnpike I-90 1400
640.2 1549.6 Greenwater Brook, footbridge 1355
640.1 1549.7 US 20, **Lee, MA** (5.0W), hotel 0.1E . . . . 42.293,-73.1614 P (0.1W) (pg. 159) 1400
639.7 1550.1 Powerline, stream to north 1583
639.3 1550.5 Tyne Rd / Becket Rd, stream to south 1797
638.8 1551.0 Becket Mountain 2180

637.8 1552.0 Walling Mountain 2214

637.2 1552.6 Finerty Pond 1940

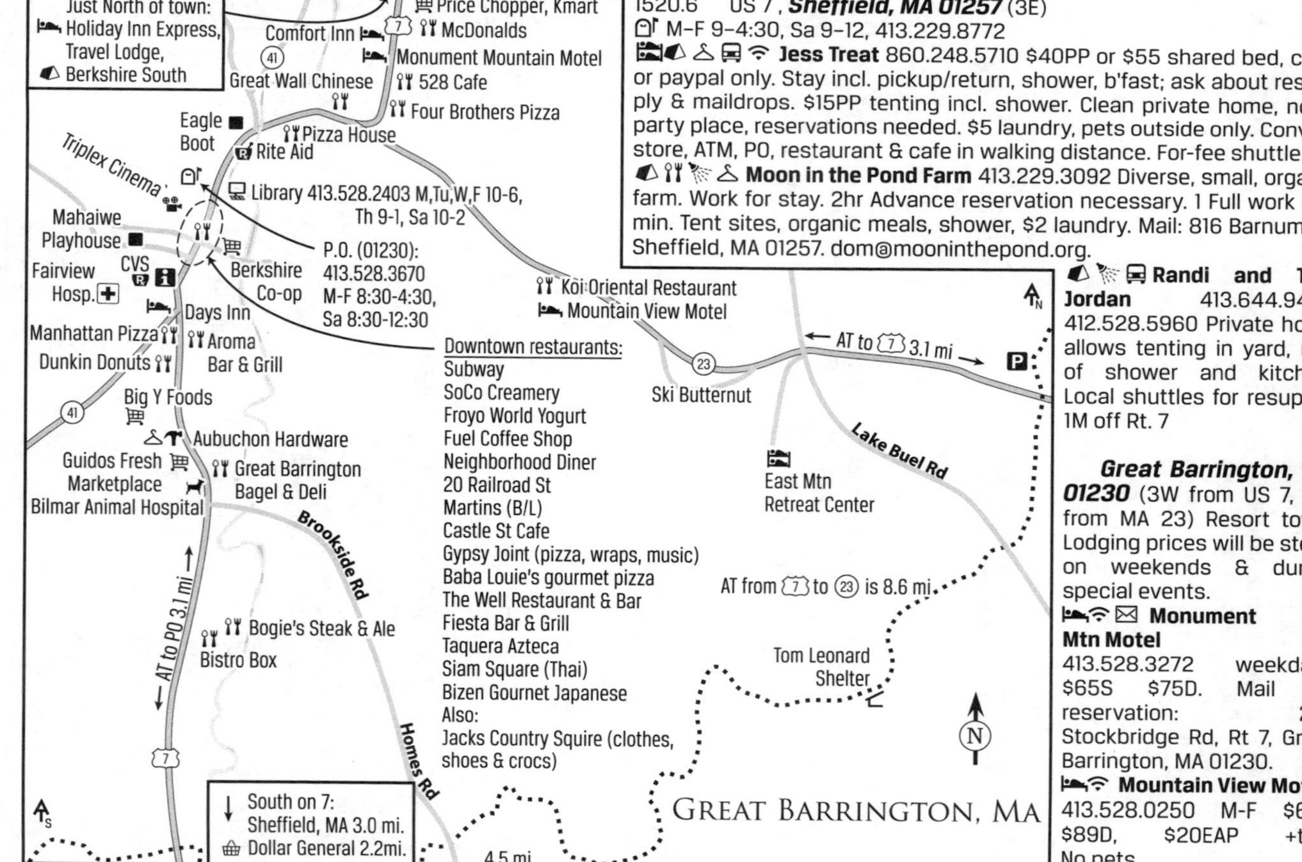

1520.6 US 7 , ***Sheffield, MA 01257*** (3E)

M–F 9–4:30, Sa 9–12, 413.229.8772

Jess Treat 860.248.5710 $40PP or $55 shared bed, cash or paypal only. Stay incl. pickup/return, shower, b'fast; ask about resupply & maildrops. $15PP tenting incl. shower. Clean private home, not a party place, reservations needed. $5 laundry, pets outside only. Conven. store, ATM, PO, restaurant & cafe in walking distance. For-fee shuttle.

Moon in the Pond Farm 413.229.3092 Diverse, small, organic farm. Work for stay. 2hr Advance reservation necessary. 1 Full work day min. Tent sites, organic meals, shower, $2 laundry. Mail: 816 Barnum St, Sheffield, MA 01257. dom@mooninthepond.org.

Randi and Tom Jordan 413.644.9474, 412.528.5960 Private home allows tenting in yard, use of shower and kitchen. Local shuttles for resupply. 1M off Rt. 7

Great Barrington, MA 01230 (3W from US 7, 4W from MA 23) Resort town; Lodging prices will be steep on weekends & during special events.

Monument Mtn Motel 413.528.3272 weekdays $65S $75D. Mail w/ reservation: 247 Stockbridge Rd, Rt 7, Great Barrington, MA 01230.

Mountain View Motel 413.528.0250 M-F $69S $89D, $20EAP +tax. No pets.

Days Inn 413.528.3150 Rates $79 /up. Cont B, non-smoking rooms, no pets.

Fairfield Inn & Suites 413.644.3200 Prices seasonal. Full B, heated pool & hot tub, no pets. Maildrops with advance reservation: 249 Stockbridge Rd, Rt 7, Great Barrington, MA 01230.

Travel Lodge 413.528.2340 Su-Th $50-89D + tax, $10EAP, cont B, coin laundry.

Berkshire South Regional Community Center 413.528.2810 15 Crissey Rd north end of town. Free tenting, check-in at front desk. $7PP use of facility (showers, saunas, pool). Free dinner M 5-6pm, donations accepted. No smoking, drugs, alcohol, or pets. On BRTA route (tell driver your destination). ⟨www.berkshiresouth.org⟩

Guido's Organic produce, cold juices, and more.

Fairview Hospital 413.528.0790

All Points Driving Service 413.429.7397 Range: Salisbury-Dalton.

1529.0 MA 23

(1.5W) **East Mountain Retreat Center** 413.528.6617 1.0W from MA 23 to corner of Lake Buel Rd. (there is a blue sign). 0.5mi up driveway. $10PP donation, no CC. Shower & hot plate. Check-in by 8:00p, 8:30a checkout. Quiet after 10p. Open May 15-Aug 15. Maildrops (FedEx & UPS only): 8 Lake Buel Rd, Great Barrington, MA 01230.

1540.1 Jerusalem Rd (0.6W to town)

1541.2 Main Rd (0.9W to town)

Tyringham, MA 01264 M–F 9–12:30 & 4-5:30, Sa 8:30–12:30, 413.243.1225

Library 413.243.1373 Adjacent to P.O. Tu 3-5, Saturday 10-12

1548.1 **Upper Goose Pond Cabin** (0.5W)

(14) On side trail north of pond. Fireplace, covered porch, bunks with mattresses. Swimming and canoeing. Open daily Sa before Memorial Day - Sa after Columbus Day (dates subject to change). When caretaker not in residence, hikers may camp on porch (no cooking) or tent platforms. Please store food in bear box. During summer, caretaker brings water; otherwise, pond is water source. Donations welcome.

1549.7 US 20

(0.1E) **Berkshire Lakeside Lodge** 413.243.9907 Weekdays $60-90, weekends $99-175 2-person room, $10EAP. Cont. b'fast, TV & fridge. No pets. Hikers welcome to get water. Sodas for sale. No services nearby but you can have Italian & Chinese food delivered. Mail (call ahead to arrange pickup): 3949 Jacob's Ladder Rd, Rt 20, Becket, MA 01223

Lee, MA 01238 (5W) Lodging busy and expensive on weekends and during Tanglewood Music Festival.

M–F 8:30–4:30, Sa 9–12, 413.243.1392

Econo Lodge 413.243.0501 Apr-May $52-55 Su-Th, $65-75 F-Sa, Jun-Oct $60-79 Su–Th, $110–$195 F–Sa, cont B.

Roadway Inn 413.243.0813 Jul-Aug Su-Th $99, F-Sa $199, (plus tax). Other months prices vary. Cont B.

Pilgrim Inn 413.243.1328 Peak rates Jun 15-Aug; Su–Th $79D, F–Sa $225D. Non-peak rates $55D-$110D. Cont B, micro, fridge. Pets $20.

Super 8 413.243.0143 Call for hiker rates.

Dunkin Donuts, Athena's Pizza House, **Friendly's**, **Joe's Diner, McDonalds**, and many more.

Price Chopper Supermarket 413.528.2408

Rite Aid

Valley Veterinary Clinic 413.243.2414

Lee Coin-Op Laundry

BRTA 800.292.2782 Commuter bus connects ***Great Barrington***, ***Dalton***, ***Cheshire***, ***North Adams***, ***Adams***, ***Williamstown***, ***Pittsfield***, ***Lee*** and **Berkshire Mall**. Buses run M-F 5:45am-7:20pm, Sa 7:15pm-7pm. Fare $1.75 for local routes (in-town and adjoining towns), or $4.50 systemwide. "CharlieCard", avail. from drivers for $5, gives you a discount per ride and allows you to make bus transfers. Drivers cannot make change. Flag bus anywhere on route.

635.4 1554.4 Washington Mountain Brook 1761

634.8 1555.0 County Rd (gravel) 1850
634.5 1555.3 Bald Top 2040

632.9 1556.9 **October Mountain Shelter,** intermittent stream, cables . . . . (12) 1907
24.6◄22.8◄8.8◄►8.8►25.7►32.3
632.2 1557.6 West Branch Rd (gravel) 1960

630.6 1559.2 AT joins dirt road and crosses . . . . . 42.377,-73.1507 P (pg. 162) 2000
Washington Mtn Rd (paved), **Becket, MA** 01223 (5.0E)

628.6 1561.2 Streams 1836

627.5 1562.3 Blotz Rd (paved), small parking lot on north side . . . . . 42.4094,-73.1503 P 1850

626.8 1563.0 Warner Hill 2050

625.2 1564.6 Tully Mountain 2082

624.4 1565.4 Powerline 1918
624.1 1565.7 **Kay Wood Shelter** (0.2E) 31.6◄17.6◄8.8◄►16.9►23.5►33.4 . . . (10) 1757
623.8 1566.0 Grange Hall Rd 1628
623.6 1566.2 Barton Brook, footbridge 1543

622.2 1567.6 Woods road 1325

621.6 1568.2 Railroad tracks, Housatonic St + Depot St 1220

621.1 1568.7 MA 8 & 9, **Dalton, MA** . . . . . **(pg. 162)** 1145

620.1 1569.7 AT on Gulf Rd / High St for 1.0 mile . . . . . 42.4818,-73.1783 P 1180

> ⚠ Many of the water sources listed in this book are springs and small streams that can go dry. Never carry just enough water to reach the next water source.

617.9 1571.9 Spring 1920

NoBo	SoBo	Feature		Elev
617.0	1572.8	Powerlines		1906
616.9	1572.9	Crystal Mountain Campsite 0.2E, water on AT just north of side trail	(5)	1950
616.1	1573.7	Gore Brook, outlet of Gore Pond		2031
615.0	1574.8	Stream.		1986
614.6	1575.2	Stream.		1815
613.9	1575.9	The Cobbles, outcroppings of marble with view of Hoosic River Valley, Mt Greylock, and the town of Cheshire.		1848
612.8	1577.0	Furnace Hill Rd (south end)		1046
612.3	1577.5	Main St + School St, **Cheshire, MA**.	(pg. 163)	978
611.8	1578.0	MA 8, **Cheshire, MA, Adams, MA** (4.0E)	(pg. 163)	992
610.7	1579.1	Outlook Ave (paved), stream and powerline to north		1317

Touch-Me-Not – Also known as "jewelweed". Trumpet-shaped flowers with a short curled tail hang horizontally like a bug in flight. Yellow with splotches of orange. Salve from crushed stems is a folk remedy for poison ivy's itch.

NoBo	SoBo	Feature		Elev
608.1	1581.7	Old Adams Rd (dirt)		2341
607.2	1582.6	**Mark Noepel Shelter** (0.2E), spring to right of shelter 34.5◄25.7◄16.9◄►6.6►16.5►23.7 Spring stronger the farther you go.	(10)	2823
606.7	1583.1	Jones Nose Trail to west		3233
604.9	1584.9	Rockwell Rd / Summit Rd to west	42.6311,-73.1783 P	3025
604.5	1585.3	Cross Rockwell Rd twice, side trails to east		3144
603.9	1585.9	Mt Greylock, highest peak in MA	(pg. 166)	3491
603.5	1586.3	Thunderbolt Trail and Bellows Pipe Trail, 75 yards apart, both to east.		3105
601.9	1587.9	Bernard Farm Trail		2780
601.6	1588.2	Mt Williams		2950
600.8	1589.0	Notch Rd (paved)		2319
600.6	1589.2	**Wilbur Clearing Shelter** (0.3W) On Money Brook Trail 32.3◄23.5◄6.6◄►9.9►17.1►23.0. Intermittent stream.	(8)	2275
600.3	1589.5	Mt Prospect Trail to west		2505
598.7	1591.1	Pattison Rd (paved)	42.6876,-73.1598 P	1018
598.1	1591.7	Phelps Ave (south end), on road 0.5 mile		732
597.6	1592.2	MA 2, Hoosic River, footbridge and RR tracks, **Williamstown, MA** (west), , **MA** (east)	42.699,-73.1535 P (0.1E) (pg. 166)	660
597.5	1592.3	Massachusetts Ave / Hoosac Rd. NoBo: east on road for 0.1 mile	(pg. 167)	689

1559.2 Washington Mtn Rd

Home of the **"Cookie Lady"** 100 yards east. 413.623.5859 Water spigot near the garage door, please sign register on the steps. Homemade cookies often avail. Soda, ice cream, boiled eggs & pick your own blueberries. Camping allowed, ask permission first. Shuttle range from Kent, CT to Manchester Center, VT. Mail: Roy & Marilyn Wiley, 47 Washington Mountain Road, Becket, MA 01223.

Becket, MA 01223 (5E) M–F 8–4, Sa 9–11:30, 413.623.8845

(6E) **Becket Motel** 413.623.8888 $95-156+tax, incl. shuttle from/to US 20 or Wash Mtn Rd. Tavern next door. Guest Mail: 29 Chester Road, Becket, MA 01223.

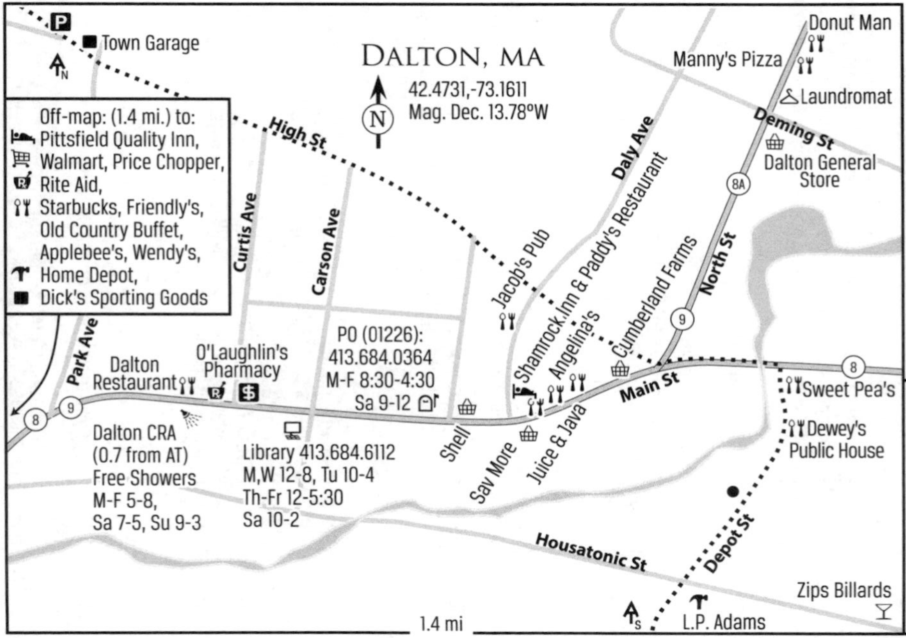

1568.7 MA 8 & 9 ***Dalton, MA 01227***

12% tax added to lodging prices.

Shamrock Village Inn 413.684.0860 Hiker rates Su-Th are $70.60S, $75D, $85 king bed. F-Sa prices $85.50/$93.60/$99 respectively. Add tax to all prices. Well-behaved pets allowed with $75 deposit. Coin laundry, free use of computer and WiFi.

Angelina's Subs

Dalton Restaurant 5:30a to 8p 7 days. Closed early on Su.

SweetPea's 413.684.9799 Lunch, ice cream. M-Sa 11:30-9, Su 2-8.

Dalton Laundry M-F 9-6, Sa 10-4, Su 10-2.

LP Adams Coleman/denatured alcohol.

Pittsfield, MA Many stores & restaurants approx. 2.0W from Dalton.

Econo Lodge 413.443.5661 prices seasonal.

Berkshire Mall on SR 8, 4 mi. north of Dalton & 7 mi. south of Cheshire has:

EMS 413.445.4967
M-Sa 10-8, Su 11-6
Regal Cinema 10 413.499.3106

1577.5 Main St, School St

Cheshire, MA 01225 (pronounced "chesh-er")

St. Mary of the Assumption Church Parish Hall 413.743.2110 (at rear of church). Indoor sleeping space w/restrooms. No laundry, showers, or cooking. No smoking/alcohol/drugs. May, Sep & Oct through the 15th check in no later than 8p. Jun, Jul, Aug no later than 9p. No facilities avail. Oct 16th - Apr 30th. Hikers must follow guidelines for useage - posted in parrish hall. Welcome to attend service in hiker attire. Please donate.

Diane's Twist Limited hours, deli sandwiches, soda, ice cream.

HD Reynolds 413.743.9512 M-W & F 8-5, Th 8-7, Sa 8-3. General store, hiker snacks, Coleman fuel/oz.

BRTA (pg. 159) stops at AT kiosk; ride to outfitter, Adams, MA, and to Berkshire Mall (has EMS) $1.75.

1578.0 MA 8

(2.2E) **Berkshire Outfitters** ⟨www.berkshireoutfitters.com⟩ 413.743.5900 M-F 10-6, Sa 10-5, Su 11-4, Full service outfitter, Coleman/alcohol/oz and canister fuel, freeze-dried foods, footwear, minor equipment repairs. Often provides return ride to Cheshire.

Adams, MA 01220 (4.2E)

M–F 8:30–4:30, Sa 10–12, 413.743.5177

Big Y Foods Supermarket

Rite Aid, Medicine Shop

Adams Veterinary Clinic 413.743.4000

Thrifty Bundle Laundromat 413.664.9007

Plan Ahead!
Be Aware of Camping
& Campfire Regulations.

Check Appalachian Trail (A.T.) guidebooks and maps for guidance and note that camping cna campfire regulations vary considerably along the Trail. Travel in groups of 10 or fewer. If you are traveling in a group of more than 5, avoid using shelters, leaving them for lone hikers and smaller groups.

SoBo	NoBo	Feature	Elev
597.2	1592.6	Footbridge, stream	756
596.0	1593.8	Petes Spring. Sherman Brook Campsite 0.1W	1352
595.3	1594.5	Bad weather bypass trail	1806
594.9	1594.9	Pine Cobble Trail to west	2113
594.8	1595.0	'98 Trail to west	2128
593.5	1596.3	**MA-VT** border, southern end of Long Trail (LT) The AT and LT are concurrent northbound for the next 105.2 miles.	2330
593.1	1596.7	Spring, stream to north	2154
591.0	1598.8	Stream	2074
590.7	1599.1	**Seth Warner Shelter** (0.2W) (8) 33.4◄16.5◄9.9◄►7.2►13.1►21.6 Brook 0.1 left of shelter, known to dry up.	2229
590.4	1599.4	Country Rd, Powerline	2290
588.7	1601.1	Powerline	2894
587.8	1602.0	Roaring Branch, pond	2479
586.6	1603.2	Consultation Peak	2833
585.5	1604.3	Woods road, Stamford Stream	2246
585.1	1604.7	Stream	2177
584.6	1605.2	Pond	2191
584.2	1605.6	Woods road	2199
583.5	1606.3	**Congdon Shelter**, creek is water source (8) 23.7◄17.1◄7.2◄►5.9►14.4►18.7	2088
582.7	1607.1	Stream	2223
581.4	1608.4	Stream	2214
581.0	1608.8	Harmon Hill	2325
580.5	1609.3	Spring	2101
579.2	1610.6	VT 9, **Bennington, VT** (5.1W) 42.8851,-73.1153 P (pg. 171) Bridge over City Stream north of road	1359
577.6	1612.2	Brook, **Melville Nauheim Shelter**, stream north of trail to shelter (8) 23.0◄13.1◄5.9◄►8.5►12.8►17.4	2424

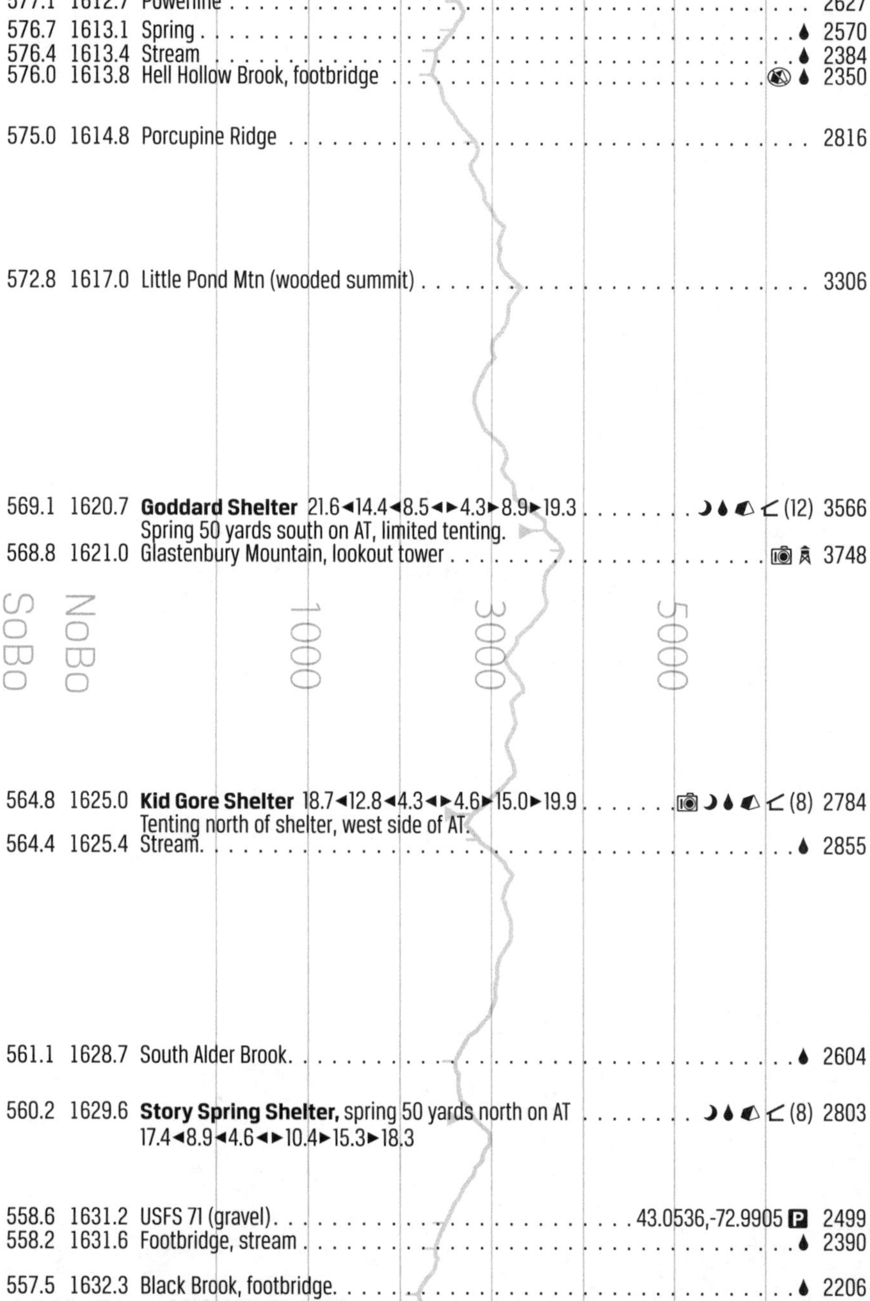

NoBo	SoBo	Location	Services	Elev
577.1	1612.7	Powerline		2627
576.7	1613.1	Spring	♦	2570
576.4	1613.4	Stream	♦	2384
576.0	1613.8	Hell Hollow Brook, footbridge	♦	2350
575.0	1614.8	Porcupine Ridge		2816
572.8	1617.0	Little Pond Mtn (wooded summit)		3306
569.1	1620.7	**Goddard Shelter** 21.6◄14.4◄8.5◄►4.3►8.9►19.3 Spring 50 yards south on AT, limited tenting.	(12)	3566
568.8	1621.0	Glastenbury Mountain, lookout tower		3748
564.8	1625.0	**Kid Gore Shelter** 18.7◄12.8◄4.3◄►4.6►15.0►19.9 Tenting north of shelter, west side of AT.	(8)	2784
564.4	1625.4	Stream.	♦	2855
561.1	1628.7	South Alder Brook.	♦	2604
560.2	1629.6	**Story Spring Shelter,** spring 50 yards north on AT 17.4◄8.9◄4.6◄►10.4►15.3►18.3	(8)	2803
558.6	1631.2	USFS 71 (gravel)	43.0536,-72.9905 P	2499
558.2	1631.6	Footbridge, stream	♦	2390
557.5	1632.3	Black Brook, footbridge.	♦	2206

1585.9 Mt Greylock (3,491') is Massachusetts's highest peak. Veterans War Memorial Tower is on the summit. There are views of the Green, Catskill, and Taconic mountain ranges and surrounding towns. No camping or fires on summit.

Bascom Lodge on summit 413.743.1591 private rooms $125/up, bunkroom $35PP. Bunkroom incl. use of shower and continental b'fast. Shower & towel w/o stay $5, some snacks in gift shop, restaurant serves B/L/D. Open May 20-Oct 22, 2017, weekends only in May.

1592.2 MA 2

Greylock Community Center Park on grass west of building, leave note with name & vehicle ID in mailbox, donations accepted.

Williamstown, MA 01267 (2.6W) All hotels expensive on peak nights, 11.7% lodging tax.

Howard Johnson 413.458.8158, Rates seasonal, cont B. Maildrops (fee for non-guests): 213 Main Street, Williamstown, MA 01267.

Willows Motel 413.458.5768 Willows Motel , $58-129, fourth night free, elaborate cont. b'fast, free pickup/return with stay, discount at adjacent Olympia restaurant. Laundry $6. Pool, some pets. Mail: 480 Main Street, Williamstown, MA 01267.

Williamstown Motel 413.458.5202 $59S $69D wkdays, $79S $89D wkends; prices higher on high-demand nights. Cont B. Laundry (done for you) $8. Will pickup at Route 2. Major CC accepted. Mail: 295 Main Street, Williamstown, MA 01267.

Maple Terrace Motel 413.458.9677 Prices seasonal, call for rates. Heated pool, all rooms non-smoking.

River Bend Farm 413.458.3121 $120D incl. b'fast. Unique experience in an authentic 1770 colonial farmhouse. Free pickup & return when avail., short term parking for guests.

Williams Inn 413.458.9371 $155D/up. Non-guests can pay $8 for use of shower, swim and sauna. Restaurant open 7 days 5p-10p (may vary). Short term parking $2/day.

Desperado's is hiker friendly.

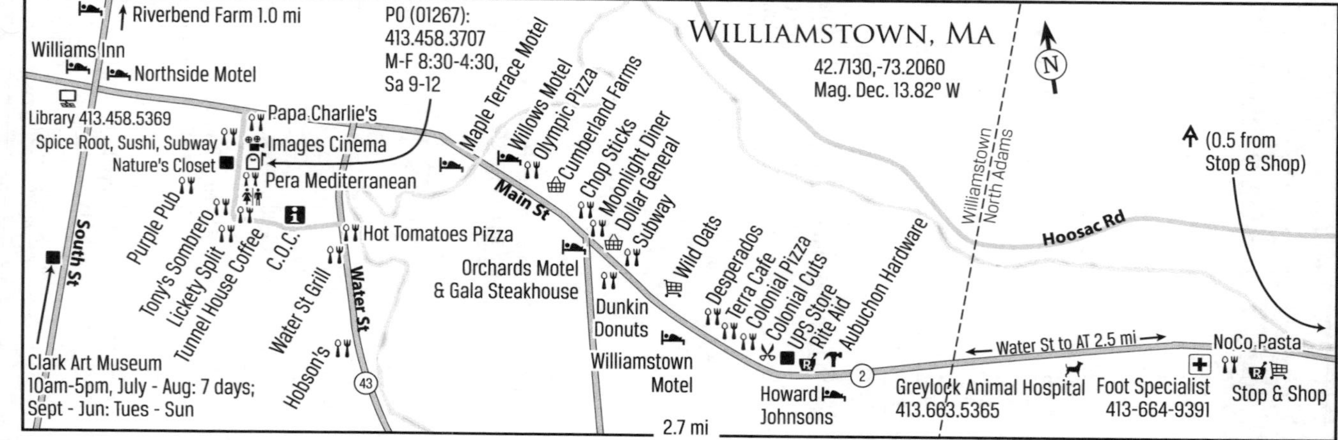

Spice Root Indian Cuisine 413.458.5200
10% hiker discount.

Water Street Grill 413.458.2175 Craft beer, L/D daily.

Nature's Closet Apparel, footwear, canister fuel and consignment sales. Mail: 61 Spring St, Williamstown, MA 01267.

Milne Public Library M-F 10-5:30, W 10-8, Sa 10-4

Greyhound Bus Service

North Adams, MA 01247 (services spread east of AT)

Holiday Inn 413.663.6500 Summer rates $169.99/up. Pool, hot tub. **Richmond Grill** on-site.

Greylock Animal Hospital 413.663.5365
M-Th 8-7, F 8-5, Sa 8-3, Su 9-3, M-F doctor on call until 11pm.

David Ackerson 413.346.1033, 413.652.9573
daveackerson@yahoo.com Shuttles to trailheads ranging from Bear Mtn Bridge to Hanover, and to/from area airports.

1592.3 Massachusetts Ave / Hoosac Rd

The Birches B&B 413.458.8134 ⟨www.birchesbb.com⟩ $125D/up. Free pickup/return from Massachusetts Ave or MA 2 with stay, advance notice required. Two night min on weekends Jun-Oct. Swimming pond, laundry, big b'fast. Ask about slackpacking (19.3mi to Bennington).

⚠Please be mindful of people's personal property. Do not camp on private land and abide by all "No Camping" signs.

Red-spotted newt is the slow-moving red salamander that can be seen anywhere along the AT. The newt lives on land for the middle stage of its life, which lasts about two years. During this stage, it's also known as a red eft. It is a tadpole in its first stage. In its last stage it returns to water and turns green, but retains its red spots.

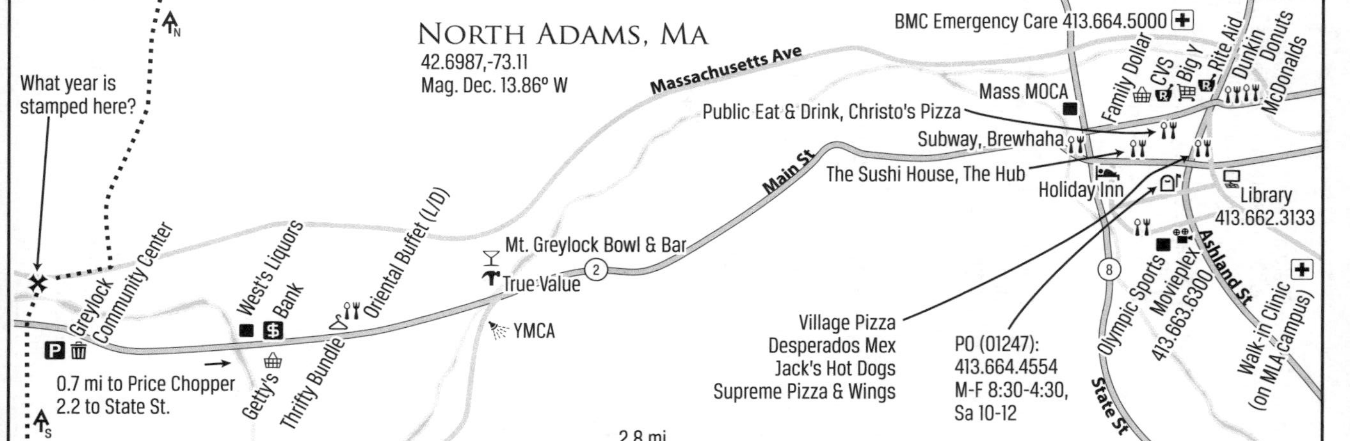

SoBo	NoBo	Feature	Elev
556.6	1633.2	Stratton-Arlington Rd / Kelly Stand Rd (gravel) . . . . . . 43.0611,-72.9681 NoBo: east on road across Deerfield River. Daniel Webster Monument 0.3E. Campsite 100 yards north of road to the east.	2230
555.1	1634.7	Logging road	2584
552.8	1637.0	Stratton Mtn, lookout tower, caretaker cabin. No camping (pg. 171) Summit on which Benton MacKaye was inspired to propose creation of the AT.	3936
552.6	1637.2	Spring to east.	3817
550.9	1638.9	Logging road	2680
550.3	1639.5	Footbridge, stream	2467
549.8	1640.0	**Stratton Pond Shelter** (0.2W) (16) 19.3◄15.0◄10.4◄►4.9►7.9►12.7 Overnight fee, no tenting, no fires.	2622
549.7	1640.1	Lye Brook Trail to west	2557
549.6	1640.2	Stratton Pond, North Shore Trail 0.5W to campsite, overnight fee	2562
548.9	1640.9	Stream.	2498
548.3	1641.5	Stream.	2447
547.8	1642.0	Winhall River, footbridge, stream	2269
546.3	1643.5	Stream.	2209
544.9	1644.9	**William B. Douglas Shelter** (0.5W) (10) 19.9◄15.3◄4.9◄►3.0►7.8►15.9 Spring to left of shelter.	2286
544.0	1645.8	Prospect Rock to west, view ⚠ NoBo: AT turns east off gravel road.	2099
541.9	1647.9	**Spruce Peak Shelter** (0.1W) 18.3◄7.9◄3.0◄►4.8►12.9►17.6 (14)	2190
541.5	1648.3	Spruce Peak 0.1W.	2040
541.1	1648.7	Stream, powerline	1819
540.9	1648.9	Stream.	1839
539.6	1650.2	Powerline, footbridge, stream	1741
539.1	1650.7	VT 11 & 30 . . . . . . 43.2068,-72.9707 (pg. 174) **Manchester Center, VT** (5.4W)	1840
538.2	1651.6	Footbridge, stream	2134

NoBo	SoBo	Location		Elev
537.1	1652.7	**Bromley Shelter** 12.7◄7.8◄4.8◄►8.1►12.8►14.3	(4) (12)	2535
536.5	1653.3	Ski slope		3090
536.1	1653.7	Bromley Mountain, no tenting or fires, okay to overnight in ski warming hut, no smoking, please keep hut clean.		3260
533.6	1656.2	Mad Tom Notch, USFS 21 (gravel)		2446
532.0	1657.8	Styles Peak		3394
530.3	1659.5	Peru Peak		3429
529.4	1660.4	Spring		2801
529.0	1660.8	**Peru Peak Shelter** 15.9◄12.9◄8.1◄►4.7►6.2►6.4 (fee)	(10)	2597
528.7	1661.1	Footbridge, stream (two)		2569
528.5	1661.3	Griffith Lake Tenting Area, camping only at designated sites within 0.5 mi.		2600
528.2	1661.6	Old Job Trail to east, Griffith Lake Trail to west		2630
526.4	1663.4	Baker Peak Trail to west, Baker Peak 0.1N on AT		2635
524.3	1665.5	**Lost Pond Shelter** 17.6◄12.8◄4.7◄►1.5►1.7►5.0	(6)	2194
523.8	1666.0	Spring		1951
522.8	1667.0	Old Job Trail to **Old Job Shelter** (1.0E), Lake Brook is water source 14.3◄6.2◄1.5◄►0.2►3.5►8.3	(8)	1531
522.6	1667.2	**Big Branch Shelter** 6.4◄1.7◄0.2◄►3.3►8.1►13.2 Close to road; heavy weekend use. Water source is Big Branch. Privy uphill.	(8)	1486
521.5	1668.3	Danby-Landgrove Rd, Big Black Branch Bridge, **Danby, VT** (3.5W)	43.3727,-72.9627 P **(pg. 175)**	1523
520.9	1668.9	Footbridge, stream		1638
519.4	1670.4	Homer Stone Brook Trail to west		1853
519.3	1670.5	**Little Rock Pond Shelter & Tenting Area** 5.0◄3.5◄3.3◄►4.8►9.9►13.6 Water source is at the caretaker's platform. Overnight fee. Tenting restricted to designated sites.		1794
518.3	1671.5	Footbridge, stream		1934

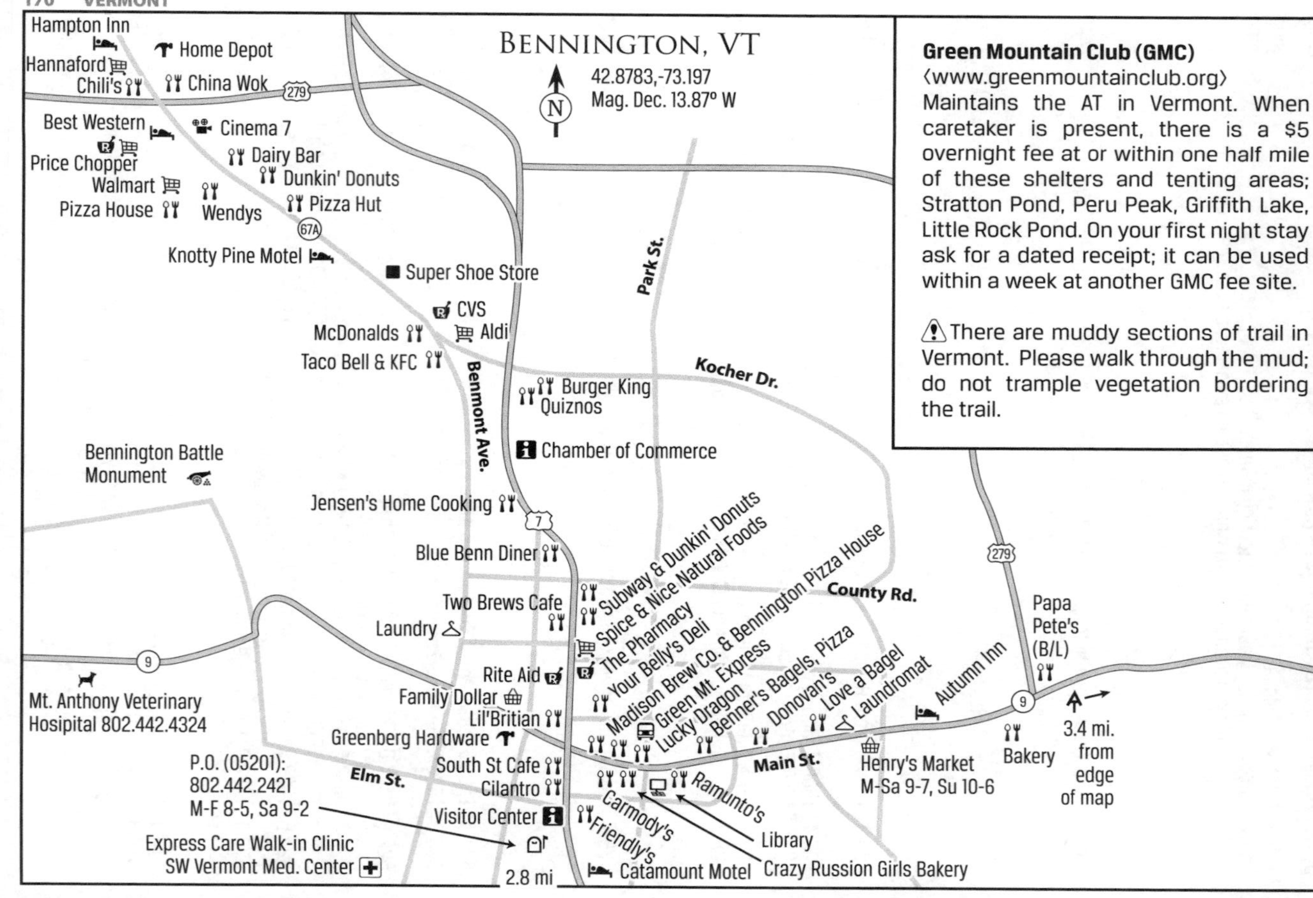

Green Mountain Club (GMC)
⟨www.greenmountainclub.org⟩
Maintains the AT in Vermont. When caretaker is present, there is a $5 overnight fee at or within one half mile of these shelters and tenting areas; Stratton Pond, Peru Peak, Griffith Lake, Little Rock Pond. On your first night stay ask for a dated receipt; it can be used within a week at another GMC fee site.

⚠ There are muddy sections of trail in Vermont. Please walk through the mud; do not trample vegetation bordering the trail.

1610.6 VT 9 ***Bennington, VT 05201*** (5.1W)

Catamount Motel 802.442.5977 $54S, $65D, $10EAP +tax. Laundry $4. One pet room, accepts cc, free maildrops, shuttle.

Autumn Inn Motel 802.447.7625 $60S $70D, Pickup or return to trail $10 (each way). Pets $10. Guest Mail: 924 Main Street, Bennington, VT 05201.

Knotty Pine Motel 802.442.5487 6.5 mi from the AT on VT 9, $88D/up, $8EAP up to 4. Incl. b'fast, pets free, pool. close to grocery/Wal-Mart. Mail (guests only): 130 Northside Dr, Bennington, VT 05201. ‹www.knottypinemotel.com›

Best Western 802.442.6311 $99/up

Hampton Inn 802.440.9862 rates seasonal, hot b'fast.

Lil' Britain Fish & chips.

Cilantro 802.768.8141 Casual, fresh, & simple taco & burrito bar

Green Mountain Express 802.447.0477 ‹www.greenmtncn.org› 215 Pleasant St. Free bus route "Emerald Line" passes between Bennington and Wilmington (17E) 3 times a day M-F. Board at town bus station, or flag the bus down at the trailhead. You may also request an unscheduled ride from town to trail for $3.

Bennington Taxi 802.442.9052

Vermont Translines 844.888.7267 ‹www.vttranslines.com› Routes cover from Albany, NY airport through towns incl. Bennington, VT, Wallingford, VT, Rutland, VT, and Hanover, NH.

Express Care Walk-in Clinic 802.440.4077. No appointment necessary, open daily 8am to 6pm.

SW Vermont Med. Center 802.442.6361 Hospital, Emg Room, Walk-in Clinic

Cinema 7 802.442.8170

Bennington Battle Monument Contains statue of Seth Warner, Revolutionary War leader of the Green Mountain Boys, for whom the shelter is named.

(3.0E) Ski Area

Greenwood Lodge & Campsites 802.442.2547 Open May 20 - Oct 26. Bunk $33, $30 for Hostelling International members. Tentsite $30 for 2. CC not accepted. Country Store nearby.

1637.0 Stratton Mountain

Stratton Mountain Resort 802.297.4000 can be reached by taking a 1.0 mi. side trail from the summit to a gondola ride. Gondola has limited days/hours; don't make the walk unless you are certain of gondola operation (or are willing to walk an additional 1.5 miles down ski slopes). The resort has a restaurant, hotel rooms starting at $84 in summer, and **First Run Ski Shop** 802.297.2200 that has limited footwear and snacks.

Leave What You Find

- Leave plants, cultural artifacts and other natural objects where you found them for others to enjoy.
- Don't build structures or dig trenches around tents.
- Do not damage live trees or plants; green wood burns poorly. Collect only firewood that is dead, down, and no larger than your wrist. Leave dead standing trees and dead limbs on standing trees for the wildlife.
- Consider using rubber tips on the bottom of your trekking poles to avoid scratch marks on rocks, "clicking" sounds, and leaving holes along the trail.
- Avoid introducing or transporting non-native species by checking your boots, socks, packs, tents, and clothing for non-native seeds that you could remove before hitting the trail.

Read more of the Leave No Trace techniques developed for the A.T.: www.appalachiantrail.org/LNT

NoBo	SoBo	Description	Elev
515.1	1674.7	Trail to White Rocks Cliff 0.2W, blue-blazed trail amid stone cairns	2283
514.5	1675.3	**Greenwall Shelter** (0.2E) 8.3◂8.1◂4.8◂▸5.1▸8.8▸14.9. Spring 0.1 mile on side trail behind shelter, prone to fail in dry seasons.	2089
513.8	1676.0	Bully Brook, Keewaydin Trail to west	1435
513.1	1676.7	Sugar Hill Rd (gravel)	1220
513.0	1676.8	VT 140, footbridge, stream 43.4567,-72.9329 (0.2E) P (pg. 175) **Wallingford, VT** (2.8W)	1119
512.0	1677.8	Short side trail to west to Domed Ledge Vista (no longer a view)	1681
511.3	1678.5	Bear Mountain	2206
510.4	1679.4	Patch Hollow	1773
510.0	1679.8	Footbridge, stream (3)	1663
509.8	1680.0	Lake Trail loop to west (yellow blazed), 100 yards north, red-blazed tr to east	1647
509.4	1680.4	**Minerva Hinchey Shelter** 13.2◂9.9◂5.1◂▸3.7▸9.8▸14.1 (10) spring 75 yards in front of shelter.	1597
507.5	1682.3	View to Rutland Airport	1418
506.8	1683.0	Clarendon Gorge, suspension bridge, swimming holes in Mill River	820
506.7	1683.1	VT 103, restaurant 0.5W 43.5214,-72.9258 P (pg. 175) **North Clarendon, VT** (4.2W) **Rutland, VT** (8.0W)	860
506.2	1683.6	View, north end of rock scramble	1378
505.7	1684.1	**Clarendon Shelter** (0.1E) 13.6◂8.8◂3.7◂▸6.1▸10.4▸12.9 (10)	1254
505.2	1684.6	Beacon Hill	1740
504.9	1684.9	Lottery Rd (gravel), powerline	1654
504.4	1685.4	Hermit Spring to east (unreliable)	1786
503.3	1686.5	Stream.	1573
503.1	1686.7	Keiffer Rd (gravel)	1513
502.8	1687.0	Cold River Rd / Lower Rd (paved) NoBo east on road 75 yards **W.E. Pierce Groceries** in North Shrewsbury (2.4E)	1385
502.0	1687.8	Gould Brook to west, AT parallel for 0.5 miles	1480
501.2	1688.6	Upper Cold River Rd (gravel)	1630
500.4	1689.4	Gravel road, Robinson Brook	1740
499.6	1690.2	**Governor Clement Shelter** 14.9◂9.8◂6.1◂▸4.3▸6.8▸8.7 (12) ⚠ Shelter's proximity to road makes it prone to use by non-hiking crowd.	1908
499.3	1690.5	AT on gravel road 0.3 miles north of shelter	2060
498.3	1691.5	Ski trail, blue diamond blazes	2577

497.3 1692.5 Spring . . . 3313
496.9 1692.9 Shrewsbury Peak Trail to east, signed. . . . 3518

495.3 1694.5 **Cooper Lodge Shelter** 14.1◄10.4◄4.3◄►2.5►4.4►16.3 (16)(**pg. 178**) 3908
Spring 60yds north on AT. Trail behind shelter 0.2 to summit, view, restaurant.
495.2 1694.6 Bucklin Trail to west . . . 3780
495.0 1694.8 Spring . . . 3592

492.8 1697.0 **Pico Camp** (0.5E) 12.9◄6.8◄2.5◄►1.9►13.8►23.7 . . . (4) 3461
Shelter on Sherburne Pass Tr where it leaves the Long Tr/AT south of Pico summit.

491.6 1698.2 Spring . . . 3133
490.9 1698.9 **Churchill Scott Shelter** (0.1W) 8.7◄4.4◄1.9◄►11.9►21.8►34.1 . . 2601
Composting privy, unreliable water at southern spur from shelter, no fires.
490.7 1699.1 Stream. . . . 2424

489.9 1699.9 Stream. . . . 2063

489.0 1700.8 US 4, **Rutland, VT** (8.5W) . . . 43.6666,-72.85 P (**pg. 178**) 1880
488.9 1700.9 Stream. . . . 1883
488.0 1701.8 Maine Junction, Tucker-Johnson camping area (0.4W). . . . 2232
⚠ The Long Trail is also white-blazed, it turns to the west.
487.8 1702.0 Spring, Deer Leap Trail to east . . . 2271
487.2 1702.6 Deer Leap Trail 0.3E to view . . . 2445
487.1 1702.7 Sherburne Pass Trail 0.5E to **Inn at Long Trail** . . . 2440

486.3 1703.5 Spring . . . 1857
485.9 1703.9 **Gifford Woods State Park** . . . (**pg. 179**) 1652
485.7 1704.1 VT 100, **Killington, VT** (0.6E) . . . 43.6743,-72.8096 P (**pg. 179**) 1618

485.1 1704.7 Kent Pond, side trail to **Killington, VT** (0.4E) . . . (**pg. 179**) 1561

483.8 1706.0 Thundering Brook Rd (gravel) . . . 1408
483.6 1706.2 Thundering Falls to west. . . . 1237
483.4 1706.4 River Rd (gravel) . . . 43.6806,-72.7822 P 1285

482.1 1707.7 Quimby Mountain. . . . 2511

481.5 1708.3 Powerline, boulder to sit on, view to Pico slopes. . . . 2328
481.2 1708.6 Gravel road . . . 2341

479.0 1710.8 **Stony Brook Shelter** (0.1E) 16.3◄13.8◄11.9◄►9.9►22.2►31.0 . (8) 1759
Tent sites behind shelter. Water from stream 0.1N on AT.
478.4 1711.4 Stony Brook Rd (gravel), Stony Brook and footbridge. . . . 1346

Marble Valley Regional Transit District (MVRTA) "The Bus" 802.773.3244, ext 117. ⟨www.thebus.com⟩ Open 7 days. Red & white bus can be flagged down; they will stop if it is safe to do so. ***Manchester to Rutland:*** ($2PP) Loops from Rultand to Manchester Center, passing through M-Sa 4 times a day. Stops include Rutland Airport, Clarendon, Wallingford, Danby, and Shaws in Manchester Center.

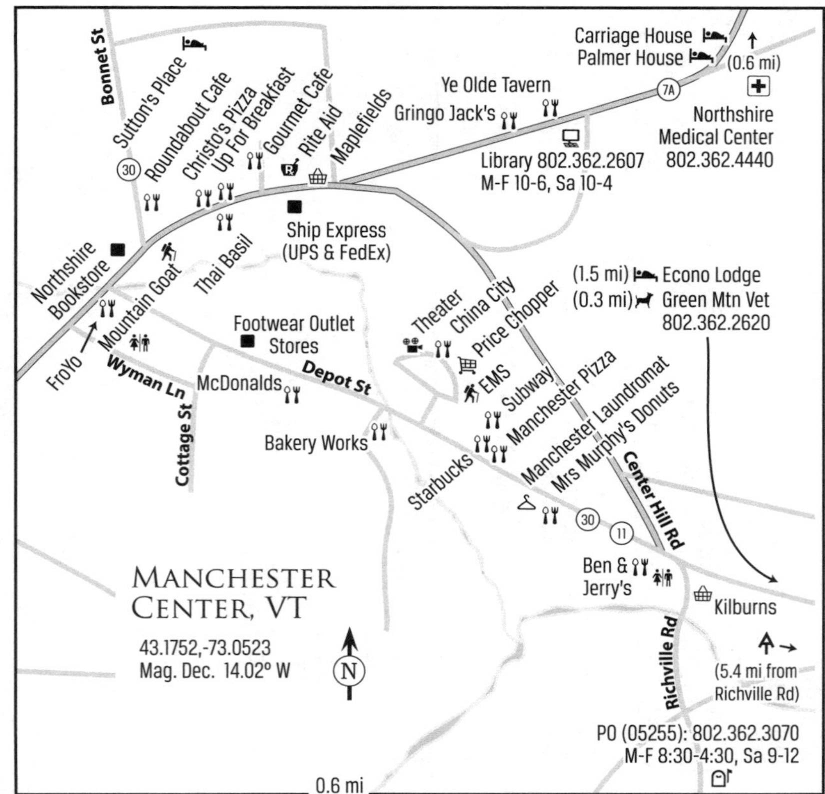

Vermont Translines 844.888.7267 ⟨www.vttranslines.com⟩ Routes cover from Albany, NY airport through towns incl. Bennington, VT, Wallingford, VT, Rutland, VT, and Hanover, NH.

1650.7 VT 11 & 30, ***Manchester Center, VT*** (5.4W)

Between trail and town:

Econo Lodge (3.4W) 802.362.3333 $90 M-F incl. cont. b'fast. Pets $15. Mail: 2187 Depot St, Manchester Center, VT 05255.

Dutton Farm Stand (3.5W) 802.362.3083 9am-7pm 7 days. Produce, sodas, baked goods, ice cream.

Call for ride:

Green Mountain House 330.388.6478 ⟨www.greenmountainhouse.net⟩ Jeff & Regina Taussig host hikers at their home. Open Jun 7 - Sep 7. Space is limited so reservations are essential. Clean bed with linens, shower, free laundry, WiFi, computer & well equipped hiker kitchen. Private room for couples. Free b'fast supplies; make your own pancakes, eggs, cereal, coffee. Not a party place, no alcohol. Hikers with reservations hitch to town, resupply, then call for pick-up. Check-in from 1pm to 7pm. Free morning shuttle back to the trail for guests. Credit cards accepted. $35+tax per person.

In town: (5.4W)

Sutton's Place 802.362.1165 $80S, $90D, $105(room for 3), pets okay on porch. Accepts MC/Visa. USPS Mail: (USPS) PO Box 142 or (UPS) 50 School St, Manchester Center, VT 05255.

Palmer House 802.362.3600 Ask for hiker discount, cont B, no pets, indoor & outdoor pool. Par-3 golf, tennis courts and trout pond (equipment provided).

Carriage House 802.362.1706 $125PP summer, no pets.

Mountain Goat Outfitter 802.362.5159, M-Sa 10-6, Su 10-5, ⟨www.mountaingoat.com⟩ Full-service outfitter, white gas/alcohol/oz canister fuel, footwear. Mail: 4886 Main St, Manchester, VT 05255.

EMS 802.366.8082, 7 days 10-6, full service outfitter, Coleman/alcohol/oz, pole repair, list of shuttlers. Bus stops here.

Leonards Taxi 802.379.5332

Northshire Taxi 802.345.9333

Green Mountain Veterinary Hospital 802.362.2620 M, Tu, Th, F 8-5:30; W-8-6; Sa 8 -1.

Peru, VT (Businesses below are to the east)

The Lodge at Bromley (2.1E) 802.824.6941 $99 hiker rate, no pets, tavern with light menu, game room, ride to/from trail w/stay. Mail: (non-guests $5) 4216 VT 11, Peru, VT 05152.

Bromley Market (2.5E) 802.824.4444 7 days 7am-7pm

Bromley View Inn (3.6E) on VA 30, 802.297.1459 $85D/up, incl. hot b'fast, shuttle to/from VT 11/30 trailhead w/stay. Mail: 522 VT 30, Bondville, VT 05340. ⟨www.bromleyviewinn.com⟩

Hapgood General Store & Eatery (4.2E) 802.824.4800 On Main St. in Peru, next to PO. Wood-fired pizza, beer and resupply. Open 7-7, weekends 7-9.

1668.3 Danby-Landgrove Rd ***Danby, VT 05739*** (3.5W)

M–F 7:15–10:15 & 11:15-2:15, Sa 7–10:30, 802.293.5105

Mt. Tabor Country Store 802.293.5641 M-Sa 5a-8p; Su 6a-7p

Nichols Store & Deli

Silas Griffith Library 802.293.5106 W 2-7 (2-5 in summer), Sa 9-noon, one computer.

1676.8 VT 140, ***Wallingford, VT 05773*** (2.8W)

M–F 8–4:30, Sa 9–12, 802.446.2140

Sal's Italian Restaurant & Pizza 802.446.2935 Serves Dinner

Wallingford Country Store & Deli

Cumberland Farms Bus stop for **MVRTA** (4 times daily) and **Vermont Translines** (see pg. 172)

Nail It Down Hardware

Gilbert Library 802.446.2685 M 10-5; W 10-8; Th-F 10-5; Sa 9-12

1683.1 VT 103

(1W) **Loretta's Deli** 802.772.7638, M–F 6am-7pm, Sa 9-6. Prepared meals & to-go trail foods. Fuel/oz, water filters.

MVRTA Stops near deli 4/day.

North Clarendon, VT 05759 (4.2W)

M–F 8–1 & 2–4:30, Sa 8–10, 802.773.7893

Mike's Country Store 802.773.7100 10a-5p M-F, weekends by appointment

Rutland, VT (8W of VT 103)

Travel and Camp on Durable Surfaces

Read more of the Leave No Trace techniques developed for the A.T. at www.appalachiantrail.org/LNT

- Stay on the trail; never shortcut switchbacks. Take breaks off-trail on durable surfaces, such as rock or grass.
- Restrict activities to areas where vegetation is already absent.
- If tree branches block the trail, move them off if possible, rather than going around and creating new trails.
- Avoid expanding existing trails and campsites by walking in the middle of the trail, and using the already impacted core areas of campsites.
- Wear gaiters and waterproof boots, so you may walk through puddles instead of walking around them and creating a wide spot in the trail.

476.1 1713.7 Streams 2013

474.5 1715.3 Chateauguay Rd (gravel), Locust Creek 2003
474.1 1715.7 Stream. 2144
473.6 1716.2 Stream. 2503

> Clintonia - Foot-tall plant with plastic-looking blue berries atop long stems.

471.6 1718.2 The Lookout, 0.1W to cabin and tower, no fires 2365

469.1 1720.7 **Wintturi Shelter** (0.2W) 23.7◄21.8◄9.9◄►12.3►21.1►28.4 . . . (8) 2058

468.3 1721.5 Woods road 1757

SoBo NoBo 1000 3000 5000

466.5 1723.3 Ascutney Mountain 1488

465.3 1724.5 VT 12, Barnard Gulf Rd (paved) . . . . 43.6552,-72.5662 P (pg. 182) 886
Gulf Stream south of road crossing. **Woodstock, VT** (4.2E)

464.4 1725.4 Dana Hill 1550

463.1 1726.7 Woodstock Stage Rd, Barnard Brook, **South Pomfret, VT** (1E). . . . (pg. 182) 820
462.8 1727.0 Stream 1035

462.3 1727.5 Totman Hill Rd, footbridge, stream. 1007

461.5 1728.3 Bartlett Brook Rd (gravel), footbridge, stream 1001

460.9 1728.9 Pomfret Rd (paved), Pomfret Brook south of road crossing, powerline. 906
460.5 1729.3 View 1538

459.7 1730.1 View 1713
459.1 1730.7 Cloudland Rd (gravel), **Cloudland Market** (0.2W) closed M & Su 1370

458.6 1731.2 Previous AT shelter (Cloudland, 0.5W) now on private land. Owners also own Cloudland Market open W-Sa. No camping. . . . 1617

457.3 1732.5 Thistle Hill . . . 1946
456.8 1733.0 **Thistle Hill Shelter** (0.2E), stream 0.1 further . . . (8) 1754
34.1◄22.2◄12.3◄►8.8►16.1►25.6
456.5 1733.3 Dimick Brook . . . 1504

455.5 1734.3 Joe Ranger Rd (gravel) . . . 1295

454.9 1734.9 Bunker Hill Rd (dirt) . . . 1406

453.1 1736.7 Bench, view to east . . . 1134
452.5 1737.3 Stream . . . 535
452.3 1737.5 Quechee West Hartford Rd, NoBo west on road 0.4 mi, cross White River . . . 474
452.0 1737.8 VT 14, White River, **West Hartford, VT** . . . (pg. 182) 392
NoBo: turn west, on road 0.3 mile.
451.6 1738.2 Tigertown Rd, NoBo: turn east, on road 0.4 mile . . . 397
451.3 1738.5 I-89 underpass . . . 43.7208,-72.4132 P 559
450.6 1739.2 Podunk Rd (gravel), Podunk Brook . . . 43.7168,-72.4002 P 860

450.1 1739.7 Woods road . . . 1048

449.7 1740.1 Woods road, stream . . . 998

SOBO NOBO 1000 3000 5000

448.0 1741.8 **Happy Hill Shelter** (0.1E) 31.0◄21.1◄8.8◄►7.3►16.8►22.5 . . . (8) 1409
Brook near shelter, known to run dry.
447.7 1742.1 Tucker Trail 3.1W to Norwich . . . 1320

446.4 1743.4 Woods road . . . 1127

445.2 1744.6 Powerline . . . 1165
444.7 1745.1 Stream . . . 819
444.6 1745.2 Elm Street, NoBo: turn east, on road 1.0 mile . . . 833

443.6 1746.2 Main St, **Norwich, VT,** NoBo: turn east, on road 1.4 miles . . . (pg. 183) 512

442.7 1747.1 **VT-NH** border, Connecticut River . . . 380
442.1 1747.7 **Hanover, NH,** Dartmouth College . . . 43.7065,-72.2776 P (pg. 185) 520
NoBo: turn east on SR 10.

441.4 1748.4 NH 120, trailhead near convenience store . . . 508

440.7 1749.1 **Velvet Rocks Shelter** (0.2W) 28.4◄16.1◄7.3◄►9.5►15.2►21.9 . . . (6) 907
Spring on northern access to shelter.
440.1 1749.7 North shelter loop trail . . . (0.2W) 959

438.4 1751.4 Pond, boardwalk . . . 800

1694.5 Trail to Killington Peak (0.2E from Cooper Lodge Shelter)

(0.2E) **Killington Peak Lodge** 800.621.6867 Food service at the summit lodge, gondola ride ($25 round trip) to the ski resort. Summer hours 10am-5pm.

1700.8 US 4

The Inn at Long Trail (0.8E) 802.775.7181 or 800.325.2540 Hiker rates, rooms include full b'fast. Limited pet rooms, reservations recommended on weekends. Overflow camping across street (no facilities). Coin laundry, outside water spigot. Closed mid-April through Memorial Day. Mail: (FedEx/UPS) 709 US 4, Killington, VT 05751.
⟨www.innatlongtrail.com⟩

McGrath's Irish Pub Inside The Inn at Long Trail. L/D 11:30-9pm, live music Fri & Sat.

Mendon Mountain View Lodge (1.4W) 802.773.4311 Seasonal rate $119 & up. $15EAP. B'fast $10. No pets. Heated pool & hot tub & sauna, bus stops here. Mail: 5654 Route 4, Mendon, VT 05701.

Rutland, VT (8.5W from US 4 trailhead)

Hikers Hostel at the Yellow Deli 802.683.9378, 802.775.9800 Run by a Twelve Tribes spiritual community. Donations accepted (financial or work). Kitchenette, laundry. No alcohol, no smoking. Free showers even w/o stay. Shuttles sometimes avail. by donation. Hostel open 24/7. Stay inc. b'fast & 15% off at **Yellow Deli**. Deli closed Fr at 3p reopens Su at noon. Open 24/7 the rest of week. Limited resupply at Hostel. Groc. PO & Library 4 min walk. EMS .50 cent bus ride. Mail: Hiker Hostel, 23 Center St, Rutland, VT 05701.
⟨www.hikershostel.org⟩

Mountain Travelers Outdoor Shop 802.775.0814 Tu–Fr 10-5; Sat 10-4. Gear, Coleman/alcohol/oz.

Rutland Food Co-op 802.773.0737 7 days, M-Sa 9-7, Su 10-6

Rutland Veterinary 802.773.2779

Amtrak 800.872.7245 Daily routes Rutland to many northeastern cities.

Rutland Taxi 802.236.3133

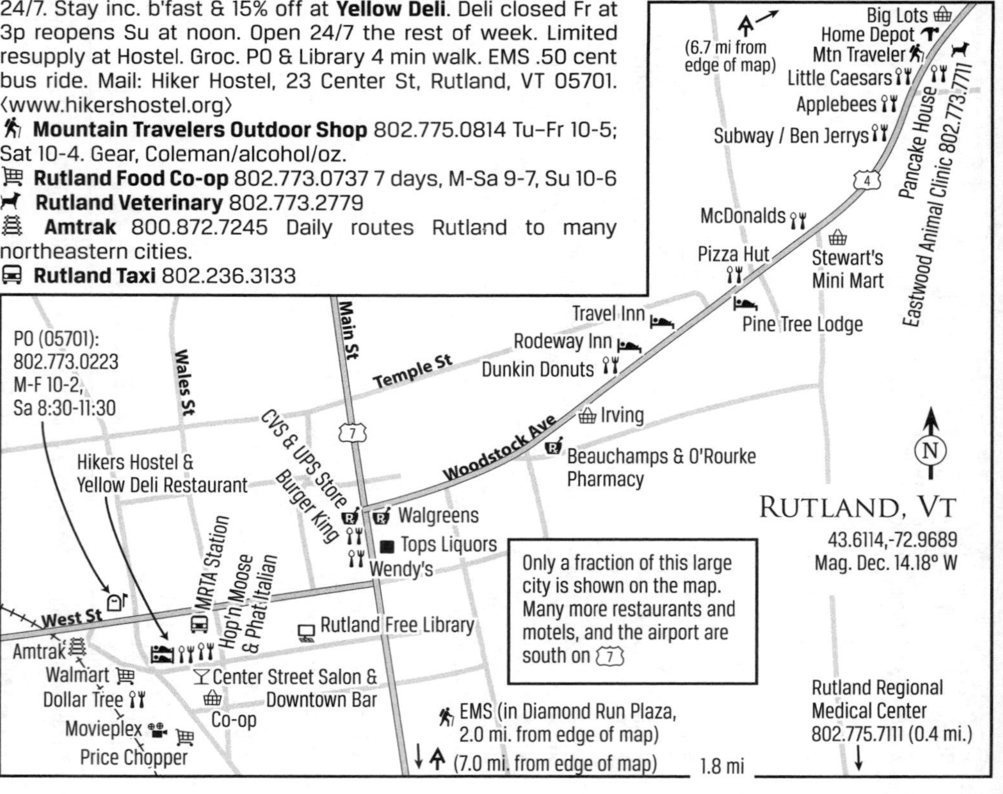

Killington, VT 05751 (1.8E from US 4, pg.177)

1703.9 The AT passes thru **Gifford Woods State Park** 802.775.5354 Shelters, discounted tent sites for AT hikers in special hiker section, coin-op showers, water spigot. Open Mem Day-Columbus Day. Fills quickly in fall.

1704.1 VT 100

Killington, VT 05751 (0.6E from VT 100, 1.8E from US 4)

Base Camp Outfitters 802.775.0166 Summer hrs: 9-5 daily. Full service outfitter, alcohol/oz & canister fuel. Also accessible by side trail from Mountain Meadows Lodge. Disc golf. Mail: 2363 Route 4, Killington VT 05751.

Greenbrier Inn 802.775.1575 15% discount for hikers, no pets.

Killington Motel 802.773.9535 Call for hiker rate, incl. cont. b'fast, pool. Next door to P.O.

Apex Shuttle Service "AT Hiker Shuttle" 603.252.8295 AThikershuttle@gmail.com. Steve "Stray Cat" Lake (AT '96) offers hikers shuttles, slack packing options, trail info and support in New England. Shuttles to or from anywhere on the trail if your hike begins or ends in the Hanover, NH area.

Marble Valley Regional Transit District (MVRTA)
"The Bus" 802.773.3244, ext 117 M-F. Red & white bus can be flagged down; they will stop if it is safe to do so. ***Rutland Killington Commuter (RKC)*** ($2PP) Loops hourly from 5:15-7:15, 7 days from Rutland to Killington, passing AT on US 4. Stops westbound at The Inn at Long Trail. ⟨www.thebus.com⟩

Vermont Translines (see pg. 172) Stops at Rutland bus station and at Long Trail Inn.

JAX Food & Games 802.422.5334 Eat/drink while-u-wash M-Sa 3p-2a, Su 12p-3a (laundry downstairs) 0.8S of US4 on Killington Rd.

Long Trail Brewing Co. (14E) 802.422.5334 802.672.5011 Open 10-7

1704.7 Kent Pond, AT crosses behind lodge near pond, 0.4E trail to **Base Camp Outfitters** ✖Dock over lake is supported by metal poles; what letters are on pole caps?

Mountain Meadows Lodge 802.775.1010 Room $69D, single room sometimes avail. for $59. Open year-round, but meals and lodging are not avail. most weekends & during events. Okay to charge phones, but please do not loiter when events are being held at the lodge. Occasional WFS. Lunch or dinner $10. No pets inside. Hot tub, sauna, game room and canoe for guests. Parking for section hiking guests. Ask about tenting. Mail free even for non-guests: 285 Thundering Brook Rd, Killington, VT 05751. ⟨www.mountainmeadowslodge.com⟩

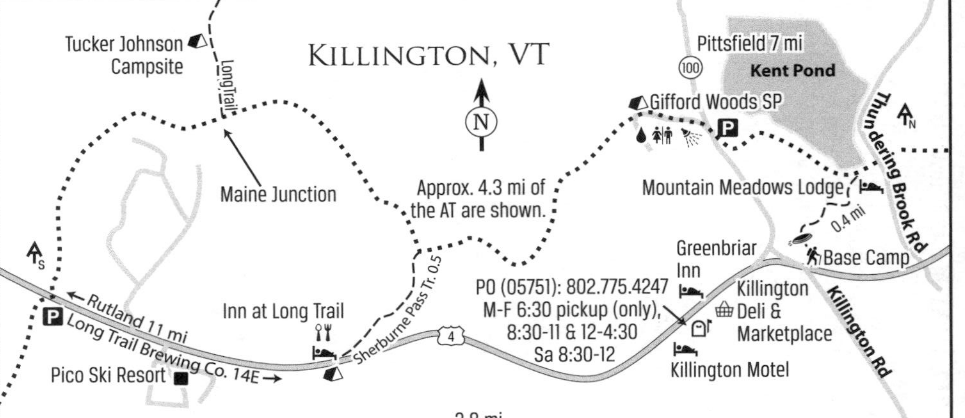

437.7 1752.1 Trescott Rd (paved). 933

436.4 1753.4 Footbridge, stream (2) 851
436.3 1753.5 Etna-Hanover Center Rd (paved), **Etna, NH** (0.8E). . . . . (pg. 185) 845
Cell phone reception at cemetery to west.

433.8 1756.0 Three Mile Rd (gravel) . . . . 43.718,-72.176 P 1414
433.6 1756.2 Mink Brook, footbridge 1348

432.0 1757.8 Moose Mountain south peak. 2290
431.4 1758.4 Woods rd ⚠ NoBo stay on AT for another 250 yards to Moose Mtn Shelter. 2004
431.2 1758.6 **Moose Mountain Shelter** (0.1E) . . . . (8) 2113
25.6◄16.8◄9.5◄►5.7►12.4►17.7 Loop trail to shelter, water at AT and northern leg intersection, tenting on northern leg of loop.
430.0 1759.8 Moose Mountain north peak 2293

428.4 1761.4 South fork of Hewes Brook 1023
428.2 1761.6 Goose Pond Rd (paved), parking to east . . . . 43.7528,-72.1233 P 945

426.1 1763.7 Holts Ledge, precipitous drop-off, views 1915

425.5 1764.3 **Trapper John Shelter** (0.2W) ⚠ Side Tr to shelter is white blazed (6) 1501
22.5◄15.2◄5.7◄►6.7►12.0►27.7 privy behind shelter
424.6 1765.2 Grafton Turnpike(paved), Dorchester Rd . . . . .43.79,-72.1 P (pg. 186) 880
Lyme Center, NH (1.3W), **Lyme, NH** (3.2W) ⚠ NoBo east on wedge of land between fork in road.

423.2 1766.6 Grant Brook 1211
422.9 1766.9 Concrete milepost 1127
422.6 1767.2 Lyme-Dorchester Rd (gravel). . . . . 43.79,-72.1029 P 1107

421.8 1768.0 Lambert Ridge, multiple views from quartzite ridge 1901

Queen Anne's Lace - White flower cluster in disk shaped doily 3-5" wide on hairy stem.

419.4 1770.4 Smarts Ranger Trail to east 2713
418.9 1770.9 Campsite, weak spring to east, fire tower north of camp, west of AT 3230

418.8 1771.0 Smarts Mountain, **Fire Wardens Cabin**. . . . . (12) 3218
21.9◄12.4◄6.7◄►5.3►21.0►27.9 Shelter is cabin north of summit, west of AT. Spring 0.2 in front of cabin. Clark Pond Loop Trail to east.

414.9 1774.9 South Jacobs Brook 1450

414.3 1775.5 Eastman Ledges 1897

413.9 1775.9 North Jacobs Brook. 1917

413.5 1776.3 **Hexacuba Shelter** (0.3E) 17.7◄12.0◄5.3◄►15.7►22.6►31.6 (2) (8) 2051
Shelter on steep side trail, unreliable stream at intersection with side trail.

411.9 1777.9 Mt Cube south peak, cross Rivendell Trail to west 2911

411.8 1778.0 Side trail 0.3W to Mt Cube north peak. 2878

410.2 1779.6 Brackett Brook 1506

409.3 1780.5 Stream. 1295

409.1 1780.7 Woods road 1197

408.5 1781.3 NH 25A (paved) NoBo east on road 300 yards . . . 43.9013,-71.9838 P (pg. 192) 911
Wentworth, NH (4.8E)

SoBo NoBo 000 000 000

406.7 1783.1 Cape Moonshine Rd (gravel). . . . . 43.9158,-71.9646 P (pg. 192) 1431
AT northbound joins Ore Hill Trail.

406.0 1783.8 Ore Hill Campsite 1878
Muddy spring 100 yards downhill from tentsites.

404.0 1785.8 Ore Hill. 1827

403.3 1786.5 Lake Tarleton Rd, NH 25C, **Warren, NH** (4E) . . . 43.9537,-71.9448 P (pg. 192) 1543
AT on road past parking area & power lines, Ore Hill Brook north of road.

401.3 1788.5 Mt Mist 2200

401.0 1788.8 View 1873

400.7 1789.1 Webster Slide Trail 0.7W to summit, view 1678

> The notation "AT: Ore Hill Tr ◄► Wachipauka Pond Tr" indicates that the AT to the south is coincident with the Ore Hill Tr; the AT to the north joins the Wachipauka Pond Tr.

398.7 1791.1 NH 25, Oliverian Brook north of road. . . . . 43.9899,-71.8995 P (pg. 193) 1043
AT: Ore Hill Tr ◄► Wachipauka Pond Tr , **Glencliff, NH** (0.3E), **Warren, NH** (5.0E)

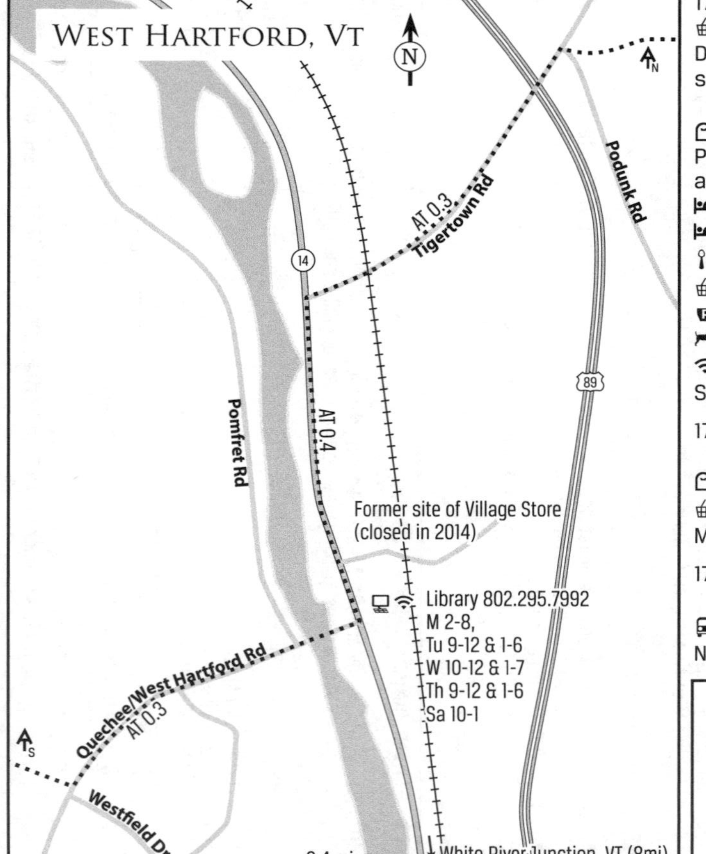

1724.5 VT 12, Barnard Gulf Rd

On The Edge Farm (0.2W) 802.457.4510 Mid-May to Labor Day 7 days 10-5:30; rest of year Th-M 10-5. Pies, fruit, ice cream, smoked meats and cheese, cold drinks.

Woodstock, VT 05091 (4.2E)

M-F 8:30-5, Sa 9-12, 802.457.1323

Pricey resort town, several motels & restaurants, movie theater, and bookstore.

Shire Woodstock 802.457.2211 $138/up

Braeside Motel 802.457.1366 $98-$168D

Bentley's, **Pizza Chef** 802.457.1444 11a-9p

Cumberland Farms, **Gillingham & Sons**

Woodstock Pharmacy

Veremedy Vet. Hospital 802.457.2229

Norman Williams Public Library 802.457.2295 M-F 10-6; Sa 10-4

1726.7 Woodstock Stage Rd

South Pomfret, VT 05067 (1E)

M-F 10-2, Sa 8:30-11:30, 802.457.1147 located inside of Teago's

Teago's General Store 802.457.1626 2035 S. Pomfret Rd. M-Sa 7-6, Su 7-4, B&J ice cream, beer, sandwiches & salads.

1737.8 VT 14, White River

West Hartford, VT 05084

Big Yellow Taxi 802.295.7878 Also covers Woodstock, Norwich, Hanover, Lebanon and White River Junction

- Bring a piece of screening to filter food scraps from your dishwater & pack them out with you.
- Bring a waterproof bag & at least 50 feet of rope to hang food & other scented articles. Or, carry a bear-resistant food container ("bear canister") to store these items.
- Repackage food in resealable bags to minimize waste.

1746.2 Main St, ***Norwich, VT 05055*** *(more services on map)*
Overnight stay may be possible with one of the many trail angels here and in Hanover. Look for list at **Norwich Library**.

Norwich Inn 802.649.1143 $109D/up, incl. free pint of ale, no smoking, reservations recommended. Rates may vary. Jasper Murdocks Ale House W–Su B/L; Dinner daily, microbrewery. Maildrops for guests: PO Box 908, Norwich, VT 04055, or FedEx to 325 Main St. Will not sign for maildrops ⟨www.norwichinn.com⟩

Dan & Whits General Store 802.649.1602, 7 days 7a-9p, 0.1W on Main St. Hikers get free day old sandwiches when avail. Small gear items, canister fuel, batteries, ponchos, hardware & grocery.

Norwich Library 802.649.1184, M 1-8; Tu-W-F 10-5:30; Th 10-8; Sa 10-3; Su, closed in summer.

Enterprise Rent-A-Car 800.736.8227 Car rental w/free pickup/return can be as economical as shuttles. ATC has arranged for hiker discount, use code W15509. Locations include Franklin, NC, Abingdon,VA, Pearisburg,VA, Roanoke,VA, Waynesboro,VA, Front Royal,VA, Charles Town,WV, Carlisle,PA, East Stroudsburg,PA, Warwick,NY, Pittsfield,MA, Bennington,VT, Rutland,VT, Hanover,NH, Gorham,NH.

Advance Transit 802.295.1824 www.advancetransit.com⟩ M-F 6-6, offers FREE bus service connecting Hanover area towns. Detailed schedule and stops are avail. on-line and at libraries. The routes are indicated on Norwich and Hanover maps and primary bus stops are:
Norwich - Dan & Whits (Brown).
Hanover - Dartmouth Book Store (Orange/Blue), Hanover Inn (Brown).
White River Junction - Amtrak.
West Lebanon - Main St. (Orange/Red), grocery stores, outfitters.
Lebanon - City Hall (Blue/Red).

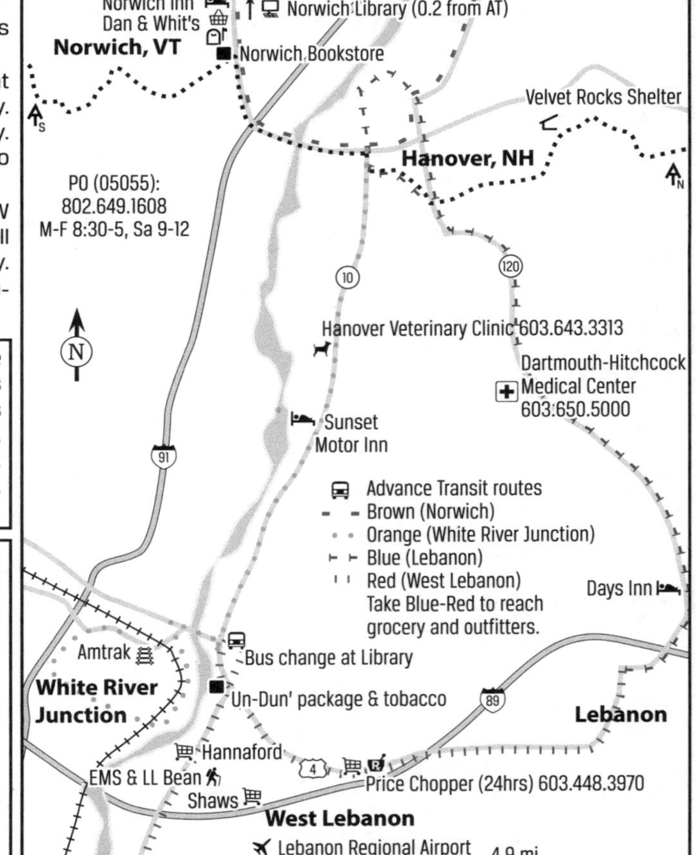

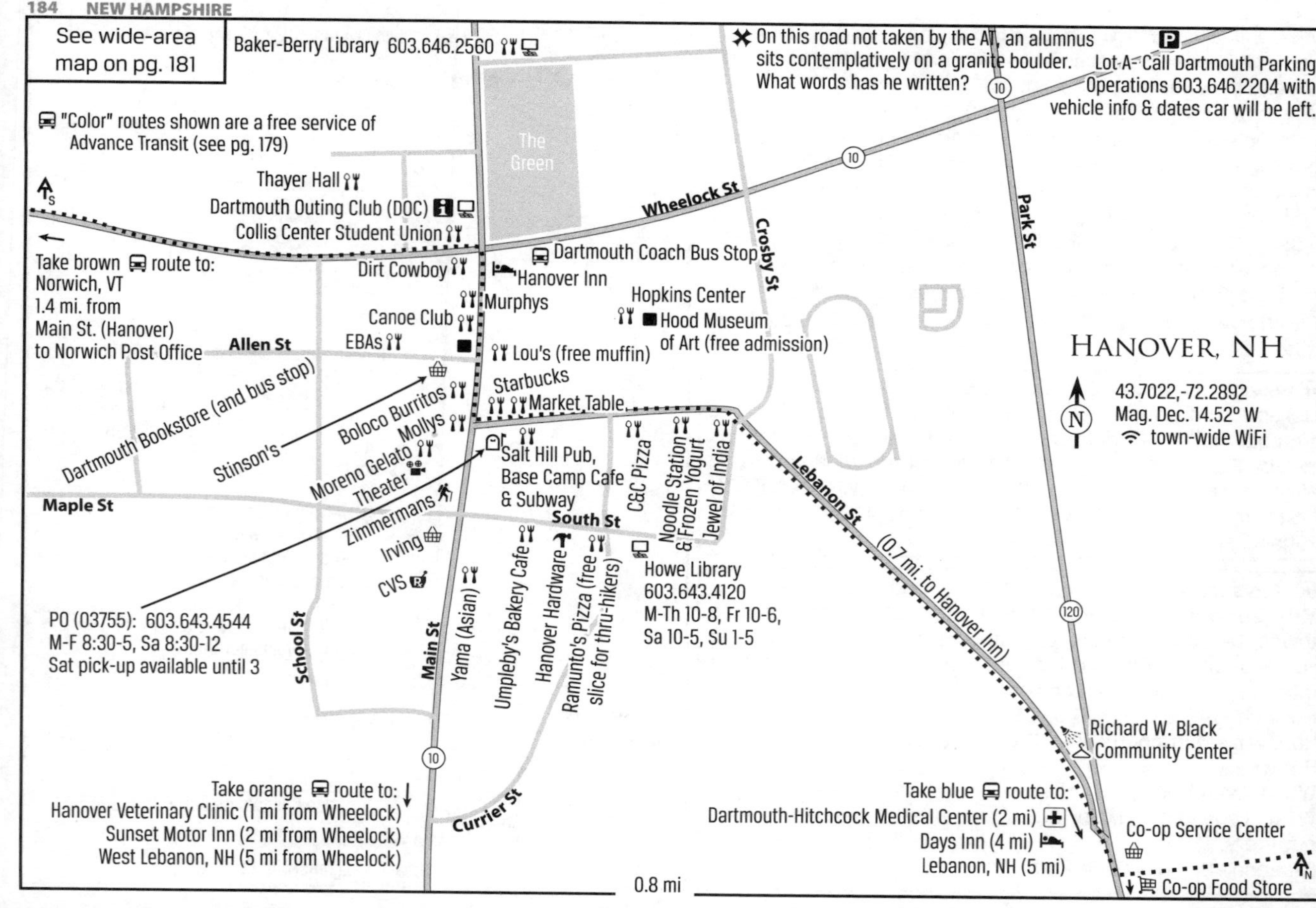

See wide-area map on pg. 181
Baker-Berry Library 603.646.2560
On this road not taken by the AT, an alumnus sits contemplatively on a granite boulder. What words has he written?
Lot-A-Call Dartmouth Parking Operations 603.646.2204 with vehicle info & dates car will be left.
"Color" routes shown are a free service of Advance Transit (see pg. 179)
The Green
Thayer Hall
Dartmouth Outing Club (DOC)
Collis Center Student Union
Wheelock St
Crosby St
Park St
Take brown route to: Norwich, VT 1.4 mi. from Main St. (Hanover) to Norwich Post Office
Dirt Cowboy
Dartmouth Coach Bus Stop
Hanover Inn
Murphys
Hopkins Center
Canoe Club
Hood Museum of Art (free admission)
Allen St
EBAs
Lou's (free muffin)
HANOVER, NH
Dartmouth Bookstore (and bus stop)
Stinson's
Boloco Burritos
Molly's
Starbucks
Market Table
43.7022,-72.2892
Mag. Dec. 14.52° W
town-wide WiFi
Moreno Gelato
Theater
Salt Hill Pub, Base Camp Cafe & Subway
C&C Pizza
Noodle Station & Frozen Yogurt
Jewel of India
Lebanon St
Maple St
Zimmermans
South St
Irving
Umpleby's Bakery Cafe
Hanover Hardware
Ramunto's Pizza (free slice for thru-hikers)
Howe Library 603.643.4120 M-Th 10-8, Fr 10-6, Sa 10-5, Su 1-5
(0.7 mi. to Hanover Inn)
CVS
PO (03755): 603.643.4544 M-F 8:30-5, Sa 8:30-12 Sat pick-up available until 3
School St
Main St
Yama (Asian)
10
120
Richard W. Black Community Center
Take orange route to: Hanover Veterinary Clinic (1 mi from Wheelock) Sunset Motor Inn (2 mi from Wheelock) West Lebanon, NH (5 mi from Wheelock)
Currier St
Take blue route to: Dartmouth-Hitchcock Medical Center (2 mi) Days Inn (4 mi) Lebanon, NH (5 mi)
Co-op Service Center
Co-op Food Store
0.8 mi

1747.7 Dartmouth College ***Hanover, NH 03755***

Hanover Friends of the AT produce a brochure with complete list of hiker services, avail. at the DOC, PO, libraries, Co-op.

Dartmouth Outing Club (DOC) 603.646.2428 Unsecured room for pack storage in Robinson Hall & in Howe Library cannot be left overnight. Not avail. during Dartmouth orientation (mid Aug - mid Sept). Both places have computers for free internet use. There are no hiker accommodations on campus.

Overnight parking on Wheelock Street Lot A, see map. No parking near Connecticut River Bridge.

Sunset Motor Inn 603.298.8721, open 8-11, Call ahead for availability; discount for hikers. Will shuttle when bus is not running, free laundry before 6pm, quiet after 10pm, $15 pet fee. Mail (guest only): 305 N Main Street, West Lebanon, NH 03874.

Hanover Inn 603.643.4300 Pricey, discount sometimes avail.

EBA's 603.643.6135 11a-2a, full menu and beer, daily specials. M-F lunch buffet $7.99. Hiker Friendly ⟨www.eba's.com⟩

Jewel of India Buffet every day 11:30-2:30

Stinson's Convenience store with $5 hiker lunch special: deli sandwich, soda & small bag of chips. Good selection of beer & tobacco.

Hanover Co-op Foodstore 603.643.4889 8a-8p, 7 days

Richard W. Black Recreation Center 603.643.5315 M-F 9a-5p. Open Saturdays Sep-Jun. Shower w/soap & towel $3, laundry w/soap $2, must finish either by 4:30p. Pack storage. Outlet outside & has list of Trail Angels.

Zimmerman's 603.643.6863 Hiker-friendly, canister fuel, Aquamira, socks & outdoor clothes. Mail: 63 Main St, Hanover, NH 03755

Hanover True Value Hardware 7 days. Coleman/alcohol/canister fuels, UPS Shipping.

Advance Transit (see pg. 181)

Big Yellow Taxi 603.643.8294

Vermont Translines 844.888.7267 Routes cover from Albany, NY airport through towns incl. Bennington, VT, Wallingford, VT, Rutland, VT, White River Junction, NH, and Hanover, NH. ⟨www.vttranslines.com⟩

Dartmouth Coach 603.448.2800 Routes to Boston, Logan Airport & NY. Schedules on website. ⟨www.dartmouthcoach.com⟩

Apex Shuttle Service 603.252.8295 AThikershuttle@gmail.com (Steve "Stray Cat" Lake) To/from anywhere if originating or ending in the Hanover area.

White River Junction, VT

Amtrak 800.872.7245 Vermonter line travels north as far as St. Albans, VT, and south through New York, Philadelphia, Baltimore and Washington, DC. There is no ticket office at this station, but you can reserve on the phone and pay when you board. ⟨www.amtrak.com⟩

Lebanon & West Lebanon, NH (see map pg. 181)

Days Inn 603.448.5070, 4 mi. south of the Co-op on Rte 120 on free bus route, cont. B, pets $20.

EMS 603.298.7716, **LL Bean** 603.298.6975

Shaw's 603.298.0388 7am-10pm, 7-9 Sunday

1753.5 Etna-Hanover Center Rd, ***Etna, NH 03750*** (0.8E)

Tiggers Tree House 603.643.9213 Private home; not a party place. No drive-ins. Advance notice ensures a place to stay. Call from trailhead, Etna General Store (will let you use phone) or Dartmouth Outing Club for pickup. Pets allowed, donations accepted or buy laundry soap or work for stay. Rides to grocery store, Walmart, EMS.

(0.8E) **Etna General Store** 603.643.1655, M-F 6-7, Sat 8-7. Deli, hot meals, closed Su.

1765.2 Grafton Turnpike, Dorchester Rd, Dartmouth Skiway

Lyme Center, NH 03769 (1.3W) M–F 8–10, Sa 8–11:30, 603.795.4037

Lyme, NH 03768 (3.2W)

M–F 7:45–12 & 1:30–5:15, Sa 7:45–12, 603.795.4421

Stella's Italian Kitchen & Market 603.795.4302 M-Th 10-9, F-Sa 10-10, Su closed. ⟨www.stellaslyme.com⟩

Dowd's Country Inn B&B 603.795.4712 Call in advance & let them know you are a hiker. PU/return avail. Rates fluctuate; mid week starting at $85S, $100D + NH taxes, wkends through Sep 20, $125S, $140D + taxes. Incl. full b'fast & afternoon tea. Pets $15, allowed in some rooms. Mail: 9 Main St, Lyme, NH 03768. ⟨www.dowdscountryinn.com⟩

Lyme Country Store (3.3W) ice cream, produce, deli, 7 days.

Lyme Veterinary Hospital (2.8W) bear right onto High St and hospital is 50 yards up on the left, 603.795.2747 M-F 8-5, Sa 8-noon.

Appalachian Mountain Club (AMC) 603.466.2727 ⟨http://www.outdoors.org/conservation/trails/appalachian-trail-white-mountains.cfm⟩ Maintains AT from Kinsman Notch, NH to Grafton Notch, ME & operates 8 walk-in only huts w/space for 30-90 people (no pets). Huts use alternative energy sources & composting toilets. No heat or showers. Huts are closed in winter. In spring & fall huts are open to "self-serve" use. Rates (member/ nonmember): $28/$34 Su-F; $40/$49 Sa. See White Mtn map for dates. "Full serve" season includes bunk, dinner & b'fast, ranging from $113PP - $135PP. Don't count on Hut stays without reservations, & camping is not allowed near huts, except at Nauman Tentsite. Reservations can be made by phone or with any AMC caretaker. Work-for-stay is available to 2 thruhikers (4 at LOC), no reservations. Arrive after 3pm and please put sincere effort into your work. **WFS** hikers get floor space for sleeping, feast on leftovers, and are typically asked to work 2 hours after breakfast. Limit WFS to 3 nights in the Whites to give other hikers the opportunity. Lakes of the Clouds Hut has 4 WFS spots and a$10 thru-hiker bunkroom called **"The Dungeon"**.

Thru-hikers stop at lunchtime for $2 bottomless bowl of soup.

AMC Hiker Shuttle (see pg. 193)

White Mountain National Forest (the "Whites")

Passage through the Whites should be planned carefully. It is one of the more heavily visited sections of the AT, and campsites are limited. The trail is rugged, so your pace may be slowed. Weather is dynamic, adding to the dangers of hiking on stretches of trail above treeline.

Take adequate cold-weather gear, check weather reports, carry maps, and know your options for overnighting. The AMC and Randolph Mountain Club (RMC) maintain camps, which are detailed in the following pages. Most have fees. Have cash on hand even if you do not plan to use them; your plans may change.

There are many trails in the Whites. The AT is the only white-blazed trail, but blazes are scant. There are no blazes in the Great Gulf Wilderness Area. The AT is always coincident with another named trail, and the other trail name may be the one you see on signs. Wherever the AT changes from one trail to another, this book uses the notation: "AT: Town Line Tr◄►Glencilff Tr." This means that the AT to the south of this point is coincident with the Town Line Trail; to the north, the AT joins the Glencliff Trail.

The area within a quarter mile of all AMC and RMC facilities and everything above treeline (trees 8' or less) are part of the Forest Protection Area (FPA). Trails are often marked where they enter or leave the FPA. Do not camp within a FPA, and camp at least 200' from water and trails. Rocks aligned to form a trail boundary (scree walls) are an indication that you should not leave the treadway. Doing so damages fragile plant life.

No fires in Forest Protection Areas, at Gentian Pond Shelter, or in Great Gulf Wilderness. Camp at designated sites, or 1/4 mi from roads, facilities & water, 200 ft from trail, below alpine zone (where trees are 8' tall or less).

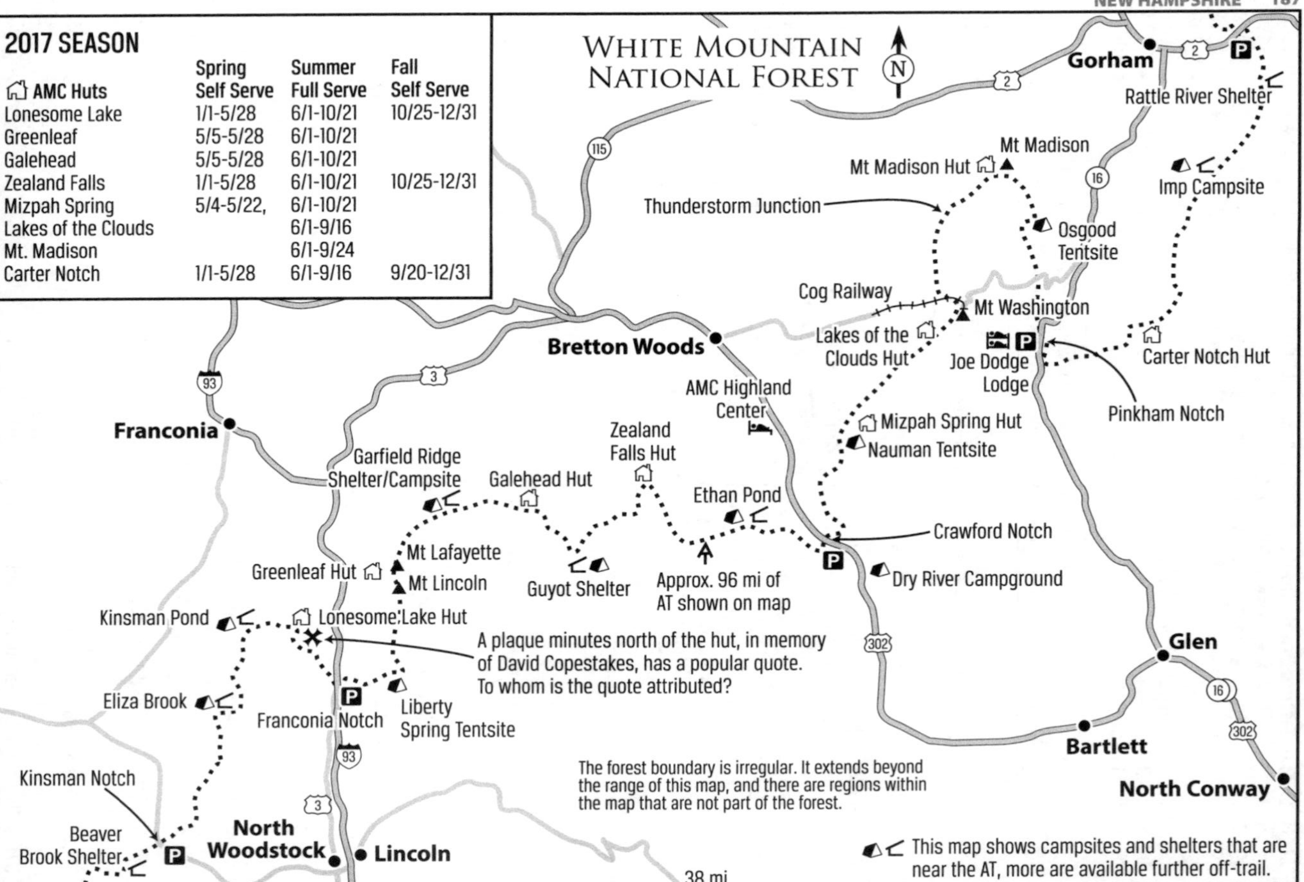

2017 SEASON

AMC Huts	Spring Self Serve	Summer Full Serve	Fall Self Serve
Lonesome Lake	1/1-5/28	6/1-10/21	10/25-12/31
Greenleaf	5/5-5/28	6/1-10/21	
Galehead	5/5-5/28	6/1-10/21	
Zealand Falls	1/1-5/28	6/1-10/21	10/25-12/31
Mizpah Spring	5/4-5/22,	6/1-10/21	
Lakes of the Clouds		6/1-9/16	
Mt. Madison		6/1-9/24	
Carter Notch	1/1-5/28	6/1-9/16	9/20-12/31

397.8 1792.0 **Jeffers Brook Shelter**, Jeffers Brook, footbridge 0.1 south . . . . ☽ 💧 ∠ (10) 1308
27.7◄21.0◄15.7◄►6.9►15.9►19.9

397.7 1792.1 Long Pond Rd ⚠ NoBo 0.1E on road AT: Wachipauka Pond Tr ◄► Town Line Tr . . . 1329

397.6 1792.2 High St (paved) ⚠ NoBo: 0.2W on road. AT: Town Line Trail ◄► Glencliff Trail . . . 1344

397.2 1792.6 Stream. . . . . 💧 1493

396.9 1792.9 Hurricane Trail to east 1661

396.1 1793.7 Stream. . . . . 💧 2484

395.6 1794.2 Spring . . . . 💧 3005

> ✿ Cattail – A tall (head-high) plant that grows in swampy areas. Characteristic part of the plant looks like a fuzzy cigar impaled lengthwise on a spear.

393.2 1796.6 Mt Moosilauke, Gorge Brook Trail to east . . . . 📷 4802

392.9 1796.9 AT: Glencliff Trail ◄► Beaver Brook Trail, Benton Trail to west 4561

391.3 1798.5 Ridge Trail to east 4048

390.9 1798.9 **Beaver Brook Shelter** 27.9◄22.6◄6.9◄►9.0►13.0►28.1 . . . . ☽ 💧 ⛺ ∠ (10) 3732
Shelter on Beaver Brook trail. Beaver Brook just past shelter.

389.6 1800.2 Beaver Brook, footbridges, streams . . . . 💧 1880

389.4 1800.4 Lost River Rd, NH 112, Kinsman Notch . . . . . 44.0398,-71.7921 🅿 🗑 🚻 (pg. 193) 1870
North Woodstock, NH (5.0E), **Lincoln, NH** (6.0E)
AT: Beaver Brook Trail ◄► Kinsman Ridge Trail

388.7 1801.1 Dilly Cliff Trail to east 2662

386.1 1803.7 Gordon Pond Trail to east 2682

384.8 1805.0 Mt Wolf east peak, summit to west . . . . 📷 3478

382.9 1806.9 Reel Brook Trail to west. 2624

382.5 1807.3 Powerline 2602

381.9 1807.9 **Eliza Brook Shelter** 31.6◄15.9◄9.0◄►4.0►19.1►24.6 . . . . ☽ 💧 ⛺ (4) ∠ (8) 2386
3 single tentpads, one double. Water source is brook.

381.1 1808.7 Eliza Brook, parallel to AT for 0.8 mi . . . . 💧 2861

380.5 1809.3 Harrington Pond 3411

379.4 1810.4 South Kinsman Mountain . . . . 📷 4358

378.5 1811.3 North Kinsman Mountain 4293

378.0	1811.8	Mt Kinsman Trail to west	3842
377.9	1811.9	**Kinsman Pond Shelter** 19.9◄13.0◄4.0◄►15.1►20.6►29.6 (4) (16) Caretaker, fee $8PP. Treat pond water. Kinsman Ridge Tr to west, Kinsman Pond Tr to east. AT: Kinsman Ridge Trail ◄► Fishin' Jimmy Trail	3746
377.0	1812.8	Stream.	2821
376.1	1813.7	Lonesome Lake Hut. **(see AMC notes, pg. 184)** AT: Fishin' Jimmy Tr ◄► Cascade Brook Tr (east), many other trail intersections	2747
375.1	1814.7	Kinsman Pond Trail to east.	2302
374.6	1815.2	Cascade Brook	2106
373.6	1816.2	Whitehouse Brook	1649
373.3	1816.5	US 3, I-93, AT underpass. Town east on US 3; better to take side trail (next entry)	1477
373.1	1816.7	Franconia Notch 44.1002,-71.6825 P **(pg. 194)** Paved trail (1.0E) to Liberty Springs trailhead parking. **North Woodstock, NH** (4.8S) left from parking area on US 3**. Lincoln, NH** (1.0E) of North Woodstock. AT: Cascade Brook Trail ◄► Liberty Springs Trail	1432
372.4	1817.4	Flume side trail to east.	1843
371.9	1817.9	Streams	2067
370.4	1819.4	Liberty Spring Campsite Overnight fee $8PP, caretaker, 7S and 3D platforms.	3905
370.2	1819.6	AT: Liberty Springs Tr ◄► Franconia Ridge Tr to west	4283
368.4	1821.4	Little Haystack Mountain, Falling Waters Trail to west NoBo: AT above treeline for next 2.0 miles.	4800
367.7	1822.1	Mt Lincoln, Franconia Ridge	5089
366.7	1823.1	Mt Lafayette, Greenleaf Hut (1.1W) (0.2W) Greenleaf Hut visible from summit of Mt Lafayette. Located down steep Greenleaf Trail. AT: Franconia Ridge Trail ◄► Garfield Ridge Trail	5263
365.9	1823.9	Skookumchuck Trail to west	4727
363.6	1826.2	Garfield Pond	3880
363.2	1826.6	Mt Garfield	4458
363.0	1826.8	Garfield Trail to west	4249
362.8	1827.0	**Garfield Ridge Shelter/Campsite** (0.2W), reliable water (7) (12) 28.1◄19.1◄15.1◄►5.5►14.5►56.5 Overnight fee $8PP, caretaker.	3933
362.3	1827.5	Franconia Brook Trail to east goes steeply down 2.2mi to 13 Falls Campsite.	3435
360.7	1829.1	Gale River Trail to west	3418
360.1	1829.7	Frost Trail to Galehead Hut AT: Garfield Ridge Trail ◄► Twinway Trail	3800
359.3	1830.5	South Twin Mountain, North Twin Spur Trail to west	4902

SoBo	NoBo	Description		Elev
357.3	1832.5	**Guyot Shelter** 0.7E on Bondcliff Tr, plus 0.3 left on spur trail. . 24.6◄20.6◄5.5◄►9.0►51.0►57.1 Overnight fee $8PP, caretaker.	(6) (14)	4515
357.2	1832.6	Mt. Guyot, view to east		4580
356.2	1833.6	Trail west to summit of Zeacliff Ridge		4037
354.9	1834.9	Zeacliff Pond to east		3788
354.5	1835.3	Zeacliff, Zeacliff Trail to east		3758
354.3	1835.5	View to east		3661
353.8	1836.0	Whitewall Brook, many streams leading to falls		3195
353.4	1836.4	Lend-A-Hand Trail to west		2667
353.2	1836.6	Zealand Falls Hut, next to falls		2617
353.0	1836.8	Ethan Pond Trail to west, AT: Twinway Trail ◄► Ethan Pond Trail		2462
351.6	1838.2	Zeacliff Trail to east.		2445
350.8	1839.0	Stream, Thoreau Falls to east		2464
350.6	1839.2	Footbridge, stream		2464
350.3	1839.5	Stream, Shoal Pond Trail to east		2509
349.6	1840.2	Footbridge, stream		2626
348.3	1841.5	**Ethan Pond Campsite** (0.2W), Ethan Pond, inlet brook to pond . 29.6◄14.5◄9.0◄►42.0►48.1►61.8 Overnight fee $8PP, caretaker, 3S and 2D platforms.	(8)	2855
347.2	1842.6	Willey Range Trail to west, stream north on AT		2621
347.0	1842.8	Kedron Flume Trail to west		2457
345.9	1843.9	Ripley Falls 0.5E		1558
345.7	1844.1	RR tracks, parking, AT: Ethan Pond Trail ◄► road walk. AT follows paved parking driveway 0.3 to US 302.	44.1771,-71.3861 P	1436
345.4	1844.4	Crawford Notch, US 302. AT: road walk ◄► Webster Cliff Trail	**(pg. 198)**	1277
345.3	1844.5	Saco River (treat), Saco River Trail to east, Sam Willey Trail to west.		1261
344.6	1845.2	Stream.		1939
343.0	1846.8	Webster Cliffs, views from many spots along 0.5 mile traverse		3288
342.1	1847.7	Mt Webster, Webster Jackson Trail to west, NoBo: AT to east		3910
340.7	1849.1	Mt Jackson, Webster Jackson Trail to west ⚠SoBo hikers turn east (left)		4052
339.0	1850.8	Mizpah cutoff to west, Mizpah Spring Hut to east, Nauman Campsite . . Tent site next to hut, overnight fee $8PP.		3800

338.2	1851.6	Mt Pierce (Mt Clinton)		4312
338.1	1851.7	AT: Webster Cliff Trail ◄► Crawford Path		4258
337.0	1852.8	Mt Eisenhower Loop Trail west to summit.		4448
336.4	1853.4	Mt Eisenhower Loop Trail west to summit.		4464
336.3	1853.5	Mt Eisenhower Trail to east		4494
335.4	1854.4	Mt Franklin		5004
335.1	1854.7	Mt Monroe Loop Trail west to summit		5080
334.4	1855.4	Mt Monroe Loop Trail west to summit		5095
334.4	1855.4	Lakes of the Clouds Hut ⚠ See map, several trails in area	(pg. 198)	5047
333.5	1856.3	Davis Path to east, Westside Trail to west		5592
333.1	1856.7	AT: Crawford Path ◄► Trinity Heights Connector		6172
332.9	1856.9	Mt Washington	(pg. 199)	6288
332.7	1857.1	AT: Trinity Heights Connector ◄► Gulfside Trail		6104
332.5	1857.3	Cross Cog Railroad, stay west on Gulfside Trail		5933
332.0	1857.8	Westside Trail to west		5504
331.7	1858.1	Mt Clay Loop Trail to east.		5441
330.9	1858.9	Mt Clay Loop Trail to east, Sphinx Trail to east		5021
330.1	1859.7	Mt Jefferson Loop Trail, summit 0.3W		5405
329.7	1860.1	Six Husband Trail 0.4W to Mt Jefferson		5336
329.2	1860.6	Edmands Col, Gulfside Spring 50 yards east on Edmands Col cutoff, Randolph Path & Mt Jefferson loop to west.		4947
328.6	1861.2	Israel Ridge Path to RMC Perch Shelter (0.9W), $7 fee	(4) (8)	5269
328.5	1861.3	Peabody Spring to east near boulder		5236
328.1	1861.7	Thunderstorm Junction, RMC cabins to west	(pg. 199)	5500
327.5	1862.3	Airline Trail, King Ravine Trail to west		5150
327.2	1862.6	Madison Spring Hut, Valley Way Trail 0.6W to VW Tent Site, no fee AT: Gulfside Trail ◄► Osgood Trail		4800
326.7	1863.1	Mt Madison, Watson Path to west		5366
326.4	1863.4	Howker Ridge Trail to east		5113
326.1	1863.7	Parapet Trail to east, Daniel Webster Trail to west		4878

⚠ **There are no blazes in the Great Gulf Wilderness area, approx. Mt. Madison to Auto Rd.**

324.1	1865.7	Osgood Tent Site to west, no fee. ⚠ AT: Osgood Trail ◄► Osgood Cutoff.		2555
323.9	1865.9	Stream.		2542
323.5	1866.3	AT: Osgood Cutoff ◄► Great Gulf Trail to east.	**(see map pg. 197)**	2341
323.5	1866.3	⚠ Parapet Brook, AT: Great Gulf Trail ◄► Madison Gulf Trail to west		2329
323.4	1866.4	⚠ West branch of Peabody River, suspension bridge. Great Gulf Tr to east		2300
322.9	1866.9	Stream.		2412
322.0	1867.8	Stream.		2582
321.5	1868.3	Lowes Bald Spot 0.1W		2849
321.4	1868.4	Mt Washington Auto Rd AT: Madision Gulf Trail ◄► Old Jackson Rd	44.2815,-71.2534 P	2734
321.2	1868.6	Nelson Crag Trail and Raymond Path to east		2679
320.4	1869.4	George's Gorge Trail to west		2570
320.1	1869.7	Peabody River, four other trails cross the AT from here to Pinkham Notch		2271
319.4	1870.4	NH 16, Pinkham Notch **Gorham, NH** (10.7W), AT: Old Jackson Rd ◄► Lost Pond Trail	44.2569,-71.2526 P (pg. 199)	2050

1781.3 NH 25A, Gov. Meldrim Thomson Scenic Hwy

Mt Cube Sugar Farm (1.9W) 603.353.4111 Owned by the Thomson family, for whom the road is named. Store is not manned, but caretaker makes frequent stops. Hikers may tent outside or may be allowed to stay in the sugar house. Sometimes more is offered. Open year-round, pets welcome.

Wentworth, NH 03282 (4.3E on NH 25A, then right 0.5 on NH 25)

M–F 9:30–12:30 & 1:30–4:30, Sa 7:15–12, 603.764.9444

Shawnee's General Store 603.764.5553 Open daily 5-8.

1783.1 Cape Moonshine Rd

Dancing Bones Intentional Community (1.4E) 802.440.1612 Water and free camping, composting toilets and good conversation. This is a residential community, so please be respectful when using shared facilities. Smoking is permitted in designated areas. Pets are welcome on a case by case basis. 〈www.dancingbones.net〉

1786.5 Lake Tarleton Rd, NH 25C

(0.2W) **Greenhouse Food & Spirits** 603.764.5708 Th,F 3-11p, Sa 12-10, Su 12-8p. Open mic Th, band on Fr & Sa.

Warren, NH 03279 (4E)

M-F 7:30-9:30 & 3-5, Sa 7:30-12, 603.764.5733

Calamity Jane's Restaurant 603.764.5288 B'fast/Lunch W-Su, Dinner F-Sa

Moose Scoops 603.764.9134 Open seasonally. Ice cream, hot dogs, soda, & hiking shirts. Free WiFi, wireless cell signal extender.

Tedeschi Food Shop 603.764.9002 Open daily 5-11. Grocery w/produce, deli w/sandwiches & pizza, deli closes 7pm Su-Th, 8pm F-Sa.

Laundry M-Su 8:30-8:30

Library (4.0E) 603.764.9072 M-Tu 10-2; W 3-7; Sa 10-1. No WiFi password, so you can use it after hours.

Burning Bush Hardware 603.764.9496 Open 7 days.

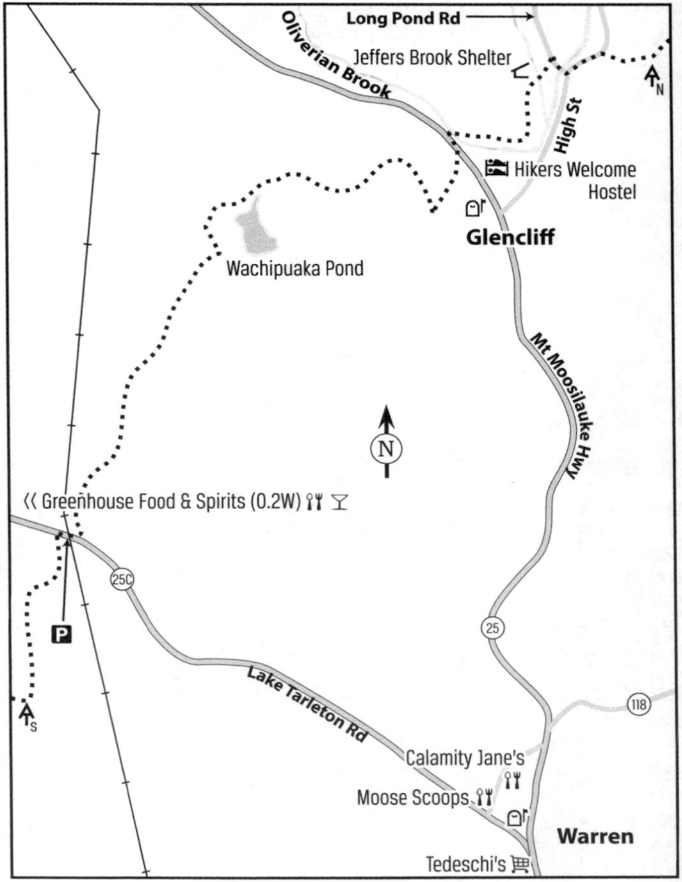

1791.1 NH 25 ***Glencliff, NH 03238*** (0.3E)
M-F 12-2, Sa 7-1, 603.989.5154
Hikers Welcome Hostel 603.989.0040 Open early May - Oct 1. Bunk ($25) & camping ($18.50) incl. shower. Shower only w/towel $3, laundry: $3 wash, $3 dry. Snacks, sodas, & ice cream. All hikers (even non-guests) are welcome to hang out & enjoy huge DVD library. Slackpacking & shuttles (5 miles to resupply in Warren). Coleman/alcohol/oz. Tools to help w/gear repair & selection of used gear avail., particularly winter wear. Pet Friendly. Both guests & non-guests are welcome to send maildrops (USPS/FedEx/UPS): c/o Hikers Welcome Hostel, 1396 NH Rt 25, PO Box 25, Glencliff, NH 03238
Warren, NH (5E) see entry pg. 190

1800.4 Lost River Rd, NH 112, Kinsman Notch
Lost River Gorge (0.5E) 603.745.8031 Tourist attraction featuring a boulder jumble similar to Mahoosuc Notch. Gift store with snacks, coffee & soda. Open early May - late Oct. ⟨www.findlostriver.com⟩
Lost River Valley Campground (3.0E) 603.745.8321, 800.370.5678 Cabin $60S, 70D, camping primitive sites $21, pets allowed but not in cabins. Showers, coin laundry, pay phone, open mid-May to Columbus Day 8-9, quiet 10pm-8am, owner Jim Kelly. Mail: 951 Lost River Rd, North Woodstock, NH 03262. ⟨www.lostriver.com⟩
Wise Way Wellness Center (16E) 603.726.7600 Open May- Oct. $85 for 1-2 persons in cabin, incl. light b'fast. $10PP for pickup & return from Franconia Notch, Kinsman Notch, North Woodstock, or Lincoln. Cabin is 10 miles south of Lincoln in Thornton, NH. This is a serene rustic cabin with no TV/phone. Bathroom and shower inside adjacent building. Amenities include pool, mini-fridge & grill. Licensed Massage by appt. Additional services: sauna and outdoor Epsom salt bath. No smoking or pets. Cash/checks/PayPal.
North Woodstock, NH (5E), ***Lincoln, NH*** (6E)
(See pg. 192)

Randolph Mountain Club (RMC)

Maintains the section of the AT from Edmands Col to Madison Hut and four shelters in the Northern Presidentials. Per-person fees for non-members: Gray Knob or Crag Camp $20, The Perch or Log Cabin $10. Fees must be paid in cash for stays at Gray Knob, Crag Camp and The Perch. Persons without cash can stay at the Log Cabin and will receive a receipt to mail in their fee. There is a caretaker year-round at Gray Knob if you need assistance or have questions. During the summer months, a second caretaker is in residence at Crag Camp. A caretaker visits Crag Camp and The Perch every evening throughout the year.

Shelter use is first-come, first-served; no reservations. Weekends are busy. If space is not avail., be prepared to camp. Camping is not permitted within a quarter mile of RMC shelters.

There is no trash disposal. Carry in, carry out. Please keep noise to a minimum after 10pm. The use of cell phones and portable TVs is not permitted. Group size is limited to ten. There is no smoking inside RMC facilities. When a camp is full, all guests are asked to limit their stay to two consecutive nights. Outdoor wood campfires are not allowed at any of the camps. Dogs are allowed at RMC's facilities, but they should be under voice control at all times.

AMC Hiker Shuttle 603.466.2727 Schedule on-line: Operates June - mid Sept daily, weekends & holidays through mid Oct. Stops at Lincoln, Franconia Notch (Liberty Springs Trailhead), Crawford Notch (Webster Cliff Trailhead), Highland Center, Pinkham Notch, & Gorham; $23 for non-members. Walk-ons if space avail. ⟨www.outdoors.org/lodging/lodging-shuttle.cfm⟩

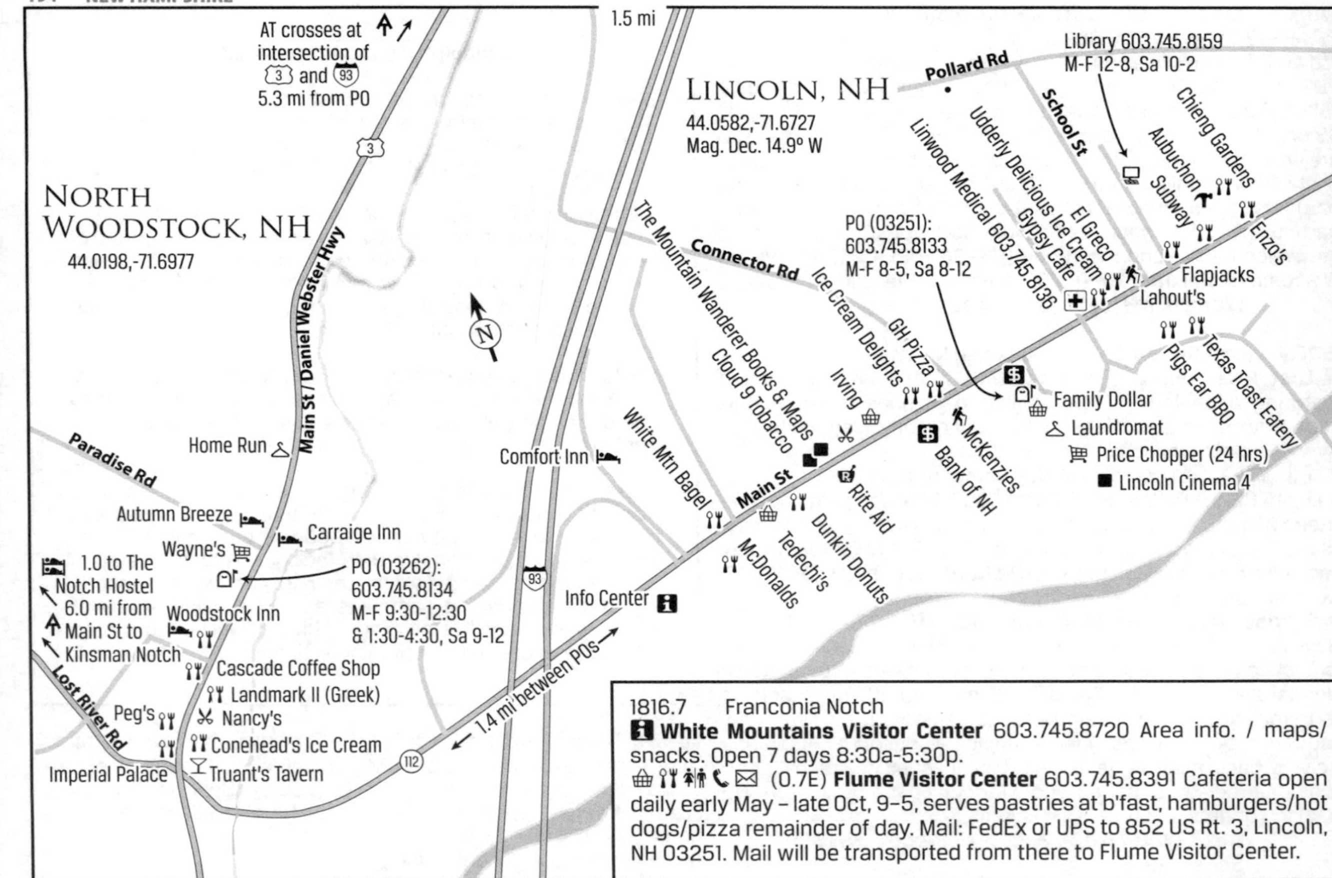

1816.7 Franconia Notch

White Mountains Visitor Center 603.745.8720 Area info. / maps/ snacks. Open 7 days 8:30a-5:30p.

(0.7E) **Flume Visitor Center** 603.745.8391 Cafeteria open daily early May – late Oct, 9–5, serves pastries at b'fast, hamburgers/hot dogs/pizza remainder of day. Mail: FedEx or UPS to 852 US Rt. 3, Lincoln, NH 03251. Mail will be transported from there to Flume Visitor Center.

(2.1W) **Lafayette Campground** 603.823.9513, tent sites $25D, limited store, no pets, quiet 10pm. Open mid May-Columbus Day. Mail: Franconia State Park, Lafayette Campground, Franconia, NH 03580.

(1.2E) **Profile Motel & Cottages** 603.745.2759 Fridge & microwave in room, grills & tables outside, open 7a-10p. Mail: 391 US 3, Lincoln, NH 03251.

(3.0E) **Mt. Liberty Motel** 603.745.3600 Open May-Oct. $85+ in season, $59+ off season incl. pickup/return from Kinsman/ Franconia Notch and town shuttle. Laundry $5. No smoking or pets. CC accepted. Mail: 10 Liberty Road, Lincoln, NH 03251 ⟨www.MtLibertyMotel.com⟩

AMC Hiker Shuttle (pg. 193)

The Shuttle Connection 603.745.3140 Shuttles between town & Kinsman or Franconia Notch or to bus terminals and airports ranging from Portland, ME to NY. Can handle large groups.

Notch Taxi Service 603.991.8777 Reservations recommended, runs 7 days. Hikers welcome.

North Woodstock, NH (4.8S of Franconia Notch)

The Notch Hostel 603.348.1483 Bunk in large, white farmhouse on Rt. 112 (Lost River Rd). 1.0W of North Woodstock/ Lincoln. Ideally situated for slackpack between Kinsman & Franconia Notch. $30PP includes bunk, linens, towel, shower, laundry service, coffee/tea, make-ur-own pancakes, WiFi, computer, guest kitchen, fridge & large yard. Beer & wine ok in moderation. No liquor. Small store: fuel, pizza, snacks & soda. Rental bikes $5/day. Check-in 4-9p, (earlier OK with text/call: follow welcome sheet if no one home). Shuttle Schedule: Jun 15-Oct 1 wkdays only. Free dropoff: Kinsman Notch 7:30a, Franconia Notch 7:45a. Free P/U: Kinsman 2:35p, Franconia (Flume Visitor's Center) 3p. Free resupply: Pricechopper 3:15. Slackpacker P/U ($5): Franconia 5:30p, Kinsman 5:50p. Please text (preferred) or call in advance to reserve P/U. Maildrops: c/o The Notch Hostel, 324 Lost River Rd. North Woodstock, NH 03262 ⟨www.notchhostel.com⟩

The Carriage Inn 603.745.2416 $69/up, no pets, pool, grills. Mail: PO Box 198, 180 Main St, North Woodstock, NH 03262. ⟨Inn32.com⟩

Autumn Breeze 603.745.8549 Open year-round. Hiker friendly. $65 hiker rate incl. kitchenette, laundry, shuttle to/ from trail until 5. One pet room. Shuttle to town if avail. CC accepted. ⟨www.autumnbreezemotel.com⟩

Woodstock Inn 603.745.3951, 800.321.3985 10% discount for thru-hikers, prices seasonal, stay incl. full b'fast. Pet rooms avail. **Woodstock Station** restaurant, outdoor bar, and a micro-brewery on-site. ⟨www.woodstockinnnh.com⟩

Wayne's Market 603.745.8819 Deli, ATM, cheap sandwiches, large beer selection. Open year-round, daily 5-10.

Fadden's General Store & Sugar House 603.745.8371 Ice cream, fudge and more. Open year-round, daily 9-5.

Lincoln, NH (5.8S of Franconia Notch)

Wise Way Wellness Center 10S of Lincoln, listing pg. 193.

■ **Mountain Wanderer** 603.745.2594 Open most days 10-5:30. Book and map store has everything you need to navigate the Whites.

Franconia, NH 03580 (11W of Franconia notch)

M-F 8:30-1 & 2-5, Sa 9-12, 603.823.5611

Gale River Motel 603.823.5655 800.255.7989 $50–$200, pets with approval, laundry wash $1, dry $1, Coleman/oz. Free pickup/return to trail w/stay, longer shuttles for a fee. Open year-round. CC accepted. Mail (fee for non-guest): 1 Main Street, Franconia, NH 03580. ⟨www.galerivermotel.com⟩

Mac's Market 603.823.7795 Open daily 7-8.

Franconia Village Store 603.823.7782 Open M-Sa 6-9, Su 6:30-7, deli.

Abbie Greenleaf Library 603.823.8424 M-Tu 2-6; W 10-12 & 2-6; Th-F 2-5; Sa 10-1.

Littleton, NH (17W)

Badass Outdoors Gear Shop 603.444.9445 Full service outfitter 17 miles west (compass north) from Franconia Notch. Thru-hiker discount. Hiker food, canister fuel & experienced staff. Open Tu-Th 11-5; F-Sa 10-6; Su 11-5. Sometimes rides are avail.

SOBO	NOBO	Feature		Elev
318.4	1871.4	AT: Lost Pond Trail ◄► Wildcat Ridge Trail		2009
318.0	1871.8	View		2860
317.4	1872.4	Rocky crevasse, stairs		3273
316.7	1873.1	Wildcat Mountain peak E.		4066
316.4	1873.4	Wildcat Mountain peak D, observation tower, ski gondola 0.1 north Gondola rides to/from the AT,$12 round trip, restaurant at base, open Jul–Oct.		3990
315.3	1874.5	Wildcat Mountain peak C.		4278
314.4	1875.4	Wildcat Mountain peak A.		4422
313.9	1875.9	Spring		3675
313.7	1876.1	AT: Wildcat Ridge Trail ◄► Nineteen Mile Brook Trail to east.		3401
313.5	1876.3	AT: Nineteen Mile Brook Trail ◄► Carter Moriah Trail, Carter Notch Hut (0.1E).		3303
312.8	1877.0	Spring to west		4308
312.3	1877.5	Carter Dome, Rainbow Trail to east		4832
311.9	1877.9	Black Angel Trail to east, Carter Dome Trail to west.		4619
311.4	1878.4	Mt Hight, view.		4653
310.9	1878.9	Zeta Pass, two Carter Dome trailheads to west		3890
308.8	1881.0	Middle Carter Mountain, view		4610
308.2	1881.6	North Carter Mountain, North Carter Trail to west, just south of summit		4539
306.3	1883.5	**Imp Campsite** (0.2W) 56.5◄51.0◄42.0◄►6.1►19.8►25.0 Overnight fee $8PP, caretaker, composting privy.	(5) (10)	3326
305.6	1884.2	Stony Brook Trail to west, Moriah Brook Trail to east		3126
304.2	1885.6	Mt Moriah, summit to west ⚠ AT: Carter Moriah Trail ◄► Kenduskeag Trail		3976
302.9	1886.9	⚠ AT: Kenduskeag Trail ◄► Rattle River Trail		3369
302.5	1887.3	Stream.		2851
301.8	1888.0	Rattle River		2004
300.4	1889.4	East Rattle River, multiple streams		1343
300.2	1889.6	**Rattle River Shelter** 57.1◄48.1◄6.1◄►13.7►18.9►23.3. No fee. Water source is Rattle River. Gently sloping trail from shelter to US 2.	(8)	1258
298.9	1890.9	Stream.		962
298.8	1891.0	Fork in trail, AT to east (not over bridge).		901

298.3	1891.5	AT 0.1W on US 2, **Gorham, NH** (3.6W)	44.4008,-71.1098 P **(pg. 203)**	780
298.2	1891.6	AT east on North Rd.	44.4064,-71.1168 P	794
297.6	1892.2	AT west on Hogan Rd (gravel)		783
296.7	1893.1	Brook		1232
294.7	1895.1	Mt Hayes, Mahoosuc Trail to west		2555
293.1	1896.7	View		2341
292.5	1897.3	Cascade Mountain		2631
291.4	1898.4	Trident Col Campsite (0.2W), no fee, spring on side trail		2020
291.1	1898.7	Spring		1909
290.4	1899.4	Page Pond.		2220
289.8	1900.0	Wocket Ledge, view.		2642
289.3	1900.5	Stream.		2589
288.6	1901.2	Dream Lake, Peabody Brook Trail to east		2610

ME camping: Dispersed camping is permitted except for specific prohibitions. Look for local postings at signposts & shelters; prohibitions listed in this guidebook are not comprehensive. Camping at non-designated locations is prohibited above treeline (where trees are less than 8' tall).

286.5	1903.3	**Gentian Pond Shelter/Campsite** (0.2E) 61.8◄19.8◄13.7◄►5.2►9.6►14.7 Junction of Mahoosuc Trail (AT) and Austin Brook Trail, inlet brook of Gentian Pond. 3S and 1D platforms.	(14)	2162
285.5	1904.3	Stream		2246
285.1	1904.7	Stream		2505

Campfires are only allowed along the AT in ME within fireplaces at designated campsites.

283.7	1906.1	Mt Success		3565
283.1	1906.7	Success Trail to west.		3171
281.8	1908.0	**NH-ME** border		2972
281.3	1908.5	**Carlo Col Shelter and Campsite** (0.3W), on Carlo Col Trail 25.0◄18.9◄5.2◄►4.4►9.5►16.4 Platforms 3S and 2D, bear box, no fee.	(16)	3191
280.9	1908.9	Mt Carlo		3565
279.5	1910.3	Goose Eye Mountain west peak, Goose Eye Mtn Trail to west		3810
279.1	1910.7	Goose Eye Mountain east peak		3790
278.8	1911.0	Wright Trail to east		3452

1844.4 Crawford Notch, US 302

(1W) **Willey House** 603.374.0999
Snack bar open 9:30am-5:00pm, 7 days, weekend before Memorial Day through weekend after Columbus Day. Located in Crawford Notch State Park.

(1.8E) **Dry River Campground** 603.374.2272
Tent sites $25 for 2 adults and children. Shelter $30D, $10EAP. Pets allowed, coin laundry & showers, sometimes rides avaiable, quiet 10pm-8am. Open May-late Oct, reduced services through Nov. ⟨www.nhstateparks.com/crawford.html⟩

(3.5W) **AMC Highland Center**
603.278.4453 Rates seasonal & are highest in summer & on holidays. Lodge $50-$150PP/up incl. dinner & b'fast. Shapleigh Bunkhouse $81 w/dinner & b'fast, $54 w/ bunkhouse only. Rates lower for AMC members. No pets/ smoking. AMC Shuttle stops daily mid- Jun to Columbus Day, Afterwards only weekends & holidays. Restaurant open to all for B/L/D. Store sells snacks, sodas, some clothing & canister fuel. Mail (include ETA): Route 302, Bretton Woods, NH 03574. Only UPS reliable. USPS & FedX do not deliver here. ⟨www.outdoors.org⟩

Crawford Notch General Store & Campground
(3.3E) 603.374.2779 Cabins $78-98, tent sites (hold 2 tents) $36. 9% lodging tax. Store carries hiker foods, ice cream & beer. Open mid May through mid October ⟨www.crawfordnotch.com⟩

Notch Taxi Service 603.991.8777 Covers northern NH. Hikers welcome.

AMC Hiker Shuttle (pg. 193)

Bretton Woods, NH (8.0W)

Fabyan's Station 603.278.2222 Open year-round 11:30-9 (limited hours in winter).

Drummonds Mountain Shop 603.278.7547 Open year-round, 7 days. Boots, packs, rain gear, hiking foods, stoves and fuel. ⟨www.drummondsmountainshop.com⟩

Bartlett, NH (13.0E from Crawford Notch)
Resort town has unique mountain roller coaster and water slide at **Attitash Resort** 800.223.7669 ⟨www.attitash.com⟩.

1855.4 Lakes of the Clouds Hut

Lodging and WFS (see AMC notes, pg. 184). Also "The Dungeon," a bunkroom avail. to 6 thru-hikers for $10PP with access to hut restroom and the common area. When the hut is closed, The Dungeon serves as an emergency shelter.

National Weather Service Wind Chill Chart

	Temperature (°F)												
Wind (mph)	35	30	25	20	15	10	5	0	-5	-10	-15	-20	-25
5	31	25	19	13	7	1	-5	-11	-16	-22	-28	-34	-40
10	27	21	15	9	3	-4	-10	-16	-22	-28	-35	-41	-47
15	25	19	13	6	0	-7	-13	-19	-26	-32	-39	-45	-51
20	24	17	11	4	-2	-9	-15	-22	-29	-35	-42	-48	-55
25	23	16	9	3	-4	-11	-17	-24	-31	-37	-44	-51	-58
30	22	15	8	1	-5	-12	-19	-26	-33	-39	-46	-53	-60
35	21	14	7	0	-7	-14	-21	-27	-34	-41	-48	-55	-62
40	20	13	6	-1	-8	-15	-22	-29	-36	-43	-50	-57	-64

Ways to Give Back
Help Conserve & Maintain the Trail

The most essential service you can perform is to volunteer to maintain the A.T. & overnight sites, or to monitor boundaries and resource conditions. To find out how or where you may assist, visit www.appalachiantrail.org or check with your local trail-maintaining club.

1856.9 Mt Washington, NH
(03589) M-S 10-4 For outgoing mail; do not send maildrops.
Second highest peak on the AT. **Sherman Adams Bldg** 603.466.3347 (part of Mt. Washington State Park) Open 8am-5pm mid-May to Columbus Day, sometimes opens earlier on wkends in season. Snack bar 9a-6p, sometimes closes earlier.
Cog Railway 603.278.5404 Runs hourly Apr- Nov. One-way tickets $48 (if space-avail.) sold at summit station. Base station 3 miles away near Bretton Woods, NH. ⟨www.thecog.com⟩

1861.7 Thunderstorm Junction
Crag Camp Cabin (1.1W) on Spur Trail, **Gray Knob Cabin** (1.2W) on Lowe Path; $20 fee for either. If you camp along these side trails, it must be at least 0.25mi. from either cabin.

1865.0 - 1866.2 Map of trail intersections

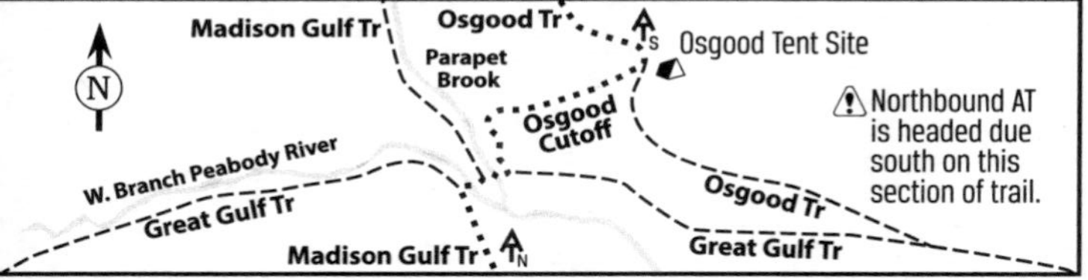

1870.4 NH 16, Pinkham Notch
Pinkham Notch Visitor Center & Joe Dodge Lodge 603.466.2721 ⟨www.outdoors.org⟩ Rates seasonal and are highest in summer and during holidays. Bunkroom starting at $63PP w/o meals; $69 with b'fast; $89 with dinner & b'fast. Private rooms also avail. Rates on lodging and meals discounted for AMC members. Meals avail. to non-guests; AYCE b'fast 6:30-9 daily, a la carte lunch, family-style dinner Sat-Thurs at 6pm, Friday dinner buffet. Open year-round. Coin-op shower avail. 24hrs, $2 towel rental. No pets. Vending machines, Coleman/alcohol/oz, canister fuel. Shuttle 7:30am daily. Accepts credit cards. Mail: AMC Visitor Center, c/o Front Desk, 361 Rte. 16, Gorham, NH 03581.

Gorham, NH (10.7W from Pinkham Notch, see pg. 201)

Mt Washington
Mt Washington Rd
Great Gulf Tr
Gulfside Tr
Cog Railway
Westside Tr
Crawford Path
Trinity Heights Connector
MT. WASHINGTON
Lakes of the Clouds Hut
Tuckerman Crossover
Davis Path
Camel Tr
Dry River Tr
1.1 mi

277.9 1911.9 Goose Eye Mountain north peak 3672

276.9 1912.9 **Full Goose Shelter and Campsite** 3S and 1D platforms. . . . . (12) 2948
23.3◄9.6◄4.4◄►5.1►12.0►15.5 No Fee, stream behind shelter.
276.4 1913.4 Fulling Mill Mountain south peak 3395

275.3 1914.5 Mahoosuc Notch south end, Mahoosuc Notch Trail to west 2492
Most difficult or fun mile of the AT. Make way through jumbled pit of boulders.

274.2 1915.6 Mahoosuc Notch north end, Bull Branch, campsite 2165

273.2 1916.6 Spring 3291
272.7 1917.1 Mahoosuc Arm 3770
272.0 1917.8 Speck Pond brook 3414
271.8 1918.0 **Speck Pond Shelter & Campsite** . . . . . . (8) 3419
14.7◄9.5◄5.1◄►6.9►10.4►20.9 Overnight fee $8PP, caretaker. Spring down Speck Pond Trail just beyond caretaker's yurt. 3S and 3D platforms
270.7 1919.1 Intersection, AT north on Old Speck Tr., south on Mahoosuc Tr. 4023
Side Trail 0.3E to Old Speck summit and observation tower.

268.4 1921.4 Eyebrow Trail to west 2508
268.1 1921.7 Stream. 2376

267.3 1922.5 Eyebrow Trail to west 1522
267.2 1922.6 Grafton Notch, ME 26 . . . . . . 44.5897,-70.9467 (pg. 208) 1495
266.4 1923.4 Stream, Table Rock Trail to east 2105

⚠ Two Night Campling Limit from Grafton Notch to Katahdin

264.9 1924.9 **Baldpate Lean-to** (0.1E), stream next to lean-to . . . . . . (8) 2665
16.4◄12.0◄6.9◄►3.5►14.0►26.8
264.1 1925.7 Baldpate west peak 3662

263.2 1926.6 Baldpate east peak, Grafton Loop Trail 3810

(NoBo) Poor cell reception at East B Hill Rd, consider calling ahead if you need ride.

261.4 1928.4 **Frye Notch Lean-to,** Frye Brook in front of lean-to . . . . . . (6) 2283
15.5◄10.4◄3.5◄►10.5►23.3►31.6

257.6	1932.2	Dunn Notch and Falls	♦	1249
256.9	1932.9	East B Hill Rd (paved), stream **Andover, ME** (8.0E)	44.6683,-70.8932 P ♦ (pg. 208)	1485
256.6	1933.2	Stream	♦	1684
255.0	1934.8	Surplus Pond. Two woods roads 100 yards apart 0.1W on southernmost road to spring near pond.	♦	2080
252.2	1937.6	Wyman Mountain		2920
250.9	1938.9	**Hall Mountain Lean-to** 20.9◄14.0◄10.5◄►12.8►21.1►32.3 Spring south of lean-to on AT, tenting and view behind shelter.	(6)	2629
249.5	1940.3	Sawyer Notch, Sawyer Rd (dirt)		1095
249.4	1940.4	Sawyer Brook, campsite	♦	1073
249.0	1940.8	View		2059
248.6	1941.2	Moody Mountain, view		2440
246.8	1943.0	South Arm Rd (paved), **Andover, ME** (9.0E) Black Brook on south side of road, campsite.	♦ (pg. 208)	1410
246.3	1943.5	View		2198
244.0	1945.8	Old Blue Mountain		3600

(SoBo) Poor cell reception at East B Hill Rd, consider calling ahead if you need ride.

242.4	1947.4	Unnamed Gap, mileage sign, water to west	♦	3005
241.1	1948.7	Spring	♦	3166
240.8	1949.0	Bemis Stream Trail to east		3350
239.8	1950.0	Bemis Mountain		3550
239.3	1950.5	View		3295

SoBo NoBo 1000 3000 5000

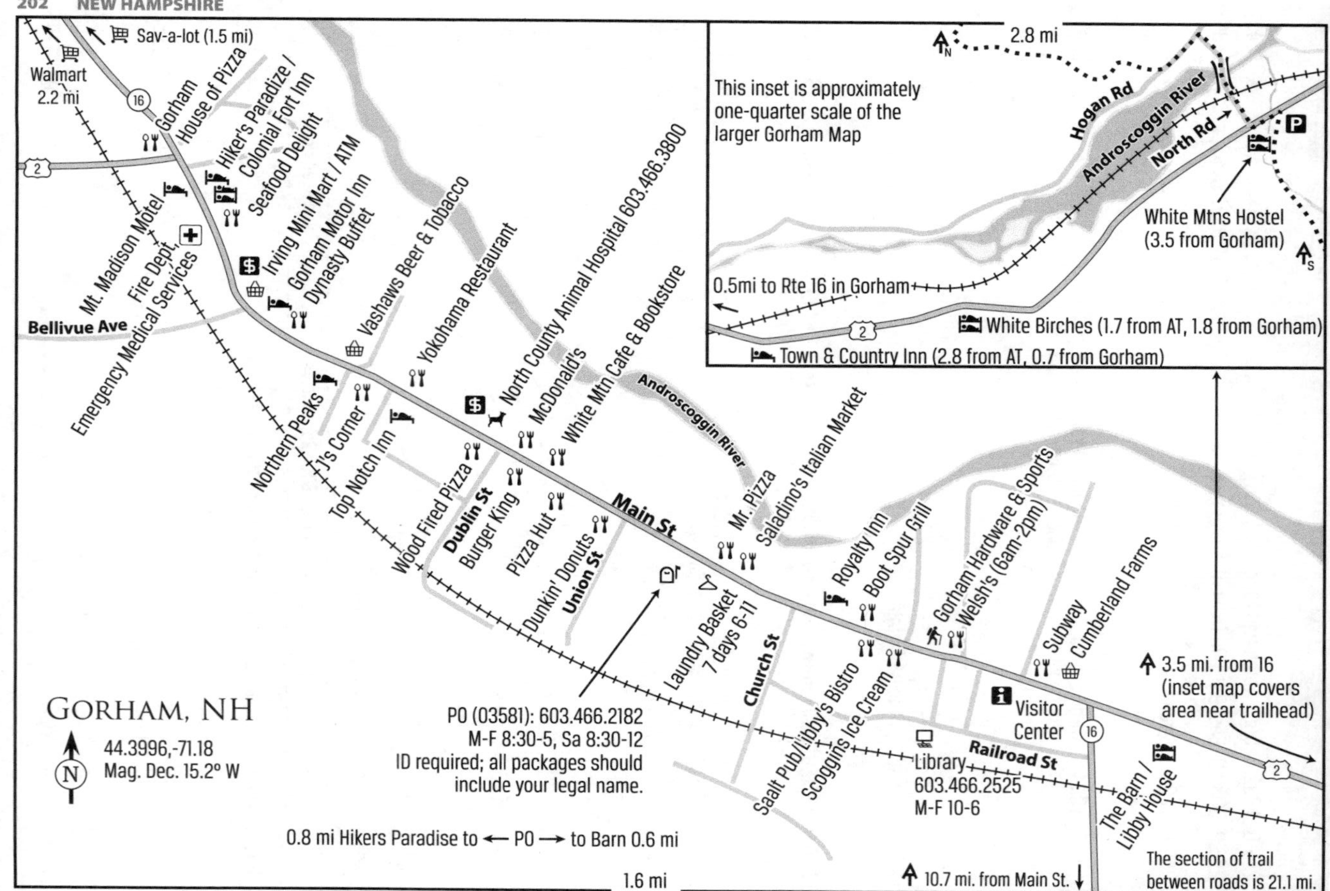

Sav-a-lot (1.5 mi)
Walmart 2.2 mi
Gorham House of Pizza
Hiker's Paradize / Colonial Fort Inn
Seafood Delight
Irving Mini Mart / ATM
Gorham Motor Inn
Dynasty Buffet
Vashaws Beer & Tobacco
Yokohama Restaurant
North County Animal Hospital 603.466.3800
McDonald's
White Mtn Cafe & Bookstore
Mt. Madison Motel
Fire Dept.
Emergency Medical Services
Bellivue Ave
Northern Peaks
J's Corner
Top Notch Inn
Wood Fired Pizza
Dublin St
Burger King
Pizza Hut
Dunkin' Donuts
Union St
Main St
Androscoggin River
Laundry Basket
7 days 6-11
Mr. Pizza
Saladino's Italian Market
Church St
Royalty Inn
Boot Spur Grill
Saalt Pub/Libby's Bistro
Scoggins Ice Cream
Gorham Hardware & Sports
Welsh's (6am-2pm)
Subway
Cumberland Farms
Visitor Center
Library
603.466.2525
M-F 10-6
Railroad St
The Barn / Libby House
GORHAM, NH
44.3996,-71.18
Mag. Dec. 15.2° W
PO (03581): 603.466.2182
M-F 8:30-5, Sa 8:30-12
ID required; all packages should include your legal name.
0.8 mi Hikers Paradise to ← PO → to Barn 0.6 mi
1.6 mi
10.7 mi. from Main St.
3.5 mi. from 16 (inset map covers area near trailhead)
The section of trail between roads is 21.1 mi.
This inset is approximately one-quarter scale of the larger Gorham Map
2.8 mi
Hogan Rd
Androscoggin River
North Rd
White Mtns Hostel (3.5 from Gorham)
0.5mi to Rte 16 in Gorham
White Birches (1.7 from AT, 1.8 from Gorham)
Town & Country Inn (2.8 from AT, 0.7 from Gorham)

1891.5 US 2, Rattle River Trailhead

White Mountains Lodge & Hostel 603.466.5049 Directly on AT at the northern Gorham trailhead (Rte. 2 & North Rd). Clean, B&B style rooms, some private, w/fresh linens & towels.Thru-hiker rate $35PP includes, huge gourmet breakfast, laundry, loaner clothes, showers, computer, town & resupply shuttles Liquid and canister fuel, sodas, ice cream, snacks for sale. Shuttle and slackpack (21 mi) from Pinkham Notch, call for free pick ups from Pinkham Notch at 8a, noon & 5p (Gorham 1 exit) free w/2 nights stay. Parking for section hikers. Open June 1-Oct 8. Maildrops (also free for non-guests): 592 State Rte. 2, Shelburne, NH 03581 ⟨www.whitemountainslodgeandhostel.com⟩

(1.7W) **White Birches Camping Park** 603.466.2022 bunks $15, tent sites $15PP, pool, air hockey, pool table, pets allowed, Coleman/ alcohol/oz & canister fuel. Free shuttle from/to trail & town with stay, open May-Oct. CC accepted. Guest mail only: 218 US 2, Shelburne, NH 03581. ⟨www.whitebirchescamping.com⟩

Gorham, NH 03581 (3.6W from US 2 RR Trailhead)

ID required; all packages should include your legal name.

(2.6W) **Town & Country Inn** 603.466.3315 Open yr-round. $64-129 seasonal, pets $10. B'ast 6:30-10:30, dinner 5-9, cocktails. Indoor pool, sauna. ⟨www.townandcountryinn.com⟩

Libby House B&B & The Barn Hikers Hostel 603.466.2271 Bunks $22, tenting $15PP, B&B rooms avail., Hot country b'fast avail. Fast, free pickup & return to Rte 2 trailhead for guests. Shuttle from Pinkham Notch free w/2 night stay to facilitate slackpacking. Celebrating more than 30 yrs of professional services, located w/in walking distance of shops & restaurants; shuttle to Walmart. Clean beds with linens, full kitchen with cookware & refrigerator, lounge w/big screen TV. Laundry $5, No pets. Visa MC accepted. Open year-round. Mail free for guests, $15 fee for non-guests: 55 Main Street, Gorham, NH 03581.

Royalty Inn (3.6W) 603.466.3312 Hiker rate $79 wkday, $89 wkend (subject to change). Indoor pool, sauna, A/C. ⟨www.royaltyinn.com⟩

Hiker's Paradise at Colonial Fort Inn 603.466.2732 603.466.2732 bunks $24 (incl. tax) w/linen, tub/shower, kitchen. Private rooms avail. Restaurants near by. Coin laundry for guests. Coleman/alcohol/oz. Free shuttle w/stay from/to Route 2, other limited shuttles. CC accepted. Smoking only on outside porch. No pets or maildrops. ⟨www.hikersparadise.com⟩

Top Notch Inn 603.466.5496 ⟨www.topnotchinn.com⟩ Guest laundry, limited shuttles, pool, hot tub, behaved dogs under 50 lbs okay, no smoking, CC accepted. 10% local restaurant discount. Open May-mid Oct. Guest mail: 265 Main St, Gorham, NH 03581.

Northern Peaks Motor Inn 603.466.2288 $70/up + tax. A/C, pets $15, no smoking, all major credit cards accepted, hiker friendly. ⟨www.northernpeaksmotorinn.com⟩

Gorham Motor Inn 603.466.3381 $58-$158 Open May-Oct.

Gorham Hardware & Sports 603.466.2312 Open M-F 8-5:30, Sa 8-4, Su 8-1. Close Su after Columbus Day. Hiking poles, Water treatment, hiking food, cold-weather clothes, White gas/alcohol/oz & canisters. Visa/MC/Disc.

Trail Angels Hiker Services 978.855.9227 Shuttles covering NH & ME.

Concord Coach 800.639.3317 Bus service 7:50am daily from Irving Mini Mart to Pinkham Notch. $7 one-way, $13 round-trip.

Berlin, NH (10W from US 2)

Androscoggin Valley Hospital 603.752.2200

Lancaster, NH (28W from US 2)

Hikers Hostel at the Yellow Deli 603.788.3031 Run by a Twelve Tribes spiritual community. Call for shuttle to (for Crawford Notch, Pinkham Notch, and Rattle River trailheads): $20 suggested donation, WFS when avail. Use of Kitchenette. No alcohol, no smoking. Stay incl. b'fast and 15% off at **Simon the Tanner** (adjacent footwear and clothing Outfitter, open 9-5 S-Th, F 9-3). Mail: Hiker Hostel, 65 Main Street, Lancaster, NH 03584. ⟨www.hikershostel.org⟩

238.1	1951.7	**Bemis Mountain Lean-to,** small spring to left of lean-to (8) 26.8◂23.3◂12.8◂▸8.3▸19.5▸28.4	2826
236.8	1953.0	Bemis Mountain Second Peak	2905
234.6	1955.2	Dirt road, campsite and stream north of road	1559
234.4	1955.4	Bemis Stream (ford)	1501
233.6	1956.2	ME 17, **Oquossoc, ME** (11.0W) 44.8364,-70.71 P (**pg. 208**) Height of Land view, bench and boulder seating	2206
232.5	1957.3	Woods road	2368
231.9	1957.9	Moxie Pond	2333
229.8	1960.0	**Sabbath Day Pond Lean-to** 31.6◂21.1◂8.3◂▸11.2▸20.1▸28.1 (8) Pond in front of lean-to. Sandy beach 0.3S on AT, swimming.	2377
229.3	1960.5	Houghton Fire Rd	2388
228.2	1961.6	Powerline	2792
225.2	1964.6	Little Swift River Pond Campsite Spring house next to pond.	2460
224.0	1965.8	Chandler Mill Stream, pond	2184
222.9	1966.9	Stream.	2305
222.5	1967.3	South Pond	2174
220.4	1969.4	ME 4, **Rangeley, ME** (9.0W) 44.8869,-70.5405 P (**pg. 209**)	1613
220.2	1969.6	Sandy River, footbridge	1664
219.7	1970.1	Old County Rd (gravel)	1867

218.9	1970.9	Stream	1978
218.6	1971.2	**Piazza Rock Lean-to,** stream through campsite (8) **(pg. 212)** 32.3◄19.5◄11.2◄►8.9►16.9►35.5 Two-seat privy and cribbage board.	2088
217.8	1972.0	Ethel Pond	2365
217.6	1972.2	Saddleback Stream	2453
216.8	1973.0	Eddy Pond, woods road passes near north bank, no camping near pond	2643
214.7	1975.1	Saddleback Mountain, trail 2.0W to ski lodge.	4120
213.1	1976.7	The Horn.	4021
212.4	1977.4	Redington Campsite to west, water 0.2W on side trail (8)	3154
211.1	1978.7	Saddleback Junior	3655
210.7	1979.1	Stream.	3230
209.7	1980.1	**Poplar Ridge Lean-to** (1961) (6) 28.4◄20.1◄8.9◄►8.0►26.6►36.8 Some tenting at lean-to, more on knoll to the north. Stream in front.	2948
207.0	1982.8	Orbeton Stream (ford)	1550
206.9	1982.9	Woods road, NoBo: walk a short distance east on road	1627
206.2	1983.6	Sluice Brook.	2088
205.6	1984.2	Barnjam Rd, private gravel road	2321
205.1	1984.7	Perham Stream, logging road to north (not accessible by car)	2300
203.9	1985.9	Lone Mountain	3260
202.7	1987.1	Mt Abraham Trail, 1.7E to summit above treeline, remnants of lookout tower	3247
201.7	1988.1	**Spaulding Mountain Lean-to,** spring on north shelter loop trail (8) 28.1◄16.9◄8.0◄►18.6►28.8►36.5	3122
200.7	1989.1	Crest NW shoulder of Spaulding Mountain Side trail 0.1E to summit.	3894
200.0	1989.8	Bronze plaque Completion of the last section of the AT from GA-ME.	3544

NoBo SoBo 1000 3000 5000

SoBo	NoBo	Feature	Elev
198.9	1990.9	View to east	3617
198.6	1991.2	Sugarloaf Mountain, stream 0.2E, Sugarloaf Mountain Trail 0.6E to summit	3645
196.6	1993.2	South Branch Carrabassett River (ford), tenting on north side of river	2147
196.5	1993.3	Caribou Valley Rd (gravel)	2220
196.0	1993.8	Spring	2440
195.5	1994.3	Crocker Cirque Campsite (0.2E), stream	2730
194.4	1995.4	South Crocker Mountain, summit 50 yards west	4040
193.4	1996.4	North Crocker Mountain	4228
192.3	1997.5	Spring	3358
188.2	2001.6	ME 27 (paved), **Stratton, ME** (5.0W) 45.1034,-70.3569 P **(pg. 212)**	1396
187.4	2002.4	Stratton Brook Pond Rd	1250
187.3	2002.5	Stratton Brook, footbridge	1203
186.5	2003.3	Footbridge, stream	1273
186.4	2003.4	Cranberry Stream Campsite	1328
185.0	2004.8	Bigelow Range Trail 0.2W to Cranberry Pond	2400
183.9	2005.9	View to east	3346
183.3	2006.5	Horns Pond Trail	3143
183.1	2006.7	**Horns Pond Lean-tos** 35.5◄26.6◄18.6◄►10.2►17.9►27.9 (16)	3165
182.7	2007.1	Trail 0.2W to North Horn, small boxed spring just south of this intersection	3712
182.6	2007.2	South Horn	3831

No Camping above the treeline in Bigelow Preserve

SoBo	NoBo	Feature	Elev
180.5	2009.3	Bigelow Mountain west peak	4145
180.1	2009.7	Avery Memorial Campsite, spring 0.2N on AT, Fire Wardens Trail to east	3838
179.8	2010.0	Avery Peak	4090

178.6 2011.2 View 2845

177.9 2011.9 Safford Brook Trail to west 2260

177.8 2012.0 Safford Notch Campsite 0.3E 2220

175.6 2014.2 View 2915

174.6 2015.2 Little Bigelow Mountain, view 3010

172.9 2016.9 **Little Bigelow Lean-to** 36.8◄28.8◄10.2◄►7.7►17.7►27.4 . . . (8) 1792
Plenty of tent sites at lean-to. Swimming in "the Tubs" along AT.

171.5 2018.3 East Flagstaff Rd, ... 45.1346,-70.1714 P (0.1W) (pg. 213) 1200
AT east on road for 0.1 mile

171.3 2018.5 Bog Brook Rd, Flagstaff Lake outlet, footbridge 1196

170.6 2019.2 Hemlock Trail to east 1257

170.3 2019.5 East Flagstaff Lake tentpads, 2 beaches, 2 firepits . . . . . . (9) 1208

169.8 2020.0 Two intersections with Hemlock Trail 1244

168.7 2021.1 Long Falls Dam Rd (paved). . . . . . . (pg. 213) 1225

168.6 2021.2 Jerome Brook 1236

"Carry" ponds are so named because they were used for portage.

165.8 2024.0 Connector trail to Great Carrying Pond Portage Trail. 1319

165.2 2024.6 **West Carry Pond Lean-to** 36.5◄17.9◄7.7◄►10.0►19.7►28.7. . . . (8) 1325
Swimming in pond. Water at spring house to left of lean-to or at West Carry Pond.

164.5 2025.3 Unmarked trail 0.5W to Arnolds Point on West Carry Pond. 1322

162.7 2027.1 Gravel road, AT to west over Sandy Stream 1276

161.8 2028.0 Gravel road 1290

161.5 2028.3 East Carry Pond, beach at north end 1261

159.5 2030.3 Scott Rd (gravel) 1337

1922.6 Grafton Notch, ME 26

The Inn at Rostay 207.824.3111 Free hot made to order b'fast (seasonal). Rates vary by season/times. Show AT Guidebook for discount. Pet fee $10. All rooms have fridge/ m'wave. Restaurants & resupply nearby.

(12.8E) **Stony Brook Camping** 207.824.2836 tentsite $28 for 4, lean-to $32 for 4. Shuttles from Grafton Notch for a fee. Pool, mini golf, zipline, rec room, campstore. 12.0E on Hwy26, then lft 0.8 mi on Rte 2. Mail: 42 Powell Place, Hanover, ME 04237 ⟨www.stonybrookrec.com⟩

Bethel, ME 04217 (12E to Rt 2, right 5 miles on Rt 2)

M-F 9-4, Sa 10-12:30, 207.824.2668

Chapman Inn 207.824.2657 Bunk space $35 incl. shower & full b'fast, $25 w/out b'fast. Rooms $79/up incl. b'fast. Kitchen use, $6 laundry. Mail: PO Box 1067, Bethel, ME 04217. ⟨www.chapmaninn.com⟩

Sudbury Inn Restaurant & Pub, 207.824.2174, Rooms $89/up. Dining Room open Th-Sa 5:30-9, seasonal Pub 11:30a till late.

Bethel Outdoor Adventure 207.824.4224 About 20 min. by car from Grafton Notch or US 2 trailheads. $22 campsites near river w/in walking distance of Bethel stores. Shuttle one-way to/from Grafton Notch tailhead $45/group.

Pat's Pizza 7 days 11-9

Bethel Shop 'n Save Su-Th 8-8, F-Sa 8-9. Grocery, deli, wine

True North Adventurewear 207.824.2201 Full line of gear, M-Th 10-6. F-Sa 9-6, Su 10-5. Leki repair, Coleman/alcohol/oz & canisters, frz-dried food.

Rodney Kneeland Shuttle Services 207.357.3083 Serves NH to Rangeley, ME. fishermanstrio@yahoo.com

Bethel Animal Hospital 207.824.2212

1932.9 East B Hill Rd ***Andover, ME 04216*** (8E)

Pine Ellis Lodging 207.392.4161 Bunks $25PP, private rooms $45S, $60D, $75T. Incl. shower, lender clothes, kitchen use, laundry & am coffee. LR with WiFi & cable. Trailhead P/U for fee-call in advance. Slackpack Grafton Notch to Rangeley, & shuttles to nearby towns, airport & bus station. No dogs. Full resupply, Coleman/ denatured/oz & canisters. Guest Mail: (USPS)PO Box 12 or (UPS)20 Pine St, Andover, ME 04216. ⟨www.pineellislodging.com⟩

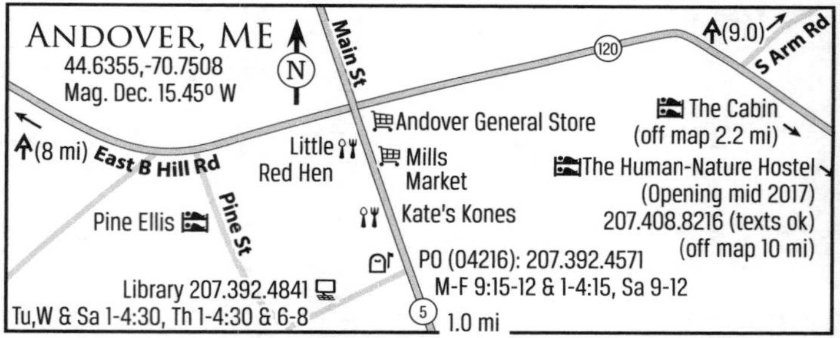

ANDOVER, ME
44.6355,-70.7508
Mag. Dec. 15.45° W
N
Main St
120
(9.0)
S Arm Rd
(8 mi)
East B Hill Rd
Pine St
Pine Ellis
Little Red Hen
Andover General Store
Mills Market
Kate's Kones
The Cabin (off map 2.2 mi)
The Human-Nature Hostel (Opening mid 2017) 207.408.8216 (texts ok) (off map 10 mi)
PO (04216): 207.392.4571 M-F 9:15-12 & 1-4:15, Sa 9-12
Library 207.392.4841 Tu,W & Sa 1-4:30, Th 1-4:30 & 6-8
5
1.0 mi

Paul's AT Camp for Hikers 207.392.4161 Contact Pine Ellis for cabin stay. $60 for 4, 15EAP incl. shower one round trip shuttle from the hostel. Located 3 mi from Andover. Slack pack shuttle service from the lodge.

Mountain Village Tiny House 207.357.7004 1 BR cottage sleeps 4 from $120/night. Discounts for solo hikers. Walk to restaurants. Kayak rental $25/day.

The Cabin 207.392.1333 Alumni hikers welcome; by reservation only. ⟨www.thecabininmaine.com⟩

Andover General Store Short-order food & pizza, ice cream. M-Sa 5-8; Su 6-8; Summer, until 9p daily.

Mills Market Open 7 days 5am-9pm.

Little Red Hen 207.392.2253 Summer Hrs: Tu-Th 6:30a-2p, F-Sa 6:30a-8p, Sun 7a-2p, closed Mon. AYCE Italian Buffet Sa 5-8. Ask about tenting. Showers & laundry $5 ea.

Kates Kones Ice cream. Summer hours 1-8:30

■ **Donna Gifford** massage therapist, 207.357.5686, call for rates. Free pickup/return to Andover.

1943.0 South Arm Rd

(3.5W) **South Arm Campground** 207.364.5155 Tent sites, store, no cc, checks okay, hot showers, pets okay, ADA comp. privy. Open May 1-Oct 1 ⟨www. southarm.com⟩

Andover, ME (9E from South Arm Rd)

1956.2 ME 17 ***Oquossoc, ME 04964*** (11W)
M–F 8–10 & 2:15–4:15, Sa 9–12, 207.864.3685
Oquossoc Grocery 207.864.3662 Su-Th, 6-8; F-Sa, 6-9; pizza,deli, bakery, wine, Coleman fuel.
Gingerbread House B/L/D, vegetarian specials.
Four Seasons Café 7 days 11–9 L/D vegetarian specialties.

1969.4 ME 4 ***Rangeley, ME*** (9W) Safest to hitch from end of guardrail 0.3W, in front of Hiker Hut. Rangeley is halfway between equator and north pole (3107 miles from either).
The Hiker Hut (0.3W) 207.670.8095 Sports Massage on site. $25 Stay incl. bunk w/mattress, pillow, hot shower, shuttle to & from Rangeley. Tea, coffee & donuts on departure. Hot meals & laundry. Separate huts $50/double, $40/single. Pet friendly. Walk-ins have preference. Cash preferred. Denatured alcohol & fuel canisters for sale. Distance shuttling avail. DIRECTLY AT TRAIL HEAD. Open May 15- Sep 15. Maildrops ($5 non-guest) C/O Steve Lynch, 2 Pine Rd., Sandy River Plantation, ME 04970. hikerhut@gmail.com.
Farmhouse Inn 207.864.3113 Hiker bunkroom for $30PP, incl. shower w/towel & return to Rte 4 trailhead. Private rooms avail. No parties. Laundry $5. Hiker supplies, Coleman/Denatured/oz, slackpacking. Clean facility w/use of a kitchen. Free shuttle B/L/D. Unscheduled shuttle for fee. Shuttle range Gorham to Monson & to airports, train, bus & car rental hubs in Portland, Bangor, Farmington, Augusta & Waterville. 0.5 S of IGA. Mail: 2057 Main St, Rangeley, ME 04970
Town & Lake Motel 207.864.3755 Hiker rates 55/1, 75/2, No discount on wkends July/Aug. Pets $5. Canoes for guest use. Mail: PO Box 47, Rangeley, ME 04970.
Rangeley Inn & Tavern 207.864.3341 Rates start at $135 in the summer, $115-after 10/9. Incl. con. b'fast. Sr discount, free calls to US & Canada.⟨www.therangeleyinn.com⟩
Rangeley Saddleback Inn 207.864.3434 $135 Incl. c. b'fast. Pets $10. Ride sometimes avail. **Pub 45th Parallel** on-site.
North Country Inn B&B 207.864.2440 $99-149 Incl. b'fast. Multi-night discount ⟨www.northcountrybb.com⟩

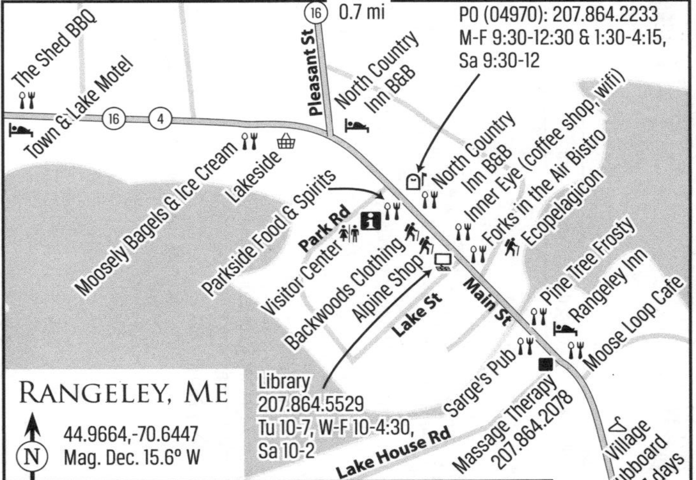

Moose Loop Cafe 207.864.3000 daily 7-2. Summer till 3.
Sarge's Sports Pub & Grub L/D & bar, daily 11a-1p, house bands Fr & Sa.
Moose Alley 207.864.9955 Bowling, billiards, darts, dance & food. Just west of The Shed BBQ on Main St.
IGA Supermarket ATM. 7 Days, 7-8.
Back Woods 207.864.2335 Gear, clothes.
Ecopelagicon 207.864.2771 Seasonal hrs. Gas/alcohol/oz & canisters. Frz-dried food, water filters, clothes, Leki poles & warranty work. Ask about shuttles. Mail: PO Box 899, 7 Pond St, Rangeley, ME 04970
Alpine Shop 207.864.3741 M-Su, 9a-8p. Full outfitter, fuel/oz.
Rangeley Health & Wellness Center 207.864.3303 & 207.864.3055 On Dallas Hill Rd south of IGA. Wellness Center $5 shower w/towel. M-Th 5-8; Fr 5-7:30; Sa-Su 8-2.

158.7	2031.1	North branch of Carrying Place Stream . . . . 💧	1200

Trails to Harrison's, before and after the dam, can be used to bypass the dam.

155.2	2034.6	**Pierce Pond Lean-to**, 27.9◄17.7◄10.0◄►9.7►18.7►22.8 ☽💧⊏(6) (**pg. 213**) Blue-blazed loop trail west to lean-to. From north end of loop, Harrison's is 0.3E.	1207
155.1	2034.7	Wooden dam, outlet of Pierce Pond . . . . 💧	1140
154.8	2035.0	Trail 0.1E to Harrison's Pierce Pond Camps, boat landing to west . . . . . (**pg. 213**)	1100
154.6	2035.2	Otter Pond Rd (gravel)	1056
154.1	2035.7	Pierce Pond Stream Falls 0.1E	980
154.0	2035.8	Waterfall 0.1E	955
153.5	2036.3	Otter Pond Stream, footbridge . . . . 💧	864

Camping on either shore of Kennebec River is prohibited.

151.6	2038.2	Kennebec River. Do not ford. Use ferry service . . . . 💧(**pg. 213**)	485
151.2	2038.6	US 201, **Caratunk, ME** (0.3E) . . . . 45.2384,-69.9963 🅿 (**pg. 213**)	520
150.9	2038.9	Woods road	674
148.6	2041.2	Holly Brook . . . . 💧	901
147.2	2042.6	Grove Rd (gravel)	1220
146.7	2043.1	Holly Brook . . . . 💧	1292
146.0	2043.8	Boise-Cascade Logging Rd to west (gravel), Pleasant Pond Rd to east	1430
145.5	2044.3	**Pleasant Pond Lean-to** 27.4◄19.7◄9.7◄►9.0►13.1►22.0. . . . . . ☽💧⊏(6) Stream left of lean-to. Beach 0.2 on side trail beyond lean-to.	1373
145.3	2044.5	Pleasant Pond Beach to east. Private property open for public use from . . . . . . May 15 - Oct 1 from 8a-8p. No camping, no fires. High quality water source.	1339
144.2	2045.6	Pleasant Pond Mountain . . . . 📷	2470

Blueberries - Abundant on open summits like Pleasant Pond Mountain and north peak of Moxie Bald.

139.7	2050.1	Stream. . . . . 💧	1034

139.3 2050.5 Moxie Pond south end (ford), road, powerlines . . . . 45.2497,-69.831 P 💧 970
139.1 2050.7 Baker Stream . . . . 💧 972
138.8 2051.0 Powerline 1015

136.5 2053.3 **Bald Mountain Brook Lean-to** (0.1E) . . . . ☽ 💧 ⊏ (8) 1312
28.7◄18.7◄9.0◄►4.1►13.0►25.0 Bald Mountain Brook in front of lean-to.
"AT Road" (gravel) 75 yards north of shelter.

135.1 2054.7 Summit bypass trail to west 2151
134.5 2055.3 Moxie Bald Mountain . . . . 📷 2629
134.2 2055.6 Summit bypass trail to west . . . . ☽ 2414
133.5 2056.3 Trail to Moxie Bald north peak (0.5W) . . . . 📷 2212

132.4 2057.4 **Moxie Bald Mountain Lean-to** . . . . ☽ 💧 ⊏ (8) 1224
22.8◄13.1◄4.1◄►8.9►20.9►28.3
Bald Mountain Pond in front of lean-to.
131.3 2058.5 Gravel road 1259
130.8 2059.0 Gravel road 1234
130.4 2059.4 Bald Mountain Stream (ford) . . . . 💧 1216

NoBo
SoBo
1000
3000
5000

128.5 2061.3 Bald Mountain Rd (gravel) . . . . 45.2762,-69.6885 P 💧 1116
bridge and stream to west

127.0 2062.8 Marble Brook . . . . 💧 985
126.5 2063.3 West Branch of Piscataquis River (ford) . . . . 💧 964
River normally knee-deep. During heavy rain periods, fording can be dangerous.

123.5 2066.3 **Horseshoe Canyon Lean-to** 22.0◄13.0◄8.9◄►12.0►19.4►24.1 . . ☽ 💧 ⊏ (8) 780
On blue-blazed trail. Stream at northern AT junction or river in front and below.
123.1 2066.7 Stream. . . . . 💧 740

121.2 2068.6 East Branch of Piscataquis River (ford) . . . . 💧 588
120.9 2068.9 Gravel road 741
120.8 2069.0 Shirley-Blanchard Rd (paved) . . . . 45.2845,-69.5871 P 850

119.7 2070.1 AT on woods road for 0.5 mile 977

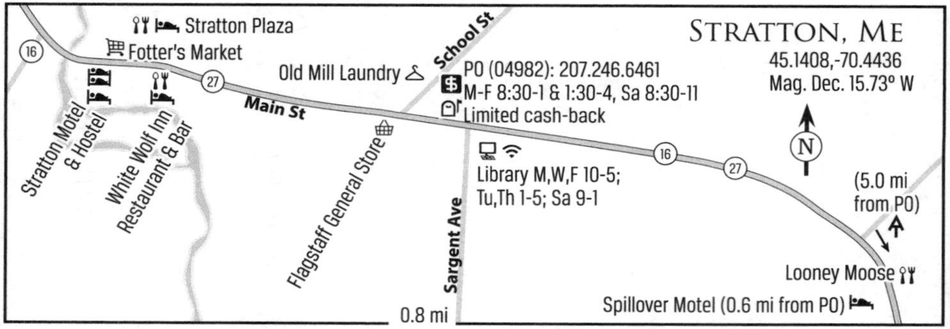

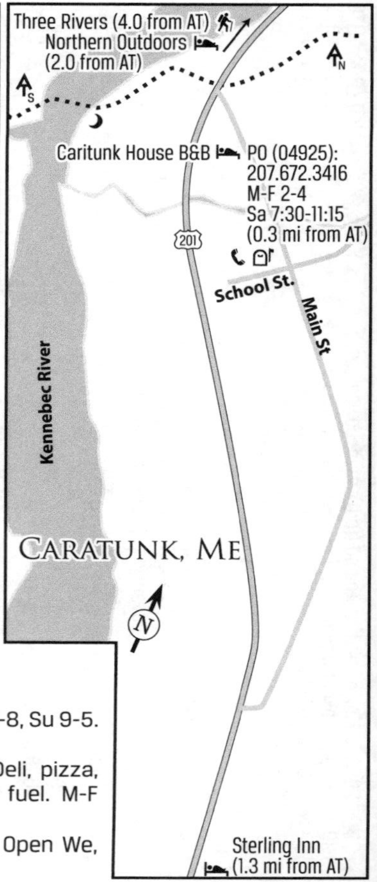

Stratton, ME

45.1408,-70.4436
Mag. Dec. 15.73° W

Stratton Plaza
Fotter's Market
Old Mill Laundry
School St
PO (04982): 207.246.6461
M-F 8:30-1 & 1:30-4, Sa 8:30-11
Limited cash-back
Stratton Motel & Hostel
White Wolf Inn Restaurant & Bar
Main St
Flagstaff General Store
Library M,W,F 10-5; Tu,Th 1-5; Sa 9-1
Sargent Ave
(5.0 mi from PO)
Looney Moose
Spillover Motel (0.6 mi from PO)
0.8 mi

1971.2 **Piazza Rock Lean-to** Two side trails north of shelter; 100 yds north: west to Piazza Rock; 0.1 north: To "The Caves", blue-blazed trail through boulders & caves.

2001.6 ME 27
(2E) **Mountainside Grocers** 207.237.2248 Open M-Sa 7:30–8, Su 7:30-6.

Stratton, ME 04982 (5W)

Stratton Motel 207.246.4171 or 207.670.5507 $30 bunk, $70 private room, Cash Only. Complimentary shuttle from trailhead (when avail.). Same owners as Farmhouse Inn of Rangeley, who facilitate supply bumps from town to town and slackpacking in area. Shuttle for fee, Gorham to Monson & to airports, train, bus & car rental hubs in Portland, Bangor, Farmington, Augusta & Waterville. Canister fuel & fuel/oz. Mail: PO Box 284, Stratton, ME 04982; FedEx & UPS 162 Main St.,Stratton, ME 04982 ⟨www.thestrattonmotel.com⟩

White Wolf Inn 207.246.2922 $59D, $69D on weekends, $10EAP + tax. Pets $10. Visa, Master Card accepted $20 min. Restaurant (closed Tuesday) serves L/D. Breakfast on weekends. Home of the 8oz Wolf Burger; Fish Fry Friday; **Wolf Den Bar** on-site. Guest Maildrop (fee for non-guests): Main Street, PO Box 590, Stratton, ME 04982.

Spillover Motel 207.246.6571 $84/up. Pets $10, continental breakfast, full kitchen for use by guests. Gas grill. Shower $5. Mail: PO Box 427, Stratton, ME 04982. ⟨www.spillovermaine.com⟩

Stratton Plaza Hotel 207.246.2000 Dining, some rooms. Closed Su-M.

Fotter's Market 207.246.2401 M-Th 8-7, F-Sa 8-8, Su 9-5. Coleman/alcohol/oz.

Flagstaff General Store 207.246.2300 Deli, pizza, subs, sodas, coffee, protein bars, beer, canister fuel. M-F 5:30am-9pm, Sa 7-9, Su 7-7.

Coplin Dinner House 207.246.0016 "Fine Food". Open We, Th, Su 5p-9p, Fri & Sa 5p-9:30p

Caratunk, ME

Three Rivers (4.0 from AT)
Northern Outdoors (2.0 from AT)
Caritunk House B&B
PO (04925): 207.672.3416 M-F 2-4 Sa 7:30-11:15 (0.3 mi from AT)
201
School St.
Main St
Kennebec River
Sterling Inn (1.3 mi from AT)

2018.3 East Flagstaff Rd
Hallowell's Hiker Helpers (18E) 207.265.6883 Free rides to resupply, free shower & laundry. Free accommodations for Neros and Zeros. Pickup Stratton, ME trailhead. Advance notice requested but not required. Will accommodate as able.

2021.1 Long Falls Dam Rd
Kingfield, ME (18E from either Rd)
Mountain Village Farm B&B 207.265.2030 Hiker rate of $60PP for room w/fridge, m'wave & private bath Incl. b'fast. Round-trip shuttle $40 for up to 4 persons from either trailhead. Pets welcome. Bed & b'fast on an organic farm; inquire about work-for-stay. Town center w/in walking distance has grocery, laundry & restaurants. Slackpack the Bigelows (Stratton to East Flagstaff Rd, either direction) $50/carload. Mail: PO Box 216, Kingfield, ME 04947

2034.6, 2035.0 Trails to camp, dam bypass
Harrison's Pierce Pond Camps 207.672.3625, 207.612.8184 May-Nov, 7 days. Bed, shower and 12-pancake b'fast for $40. For b'fast only, ($9-12 served 7am), reserve a seat the day before. Cash only, no reservations for overnight stay. Pets welcome. Okay to get water at camp and dispose of trash. Shortest route to camp is west from the north end of blue-blaze shelter loop trail.

2038.2 Kennebec River. The ferry is the official AT route. Do not ford; current is unpredictable due to an upstream dam.
The Kennebec Ferry 207.858.3627 Free ferry service provided seasonally by the ATC & MATC. Ferry holds 1 or 2; hikers are required to sign a release form. Scheduled Hours:

- May 26-June: 9a-11a
- July 1-Sept 30: 9a-2p
- Oct 1-Oct 9: 9a-11a

$50 fee for on call ferry service outside of scheduled hours, weather permitting, provided by **Maine Guide Services**.
Cheryl Anderson 207.672.3997 Privately run ferry service $30. Can take up to 4.

2038.6 US 201 ***Caratunk, ME 04925*** (0.3E)
Post office accepts debit cards with limited cash back. Note limited hours; consider businesses below for maildrops.
The Caratunk House B&B (150yds E) 207.672.4349 Open Jun 1 - Sep 30. Closest to ferry. Beds: $20/twin rooms, $25 to $40/private rooms. No tenting. Full family style b'fast, $7. Shuttle service, WiFi. CC ok. Pet friendly. Laundry $5, Shower $5 for non-guests. Long term resupply. All fuels, homemade baked goods, milk shakes. A quiet, non party house. Free maildrop: 218 Main St. (PO Box 98) Caratunk, ME 04925
The Sterling Inn (1.3E) 207.672.3333 Bunk room $25, private $40S, $55D (shared bed), $90/4. All include b'fast buffet. Multi-night discount, cc/debit OK, pets welcome, open yr-round. **Caratunk Country Store** has everything a hiker needs, incl. fuel/oz, canister fuel, batteries & candy bars, ice cream, sodas, cook-yourself options & more. Free shuttle to/from trail, PO & nearby restaurants. Resupply, showers ($2.50) & laundry ($5) avail. even if you are not staying. Address: 1041 Route 201. Maildrops & shipping (also free for non-guests): PO Box 129, Caratunk Maine 04925. ⟨www.mainesterlinginn.com⟩
Northern Outdoors (2W) 800.765.7238 Hikers welcome, free shuttle (coincides w/ferry schedule), use resort facilities with or w/out stay; hikers receive 30% lodging discount; prices vary, call for rates. No pets in campground. Coin laundry, hot tub, free WiFi, limited hiker resupply, food & ale in **Kennebec River Brewpub**, Home of the exterminator burger challenge! Finish the meal in 30 min, get it free. Mail: C/O Northern Outdoors, 1771 Route 201, The Forks, ME 04985.
Three Rivers Trading Post (4W) 207.663.2104 Store open yr-round 7-8 w/variety of packaged food, beer & wine. Bunks, tenting & restaurant open May-mid Sep. Bunk $25PP, tenting $12PP. Rafting trips w/reservation. **Boatman's Bar & Grill** on-site 4p-1a. Mail: 2265 US Route 201, The Forks, ME 04985
Berry's General Store (7.5W) 207.663.4461 5a-7p daily, yr-round. Open till 8 in summer.

SoBo	NoBo	Description		Elev
119.3	2070.5	Gravel road		895
117.8	2072.0	Historic AT route near Lake Hebron. 45.2907,-69.5333 🅿 (pg. 220)		900
		0.2E on woods road to Pleasant St & parking, then left 1.6 mi to **Monson, ME.**		
117.4	2072.4	Dirt road		1033
115.9	2073.9	Side trail to Doughty Ponds (0.1W), 180' footbridge built in 2014	💧	1229
115.8	2074.0	Stream.	💧	1251
115.2	2074.6	Gravel road		1386
114.5	2075.3	ME 15 (paved), **Monson, ME** (3.6E) 45.3309,-69.5354 🅿 (pg. 220)		1215
		South end of 100-Mile Wilderness.		
114.4	2075.4	Spectacle Pond outlet	💧	1180
113.6	2076.2	Old Stage Rd (dirt) Once a stagecoach road and part of the original AT		1291
113.3	2076.5	Bell Pond	💧	1278
112.6	2077.2	Lily Pond	💧	1130
111.5	2078.3	**Leeman Brook Lean-to**	☽ 💧 ∠ (6)	1062
		25.0◄20.9◄12.0◄►7.4►12.1►16.1 Stream in front of lean-to.		
110.7	2079.1	North Pond outlet	💧	1013
110.4	2079.4	North Pond Tote Rd		1090
109.3	2080.5	Mud Pond		1031
108.9	2080.9	Bear Pond Ledge		1208
108.5	2081.3	James Brook	💧	946
108.1	2081.7	Woods road		938
108.0	2081.8	Little Wilson Falls, west 30 yards	💧	844
107.7	2082.1	Little Wilson Stream (ford), campsite	💧 ⛺	750
107.3	2082.5	Follow gravel road for 100 yards, pond		925
105.4	2084.4	Big Wilson Tote Rd		566
105.2	2084.6	Thompson Brook	💧	563
104.8	2085.0	Big Wilson Stream (ford)	💧	600
104.5	2085.3	Railroad tracks		883
104.1	2085.7	**Wilson Valley Lean-to** (1993)	☽ 💧 ∠ (6)	951
		28.3◄19.4◄7.4◄►4.7►8.7►15.6 Spring on opposite side of AT.		
103.4	2086.4	Woods road		1180
102.1	2087.7	Stream	💧	924
101.8	2088.0	Stream	💧	914
101.0	2088.8	Wilber Brook	💧	595
100.8	2089.0	Vaughn Stream	💧	617
100.3	2089.5	Bodfish Farm/Long Pond Tote Rd (gravel), ford Long Pond Stream north of road	💧	638

99.4	2090.4	**Long Pond Stream Lean-to** 24.1◄12.1◄4.7◄►4.0►10.9►20.8	(8)	914
99.2	2090.6	Trail 0.8E to Otter Pond parking	P	1059
98.2	2091.6	Barren Slide to east, view		1971
98.1	2091.7	Barren Ledges		2017
96.3	2093.5	Barren Mountain, remnants of tower		2660
95.4	2094.4	Side trail to **Cloud Pond Lean-to** (0.4E) 16.1◄8.7◄4.0◄►6.9►16.8►24.0 Cloud Pond is water source.	(6)	2483
93.9	2095.9	Fourth Mountain Bog		1931
93.3	2096.5	Fourth Mountain		2380
92.1	2097.7	Mt Three and a Half		1958
91.7	2098.1	Third Mountain Trail to west		1800
90.8	2099.0	Third Mountain, Monument Cliff		2097
90.2	2099.6	Trail 0.1E to West Chairback Pond, stream crosses AT north of side trail		1770
89.3	2100.5	View		2150
89.2	2100.6	Spring		2237
88.9	2100.9	Columbus Mountain		2325
88.5	2101.3	**Chairback Gap Lean-to** 15.6◄10.9◄6.9◄►9.9►17.1►20.7 Spring on AT north of shelter.	(6)	1960
88.0	2101.8	Chairback Mountain		2180
85.9	2103.9	0.2W to East Chairback Pond	(0.2W)	1709
85.3	2104.5	Spring		1460
84.7	2105.1	Katahdin Ironworks Rd (gravel) 45.4772,-69.2851	P (0.4E)	783
84.2	2105.6	West Branch Pleasant River (ford). Wide ford with slick rocky bottom. Campsites to south; no camping/fires for 2.0N.		663
83.3	2106.5	Stream.		748
82.8	2107.0	Gulf Hagas Trail to west, 5.2 mile loop trail whose ends intersect the AT 0.7 mile apart. Features narrow, deep gorge with many waterfalls.		875
82.1	2107.7	Gulf Hagas Trail to west		1050

All 100 M.W. roads are privately owned, gated, and have fees. Road names vary on maps and in local use. Both roads that pass by Logan Brook & Cooper Brook Shelters may be referred to as "B Pond Road". If getting shuttles or drops be clear about the destination.

78.6	2111.2	**Carl A. Newhall Lean-to** 20.8◄16.8◄9.9◄►7.2►10.8►18.9 Gulf Hagas Brook, south of shelter, is water source.	(6)	1923
77.7	2112.1	Gulf Hagas Mountain		2681
76.8	2113.0	Sidney Tappan Campsite, water 0.1E		2434
76.1	2113.7	West Peak		3178
74.5	2115.3	Hay Mountain		3244
73.7	2116.1	White Brook Trail to east		3004
72.8	2117.0	White Cap Mountain		3650
71.9	2117.9	View of Katahdin from north side of mountain		2730
71.4	2118.4	**Logan Brook Lean-to** 24.0◄17.1◄7.2◄►3.6►11.7►23.1 Some tent sites; better sites 0.1N on AT. Logan Brook in front of lean-to; cascades upstream.	(6)	2386
69.8	2120.0	Logan Brook Rd (dirt). Piped spring 50 yards south of road, west of AT		1602
67.8	2122.0	**East Branch Lean-to,** Pleasant River in front 20.7◄10.8◄3.6◄►8.1►19.5►29.6	(6)	1242
67.5	2122.3	East branch of Pleasant River (ford).		1208
65.9	2123.9	Mountain View Pond outlet		1574
65.6	2124.2	Spring to east		1561
64.3	2125.5	Side trail 100 yards to Little Boardman Mountain		1980
63.0	2126.8	Kokadjo-B Pond Rd (gravel)		1222
62.7	2127.1	West to beach on Crawford Pond (no camping)		1249
62.1	2127.7	Cooper Brook		1206
60.2	2129.6	Stream		1000
59.7	2130.1	**Cooper Brook Falls Lean-to** 18.9◄11.7◄8.1◄►11.4►21.5►29.6 Brook, falls, swimming hole in front of lean-to. Privy across trail and up hill.	(6)	928

59.1 2130.7 Large tributary to Cooper Brook 821

56.0 2133.8 Jo-Mary Rd . . . . . 45.6515,-69.0317 P (pg. 221) 625

54.6 2135.2 Footbridge, snowmobile trail 585

53.5 2136.3 Side trail 0.2E to north shore of Cooper Pond 516
53.1 2136.7 Mud Pond to west, footbridge over Mud Brook 508

51.8 2138.0 Antlers Campsite 500
Campsites on edge of Jo-Mary Lake. Fort Relief two seat privy.

50.3 2139.5 Potaywadjo Ridge Trail 1.0W 514
50.1 2139.7 East to sandy beach on lower Jo-Mary Lake 499

48.3 2141.5 **Potaywadjo Spring Lean-to** (1995) . . . . . (8) 637
23.1◄19.5◄11.4◄►10.1►18.2►29.7 Potaywadjo Spring to right.
48.0 2141.8 Tirio Access Rd (gravel). 555
47.7 2142.1 Twitchell Brook, footbridge, east to Pemadumcook Lake, view of Katahdin. . . 493

46.5 2143.3 Deer Brook 502

45.8 2144.0 Woods road 510
45.7 2144.1 Mahar Tote Tr, Blue-blazed tr 0.2E **White House Landing** pickup . . . (pg. 221) 510
45.6 2144.2 Tumbledown Dick Stream (ford) 501
45.1 2144.7 High water trail to west 496
44.5 2145.3 Ford branch of the Nahmakanta Stream 512
44.0 2145.8 Nahmakanta Stream Campsite 520

Indian pipe – A plant without chlorophyll that grows in moist duff. Translucent white candy cane shape 3-4" tall, grows in clusters. Scale-like leaves/petals.

42.0 2147.8 Stream. 616

41.2 2148.6 Gravel Road near south end of Nahmakanta Lake . . . . . 45.736,-69.1035 P 638
Camping on shore of Nahmakanta Lake is prohibited.

40.0 2149.8 Prentiss Brook 661

SoBo	NoBo	Description	Elev
38.6	2151.2	Side trail east to sand beach on shore of Nahmakanta Lake	657
38.2	2151.6	**Wadleigh Stream Lean-to,** stream can be dry during summer (6) 29.6◄21.5◄10.1◄►8.1►19.6►33.0	685
37.2	2152.6	Spring	819
36.3	2153.5	Nesuntabunt Mountain, short side trail east to view of Katahdin, 16 mile line-of-sight distance to Katahdin summit from here.	1520
35.7	2154.1	View	1181
35.1	2154.7	Wadleigh Pond Rd (gravel)	1022
34.3	2155.5	Crescent Pond west end	1000
33.6	2156.2	Pollywog Gorge, side trail overlooking gorge	891
32.6	2157.2	Pollywog Stream 45.7796,-69.172 P Cross stream on logging road bridge.	668
30.6	2159.2	Outlet stream from Murphy Pond	954
30.1	2159.7	**Rainbow Stream Lean-to,** baseball bat floor (6) 29.6◄18.2◄8.1◄►11.5►24.9►0.0 Tenting on hill behind lean-to. Excellent swimming hole upstream.	1002
28.2	2161.6	West to Rainbow Lake dam	1100
28.0	2161.8	Stream.	1062
26.3	2163.5	Rainbow Lake Campsite, spring west 30 yards	1100
25.1	2164.7	Stream.	1079
24.8	2165.0	Unmarked trail leads 0.2W to Rainbow Lake Camps (private)	1125
24.5	2165.3	Trail 0.7E to Rainbow Mountain	1145
22.9	2166.9	Side trail 0.1E to Little Beaver Pond, 0.7E to Big Beaver Pond	1085
21.1	2168.7	Rainbow Ledges, view of Katahdin	1517

18.6 2171.2 **Hurd Brook Lean-to,** baseball bat floor . . . . (6) 701
29.7◄19.6◄11.5◄►13.4►0.0►0.0
18.1 2171.7 Small spring. 774

15.9 2173.9 Bog bridge 606
15.4 2174.4 Golden Rd (paved), NoBo east on road, **Millinocket, ME** (19E) . . . . (pg. 222) 591
15.1 2174.7 Abol Bridge crosses west branch . . . . 45.8352,-68.9693 P (pg. 222) 560
of Penobscot River. Parking on east side of road between bridge and trailhead.
14.7 2175.1 End of Golden Rd, NoBo veer left on dirt road. 603
14.6 2175.2 Abol Stream Trail to east, footbridge, Baxter State Park Boundary 589
14.3 2175.5 Information board, Abol Pond Trail east, registration for The Birches Campsites. . 577
14.0 2175.8 Footbridge, Katahdin Stream, Foss and Knowlton Trail to east 573
13.2 2176.6 Foss and Knowlton Brook, footbridge 580

> **Baxter State Park - Fires & other cooking/heating devices permitted only in designated campsites & picnic areas. Camping at designated campsites only. Camp/Shelter reservations strongly recommended for those starting SoBo from Baxter, flip-flop thru-hikers, & NoBo hikers who started less than 100 mi from Baxter.**

10.5 2179.3 Lower fork of Nesowadnehunk Stream 606
Both forks of this stream may require fording. There is a highwater bypass.

9.5 2180.3 Upper fork of Nesowadnehunk Stream 790

8.7 2181.1 Short side trail to view of Big Niagara Falls 930
8.4 2181.4 Side trail west to Toll Dam and Little Niagara Falls 1042

7.7 2182.1 Daicey Pond Nature Trail to west, parking area and privy north of trailhead . P 1078

6.9 2182.9 Tracy and Elbow Pond Trails to west, Daicey Pond Nature Trail to east. 1100

6.2 2183.6 Grassy Pond Trail to west (two intersections). 1063
5.8 2184.0 Footbridge, stream 1040
5.3 2184.5 Perimeter Rd 1073
5.2 2184.6 Katahdin Stream Campground. . . . . (12) (pg. 222) 1089
The Birches Lean-tos & Campsite (0.2E) thru-hikers only, $10PP pay at KSC ranger station or info board. 1 Night limit (9.1S). 33.0◄24.9◄13.4◄►0.0►0.0►0.0
4.0 2185.8 Owl Trail to west, footbridge, stream 1548
3.9 2185.9 Katahdin Stream Falls. 1634

3.0 2186.8 Spring 2392
2.6 2187.2 Pass "The cave" small slab cave 2842
✖ Where are the northernmost bear cables on the AT?

1.6 2188.2 The Gateway, The Tableland 4522

1.0 2188.8 Thoreau Spring, Abol Trail to east 4620

0.0 2189.8 **Katahdin**, Baxter Peak, Northern Terminus of the AT . . . . (pg. 222) 5268

2072.0 Historic AT route, side trail 0.2E to Pleasant St., then left 1.7 to ***Monson***

Monson AT Visitor Center (3.6E) Downtown Monson. Open daily Jun 5 - Oct 15, from 8a-11a & 1p-5p (hrs subject to adjustment). The Visitor Center is a critical source of info for all hikers on the trail in Maine. NoBo hikers should stop in & make plans for entering & staying in BSP, permits, climbing Katahdin & leaving the Trail.

2075.3 ME 15 ***Monson, ME 04464*** (3.6E)

Strictly enforced: *No stealth camping in town*

Lakeshore House Lodging & Pub 207.997.7069, 207.343.5033 Bunkroom $25PP cash or $32.40PP with cc. Private rooms $45S/$60D w/shared bath. Well-behaved dogs ok. Reservations appreciated, packs out by 10:30a; full check-out/vacate by noon unless otherwise arranged. CC, ATM on-site. Free for guests: trailhead P/U & return (only till 11:00a for return), loaner laptop, loaner clothing, WiFi, kayaks, paddleboat, swimming. Parking $1/day. Laundry $5 & shower $5 avail. to non-guests. Pub hours: Tu-Su 11:30-9, bar open later, open mic Th, closed M. Live music Su 3-6p. House quiet by 10:00p & NO BINGE DRINKING, social drinking okay. Guests welcome at **Shaws** for b'fast. Guest mail (non-guests $5): PO Box 215, C/O Lakeshore House, Monson, ME 04464 or UPS/FedEx (no Sa delivery): 9 Tenney Hill Rd ⟨www.thelakeshorehouse.com⟩

Shaw's Hiker Hostel 207.997.3597 Celebrating 40 yrs of continuous operation. Per Bryson's, *A Walk in the Woods*, "the most famous guesthouse on the AT." Mid-May through Oct, bunks $25, private room $50S $60D, $12 tenting/hammock. Free P/U &return w/stay. $9 B'fast, $5 laundry, $5 shower (w/o stay), high speed WiFi. Food drops, licensed & insured slackpacking & shuttles all over Maine. Full resupply & Gear Shop: Hyperlite, ULA, Big Agnes Darn Tough, Leki, etc. Gear repair & shakedowns. Guest use of Kayak or Canoe. CC accepted. Maildrops (nonguests $5): PO Box 72 or 17 Pleasant St, Monson, ME 04464. ⟨www.shawshikerhostel.com⟩

John Baptist Mission 207.997.3753 Limited bunks & tenting in yard of Mission house on Main St. Shower, laundry, use of kitchen. Donation required. No drugs or alcohol.

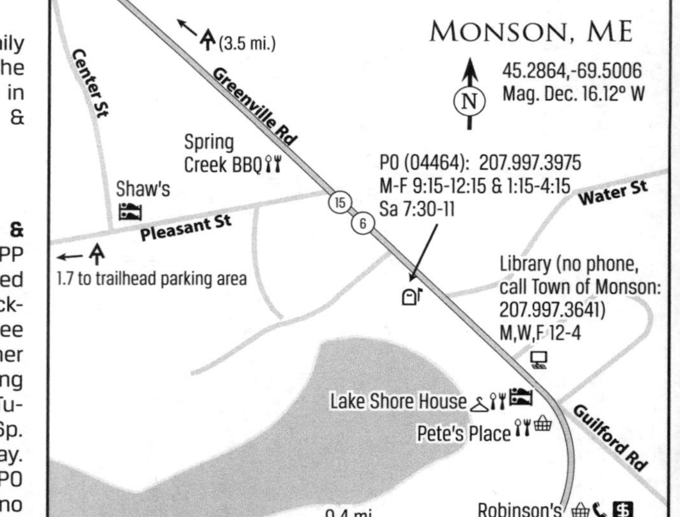

Pete's Place 207.997.3400 Open May 1 thru mid Dec; F-M. 6a-7p, Tu-Th 6a-5p. Lodging (private/ bunks) for up to 5 in home. Restaurant, bakery, ice cream. Resupply: hiker foods, small gear items, dog food. Coleman/denatured/oz, canisters.

A.E. Robinson's 207.997.3700 3a-10p 7 days. ATM fee $2. **Country Cafe Deli** inside serves burgers, pizza, b'fast.

Spring Creek Bar-B-Q 207.997.7025 Th-Sa 11a-8p, Su 11a-5p, or until the food runs out!

Greenville, ME 04485 (10W from ME 15)

Kineo View Motor Lodge 207.695.4470 $89-$109D, $10EAP incl. c. b'fast. Clean, quiet motel w/nice view, 7.5 mi. from trailhead.

White House Landing Camps 207.745.5116 Reservations recommended. Arrival date flexible. P/U & return at boat dock incl. Call/text. Open Mem Day-Oct 15. Bunk $35PP, semi-pvt $45S, $85D +tax. Shower, towel & pillowcase incl, linens extra. Resupply. Dinner menu for overnight guests incl. burgers, pizza & more. AYCE b'fast. Device recharge. Free use of canoes. CC ok. Mail: allow 7-10D for arrival. PO Box 1, Millinocket, ME 04462.

Kineo Coffee Station 207.695.2167 Open Tu-SA 7a-1p. Baked goods, B'fast sandwiches, Paninis, Coffee, cold brew.

Kelly's Landing 207.695.4438 7 days 7-9, Su AYCE b'fast.

Dairy Bar ice cream

Northwoods Outfitters 207.695.3288 Full service outfitter with fuel/oz and canister fuel. Espresso bar, pastries, internet. 7 Days 8-5. ⟨www.maineoutfitter.com⟩

Indian Hill Trading Post & Supermarket 207.695.2104 Open daily 8-8.

Jamieson's Store supplies, pizza and subs.

Harris Drug Store 207.695.2921 Ice cream counter inside.

Charles Dean Memorial Hospital 207.695.5200

Also: two banks w/ATMs in Greenville

2133.8 Jo-Mary Rd. (little traffic on road) 12.0E to ME 11.

Manufacturers & Retailers

AntiGravityGear	910.794.3308
Arc'Teryx	866.458.2473
Asolo/Lowe Alpine	603.448.8827
Backcountry.com	800.409.4502
Big Agnes	877.554.8975
Black Diamond	801.278.5552
CamelBak	800.767.8725
Campmor	888.226.7667
Camp Trails	800.345.7622
Cascade Designs (MSR/Therm-a-Rest/Platypus)	800.531.9531
Cedar Tree (Packa)	276.780.2354
Columbia	800.547.8066
Dana Designs	888.357.3262
Danner	877.432.6637
Eagle Creek	800.874.1048
Eastern Mountain Sports	888.463.6367
Etowah Outfitters	770.975.7829
Eureka!	800.572.8822
Ex Officio	800.644.7303
Feathered Friends	206.292.2210
First Need	800.441.8166
Frogg Toggs	800.349.1835
Garmin	800.800.1020
Garmont	800.943.4453
Gossamer Gear	512.374.0133
Granite Gear	218.834.6157
Gregory	877.477.4292
Hi-Tec	800.521.1698
Hyperlite Mountain Gear	800.464.9208
Jacks 'R' Better	757.643.8908
JanSport	800.552.6776
Katadyn/PUR	800.755.6701
Keen	866.676.5336
Kelty	866.349.7225
Leki	800.255.9982
Limmer	603.694.2668
LL Bean	800.441.5713
Marmont	888.357.3262
Merrell	800.288.3124
Montbell	877.666.8235
Montrail	800.826.1598
Mountain Hardwear	800.953.8398
Mountainsmith	800.551.5889
Mystery Ranch	406.585.1428
NEMO	800.997.9301
North Face	866.715.3223
Osprey	866.314.3130
Outdoor Research	888.467.4327
Patagonia	800.638.6464
Peak 1/Coleman	800.835.3278
Petzl	877.807.3805
Photon	877.584.6898
Primus	307.857.4700
Princeton Tec	800.257.9080
REI	800.426.4840
Royal Robbins	800.587.9044
Sawyer Products	727.725.1177
Salomon	800.654.2668
Sierra Designs	800.736.8592
Sierra Trading Post	800.713.4534
Six Moon Designs	503.430.2303
Slumberjack	800.233.6283
SOTO Outdoors	503.314.5119
Speer Hammocks	252.619.8292
Suunto	800.543.9124
Tarptent / Henry Shires	650.587.1548
Tecnica	800.258.3897
Teva	800.367.8382
The Underwear Guys	570.573.0209
ULA	435.753.5191
Vasque	800.224.4453
Warmstuff/ Adventurelite	570.573.0209
Western Mountaineering	408.287.8944
Zip Stove	800.594.9046

2174.4, 2174.7 Golden Rd, Abol Bridge

Abol Bridge Campground & Store 207.447.5803 Store hrs 7-7. Open May 15-Oct 15. Campsites $25PP+tax, inc. showers & b'fast buffet. Private bunk cabins $60D+tax inc. shwr & b'fast, $30EAP up to 6. Visa/MC accepted. B'fast sandwiches, subs, sodas & ice cream. Long-term resupply. Coin laundry. Shower non-guests $5. Satellite pay phone avail. Shuttle to Millinocket & Baxter Park. ⚠ $10 maildrop fee, call before sending & send well in advance: P.O. Box 536, Millinocket, ME 04462. ⟨www.abolcampground.com⟩

The Northern Restaurant adjacent to Abol Bridge Store, open Jun 15-Sep 30, 11a-7p. Food & full bar w/local & microbrewed beer. B'fast buffet 7-9a free w/campground stay.

Abol Pines 207.287.3821 Abol Pines $12+tax ($6+tax ME residents) self-register tent sites & shelters across the street from Abol Bridge Store, south of Golden Road. Provided by Maine Dept. of Conservation.

CPM Pet Care 207.723.6795, 207.731.3111 In house, privately run kennel service; pickup/drop-off at Millinocket, Abol Bridge and other campgrounds.

2184.6 Katahdin Stream Campgrd & The Birches (see pg 224)

2189.8 Katahdin, Baxter Peak

Between Baxter & Millinocket (16E from Katahdin Stream Campground (KSC), 8 miles north of Millinocket)

North Woods Trading Post 207.723.4326 Open Mem. Day - mid-Oct. 8–8 most days; hrs vary. Good selection of trail foods, many gear items. Sandwiches & pizza made on-site.

Big Moose Inn 207.723.8391 Open Memorial Day - Columbus Day, prices listed incl. tax. Rooms w/ shared baths for $65.40PP, suites w/private baths $163.50/up, cabins $119.90/up. Tenting $13.08PP, lean-to $16.35PP. WiFi in lobby, pets allowed at campsites only & must be attended at all times. **Fredericka's Restaurant** on-site open W-Sa 5:30p-close. B'fast avail. for guests daily. **Loose Moose Bar & Grill** open every night 5p-10p. B'fast avail Sa–Su. ⟨www.bigmoosecabins.com⟩

Millinocket, ME 04462 (24E from KSC)

Trail's End Festival (24E) 207.723.4443 Verify dates with Katahdin Chamber of Commerce. Typically second weekend after Labor Day with vendors, food & entertainment/live music. Hardcore trail work on Friday. ⟨www.trailsendfestival.org⟩

Millinocket: Paul (OleMan) & Jaime (NaviGator) Renaud 207.723.4321 Provide services in this text block from Mem Day-Oct 24. Credit cards accepted. ⟨www.appalachiantraillodge.com⟩

The Appalachian Trail Lodge Bunkroom $25, private room $55, family suite $95D $10EAP. Showers for nonguests $5. Coin laundry. Free daily shuttle from Baxter SP from Sep 1 - Oct 24, between 3:30p – 4:30p. Licensed & insured shuttle service for hire to & from bus in Medway, into 100-Mile Wilderness or Monson, food drops, slackpack in 100-Mile Wilderness, other shuttles by arrangement. Free parking. No pets. SoBo special: pickup in Medway, bed in bunkroom, b'fast at AT Cafe, & shuttle to KSC. $70pp, by reservation. Mail (guests only), we DO NOT sign for mail: 33 Penobscot Ave, Millinocket, ME 04462.

Ole Man's Gear Shop Full line of gear; ULA & Hyperlite packs, bags, fuel, stoves, poles, Southbound A.T. Guide and more. No clothing or shoes.

The Appalachian Trail Cafe Serves b'fast & lunch

Trail Connection Wifi, specialty coffee and gifts.

Maine Quest Adventures 207.447.5011 Lodging and tenting. Pickup at Medway bus station and drop-off at Katahdin Stream or Abol Bridge. Shuttles to Monson and parts of the 100-Mile Wilderness. Food Drops can be arranged. ⟨www.mainequestadventures.com⟩

Katahdin Cabins 207.723.6305 Skip & Nicole Mohoff run eco-friendly cabins with continental b'fast, TV, DVD, fridge & m'wave. $65 up to 3 persons, $85 up to 5. Cafe and bakery on-site. No smoking. Gas grill, mountain bikes and fishing tackle free for use,. Community room. Accepts CC/cash/checks. Mail: 181 Medway Rd, Millinocket, ME 04462. ⟨www.katahdincabins.com⟩

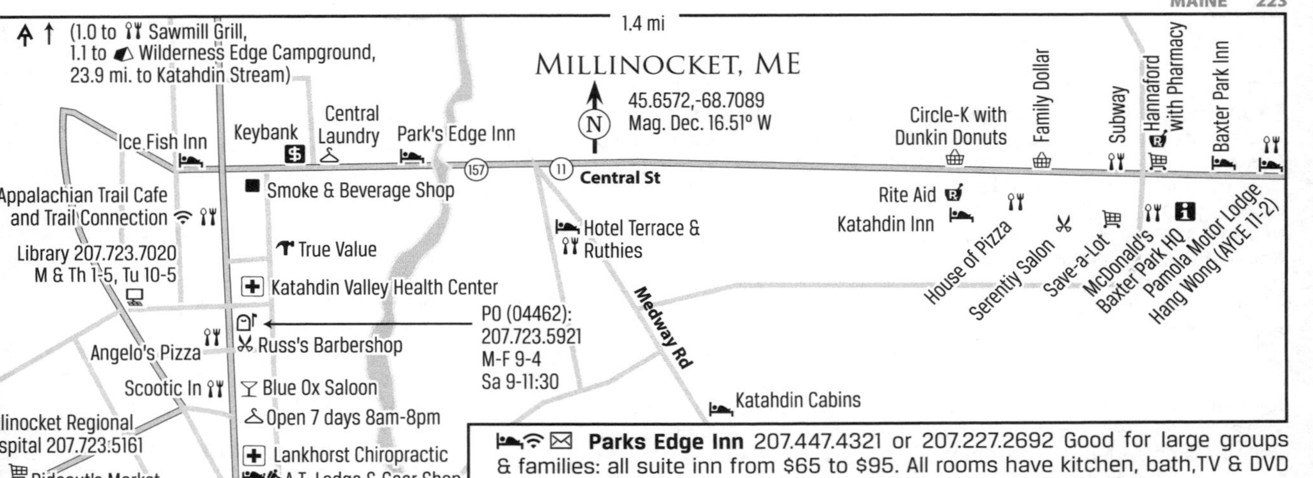

Baxter Park Inn 207.723.9777 $89.99D + tax, $10EAP, pets $25, sauna, pool.

Pamola Motor Lodge 800.575.9746 $69S $10EAP up to 4. Pets $10. Cont. b'fast. **Hang Wong Chinese Restaurant** and **Highlands Tavern** on site. Mail with reservation: 973 Central St, Millinocket, ME 04462.

Katahdin Inn 207.723.4555 Cont b'fast. Indoor heated pool and hot tub. ⟨katahdininnandsuites.com⟩

Ice Fish Inn 207.723.9999 $99S-$109D. Mail: PO Box 136, Millinocket, ME 04462.

Hotel Terrace & Ruthie's Restaurant 207.723.4545 Rates subject to change. Ruthie's serves B/L/D.

Parks Edge Inn 207.447.4321 or 207.227.2692 Good for large groups & families: all suite inn from $65 to $95. All rooms have kitchen, bath,TV & DVD players. Mail with reservation: 19 Central St, Millinocket, ME 04462.

Wilderness Edge Campground 207.447.8485 Tent site $14PP, incl. free hot shower & swimming pool. Cabin tents $17PP, up to 4 per cabin. Open May 15-Oct 15. Shuttle to trailheads and Medway bus depot avail. WiFi in office, coin laundry, Campstore: coleman/cannister fuel, soda, candy, ice cream. ⟨wildernessedgecampground.com⟩

Sawmill Grill 207.447.6996 Open Tu-Th 4p-11p; Fr-Sa 11a-11p; Su 11a-9p. Burgers, pizza & beer. "Mile High Club"; $20 for t-shirt. Return from Katahdin w/photo to get another t-shirt & a free meal.

Katahdin Kritters Pet Resort (32E) 207.746.8040 Kennel free w/24 hr supervision. Rabies, distemper & kennel cough vaccine required. Can register on-line. may assist w/pick up. ⟨katahdinkritters.com⟩

Millinocket Municipal Airport 207.731.9906 Car rental avail. from airport on Medway Rd. one mile south of Central St.

Katahdin Air 866.359.6246 fly@katahdinair.com One-way flights to 7 trailheads in ME's 100M wilderness. Flights from base on Ambajejus Lake w/ free shuttle from Abol Bridge. $75-$140. ⟨www.KatahdinAir.com⟩

Baxter State Park

baxterstateparkauthority.com | facebook.com/baxterstatepark

AT Hikers MUST obtain a Hiker Permit card in order to complete their hike to Katahdin. You can pre-register for the card at the Monson Visitor Center. Cards are issued at the **Katahdin Stream Campground (KSC)** prior to their summit hike. Hikers must also sign in & out on the Trail head register on their way up/down Katahdin. For park information and reservations call 207.723.5140. Memorial Day - Columbus Day 8-4 x 7D, Columbus Day to Memorial Day 8-4 M-Fr. When driving, tune to AM 1610 for recent reports. Dates vary based on weather, but the hiking season is approximately May 15 - Oct 15. Weather conditions may prompt trail closure at any time to protect alpine habitat or other park resources, subject to Park Director's approval. Weather reports are posted at KSC at 7a daily, along with "Trail Status and Alerts." Consequences for hiking when the trail is closed include fines, eviction, loss of park visitation privileges & reimbursement of search & rescue costs. Daily recommended cut-off times for starting hikes to Baxter Peak are noon in Jun & Jul, 11a in Aug, 10a in Sep, and 9a in Oct. Overnight camping above treeline is against park regulations & can damage rare alpine plants. Hikers are welcome to leave their backpack at KSC; loaner daypacks are available at no charge from the ranger's station. Northbound thru-hikers completing their hike in late summer or early fall usually have an easy time hitching from KSC into Millinocket. There are fees for nonresidents entering the park by car & fees for campsites that also apply to residents. Fees must be paid in cash; no cc & no work-for-stay. Pets are not allowed in the park. Cell phone reception is unlikely anywhere in the park other than on Katahdin. Please do not place calls from the summit or within earshot of other hikers. Please use a cell phone only if there is an emergency. Maine law prohibits the drinking of alcohol in public places.

The Birches near KSC has 2 shelters & one tent site, open to northbound long distance hikers who have hiked a minimum of "the 100 mile wilderness" immediately prior to entering the Park. Stay is limited to a single night, is limited to 12 persons (combined tenting & shelter) & the fee is $10PP. All other hikers, including flip-floppers & southbound thru-hikers, who wish to overnight in the Park should make reservations in advance. Common options, listed in order of their proximity to KSC are Abol Campground, Daicey Pond Campground (cabins $55D/up) & Foster Field Group Area, north of Katahdin. Note that Abol Campground in the Park, Abol Pines at Abol Bridge & privately run Abol Bridge Campground are three distinct entities.

Baxter gates open at 6a. ME residents enter for free; $14/vehicle for non-residents. KSC parking is limited & you will not be allowed to enter if the lots are full. Day-use parking reservations are highly recommended & can be obtained for KSC, Abol or Roaring Brook Campgrounds by phone up to 3 wks in adv, for a $5 fee. No long-term parking in Baxter. Check w/local taxi & shuttle services for info on long term parking outside Park. Park Fees expected to increase slightly.

Getting to Katahdin

Most routes to Katahdin are through Bangor, ME, 91 mi from Baxter SP. Bangor has an airport & bus terminal. Shuttle services will pick you up in Bangor, but it is more economical to take **Cyr Bus Lines** to Medway, 31 mi from Baxter. Hikers often layover in Millinocket, 24 mi from KSC, the closest parking area to Katahdin.

Cyr Bus Lines 800.244.2335 ⟨www.cyrbustours.com⟩ One-way routes 7D $12. Cash & CC accepted. Routes below are to Concord Hub near airport; bus also stops at Greyhound station 20 min later on arrival, sooner on departure.

- Medway 9:30am (station at Irving store) to Bangor 10:50
- Bangor 6:30pm to Medway 7:40pm

Concord Trailways 207.945.4000 Bangor airport hub, svc to South Station in Boston ⟨www.concordcoachlines.com⟩.

The Appalachian Trail Lodge, Maine Quest Adventures, & Bull Moose Taxi, all listed in Millinocket, provide transportation from Medway to Millinocket & Katahdin.